Volume 6 (2021)

Contents

IN MEMORIAM

MAHMOUD M. AYOUB (1935–2021)

FRED LEEMHUIS (1942–2021)

JIQSA *intends to run obituaries of these scholars in a future issue.*

OBITUARY: ALAN JONES (1933–2021)

NICOLAI SINAI
University of Oxford, UK

On September 25, 2021, Professor Alan Jones, a scholar of Arabic literature and the Qur'ān, died at his home in Oxford, surrounded by his children and the last one of a sequence of beloved cats. Born into a humble working-class background, a family of shopkeepers in Oldham, Alan passed the entrance examination to Manchester Grammar School at the age of eleven towards the end of the Second World War and then went on to win a scholarship to read Classics at St John's College, Cambridge. According to his children, Alan's decision to shift his attention to Arabic during the course of his studies was motivated by the estimation that it seemed "more of a challenge." Having completed his Cambridge BA in Classics and Oriental Languages in 1955, Alan moved to Oxford and in 1957 began teaching Arabic and Islamic Studies at the Faculty of Oriental Studies. Alan served two four-year terms as the director of Oxford's Oriental Institute, and from 1980 until his retirement in 2000 was Pembroke College's first Tutorial Fellow in Arabic (a capacity in which he was succeeded by Christopher Melchert). During a teaching career spanning more than forty years, Alan trained and supervised generations of British and international students, including members of the Jordanian royal house. Quite a few of his students went on to become well-known scholars in their own right; the list of contributors to a *Festschrift* from 2004 reads like a *Who's Who* of Arabic studies in the UK in the early 2000s.[1]

Anecdotes about Alan's pedagogical persona stress not only his occasionally intimidating linguistic rigor and his aversion to academic jargon but also his profound generosity and kindness. Alan's dry humor is noted, too: Elisabeth Kendall transmits the matchless gem that "the first twenty-five years of Arabic are the hardest"—words of encouragement that were received during the first week of an undergraduate degree in Arabic. Up until the outbreak of the COVID-19 pandemic, Alan would regularly take

1. *Islamic Reflections, Arabic Musings: Studies in Honour of Alan Jones*, edited by Robert Hoyland and Philip F. Kennedy (Cambridge: Gibb Memorial Trust, 2004).

doi: http://dx.doi.org/10.5913/jiqsa.6.2021.o01

his Friday lunch (invariably fish and chips) at Pembroke College, ever ready to debate obscure issues of Arabic grammar and qurʾānic exegesis with alacrity and erudition. When he welcomed me to Oxford by kindly extending an invitation to join him for a formal dinner at St Cross College, my sheepish confession to lacking suitable attire was met with shrewd advice about where to purchase an inexpensive but good-quality dinner jacket. I cherish the honor of having been introduced by him, to another dinner guest, as a fellow specimen of that rare academic species, "the Qurʾān-probing ilk."

Despite what was, in the 1980s, a pioneering interest in exploring how personal computers might aid scholars of Arabic, Alan was an Oxford tutor of the traditional sort, with a strong ethos of devotion to teaching and pastoral care. His scholarly output was nonetheless groundbreaking. Alan's pedagogical concerns and ability are masterfully displayed in his *Arabic through the Qurʾān* (2005), a splendid textbook that includes lucid discussions of many of the more arcane points of qurʾānic Arabic, such as the use of *an* in the sense of *allā* or special uses of the phrase *mā kāna.*[2] Alan's scholarship embodies the need to study the language of the Qurʾān, and early Arabic more generally, with a keen eye for archaic usage and non-conformity to later grammatical postulates. In this spirit, he notes, for instance, that *laʿalla* frequently means "so that" rather than "perhaps" in the Qurʾān, often serving to maintain verse-final rhyme, or that early Arabic quite freely employs asyndetic relative clauses after a definite antecedent.[3] A programmatic albeit inaccessibly published article from 1993 on "The Language of the Qurʾān" argues against "the traditional view that the language of the Qurʾān is identical with the *ʿarabiyya* of early poetry on the one hand and with the dialect of Qurayš, the spoken language of Muḥammad, on the other," and instead suggests that scholars contextualize the Qurʾān's language with the linguistic registers of soothsayers, orators, and storytellers.[4] If the field will ever succeed in producing a proper grammar of Qurʾānic Arabic, it will be to a significant degree by following in Alan's trailblazing footsteps.

Likewise of outstanding didactic and scholarly value are two volumes containing line-by-line commentaries on a selection of pre-Islamic and early Islamic poems, entitled *Early Arabic Poetry.*[5] The two books remain arguably the best available resource for teaching Anglophone students to read early poetry with its plethora of linguistic and other difficulties, but they

2. Alan Jones, *Arabic through the Qurʾān* (Cambridge: Islamic Texts Society, 2005).
3. Jones, *Arabic through the Qurʾān*, 243 and 146.
4. Alan Jones, "The Language of the Qurʾān," *Arabist: Budapest Studies in Arabic* 6–7 (1993): 29–48 (quoting p. 29).
5. Alan Jones, *Early Arabic Poetry* (2 vols.; Reading: Ithaca Press, 1992–1996).

also have much to offer to specialists. In particular, they showcase the importance and profitability of a comparative and contrastive analysis of the Qur'ān and Arabic poetry, an abiding interest of Alan's that is also exhibited by a brief 1994 article entitled "Narrative Technique in the Qur'ān and in Early Poetry."[6] A crowning achievement of Alan's work on the Qur'ān is his full translation of the Islamic scripture, published in 2007 by the Gibb Memorial Trust.[7] It combines philological acumen and readability, and prefaces each *sūrah* with succinct opening remarks on their compositional structure and main themes. That Alan's erudition went far beyond the Qur'an is evidenced by his editions of two anthologies of Andalusian stanzaic poetry by Ibn Bishrī and Ibn al-Khaṭīb, published in 1992 and 1997.

6. Alan Jones, "Narrative Technique in the Qur'ān and in Early Poetry," *Journal of Arabic Literature* 25 (1994): 185–191.
7. Alan Jones (trans.), *The Qur'ān* (Cambridge: Gibb Memorial Trust, 2007).

OBITUARY: URI RUBIN (1944–2021)

ALIZA SHNIZER
Tel Aviv University

Uri Rubin, one of the most significant and pioneering scholars of Islam of our times, passed away on October 26 in his Tel Aviv home at the age of seventy-seven. The death of such a humble and brilliant scholar will leave a significant mark on all those who knew him either personally or professionally.

Rubin became interested in the Arabic language and the world of Islam as a high-school student. He continued to pursue this interest during his studies at Tel Aviv University, where he went on to complete all of his academic studies and research activities. Initially, Rubin studied towards a BA in Middle Eastern Studies and Biblical Studies. The completion of his undergraduate degree coincided with the establishment of the Department of Arabic Studies of Tel Aviv University. Rubin then embarked upon a second BA in this department, where he continued up until his doctorate and beyond. His doctoral work, which he completed *magna cum laude* under the supervision of Prof. M. J. Kister, addressed aspects of the figure of Muḥammad in early Islamic tradition. Rubin's first paper, which concerned the symbolism of light in the figure of the prophet Muḥammad, was based on a chapter of his doctorate. [1]

Near the end of his doctorate, Rubin began to teach in the Arabic Studies department at Tel Aviv University. He later served as the department chair for three terms, during which he played a critical role in the department's formation and development. In 2012, Rubin retired from his position as a full professor yet continued engaging in research and teaching at Tel Aviv University until his passing. His continued contribution to the University is testament to his unstinting dedication and devotion.

Throughout his research career, Rubin published numerous books and articles. He was a member of the advisory committee of the *Encyclopaedia of the Qur'ān* and wrote dozens of entries for it as well as for the second and

1. "Pre-Existence and Light—Aspects of the Concept of Nūr Muḥammad," *Israel Oriental Studies* 5 (1975): 62–119.

doi: http://dx.doi.org/10.5913/jiqsa.6.2021.o02

third editions of the *Encyclopaedia of Islam*, the *Encyclopaedia Hebraica*, and additional encyclopedias. Rubin also published a new Hebrew translation of the Qurʾān, which once again underlined his essential contribution to the study of Islam.

Uri Rubin's work dealt with the Qurʾān and its interpretation as well as the early Islamic tradition in general. Over the years, he told his close students that his sojourn at the Department of Biblical Studies had contributed significantly to his study of the Qurʾān. The aim of Rubin's scholarship, as embodied by his articles and books, was to reveal Muslim views on the early Islamic past and on Muslim religion and culture as reflected in early Islamic sources. Rubin did not aim to distinguish between "history" and "legend" but rather between various layers of tradition and between the different perspectives and beliefs that generated the sources available to us today. He sought to illuminate the ways in which those who compiled and disseminated the Islamic tradition had molded the historical memory of Islam.

Rubin's first book focused on the life of Muḥammad.[2] In it, he examined the literary composition of traditions concerning the prophet Muḥammad and the underlying views that they reflected. Rubin demonstrates that Muḥammad's biography was largely constructed from the following two sources: (i) an extra-qurʾānic stratum consisting of the names of specific figures, places, and battles, which provided a structural framework of events for the story of Muḥammad's life; and (ii) a qurʾānic stratum, that is, verses from the Qurʾān that were incorporated by the compilers of Muḥammad's biography into the extra-qurʾānic framework in order to anchor obscure qurʾānic passages in a concrete series of events.

Rubin's second book examined the portrayal of the Children of Israel and the Islamic self-image.[3] In this book, Rubin compares Muslim depictions of the Israelites as shaped by biblical and qurʾānic models, discussing the ambivalent attitude of early Muslim traditions toward the Children of Israel. On the one hand, it is possible to discern a positive image of the Children of Israel in the form of a messianic model adapted to the Islamic community; on the other hand, the sources also highlight the factionalist character of the Children of Israel by way of a negative model that the Islamic community must take care to eschew. Rubin notes that the negative traditions make greater use of qurʾānic motifs in order to replace biblical ones.

2. *The Eye of the Beholder: The Life of Muḥammad as Viewed by the Early Muslims; A Textual Analysis* (Princeton: Darwin Press, 1995).
3. *Between Bible and Qurʾān: The Children of Israel and the Islamic Self-Image* (Princeton: Darwin Press, 1999).

Two years ago, in 2019, Rubin published two books in Hebrew with the Hebrew University's Magnes Press. The first book is a brief introduction to the Qurʾān.[4] The second book addresses the holy status of Mecca and Jerusalem in the Qurʾān and in the Islamic tradition.[5] It discusses central aspects of Jerusalem's sanctity and the fluctuation between the sanctity of Jerusalem and that of Mecca and the Kaʿbah. According to Rubin, an axis of holiness connecting Mecca and Jerusalem had been an accepted fact well before the appearance of Islam on the historical stage. An English translation of the book is forthcoming; in the final year of his life, Rubin invested considerable efforts in translating the book into English and preparing it for print.

The articles that Rubin wrote over the course of his rich and diverse research career cover a broad range of topics, including the image and life of the prophet Muḥammad,[6] the history of Islamic prayer, the Meccan pilgrimage rites, Abrahamic religion in pre-Islamic Arabia and its connection to the Kaʿbah rituals in Mecca, the Kaʿbah as a direction of prayer, the sanctity of Jerusalem in Islam, relations between Muslims and non-Muslims, biblical models in the Islamic tradition, prophets and prophecy, governmental authority in Islam, and the meaning of numerous qurʾānic verses.[7] Rubin also edited an anthology of articles examining various aspects of the life of Muḥammad and was the coeditor of a volume on the status of *dhimmīs*.[8]

Rubin's translation of the Qurʾān was well received by researchers, students, and seekers of knowledge in Israel and also in the Arab world. In 2001, the head of Tel Aviv University Press had turned to Rubin with a request to translate the Qurʾān for readers of Hebrew. The first edition of the translation was published in 2005. A decade later, in 2016, a new, updated and expanded edition was published. The translation was praised for its meticulousness, its thoroughness, and for its extensive and valuable annotation. Rubin sought to reflect the accepted traditional interpretations; in footnotes, he described various additional meanings that were not reflected

4. *The Qurʾān: The Divine Voice Speaks to Muḥammad the Messenger* [in Hebrew] (Jerusalem: Magnes Press, 2019).
5. *Between Jerusalem and Mecca: Sanctity and Salvation in the Qurʾān and the Islamic Tradition* [in Hebrew] (Jerusalem: Magnes Press, 2019).
6. For a selection of Rubin's articles on Muḥammad and pre-Islamic Arabia from the years 1975–2009, see *Muḥammad the Prophet and Arabia* (Farnham: Ashgate, 2011).
7. Rubin wrote multiple articles on each of the topics listed above. For a complete list of Prof. Uri Rubin's publications and files of the articles, see http://www.urirubin.com/publications.
8. Uri Rubin and David J. Wasserstein (eds.), *Dhimmis and Others: Jews and Christians and the World of Classical Islam = Israel Oriental Studies* 17 (1997).

in the body of the translation as well as parallels from Jewish and Christian sources. The translation also contains appendices and a detailed index.

Rubin provided a foundation for generations of students and researchers, making an important and essential contribution to Islamic studies through his books and articles. His students—past, present, and future—are fortunate to have learned from the work of such a remarkable lecturer and mentor, whose benevolence and devotion toward his students were profound and limitless.

JIQSA 6 (2021): 12–15

OBITUARY: JOSEF VAN ESS (1934–2021)

CHRISTIAN LANGE
Utrecht University, Netherlands

On 20 November 2021, Josef van Ess, doyen of Islamic Studies, passed away in Tübingen at the age of eighty-seven. He was born in Aachen/Aix-la-Chapelle to Dutch working-class parents, and as a ten-year old he witnessed the destruction of his hometown by Allied air raids—an event he often reminisced about later in life. Despite these difficult beginnings, he had a delightfully dry and warm sense of humor, full of witticisms and subtle irony, which he leveled at others as well as himself. He did not know how to drive a car or ride a bicycle. "I just missed the right moment to learn it," he quipped, "just like I never got into smoking, watching TV, or using Powerpoint."[1]

His mind was occupied with more important things. At Bonn, he studied Classics, but soon switched to Arabic, Persian, Turkish, and comparative Semitic languages, as these fields seemed to offer him more freedom and greater chances of success. Hellmut Ritter (1892–1971), writing from Istanbul, suggested his PhD topic: the early Muslim ascetic and theorist of the human soul (*nafs*), al-Ḥārith al-Muḥāsibī (d. 243/857). This resulted in his first monograph, *Die Gedankenwelt des Ḥāriṯ al-Muḥāsibī* (1961)—a work that remains, testament to his greatness, fundamental for the study of al-Muḥāsibī. He admired Ritter's "effortless combination of intellectual discipline and elegance of expression."[2] He himself came to embody this combination like no other. A master stylist and orator, he is widely acclaimed as the most brilliant Islamicist of the second half of the twentieth century. Coming full circle with *Die Gedankenwelt des Ḥāriṯ al-Muḥāsibī*, his last monograph, *Im Halbschatten* (2013), is a richly colored biography of Ritter, and simultaneously a *tour de force* through twentieth-century European Orientalism.

1. Josef van Ess, *Kleine Schriften by Josef van Ess*, ed. Hinrich Biesterfeldt (3 vols.; Leiden: Brill, 2018), 3.2407.
2. Ibid., 3.2403.

doi: http://dx.doi.org/10.5913/jiqsa.6.2021.o03

At first, he thought he would devote his scholarly career to the study of Islamic mysticism, but then Islamic theology, or *kalām*, became his main area of specialization. Again, he appears to have been attracted by the prospect of unfettered freedom, of pioneer research in a field largely unencumbered by disciplinary baggage, such as a set of mandatory methods. As he remembered, in the early 1960s, next to himself there were only three other scholars of Islamic theology in the West, two in the United States, and one in Paris. "Nobody interfered with the other person's work, and we were all good friends."[3] In his *Habilitationsschrift*, submitted at Frankfurt, he studied the epistemological prolegomenon of ʿAḍud al-Dīn al-Ījī's (d. 756/1355) Ashʿarī *summa theologica, al-Mawāqif* (*Die Erkenntnislehre des ʿAḍudaddīn al-Īcī*, 1966), meticulously tracing the genealogy of ideas and *en passant* inventing a whole new arsenal of terms to translate the intricacies of Arabic *ʿilm al-kalām*.

During his years as *Referent* at the German *Orient-Institut* in Beirut (OIB) in the mid-sixties, he edited volume 9 (published in 1974) of the OIB's 30-volume edition of the biographical dictionary of al-Ṣafadī (d. 764/1362), worked on al-Jāḥiẓ (d. 255/869) and other thinkers of the "classical" period of Islamic intellectual history, acquainted himself with Druze, Ismāʿīlī, and Sufi traditions (an interest that sparked a number of publications in the 1970s, such as his book on the chiliastic reign of the Fāṭimid caliph al-Ḥākim [386–411/996–1021], published in 1977), and became a keen observer of interconfessional dialogue, a preoccupation he continued to nurture in his later years in exchange with Hans Küng (1928–2021), his colleague at Tübingen, with whom he published *Christentum und Weltreligionen* (1984, with Heinrich von Stietencron and Heinz Bechert).

Having been appointed professor at Tübingen in 1968, he increasingly turned his attention to the beginnings of Islamic theology. Two important early milestones were *Zwischen Ḥadīṯ und Theologie* (1975), in which he elevated what later came to be known as the *isnād-cum-matn* analysis to unsurpassed heights, and *Anfänge muslimischer Theologie* (1977), in which he examined the textual evidence for an early dating (to the seventh century CE) of the activities of the Qadarīs, defenders of free will in Islam's formative period. However, plumbing the early history of Islam, he rarely ventured beyond the turn of the first century of Islam, and only occasionally wrote about the Qurʾān. Nonetheless, his contributions to Qurʾānic Studies were significant. One thinks, for example, of the chapter on Sūrat al-Najm

3. Ibid., 3.2412.

included in *Les prémices de la théologie musulmane* (2002), translated into English as *The Flowering of Islamic Theology* (2006).

Rudi Paret (1901–1983), the well-known translator of the Qurʾān and his predecessor at Tübingen, had encouraged him to pursue a major project, warning him that it would require patience and stamina. "To write a six-volume work," he later mused in the foreword to the volume that concluded his *opus magnum*, *Theologie und Gesellschaft im 2. und 3. Jahrhundert Hidschra* (1991–1997), "is playing with one's life; but ... a happy corollary of studying Islamic theology is that one is left alone and in peace."[4] In *Theologie und Gesellschaft*, he almost single-handedly reconstructed the thought of a vast array of early Muslim theologians of all stripes and colors, mostly on the basis of the scattered reports preserved in the later heresiographical literature: a mind-bogglingly complex undertaking. The splendid isolation of Tübingen certainly helped, and it is telling that he declined offers of professorships from both Princeton and Harvard, preferring the quiet backwaters of Swabia's *Insel der Seligen* and its excellent library. Not that he kept out of everything, or that he shunned administrative responsibility. Far from it. By surrounding himself with a stellar line-up of colleagues, he fashioned Tübingen's *Orientalisches Seminar* into a veritable bastion of Islamic Studies in Germany. At the same time, it is true that he never had more than a handful of students, wasted little time on edited volumes, and never even thought of running research projects and organizing regular workshops and conferences. Instead, he wrote, and he traveled, both zealously.

A life-long singer and one-time member of Aachen Dome's boy choir, he was deeply imbued with music. At his retirement ceremony in 1999, he spoke about how music had taught him creativity and structure, how he thought about his own writing in terms of exposition, development, and recapitulation, as in the Sonata form, of *crescendos*, *decrescendos*, and *ritardandos*. As emeritus, he continued to sing; if anything, he became more vocal and prolific. In his two-volume *Der Eine und das Andere* (2011), *Theologie und Gesellschaft*'s companion piece, he studied the heresiographers from whom he had so painstakingly gleaned the information that formed the bedrock of *Theologie und Gesellschaft*. In 2018, a massive collection of his "short writings" appeared, curated by himself and edited by Hinrich Biesterfeldt, the three-volume *Kleine Schriften*. *Kleine Schriften* features many gems, including previously unpublished materials and a string of autobi-

4. Josef van Ess, *Theologie und Gesellschaft im 2. und 3. Jahrhundert Hidschra: Eine Geschichte des religiösen Denkens im frühen Islam* (Berlin: de Gruyter, 1991–1997), 4.vii.

ographical essays. The bibliography of his works, including twenty-three monographs, 138 articles and book chapters, numerous encyclopaedia entries, and over 250 book reviews, serves as a lesson in humility to all. *Theologie und Gesellschaft*, *Der Eine und das Andere*, and *Kleine Schriften* are monuments of brilliance and erudition.

He was not denied the national and international recognition to which his achievements entitled him. The crowning moment arrived in 2009, when he was inducted in the *Orden Pour le mérite für Wissenschaften und Künste*, established in 1740 by Frederick II of Prussia. To this day, he remains the only German *Islamwissenschaftler* to have been decorated with this supreme honor. In Tübingen, his students respected him a lot, and to those who were willing to put in the hard work, he extended his genuine interest and support. His seminars were daunting affairs, but also exquisitely entertaining. His colleagues and friends will miss him immensely, as he meant a great deal to a great number of people. He will be remembered with gratitude and fond admiration. Survived by his wife Marie Luise and three of his four children, he lies buried on the Bergfriedhof in Tübingen.

JIQSA 6 (2021): 17–67

NOAH'S BOAT AND OTHER MISSED OPPORTUNITIES (2019 IQSA PRESIDENTIAL ADRESS)

DEVIN STEWART
Emory University, USA

Abstract

This essay addresses the ways in which several of the most popular English translations of the Qur'ān treat cases in which the text draws on key biblical concepts and vocabulary. It suggests that when determining how such passages ought to be translated, one must take into account not only the meaning that fits the passage generally but also the extent to which the text reflects an intention to invoke, modify, alter, or ignore biblical precedent. In a number of cases, it is argued, many English translations adopt an anti-biblicizing translation, often a literal rendition, such as reference to the "ship" of Noah, that obscures the connection of the qur'ānic passage with biblical tradition. The adoption of a biblicizing translation, such as referring to Noah's "ark" instead, would in many cases render tangible a connection with biblical texts that was originally intended.

Introduction

It is not surprising to claim that the Qur'ān is closely related to biblical tradition and that particular aspects of qur'ānic language are related to biblical language. A cursory reading of the Qur'ān is enough to show this, and any interested reader may find it out from a number of accessible secondary works. The majority of the characters that appear in the Qur'ān appear in the Bible. The biblical figures Moses and Abraham appear more frequently than any other figures in the text, and both are presented as models for the prophetic mission of Muḥammad. Judging on the basis of narrative prominence, one may argue that the hero of the Qur'ān is, in fact, Moses. The qur'ānic conceptions of creation, the flood, prophecy, sin, the eternal soul, angels, Satan, judgement, paradise, and hell all have obvious connections with biblical tradition. Key qur'ānic terms such as *jahannam* ("hell") and *al-ṭūr* ("the mountain," namely, Sinai) derive ultimately from Hebrew and Ar-

doi: http://dx.doi.org/10.5913/jiqsa.6.2021.a001

amaic or Syriac scriptural terms. Nevertheless, even specialists in Qurʾānic and Islamic Studies, both those who underestimate the indebtedness of the Qurʾān to biblical tradition and those who embrace it wholeheartedly and perhaps even exaggerate it in certain cases—let alone lay readers—often fail to see the forest for the trees. Much Qurʾānic Studies scholarship appears to dance around certain basic issues without stating the obvious, and related to this set of blind spots regarding the relation of qurʾānic to biblical material is the failure of some, many, or most English translations to capture the biblical valences of particular qurʾānic terms.

All translators of the Qurʾān repeatedly face the following issue: when a qurʾānic term is related in some fashion to salvation history and to earlier texts or concepts in the Jewish and Christian traditions, to what extent should the translator make those connections obvious in the English rendition? Translators have grappled with this problem in different ways, often unsuccessfully, in my view. Such translations may have occurred through lack of insight or limited background knowledge. They are certainly facilitated by recourse to qurʾānic commentaries that ignore biblical references. They may have resulted from an active desire to maintain a distance between the Qurʾān and the Bible, whether on the part of Muslim translators seeking to uphold the superiority of the Qurʾān and Islam to other scriptures and religions or on the part of Jewish and Christian translators seeking to protect biblical tradition from outside encroachment. In the following remarks, I address several examples in which, in my view, at least a few and sometimes most or all of the English translations fail to convey a biblical allusion or invocation that was intended in the text.

"Noah's Ship" (I)

fa-anjaynāhu wa-aṣḥāba ʾl-safīnati wa-jaʿalnāhā āyatan liʾl-ʿālamīn
And We rescued him and those with him in the ship, and made of it a portent for the peoples. (Q 29:15)[1]

1. This essay draws on a limited number of translations of the Qurʾān into English. I could have cited dozens more English translations, not to mention translations of the Qurʾān into French, German, Italian, Spanish, and other European languages, but that would not have changed the overall point, since they all share, *grosso modo*, the same issues that are raised here, only varying in degree. The English translations I will cite include the following: Richard Bell (trans.), *The Qurʾān, Translated, with a Critical Re-arrangement of the Surahs* (2 vols; Edinburgh: T&T Clark, 1937–1939); Marmaduke Pickthall (trans.), *The Meaning of the Glorious Koran* (New York: Alfred A. Knopf, 1992); Abdullah Yusuf Ali (trans.), *The Holy Qurʾān: Text, Translation and*

Thus, Marmaduke Pickthall renders the conclusion to a brief account of Noah and the flood in Sūrat al-ʿAnkabūt (Q 29). Arthur John Arberry and Alan Jones render the verse in similar fashion:

> Yet We delivered him, and those who were in the ship, and appointed it for a sign unto all beings. (Arberry)

> We rescued him and those [with him] in the ship, which We made a sign for created beings. (Jones)

All three translators render the Arabic term *safīnah* here as "ship." One might wonder how they justified their choice of the term "ship" instead of "ark," which one would expect in a retelling of Noah's story. These translators may have been influenced by the fact that the terms used to designate Noah's ark in the Qurʾān also refer to ordinary ships. For example, the ordinary boat in the story of Moses's mysterious teacher in Sūrat al-Kahf is also designated as a *safīnah* (Q 18:71.79). Similarly, while Noah's vessel is most frequently termed *al-fulk* in the Qurʾān (Q 7:64, 10:73, 11:37.38, 23:27, 26:119, 36:41), the same word, *fulk*, is used for other types of boats in several other verses (e.g., Q 2:164, 14:32). Perhaps on this account, Pickthall chose to render Noah's *fulk*, as well as *safīnah*, throughout as "ship." One could also argue that this situation contrasts with that found in the Bible, since the common word for "ship" or "boat" is *ʾoniyyâ* (e.g., Prov 30:19, Jonah 1:3.4), while, in contrast, Noah's ark is designated by a distinct term, *tēbâ*. Keeping the English rendering consistent across the two categories of Noah's vessel and of other ordinary vessels might signal to the audience a distinct difference from the biblical presentation.

While the translations of Pickthall, Arberry, and Jones are in a sense technically correct, because the word *safīnah* does mean "ship" and the vessel portrayed in Q 29:15 certainly has the basic features of a ship, I consider them tactical blunders. There is something disturbing about this rendition of the verse, because the ship in question is clearly Noah's ark, the same one that appears in Genesis. To call it otherwise somehow does violence to the story, as if to drive a wedge between the qurʾānic and the biblical version of the story. In this particular case, many other translators did not choose

---

Commentary, new revised ed. (Brentwood: Amana Corporation, 1989); M. H. Shakir (trans.), *Qur'an: The Translation* (New York: Tahrike Tarsile Qur'an, 1993); Arthur John Arberry (trans.), *The Koran Interpreted* (London: Allen & Unwin, 1955); Alan Jones (trans.), *The Qur'ān* (Cambridge: Gibb Memorial Trust, 2007); M. A. S. Abdel Haleem (trans.), *The Qur'an: A New Translation* (Oxford: Oxford University Press, 2007); Tarif Khalidi (trans.), *The Qur'an* (London: Penguin Books, 2008).

the path adopted by Pickthall, Arberry, and Jones, and instead translated *safīnah* as "ark."

> But We saved him and the companions of the Ark, and We made the (Ark) a Sign for all peoples! (Abdullah Yusuf Ali)
>
> We saved him and those with him on the Ark. We made this a sign for all people. (Muhammad Abdel Haleem)
>
> But him We saved, as also the passengers in the Ark, making it a wonder to mankind. (Tarif Khalidi)

In my view, these translations are more satisfying because they render transparent the connection of this particular passage with the biblical story of Noah's ark and the flood.

In order to decide which translation is preferable, one must consider the intention behind the qurʾānic passages in question. Is the scene in which Noah and his companions are saved supposed to recall the biblical story of Noah's ark, is it intended to highlight a significant distinction between the two accounts, or is it purposefully ignoring the biblical account? In my view, the answer to this question is obvious: this scene is intended to recall its biblical counterpart, as many other passages do. This does not mean that such recall is always intended or that contrasts are not intended in other cases. Translating *safīnah* or *fulk* as "ark" is therefore preferable by far, on the grounds that it makes the intended connection all the more obvious, rather than obscuring or concealing it.

Noah's ark is an inspiring symbol in the Qurʾān and in Islamic literature generally. For example, a recently published work on Shāfiʿī law bears the title *Safīnat al-najāh fī mā yajibu ʿalā ʾl-ʿabd li-mawlāh*, "The Ark of Salvation, on the Obligations of the Worshiper to His Lord."[2] This title, like hundreds of others throughout Islamic history, invokes the symbol of Noah's ark as an indication that the book is indispensable for the reader's religious instruction and soteriological needs. Ibn Qayyim al-Jawziyyah (d. 751/1350) authored *al-Kāfiyah al-shāfiyah*, "The Curative and Sufficient Treatise," a theological treatise in which he championed orthodox Islamic theology, that of the "true monotheists" (*muwaḥḥidūn*), against the heretical theology of "anthropomorphists" (*mushabbihūn*), meaning extreme literalists, and "nullifiers" (*muʿaṭṭilūn*), meaning the Muʿtazilīs, who in his opinion did not give God's attributes their full due. In it he wrote, "the nullifier has fallen

2. Sālim b. Samīr al-Ḥaḍramī, *Safīnat al-najāh fī mā yajibu ʿalā ʾl-ʿabd li-mawlāh* (Jedda: Dār al-Minhāj, 2009).

behind and has missed the ark of salvation, but the true monotheist has embarked on Noah's ark."[3] This fourteenth-century author is taking up a common trope that likens "the saved sect" (*al-firqah al-nājiyah*), the one sect that has adopted the correct doctrine—of the seventy-two into which Islam was predicted to divide in a famous *ḥadīth* report—with the passengers on Noah's ark.

Another large set of examples related to the doctrinal use of Noah's ark is provided by Shīʿī tradition. Shīʿīs regularly refer to the Imams as Noah's ark—the point being that the believer can only hope for salvation if he or she pledges allegiance to the Imam of the age. They often cite the *ḥadīth* report, "The likeness of my descendants (*ahl baytī*) is that of Noah's ark (*safīnat nūḥ*): whoever embarks on it will be saved, and whoever fails to do so will be drowned."[4] The Shīʿī comparison of their own sect with Noah's ark is a fundamental feature of their theology.[5] It resembles the Christian comparison of the Church to Noah's ark, also ubiquitous, occurring perhaps most famously in the papal bull of Boniface VIII (1294–1303), *Unam sanctam* (1302).[6] And with the symbol of Noah's ark is associated the principle, parallel to Shīʿī doctrine of the Imamate, of *nulla salus extra ecclesiam*, "there is no being saved outside the church." Without engaging in a grand tour of medieval Islamic theology, one may recognize that the image of Noah's ark, in the Qurʾān and in ideas inspired by the Qurʾān throughout Islamic culture, carries with it the same sorts of symbolic value that it does in Jewish and Christian tradition. And while these are obviously post-qurʾānic

3. Ibn Qayyim al-Jawziyyah, *al-Kāfiyah al-shāfiyah fī 'l-intiṣār li'l-firqah al-nājiyah* (4 vols.; Mecca: Dār ʿĀlam al-Fawāʾid, 1428 AH), 1.46–47.

4. Muḥsin al-Amīn, *al-Shīʿah bayn al-ḥaqāʾiq wa'l-awhām: Naqḍ al-Washīʿah* (Beirut: Mu'assasat al-Aʿlamī, 1983), 30; Ibn Qutaybah, *ʿUyūn al-akhbār*, ed. Yūsuf ʿAlī Ṭawīl (4 vols.; Beirut: Dār al-Kutub al-ʿIlmiyyah, 2009), 1.310. The report occurs in many variant versions.

5. Khalid Sindawi, "Noah and Noah's Ark as the Primordial Model of Shīʿism in Shīʿite Literature," *Quaderni di Studi Arabi* (n.s.) 1 (2006): 29–48.

6. For the Latin text, see Wilhelm Römer, *Die Bulle* unam sanctam (Schaffhausen: Johannes Bachmann, 1889). For the English translation, see Philip Schaff, *The Creeds of Christendom with History and Critical Notes*, vol. 2: *The Greek and Latin Creeds, with Translations* (New York: Harper Brothers, 1919), 605–607. For historical and theological context, see Don Louis Tosti, *History of Pope Boniface VIII and His Times, with Notes and Documentatry Evidence*, trans. Eugene J. Donnely (New York: Christian Press Association Publishing Company, 1911), 349–356; Walter Ullmann, "Boniface VIII and His Contemporary Scholarship," *The Journal of Theological Studies* 27 (1976): 58–87; R. M. Johannessen, "Cardinal Jean Lemoine and the Authorship of the Glosses to Unam Sanctam," *Bulletin of Medieval Canon Law* 33 (1988): 33–42.

examples, this particular symbolic use of Noah's ark is in keeping with and inspired by the Qurʾān's presentation. In Noah's story as in many other cases in the qurʾānic punishment stories, a tiny group of believers are saved, while those who did not embark on the ark are annihilated (cf. Q al-Shuʿarāʾ 26). There is thus a very compelling reason to make that connection apparent when one is translating the Qurʾān into English.

This is not to say that no significant differences exist between the qurʾānic and the biblical versions of Noah's story (or between the qurʾānic and biblical versions of many other stories). In fact, a quite radical difference is associated with the denouement of the two versions, which seem to be diametrically opposed. Both accounts end with prominent reference to a sign from the Almighty, but whereas the sign of the rainbow in the biblical account signals God's promise that He will never again destroy the world by flood, in the qurʾānic account God leaves the ark as a sign to indicate that He will continue to annihilate future peoples who reject the teachings and warnings of their prophets. The point here, though, is that the role the ark plays in saving Noah and his companions is parallel and similar in the Bible and the Qurʾān, and thus a biblicizing translation, calling attention to that similarity, is entirely appropriate. Noah's ark is the sole means available of escaping all-encompassing destruction, and this is as true of the qurʾānic version of the story as it is of the biblical version. The ark is no ordinary ship.

Questions of Etymology, Influence, and Translation

Deciding how to translate qurʾānic terms that resonate with biblical texts is not a simple matter, and it is tied to general views of the extent of biblical influence on the Qurʾān and views of etymology and borrowing. The question of the existence of foreign vocabulary in the Qurʾān is an old one, both in Islamic letters and in Western scholarship. Medieval Muslim scholars realized that a number of terms in the Qurʾān were related to Hebrew, Aramaic/Syriac, Persian, Greek, Latin, South Arabian, and Ethiopic words. They were conscious that this was potentially problematic for two reasons. First, it opened up the possibility that the Qurʾān contained borrowings from Jewish and Christian texts, and secondly, it threatened to contradict the explicit text of the Qurʾān, which states in several passages that it is *qurʾānan ʿarabiyyan*, "an Arabic Qurʾān" (Q 12:2, 20:113, 39:28, 41:3, 42:7, 43:3). The main argument put forward by medieval Muslim commentators was that, even if some qurʾānic words were related to foreign etyma, they had been assimilated into Arabic before the Qurʾān was revealed and so, since they were *bona fide* Arabic words, the Qur'ān's characterization of itself as an Arabic Qur'ān could not be impugned.

In the European tradition of Qur'ānic Studies, the investigation of foreign words in the Qur'ān and biblical influence on Islam's sacred text have been strongly linked.[7] However, it must be recognized that the matter is a bit tricky, in part because the main biblical languages of Hebrew, Aramaic, and Syriac are Semitic languages that have many cognates in common with Arabic. It is thus possible that certain qur'ānic words are similar to corresponding words in the Bible simply because they derive from the same original etymon in proto-Western Semitic and were not borrowed into the Qur'ān from biblical texts. This is obviously the case for numbers, basic kinship terms, the words for day, night, year, the sun, and so on. Less obvious, perhaps, is the term *ḥajj*, designating the pilgrimage to Mecca in the Qur'ān (Q 2:189–197, 22:27), which phonetically resembles the Hebrew word *ḥag* ("festival" or "feast day"; e.g., Exod 10:9 and 12:14, Num 28:17). This is not a borrowing from the Hebrew Bible or from other texts in Jewish tradition but rather, in all likelihood, already designated a religious ritual of some sort in proto-West Semitic. That original etymon came eventually to designate pilgrimage in Arabic and a religious festival in Hebrew. Similarly, Arabic *salām* ("peace") and Hebrew *šālôm* ("peace") occur as greetings in the Qur'ān (e.g., Q 4:94, 6:54, 7:46, 10:10, 13:24) and the Hebrew Bible (Gen 43:23, Judg 6:23, Dan 10:19), respectively.[8] It seems likely that this is not a case of the borrowing of biblical texts or concepts into the Qur'ān. Rather, *salām* and *šālôm* have a common origin in proto-Western Semitic. *Salām* ("peace") was probably already a standard form of greeting in the ancestral language, and the usage lived on in the daughter languages.

There are, however, intermediate cases, in which similar terms may be signs of borrowing even though they happen to be cognate words. The words for cucumbers—Arabic *qiththā'*, Hebrew *qiššū'â*—and onions—Arabic *baṣal*, Hebrew *bāṣāl*—are obvious cognates that derive from an ancient, common origin in the Semitic language tree. One should not suppose that these words owe their existence in the Arabic lexicon to the fact that they

7. Josef Horovitz, "Jewish Proper Names and Derivatives in the Koran," *Hebrew Union College Annual* 2 (1925): 145–227, 208–209; Arthur Jeffery, *The Foreign Vocabulary of the Qur'ān* (Leiden: Brill, 2007 [1938]); D. S. Margoliouth, "Some Additions to Professor Jeffery's *Foreign Vocabulary of the Qur'ān*," *JRAS* 71 (1939): 53–61; Andrew Rippin, "Foreign Vocabulary," *EQ*, s.v. (2002). For a historical overview of this topic, see the works of Jeffery and Rippin cited here.

8. Irene Lande, *Formelhafte Wendungen der Umgangsprache im Alten Testament* (Leiden: E.J. Brill, 1949), especially "Die Grüssformel," pp. 2–12.

have been imported into the Qurʾān from biblical Hebrew. It is nevertheless clear that the single verse that includes these words in the Qurʾān, "And recall when you said, ʿO Moses, we can never endure one kind of food, so call upon your Lord to bring forth for us from the earth its green herbs and its cucumbers and its garlic and its lentils and its onions'" (Q al-Baqarah 2:61), is closely related to a particular biblical passage, Num 11:4–5. That text reads, "The rabble who were among them had greedy desires; and also the sons of Israel wept again and said, 'Who will give us meat to eat? We remember the fish we ate in Egypt at no cost—also the cucumbers (*haqqiššuʾîm*), melons, leeks, onions (*habbəṣālîm*), and garlic.'" Comparison of the two texts show that, while they differ somewhat in terms of both content and order, the Arabic text is clearly a version of the biblical statement, including these prominent cognates. Another mixed example is that of the *mathal*, which has most often been translated as "parable" in Qurʾānic Studies, even though it also designates "proverb, comparison, exemplum" in the text, in addition to "parable." *Mathal* is cognate with Hebrew *māšāl*, which has a similarly wide range of meanings, and both presumably go back to the proto-West Semitic **mathal*, which, in all likelihood, originally meant "proverb." Even though parables were important in both Jewish and Christian tradition before the advent of Islam, the term *mathal* cannot be a borrowing from Hebrew *māšāl*, since it would not have contained a *-th-* in that case; instead, proto-Semitic *-th-* remained *-th-* in Arabic but changed to *-š-* in Hebrew. However, even if this is true, the qurʾānic parables may have been influenced to some degree by rabbinic parables or the parables of Jesus.

In other cases, however, certain foreign terms in the Qurʾān clearly derive from biblical tradition and have been borrowed along with more or less their same, original meanings. So, for example, *al-asbāṭ* refers in the Qurʾān to the "tribes," that is, the twelve tribes of Israel (Q 2:136.140, 3:84, 4:163, 7:160). This word derives from the Hebrew *šəbāṭîm*, "tribes," and is obviously distinct from the ordinary Arabic word for tribe, *qabīlah*. The word *al-ṭūr* is used in the Qurʾān to refer to Mount Sinai (Q 2:63.93, 4:154, 19:52, 20:80, 23:20, 28:29.46, 52:1, 95:2). It derives from Aramaic *ṭūrā* ("the mountain"), and it is substituted instead of the ordinary word for mountain in Arabic, *jabal*, or Hebrew *har*. After *al-nār*, "the fire," the most frequently used term for hell in the Qurʾān is *jahannam*, which derives ultimately from *gêʾ [ben-] hinnōm* ("the Valley of [the Son of] Hinnom"; Jer 7:31 and 19:2–6).[9] In these and other cases, there is little to suggest that these words were simply cog-

9. It has been suggested that the Arabic term derives indirectly from Hebrew

nates that had been passed down the Semitic language tree or that they had been borrowed into Arabic long before the Qur'ān was produced. It seems clear that they derive from biblical or other Jewish and Christian texts.

However, one must exercise caution in interpreting such terms, for certain borrowed words may be used in entirely different senses. As Walid Saleh has explained, the field of Qur'ānic Studies is plagued by a collection of bad interpretive habits that he labels "the etymological fallacy." The fallacy includes, first, the assumption that whenever the Muslim exegetes do not agree on the meaning of a qur'ānic term, then it must derive from a foreign term. The second assumption is that whenever a foreign etymon has been identified, the interpretive problem has been completely solved. Saleh points out that neither of these assumptions is warranted and that the procedure is flawed, especially because it does not take into account the meanings of the terms in the contexts in which they occur. Among a number of examples, he cites the term *ḥanīf*, which, many scholars agree, is related to the Syriac *ḥanpā* ("heathen"), but which obviously has a positive and quite distinct meaning in the Qur'ān. On the basis of the qur'ānic evidence, for example, the term *ḥanīf* "reflects a notion of basic religious impulse in humanity towards dedication to the one God." The point is that understanding the term *ḥanīf* as meaning "heathen" does not at all explain its correct meaning in the Qur'ān. This entire discussion is directly relevant to the topic addressed here because most of the "foreign" terms identified in such investigations are related to biblical and post-biblical Jewish and Christian traditions. Having identified a particular qur'ānic term as being related in some fashion to Jewish and Christian texts, one may not assume that it is being used with the same or even with a similar meaning, without examining carefully the contexts in which it occurs.[10] Even if the term is clearly related to a biblical precedent, the qur'ānic text may be recognizing, accentuating, playing down, modifying, distorting, or even completely ignoring a term's biblical origin. Knowing the original usage, or an earlier us-

---

through Gəʿəz. Jeffery, *The Foreign Vocabulary of the Qur'ān*, 57–58, 105–106, 206–207.

10. Walid A. Saleh, "The Etymological Fallacy and Qur'anic Studies: Muhammad, Paradise, and Late Antiquity," in Angelika Neuwirth, Nicolai Sinai, and Michael Marx (eds.), *The Qur'ān in Context: Historical and Literary Investigations into the Qur'ānic Milieu* (Leiden: Brill, 2011), 649–698, esp. 659; Andrew Rippin, "RḤMNN and the Ḥanīfs," in Wael B. Hallaq and Donald P. Little (eds.), *Islamic Studies Presented to Charles J. Adams* (Leiden: Brill, 1991), 153–168, esp. 161. On etymology and interpretation of the Qur'ān, see also Ghassan El Masri, *The Semantics of Qur'anic Language:* al-Āḫira (Leiden: Brill, 2020), 7–50.

age, of a word does not guarantee that one understands its later usage. For example, "manufactured" decidedly does not now mean "made by hand," even though that was the original sense.[11]

The anti-biblicizing or alienating rendering of the references to Noah's vessel is emblematic of the practice of many qur'ānic translators with regard to elements of biblical tradition that are invoked in the Qur'ān. They regularly opt for a literal translation, often the most common sense of the word in question. They may not have noticed that the word could be rendered otherwise. They may have neglected or overlooked the connection of particular vocabulary with the Bible, something that could be due to lack of familiarity with certain aspects of the biblical tradition. Alternatively, they may have decided to avoid a particular translation out of an intention to create some distance between the Qur'ān and the Bible. This type of translation practice occurs from both directions: Muslim translators may strive to separate the Qur'ān from the Bible so that the text does not appear derivative and so that Islam as a whole maintains a more distinct profile. Jewish and Christian translators may strive to make the Qur'ān appear more distinct and distant from biblical tradition and similarly may stress Islam's distance from Judaism and Christianity. In either scenario, translators may have ideological biases or goals behind their overall approach, using the distinctive nature of Islam to argue for its superiority on the one hand and its inferiority—or at least its failure to merit inclusion with the other "Abrahamic" faiths—on the other hand.

This strategy of division is taken to an extreme when *allāh*, the Arabic term for the biblical God, is not translated as God, but left in transliterated Arabic form, a practice that is quite common. For example, a revised version of Yusuf Ali's Qur'ān translation was produced in 1989 by Amana Publications with official backing of the government of Saudi Arabia. One of the striking features of this version was that all of Yusuf Ali's mentions of "God" were corrected, so to speak, to "Allah."[12] In a typical answer to the question whether the name *allāh* can be translated, one pundit in a Kuwaiti newspaper argues that, since the names of God are known by direct designation in scripture (*tawqīf*), translations must therefore take into account the original contexts in which they occur and the meanings intended in those contexts. He argues that use of the English word "God"

11. Wilfred Cantwell Smith, "The True Meaning of Scripture: An Empirical Historian's Nonreductionist Interpretation of the Qur'an," *IJMES* 11 (1980): 487–505, esp. 501.
12. Bruce Lawrence, *Who Is Allah?* (Chapel Hill: University of North Carolina Press, 2015), 174.

can conjure up worshipped beings other than Allah, whose definitions and characteristics do not correspond to those of Allah. In his view, the God that the Christians worship is not the single and singular being worshipped by Muslims, by which he apparently—and typically—refers to the Christian Trinity. Therefore, the word *allāh* in foreign language translations should either be retained in the Arabic script or presented as "Allah" in Roman letters.[13] Some Christian authors make the same argument from the other side. Even if one sets aside alarmist evangelical polemics such as *Allah, God of the Moon: Why We Should Fear the Islamic Cult*,[14] somewhat more careful writers such as the Catholic theologian Felix Körner argue that one must not assume that *allāh* can be translated as "God" on account of the different theological understandings attached to those terms in Christianity and Islam.[15] Despite the obvious importance of Judaism for a discussion of this topic, it is interesting to note that it is framed, on both sides, primarily as a conflict between Christian and Islamic theology.

A similar difference of opinion may be seen with regard to the translation of biblical personal names that occur in the Qur'ān. Perhaps the most consistent of the popular English translations in this regard, Muhammad Habib Shakir's translation keeps all of the names of biblical characters in their Arabic forms, using "Ibrahim" instead of "Abraham," "Musa" instead of "Moses," "Yusuf" instead of "Joseph," and so on, as if to suggest to Jewish or Christian readers: Don't think that *our* Ibrahim and *our* Musa are the same as *your* Abraham and *your* Moses. Similarly, Michel Lagarde's decision to retain the Arabic forms of biblical names in his translation of al-Suyūṭī's substantial manual of the qur'ānic sciences, *al-Itqān fī ʿulūm al-Qur'ān*, apparently reflects a similar view, that Ibrahim and Abraham cannot, in fact, be considered the same character on account of differences in interpretation between the Bible and the Qur'ān.[16] With regard both to *allāh* and to the Ar-

13. Nāẓim al-Misbāḥ, "*Lafẓ al-jalālah*," *Jarīdat al-Anbā'* (Kuwait), May 3, 2013, https://www.alanba.com.kw/ar/kuwait-news/islamic-faith/378850/03-05-2013.

14. Steve Preston, *Allah, God of the Moon: Why We Should Fear the Islamic Cult* (Scott Valley: Create Space Independent Publishing Platform, 2014).

15. Felix Körner, "JHWH, Gott, Allāh: drei Namen für dieselbe Wirklichkeit?" *Theologisch-praktische Quartalschrift* 158 (2010): 31–38; idem, "Der Gott Israels, Jesu und Muḥammads? Trinitätstheologie als Regula im interreligiösen Gespräch," *Gregorianum* 92 (2011): 139–158; Klaus von Stosch, "Does Allah Translate 'God'? Translating Concepts between Religions," in Michael P. De Jonge and Christiane Tietz (eds.), *Translating Religion: What Is Lost and Gained?* (Abingdon: Routledge, 2015), 123–136.

16. Michel Lagarde (trans.), *Le parfait manuel des sciences coraniques:* al-Itqān fī

abic names of biblical figures, however, there are inconsistencies in translation practices. Pickthall's translation uses both "Allah" and "God" frequently, and the logic behind the alternation is not clear. Many translations, such as that of Pickthall, regularly give the ordinary English versions of most biblical names, such as "Noah," "Moses," "Abraham," "Lot," and so on while at the same time retaining the Arabic form "ʿImrān" without rendering it as "Amram," the ordinary English version of the name of Moses's father.

While theological considerations clearly play a part in qurʾānic translation practices regarding the name of God and the biblical personal names, I do not believe that they are the major deciding factor in the other examples examined here. In most cases, the translators are choosing the most common literal translation for a term that has biblical associations, so it may be that they simply were unaware of the connection. Most instances in which I argue that the translations fail to emphasize the biblical valences of terms are simply cases of a type of inertia. With regard to most of the examples examined here, translators have tended to follow the interpretive choices of earlier translators or common usage in secondary scholarship in Islamic Studies. This tradition has been influenced ultimately both by Muslim commentaries on the Qurʾān and by Western scholarship in Islamic Studies generally. The examples presented suffice to indicate that there is no simple divide with regard to the treatment of biblical allusions in the Qurʾān between Muslims and Christians, conservatives or liberals, traditionalists or modernists, nor is it the case that some translators consistently capture all the biblical allusions, while others consistently miss or conceal them. The point is, rather, that even translators whom one might expect to be favorably disposed to a biblicizing rendition often miss the opportunity, for whatever reason, to employ such a translation. In the end, many of these cases are simply the consequence of following the tradition of earlier Qurʾān translations. Whatever the cause of the adoption of anti-biblical or alienating translations, in many cases they go against both the letter and the spirit of the qurʾānic text.

Several aspects of Western Qurʾānic Studies' historical development may have contributed to the neglect of biblical valences in Qurʾān translations into English and the European languages. Some of the blame lies with the lack of attention to the relationship between the Qurʾān and the biblical tradition that was a by-product of a general slump in Qurʾānic Studies in the mid-late twentieth century. One cause of this was the break-up of the

---

ʿulūm al-Qurʾān *de Ǧalāl ad-Dīn as-Suyūṭī (849/1445–911/1505)* (2 vols.; Leiden: Brill, 2018).

critical mass of Qurʾānic Studies scholars in Germany following the rise of the Nazi party. In addition, Qurʾānic Studies early on developed distinct silos or sub-genres of scholarship, such that discussions of the relationship of the Qurʾān and the Bible tended to be excluded from general introductions to the Qurʾān. The topic was absent from Gustav Weil's *Historisch-Kritische Einleitung in den Koran* (1844), Nöldeke's influential *Geschichte des Qorans* (1860 and 1909–1930), and Régis Blachère's *Introduction au Coran* (1947, 1959). Richard Bell included a short discussion of the topic in his *Introduction to the Qur'ān* (1953), but Montgomery Watt effectively edited it out of his revised version of Bell's work, published 1970, because he felt that discussion of the topic would offend Muslims and work against cordial Christian-Muslim dialogue. In the field of religious studies in the latter half of the twentieth century, many scholars interested in the Qurʾān were influenced by the ideas of Wilfred Cantwell Smith, who argued that, in order to take non-Christian religions seriously, scholars in religious studies needed to examine non-Christian scriptures such as the Qurʾān with particular attention to the ways in which Muslims have understood the text over the centuries. One practical consequence of his ideas was to shift attention of scholars whose interests lay in Islamic scripture from the qurʾānic text to *tafsīr*.[17] Moreover, most translations of the Qurʾān have not been undertaken by experts in Qurʾānic Studies, but by scholars in other fields, such as literature, history, and philosophy, who did not incorporate advances in Qurʾānic Studies into their translations. It is difficult to assign particular translation decisions to any of these factors, but they all worked to downplay attention to the influence of biblical texts on the Qurʾān. In the end, as mentioned, the main factor for the persistence of anti-biblicizing, or non-biblicizing, translations may simply be inertia in the history of Qurʾān translation, in which the common practice of many who have undertaken new translations has

---

17. Nicolai Sinai and Angelika Neuwirth, "Introduction," in Neuwirth, Sinai, and Marx, *The Qur'ān in Context*, 1–24, 5–6; Devin J. Stewart, "Reflections on the State of the Art in Western Qur'anic Studies," in Carol Bakhos and Michael Cook (eds.), *Islam and Its Past: Jahiliyya, Late Antiquity, and the Qur'an* (Oxford: Oxford University Press, 2017), 4–68; Theodor Nöldeke, *Geschichte des Qorans* (Göttingen: Verlag der Dieterichschen Buchhandlung, 1860); Régis Blachère, *Introduction au Coran* (Paris: G.-P. Maisonneuve, 1947 [2nd ed., 1959]); Richard Bell, *Introduction to the Qur'ān* (Edinburgh: Edinburgh University Press, 1953); Richard Bell and William Montgomery Watt, *Bell's Introduction to the Qur'ān*, completely revised and enlarged (Edinburgh: Edinburgh University Press, 1970); Smith, "The True Meaning of Scripture." I hope to address this topic in more detail in a future study.

been simply to adopt one of the earlier translations as a basis and modify it in some respects.

"God's House" (II)

Bayt is the ordinary word for house in Arabic, though it can take on senses such as "room," "tent," "spiderweb," "beehive," and a host of others. In one set of passages in the Qurʾān, this term is used to refer to the Kaʿbah, the rectangular building that was Mecca's main shrine before the advent of Islam and later the focus of daily Islamic prayer. In these verses, English translations most often render the term as "house." However, I suggest that it means "temple" in this context and that it ought to be translated as such. The most common word for temple in the Semitic languages is in fact *bayt*, and this usage presumably goes back to proto-Semitic. The Akkadian cognate *bītu*, for example, means "house, dwelling, temple, sanctuary, palace, region, household, family, property," and the genitive construct *bīt ili*, literally, "house of god," is a standard Akkadian term for "temple." In Hebrew, the temple in Jerusalem is *bêt hammiqdāš*, literally, "the house of holiness" (2 Chr 36:17), which becomes *bayt al-maqdis* in Arabic, though that term does not occur in the Qurʾān. Significantly, the biblical text also refers to the temple in Jerusalem as *bêt YHWH*, "the house of Yahweh" (e.g., 1 Kgs 3:1, 2 Kgs 24:13). The term "the house of God" (*bêt hāʾĕlōhîm*), a label that corresponds closely to *bayt allāh* in the Qurʾān, is used to refer to the tabernacle at Shiloh (Judg 18:31).

Use of the term *bīt/bêt/bayt* to mean "temple" obviously originates in an analogy between a human master's house and the house of a god. The divinity lives in this house, which is recognized as his or her special property. Like the owner of a mundane estate, he or she has servants who run the household, clean the rooms, tend the grounds, prepare and serve meals, and entertain, pamper, and flatter their master or mistress. The emphasis on God's transcendence in later Jewish and Christian tradition and in the Qurʾān made such analogies between house and temple less obvious, apt, and doctrinally acceptable. In modern English, the close connection between an ordinary house and a temple is mainly lost. One can still refer to a center of worship as a house of God, with the difference that one is not signaling that He actually resides at that address. Despite the existence of that turn of phrase, when the Kaʿbah is referred to as a "house" in English, this fails to carry the weight of veneration that the designation "temple" does.

Muslims do not pray towards Mecca because it is the native town of the Prophet, but rather because it is the location of a biblical temple. The early

Muslims originally prayed toward Jerusalem on the grounds that it was the site of Solomon's temple. When it was revealed in the Qurʾān that the Kaʿbah had been built by Abraham and Ishmael but subsequently corrupted by Arab pagans, this was connected with the idea that it had originally been consecrated as a temple to the biblical God.[18] The Prophet Muḥammad's mission was framed in part as a project to restore Abraham's temple to its original purpose. Moreover, the Kaʿbah was the first temple, since Abraham lived centuries before Solomon, whose grand monument was actually the second temple. As Angelika Neuwirth puts it succinctly: "Mecca is thus 'the first temple of God.'"[19] This understanding is clear from Q Āl ʿImrān 3:96: *inna awwala baytin wuḍiʿa li'l-nāsi la'lladhī bi-bakkata* ("The first temple erected for mankind is certainly that at Bakkah"), Bakkah being understood as an alternative designation of Mecca. Since the Kaʿbah is portrayed as a precursor of other biblical temples, the many references to the Kaʿbah as a "house" (Q 2:125.127.158, 3:96, 5:2.97, 8:35, 14:37, 22:26, 106:3) should preferably be rendered as "temple." Accordingly, the epithet *al-bayt al-ḥarām* (Q al-Māʾidah 5:97) should be "the sacred temple" or "the inviolable temple," and the epithet *al-bayt al-ʿatīq* (Q al-Ḥajj 22:29.33) should be "the ancient temple."

The view that *bayt* in qurʾānic usage means "temple" has been rejected by at least one investigator in the field of Qurʾānic Studies, on the basis of what is, in my view, an ultimately unconvincing argument. In *Le Seigneur des tribus: L'Islam de Mahomet*, Jacqueline Chabbi undertakes an analysis of the rise of Islam that concentrates on its setting in the geography of the Ḥijāz and in tribal society of the time. This attempt to emphasize the Arabian background of Islam and the Qurʾān is an important corrective to the works of Wansbrough and other scholars who treat both as related entirely to biblical traditions and downplay or completely ignore the influence of pre-Islamic Arabian pagan religion. At the same time, an exclusive emphasis on the Arabian background risks downplaying the strategies of adopting biblical history as the central framework of qurʾānic salvation history and of rejecting certain pre-Islamic Arabian concepts such as the poetic virtues of extravagant generosity, violence, and pride and loyalties based primarily on solidarities of clan and tribe that clearly play an important role in the Qurʾān and in the early Islamic movement. In one chapter of her work, Chabbi describes the physical space of Mecca, addressing, among

18. Gerald R. Hawting, "Kaʿba," *EQ*, s.v. (2003); Angelika Neuwirth, *The Qur'an and Late Antiquity: A Shared Heritage*, trans. Samuel Wilder (Oxford: Oxford University Press, 2019), 398–402.
19. Neuwirth, *The Qur'an and Late Antiquity*, 401.

other things, the nature of the Kaʿbah. She argues that the Kaʿbah was not a temple, suggesting that the term *bayt* in Arabic differs considerably from its Hebrew counterpart in that *bayt* is much less concrete in conception, because it means "tent" or any place where one spends the night. She argues that in it were combined two conceptions, neither of which corresponds to that of a temple: a sacred enclosure and a betyl or sacred stone in which the power of the divinity was concentrated. Neither is an actual building.[20] This argument is based on certain important observations, such as the fact that the Kaʿbah is associated with a betyl, the black stone that is embedded in its wall, and that the term *bayt* was applied to sacred stones—betyl derives from *bet el* ("a house of god")—which were conceived of as receptacles for the powers of particular gods. It is also an argument from silence: Chabbi is reluctant to term the Kaʿbah a temple not only because she is engaged throughout her work in downplaying the connections of Islam and the Qurʾān with biblical tradition and correspondingly emphasizing the distinct Arabian tradition but also because little information has been preserved about what used to occur inside the Kaʿbah, suggesting that all the important ritual activity, and primarily circumambulation, took place *around* the Kaʿbah. This ignores a number of reports about the idols that were housed inside the Kaʿbah, such as a statue of the god Hubal, along with other decorations, such as paintings of Mary and Jesus, Abraham and Ishmael.[21] Even if those accounts are apocryphal, it is not unreasonable to suppose the use of the interior of the Kaʿbah for ritual activity on the basis of analogy with other shrines and scattered hints in Islamic literature such as Hishām b. al-Kalbī's (d. c. 206/821) *Kitāb al-Aṣnām.*[22] Crucial, also, is the recognition that, whatever the pre-Islamic notions of the Kaʿbah were, it was transformed in the Qurʾān and early Islamic tradition and reinterpreted as a biblical temple dedicated to the worship of the one God.

"The Disasters" (III)

The term *al-muʾtafikāt* occurs three times in the Qurʾān, in all cases in a list of earlier rebellious peoples who were punished through God's wrath. The singular form *al-muʾtafikah* appears once (Q al-Najm 53:53), and the

20. Jacqueline Chabbi, *Le Seigneur des tribus: L'Islam de Mahomet* (Paris: Éditions Noesis, 1997), 31–55, esp. 36–39, 51.
21. G. R. D. King, "The Paintings of the Pre-Islamic Kaʿba," *Muqarnas* 21 (2004): 219–229.
22. Hishām b. al-Kalbī, *The Book of Idols*, trans. Nabih Amin Faris (Princeton: Princeton University Press, 1952), passim.

plural form *al-mu'tafikāt* twice (Q 9:70, 69:9). In Q 53:53, *al-mu'tafikah* occurs immediately after reports of God's destruction of ʿĀd, Thamūd, and Noah's people (Q 53:50–52). In Sūrat al-Ḥāqqah, *al-mu'tafikāt* occurs after a description of the destruction of Thamūd and ʿĀd (Q 69:4–8). It is mentioned along with "Pharaoh and those before him" (Q 69:9–10), suggesting that they represent one of the communities that were destroyed before the time of Moses and Pharaoh. In Q al-Tawbah 9:70, *al-mu'tafikāt* occurs in a list of annihilated communities, after mention of the folk of Noah, ʿĀd, Thamūd, the folk of Abraham, and the dwellers of Midian. In all cases, then, the term occurs together with names of earlier peoples who were destroyed by God, and so likely refers to a parallel, historical people who were subjected to God's wrath.

With regard to form, the word *mu'tafikah* is an active participle of form VIII, from the root combination *'-f-k*. It thus appears, at first glance, to be related to the term *ifk* ("lying, deception"; Q 24:11.12, 25:4, 29:17, 31:43, 37:86.151, 46:11.28) and *affāk* ("inveterate liar"; Q 26:222, 45:7), but these cognates do not appear to give an appropriate meaning for the contexts in which *al-mu'tafikah* and *al-mu'tafikāt* occur. Mohammed Marmaduke Pickthall renders the term variously in his translation. In Q 53:53, he interprets *al-mu'tafikah* as a proper noun, refraining from translating it: "And Al-Mu'tafikah He destroyed." In Q 69:9 he translates it as "the communities that were destroyed": "And Pharaoh and those before him, and the communities that were destroyed, brought error." In Q 9:70, he translates the term as "the disasters": "Hath not the fame of those before them reached them—the folk of Noah, A'ad, Thamud, the folk of Abraham, the dwellers of Midian and the disasters (which befell them)?" First, these are three distinct translations for as many verses, and while that might be required in other circumstances, it appears that the three contexts here do not differ considerably, and a single rendition would have been appropriate. Secondly, "disasters" is certainly wrong, for the context does not suggest that *al-mu'tafikāt* are the means by which the nations of the past that appear earlier in the verse were destroyed. Rather, the fact that they occur in a list along with various destroyed nations of the past, parallel with them, suggests that the term must refer to another destroyed nation.

Scholars of Qur'ānic Studies have long recognized that *al-mu'tafikah/al-mu'tafikāt* derives ultimately from biblical Hebrew and that it refers to the cities of Sodom and Gomorrah. Abraham Geiger did not address the term in his 1833 work, *Was hat Mohammed aus dem Judenthume aufgenommen?*, but Aloys Sprenger suggested that *al-mu'tafikah/al-mu'tafikāt* derives from rabbinic uses of the verb *h-p-k* ("to overthrow") to describe the act by which

God destroyed Sodom and Gomorrah.[23] Hartwig Hirschfeld suggested that *al-mu'tafikah* derives from the Hebrew noun *mahpēkâ* ("the overthrow"), a term used to describe the destruction of Sodom and Gomorrah.[24] Josef Horovitz suggested that the *al-mu'tafikah/al-mu'tafikāt* derives from Aramaic *mahpektā* in the Targums or *hafektā* or other nominal forms, arguing that it was assimilated by being couched in the form of a participle of the form-VIII Arabic verb.[25] Heinrich Speyer and Arthur Jeffery mentioned these interpretations without, however, endorsing them explicitly, and Jeffery pointed out that the term is "certainly Arabic in its form."[26] Richard Bell viewed the derivation from Hebrew *mahpēkâ* proposed by Hirschfeld probable,[27] and Paret accepted it as established.[28] Overall, a compelling case can be made that *al-mu'tafikah/al-mu'tafikāt* derive ultimately from Hebrew *mahpēkâ*, perhaps through Aramaic.[29]

In the Bible, the story of Sodom and Gomorrah is not simply an etiological account explaining the desolation of the southern plain of the Dead Sea; it also serves as an exemplum of divine punishment for sin and disobedience. It is used in later biblical accounts in a typological fashion, serving as the model or analogue for Babylon, Edom, Jerusalem, or other cities, suggesting that the present corruption of society would, if it continued,

---

23. Aloys Sprenger, *Das Leben und die Lehre des Mohammad: Nach bisher größtentheils unbenutzten Quellen* (3 vols.; Berlin: Nicolai'sche Verlagsbuchhandlung, 1861–1865), 1.492.

24. Hartwig Hirschfeld, *Beiträge zur Erklärung des Ḳorân* (Leipzig: Otto Schulze, 1886), 37.

25. Josef Horovitz, *Koranische Untersuchungen* (Berlin: Walter de Gruyter, 1926), 13–14; idem, "Proper Names," 187–188.

26. Heinrich Speyer, *Die biblischen Erzählungen im Qoran* (Gräfenhainichen: Schulze, 1931 [late 1930s]), 156; Arthur Jeffery, *The Foreign Vocabulary of the Qur'ān*, 274.

27. Bell, *Introduction to the Qur'ān*, 124.

28. Rudi Paret, *Der Koran: Kommentar und Konkordanz* (Stuttgart: Kohlhammer, 1980), 207.

29. The exact process by which *mahpēkâ or mahpektā* ended up as *al-mu'tafikah/al-mu'tafikāt* in Arabic by being modified and adapted to the particular Arabic participial pattern *mufta'ilah* and the reason for this occurrence remain unclear. Despite the phonetic similarity, there is a certain semantic discrepancy of shift between the two forms, since *mahpēkâ* refers to God's act of destruction, whereas *al-mu'tafikah/al-mu'tafikāt* evidently refer to the cities that were destroyed. The common Arabic nominal pattern *maf'alah* would match Hebrew *mahpēkâ* more closely in form. Perhaps that form was not favored because it usually serves as a noun of place and the intention was to create a cognate form that would ostensibly describe the cities that were destroyed.

cause the city in question to meet the same fate that Sodom and Gomorrah had met centuries earlier. It is joined suggestively in various passages of the New Testament with Noah's flood and the plagues inflicted on the Egyptians as examples of the dire consequences of disobedience to God (e.g., Luke 17:26–32, Rev 11:8). This typological usage continues to appear in later Jewish and Christian literature.

Sodom and Gomorrah are regularly invoked in the Hebrew Bible, especially by the later prophets, most often to make analogical arguments about contemporary society in Jerusalem. The prophet Isaiah addresses his audience as follows (Isa 1:9–10):

> Unless the Lord Almighty had left us some survivors, we would have become like Sodom, we would have been like Gomorrah. Hear the word of the Lord, you rulers of Sodom; listen to the instruction of our God, you people of Gomorrah!

Here Isaiah refers metaphorically to the rulers and the people of the kingdom of Israel as the rulers of Sodom and the people of Gomorrah, making the point that their general sinfulness would have caused their doom had it not been for a small group of the righteous who continued to exist within the community, upholding correct behavior and thus averting disaster. Ezekiel also uses an analogical argument to denounce his contemporaries, inhabitants of the southern kingdom of Judah (Ezek 16:46–48):

> Your older sister was Samaria, who lived to the north of you with her daughters; and your younger sister, who lived to the south of you with her daughters, was Sodom. You not only followed their ways and copied their detestable practices, but in all your ways you soon became more depraved than they. As surely as I live, declares the Sovereign Lord, your sister Sodom and her daughters never did what you and your daughters have done.

The message is that the cities of Judah are even more sinful than Sodom and its counterparts, the implication being that they risk an analogous destruction. Jeremiah makes a similar comparison of the city of Jerusalem (Jer 23:14):

> I have seen also in the prophets of Jerusalem a horrible thing: They commit adultery and walk in lies; they strengthen also the hands of evildoers, that none doth return from his wickedness. They are all of them unto me as Sodom, and the inhabitants thereof as Gomorrah.

Here he complains specifically about sinful and evildoing prophets, as well as ordinary inhabitants of Jerusalem, comparing them to the inhabitants of Sodom and Gomorrah.

The catastrophic end of Sodom and Gomorrah came to be known in later strata of the Bible as *hammahpēkâ*, "the overthrowing." The term *mahpēkâ* derives from the accounts in Gen 19 of God's destruction of Sodom and Gomorrah.[30] At several points in the narrative, the text employs forms of the verb "to overthrow" in order to describe God's act of destruction: "that I will not overthrow (*hāpkî*) the city of which you have spoken" (Gen 19:21), … "and He overthrew (*wayyahăpōk*) those cities, and all the plain …" (Gen 19:25); "And God sent Lot out of the midst of the overthrow (*hahăpēkâ*), when He overthrew (*behăpōk*) the cities in which Lot dwelt" (Gen 19:29). On account of such uses of derivatives of the tri-consonantal root *h-p-k*, the destruction of Sodom and Gomorrah—and of the other cities of the plain at the southern end of the Dead Sea—became known as *hammahpēkâ*, "the overthrowing," as a pithy characterization of the historical event.

Analogical references to Sodom and Gomorrah in later books of the Bible regularly use the term *mahpēkâ* to describe the particular act of their destruction:

> And Babylon, the glory of kingdoms, the beauty of the Chaldeans' pride, shall be like God's overthrow (*kəmahpēkat ĕlōhîm*) of Sodom and Gomorrah. (Isa 13:19)

> I have overthrown some of you as when God overthrew (*kəmahpēkat ĕlōhîm*) Sodom and Gomorrah. (Amos 4:11)

> As God overthrew (*kəmahpēkat ĕlōhîm*) Sodom and Gomorrah and the neighbor cities thereof, the Lord says that no man shall abide there, nor shall any son of man dwell therein. (Jer 50:40)

In all of these cases, the phrase *kəmahpēkat* … ("like the overthrow of …") is used regularly to designate the destruction of Sodom and Gomorrah while threatening later societies with a comparable fate. It is this usage from which the qur'ānic term for Sodom and Gomorrah apparently derives.

Typological usage ties the qur'ānic *mu'tafikāt* with the biblical *mahpēkâ*. The passages in which the term *al-mu'tafikāt* occurs make similar analogical arguments, holding up the destructions of bygone nations as examples of what will happen to the contemporary audience if they fail to heed the

30. I would like to thank my colleague Shalom Goldman for first pointing this out to me.

warning of the Prophet Muḥammad. It is therefore clear that *al-muʾtafikāt* is related to the biblical *mahpēkâ* ("the overthrowing") and refers to Sodom and Gomorrah, which are never referred to explicitly by those names in the Qurʾān. *Al-muʾtafikāt* must mean, literally, "the overturned cities," referring to God's method of destruction, and the fact that the term is related to *mahpēkâ* has to do with the fact that the Qurʾān is drawing on biblical tradition in framing the entire genre of the punishment stories that play such a prominent role in the text.

The Qurʾān provides some corroboration that *al-muʾtafikāt* is not just etymologically related to the Hebrew terms for biblical destruction of Sodom and Gomorrah. Several qurʾānic passages make it clear that the qurʾānic understanding of the act of destruction corresponds to the "overthrow" that appears in the Bible. Q 53:53 uses the verb *ahwā* ("cast down, cause to fall") to describe the destruction: *wa'l-muʾtafikata ahwā* ("and He cast down the *muʾtafikah*"; Q 53:53). Two other verses describe the act of destruction using the explicit phrase *jaʿalnā ʿāliyahā sāfilahā* ("We made its uppermost part its lowermost part" or "We made its high part its low part"; Q 11:82, 15:74). Especially the last two verses go along with the sense of "overthrowing," and this may indicate an understanding that the term *al-muʾtafikāt* was connected with that idea.

In contrast to Pickthall's rendition, some other translations capture the meaning of "overturned" cities found in the Hebrew Bible, and Yusuf Ali refers to Sodom and Gomorrah explicitly once. Thus Yusuf Ali:

> Hath not the story reached them of those before them?—The people of Noah, and ʿĀd, and Thamūd; the people of Abraham, the men of Midian, and the Cities overthrown. (Q 9:70)
>
> And He destroyed the Overthrown Cities (of Sodom and Gomorrah). (Q 53:53)
>
> And Pharaoh, and those before him, and the Cities Overthrown, committed habitual Sin. (Q 69:9)

And thus Bell:

> And the overturned (cities) He cast down. (Q 53:53)
>
> Pharaoh, and those before him, and the overwhelmed (cities) committed fault. (Q 69:9)

Shakir's translation has the following renderings:

> Has not the news of those before them come to them; of the people of Nuh and Ad and Samood, and the people of Ibrahim and the dwellers of Madyan and the overthrown cities. (Q 9:70)
>
> And the overthrown cities did He overthrow. (Q 53:53)
>
> And Pharaoh, and those before him, and the Cities Overthrown, committed habitual Sin. (Q 69:9)

Finally, here is Alan Jones:

> And he also overthrew the overturned settlements. (Q 53:53)
>
> And Pharaoh and those before him and the overturned settlements brought error. (Q 69:9)

The translations "overturned" or "overthrown," modifying "cities" or "settlements," captures quite directly the connection with the biblical image of the destruction of Sodom, Gomorrah, and the other cities of the plain.

Several other translations render *al-muʾtafikah/al-muʾtafikāt* in somewhat different fashions. Arberry uses "subverted," which in one sense is synonymous with "overturned":

> Has there not come to you the tidings of those who were before you—the people of Noah, Ad, Thamood, the people of Abraham, the men of Midian and the subverted cities? Their Messengers came to them with the clear signs God would not wrong them, but themselves they wronged. (Q 9:70)
>
> ... and the Subverted City He also overthrew. (Q 53:53)
>
> Pharaoh likewise, and those before him, and the Subverted Cities – they committed error. (Q 69:9)

I would prefer "overturned" to "subverted" on the grounds that "subvert" is often understood to mean "undermine," which would be incorrect here, since the understanding is that the city is being raised up, inverted, and smashed to the ground.

In yet other cases, translators have chosen "overwhelmed" rather than "overturned":

> Has there not come to them the report of those before them, the people of Noah, and ʿĀd and Thamūd, and the people of Abraham, and those of Midian, and the overwhelmed (cities)? (Q 9:70; Richard Bell)

> Have they not heard the tidings of those before them: the people of Noah, ʿĀd, Thamūd, the people of Abraham, the men of Madyan, and the overwhelmed settlements? (Q 9:70; Jones)

In my view, this particular diction does not fit the context. The use of "overwhelmed" suggests that the cities were flooded or covered over, whereas the biblical *mahpēkâ* appears to describe God's act of raising them up, inverting them, and smashing them to the ground. Muhammad Abdel Haleem uses the more generic term "ruined cities" to render *al-mu'tafikah/al-mu'tafikāt*:

> Have they never heard the stories about their predecessors, the peoples of Noah, ʿAd, Thamud, Abraham, Midian, and the ruined cities? (Q 9:70)

> ... that it was He who brought down the ruined cities. (Q 53:53)

> Pharaoh, too, and those before him, and the ruined cities: these people committed grave sins. (Q 69:9)

While this translation certainly fits in with the general logic of the punishment stories, in which nations of the past are in fact ruined, this translation is less than ideal. First, it breaks or conceals the connection with biblical diction, and secondly, it obscures one of the crucial features of the punishment stories. The annihilations of past nations occur in specific ways. One realizes from the beginning of these accounts that those who disobey God and reject the Prophet will inevitably meet their fate and be destroyed, but the particular mode of destruction visited upon them is a point of acute interest: Noah's people are destroyed by a flood, ʿĀd by a wind, and Sodom and Gomorrah by being overturned. Abdel Haleem's generic reference to ruination thus removes a key element of the story.

"The Burning Tree" (IV)

The scene in which God selects Moses to be his prophet is well known from the Book of Exodus, and it is generally known by reference to its most striking element, "the burning bush" (Exod 3:1 – 4:17). It is a crucial scene in the Hebrew Bible, for it recounts God's commission of Moses as a prophet, whereby he is assigned the task of confronting Pharaoh and rescuing the Hebrews from oppression. It stands as a model for prophecy in general, and it presents God speaking directly to a human prophet, stressing the intimate contact between Moses and God and at the same time the overpowering presence of the Lord on hallowed ground. It provides the archetype of prophetic miracles—the snake turning into a staff and Moses's hand turning white—through which the legitimacy of prophecy is established.

Versions of this scene in which God commissions Moses as his messenger to Pharaoh occur in five qurʾānic passages of varying length (Q 19:51–53, 20:9–48, 26:10–16, 27:7–12, 28:29–35). The scene is crucial in the same ways, and for the same reasons, as it is in the Bible. Three of the five passages refer explicitly to the fire that attracts Moses's attention (Q 20:9–11, 27:7–8, 28:29–30). A notable difference is that whereas in Exodus Moses goes to investigate the fire in the wilderness out of curiosity, because the bush is not being consumed by the fire, in the Qurʾān he goes in order to fetch a firebrand or live ember for his family (*ahl*)—probably meaning here his wife—evidently to help start their own fire to cook a meal (Q 20:9, 27:7, 28:29). All three passages imply that some sort of wood is burning, but only one, Q al-Qaṣaṣ 28:30, refers explicitly to the burning bush. Given the close connection of these passages with the events portrayed in Exod 3–4, it is surprising that most translations of the Qurʾān into English refer to a "tree" that burns, and not a bush. To refer to "the burning tree" is to make the scene somehow strange and unfamiliar, as if it referred to a forest fire and not to one of the most striking and dramatic scenes of God's presence in the Hebrew Bible.

At the outset, it is worth pointing out that "bush" is a perfectly fine translation of the word that occurs in the qurʾānic text, Arabic *shajarah*. *Shajarah* is indeed rendered commonly as "tree," and this is certainly the first sense that appears in the dictionary. However, the Arabic term may refer to leafy plants that vary greatly in size. For example, Q al-Ṣāffāt 37:147 depicts Jonah being cast up on the seashore, where he is protected by a gourd vine (*shajarah min yaqṭīn*) that grows over him to conceal his body from the view. The context indicates that the "tree" in question is a plant that grows low to the ground. *Shajarah* can thus be translated as "bush" while adhering closely to the original text and without doing any violence to it, but this option is rarely taken in English translations of the Qurʾān.

Some of the widely used English Qurʾān translations render Q 28:30 as follows:

> And when he reached it, he was called from the right side of the valley in the blessed field, from the tree: "O Moses! Lo! I, even I, am Allah, the Lord of the Worlds." (Pickthall)

> But when he came to the (Fire), a voice was heard from the right bank of the valley, from a tree in hallowed ground: "O Moses! Verily I am Allah, the Lord of the Worlds." (Yusuf Ali)

> But when he reached it, a voice called out to him from the right-hand side of the valley, from a tree on the blessed ground: "Moses, I am God, the Lord of the Worlds." (Abdel Haleem)

> When he came to it, a voice cried from the right of the watercourse, in the sacred hollow, coming from the tree: "Moses, I am God, the Lord of all Being." (Arberry)

> Arriving at the fire, a voice called out to him from the right side of the valley, at a blessed spot, and coming from the tree: "O Moses, it is I, God, Lord of the Worlds." (Khalidi)

All of these examples use the term tree to refer to what is evidently the burning bush. Only a few translators whose translations I have examined use "bush." Richard Bell has the following:

> When he came to it, a voice called to him from the right-hand bank of the wādi, in the blessed vale, out of the bush: "O Moses, lo, I am Allah, Lord of the worlds."

Muhammad Habib Shakir, though he in many other cases shows a tendency to avoid biblical vocabulary, renders this passage as follows:

> And when he came to it, a voice was uttered from the right side of the valley in the blessed spot of the bush, saying: O Musa! Surely I am Allah, the Lord of the worlds.

In my view, the translations of Bell and Shakir are in this respect superior to the others, since they preserve the critical term "bush" as the exact site of Moses's direct encounter with God.

In this case, the qurʾānic text certainly does not evince a strategy of separating this scene from its biblical forerunner, despite some obvious differences between the two accounts, including the fact that the Hebrew text uses the term *hassəneh*, "the bush" (Exod 3:2.3), and not *hāʿēṣ*, the common Hebrew word for "tree," and the fact that the scene opens with a statement that *the angel of* the Lord, that is, the angel of Yahweh, appeared to Moses in the flames coming out of the midst of a bush (Exod 3:2), whereas in the Qurʾān there is no mention of an angel. The general equivalence of the scenes and the role they play in establishing Moses's prophecy and setting up his later confrontation with Pharaoh are clear, and this equivalence is corroborated by many other more specific correspondences. For example, God's statement to Moses in Exod 3:14, *ʾehyeh ʾăšer ʾehyeh* ("I am that I am"), is certainly reflected in the Qurʾān's emphatic statement *innī anā ʾllāhu rabbu ʾl-ʿālamīn* ("I, indeed I, am God, Lord of the Worlds"; Q 28:30). The emblematic nature of this scene is made poignant by the Islamic tradition's assignment to Moses of the epithet *kalīm allāh* ("the one to whom God spoke") on the basis of their interaction in this scene and by several other verses that refer to it, such as Q 28:44: "You [Muḥammad] were not present on the western side of the mountain when We gave Our command to Moses: you were not there." Insisting on translating the term *shajarah* here as "tree" rather than "bush" obscures the invocation of the scene in Exodus that is obviously intended.

"The Chest of Tranquility" (V)

The ark of the covenant appears prominently in Q 2:248, in the course of an account of the exploits of Saul (Arabic *ṭālūt*). The verse features a prophet who arose after the time of Moses and who corresponds to Samuel but is unnamed in the text.[31] The qurʾānic passage presents in a few verses, Q 2:246–251, a highly condensed version of the events recounted in 1 Sam 4–17. The verse of interest for the present discussion occurs after the prophet, again, presumably Samuel, has appointed Saul king of the Israelites (Q 2:247; cf. 1 Sam 10:24–25, 11:14 – 12:4). In Q 2:248, the unnamed prophet promises the Israelites future victory over their enemies. This is followed by a description of one of Saul's military campaigns, before the momentous battle in which David defeats Goliath, sealing Israel's victory over the Philistines (Q 2:250–251; cf. 1 Sam 17).[32] Shakir translates the key verse as follows:

> And the prophet said to them: "Surely the sign of His kingdom is, that there shall come to you *the chest* in which there is *tranquility* from your Lord and residue of the relics of what the children of Musa and the children of Haroun have left, the angels bearing it; most surely there is a sign in this for those who believe."

31. Speyer, *Die biblischen Erzählungen*, 364–371.

32. In Q 2:249, Saul is described as forbidding the Israelites from drinking from a river when they cross it. Some scholars have argued that this scene is based on an erroneous conflation of the story of Gideon with the story of Saul's campaign, which differs at this point. Saul ill-advisedly makes the members of the army swear that they will not eat, and as a result they become weak. The temptation is honey in a forest, and not the river water. Neal Robinson and Walid Saleh, however, have argued that such quibbles miss the point of the qurʾānic story. See Neal Robinson, *Discovering the Qurʾan: A Contemporary Approach to a Veiled Text* (London: SCM Press, 1996), 217–218; Walid Saleh, "In Search of a Comprehensible Qurʾān: A Survey of Some Recent Scholarly Works," *Bulletin of the Royal Institute for Inter-Faith Studies* 5 (2003): 143–162, 155–157.

First, the "chest" here is clearly meant to be the ark of the covenant. The qurʾānic term for the ark of the covenant is *al-tābūt*, which occurs in this sense only in this verse. In Q 20:39, the word's only other occurrence in the Qurʾān, *tābūt* refers to the vessel in which Moses's mother placed him when she set him afloat on the river (cf. Exod 2:3). Geiger identifies *tābūt* as a borrowing from Aramaic *tābūtā* ("ark"), though Nöldeke argues that it derives from Ethiopic *tābōt*. Though the Hebrew in the Bible for "ark of the covenant," *ʾărôn habbərît*, is quite different, the noun *tēbâ*, the same word used for Noah's ark and the vessel of reeds in which Moses was placed by his mother, a cognate of *tābūt*, is used for the ark of the covenant in the Mishnah.[33] Most other English translations of the Qurʾān capture the connection of the term *tābūt* in this verse with the ark of the covenant, but they regularly fail to capture the biblical allusion to God's "presence" in the ark, conveyed by the term *shekhinah* in rabbinic Hebrew, which corresponds to Arabic *sakīnah* in the qurʾānic text. Most English translations of the text render *sakīnah* with a term related to "calm" or "tranquility" instead:

> Their prophet said to them, "The sign of his authority will be that the Ark [of the Covenant] will come to you. In it there will be [*the gift of*] *tranquility* from your Lord and relics of the followers of Moses and Aaron, carried by the angels. There is a sign in this for you if you believe." (Abdel Haleem)

> And their Prophet said unto them: Lo! The token of his kingdom is that there shall come unto you the ark wherein is *peace of reassurance* from your Lord, and a remnant of that which the house of Moses and the house of Aaron left behind, the angels bearing it. Lo! Herein shall be a token for you if (in truth) ye are believers. (Pickthall)

> Their prophet said to them, "The sign of his sovereignty is that the ark, in which there is *an assurance* from your Lord, will come to you, and a remnant of that which the family of Moses and Aaron left behind, borne by the angels. In that there is a sign for you if you are believers." (Jones)

> And (further) their Prophet said to them: "A sign of his authority is that there shall come to you the Ark [of the Covenant], with *(an assurance) therein of security* from your Lord, and the relics left by the family of Moses and the family of Aaron, carried by angels. In this is a Symbol for you if ye indeed have faith." (Abdullah Yusuf Ali)

33. Theodor Nöldeke, *Neue Beiträge zur semitischen Sprachwissenschaft* (Strassburg: Trübner, 1910), 49; Speyer, *Die biblischen Erzählungen*, 367–368; Jeffery, *Foreign Vocabulary*, 88–89; Uri Rubin, "Traditions in Transformation: The Ark of the Covenant and the Golden Calf in Biblical and Islamic Historiography," *Oriens* 36 (2001): 196–214.

All of these translations render *al-tābūt* as "the ark" or "the ark of the covenant." However, they render the term *sakīnah* "[the gift of] tranquility" (Abdel Haleem); "peace of reassurance" (Pickthall); "an assurance" (Jones); and "(an assurance) therein of security" (Abdullah Yusuf Ali). In doing so, they are in agreement with many commentaries on the Qur'ān, which gloss *sakīnah* as *ṭuma'nīnah* ("reassurance").[34] The meaning "tranquility" derives from one of the main meanings of the triconsonantal root *s-k-n* in Arabic, "to be quiet, calm," and the translations of "assurance" or "reassurance" derive from a combination of the understanding of this Arabic root and a consideration of the context, probably influenced by commentaries on the verse. In my view, these translations of the term *sakīnah* do not adequately capture the image invoked, which is related to the representation of the ark of the covenant in the Hebrew Bible.

The Qur'ānic term *sakīnah* has long been recognized as a borrowing from Jewish tradition, and the general interpretation of its use in the Qur'ān has followed for the most part the same lines from the beginning. Silvestre de Sacy identified *sakīnah* as a borrowing from Hebrew already in 1829, explaining, "Or qui ne voit que ce n'est autre chose que la *schékina*, שכינה c'est-à-dire *la présence de la majesté divine* ou, comme s'exprime Moïse, *la gloire de Dieu* qui, reposant sur le tabernacle, annonçait la présence de la divinité." He added, "On peut conjecturer, par les deux passages de la surate 48, que Mahomet lui-même attachait à ce mot une idée de calme et de sécurité."[35] Subsequently, Abraham Geiger and many other scholars recognized Hebrew *shekhinah* as the etymon of *sakīnah*.[36]

---

34. See, for example, al-Thaʿlabī, *al-Kashf wa'l-bayān*, ed. Abū Muḥammad Ibn ʿĀshūr (10 vols.; Beirut: Dār Iḥyā' al-Turāth al-ʿArabī, 2002), 2.213.
35. Silvestre de Sacy, "Lettre de M. le baron Silvestre de Sacy, à M. Garcin de Tassy," *Journal Asiatique* 4 (1829): 161–179, 177–178.
36. Abraham Geiger, *Was hat Mohammed aus dem Judenthume aufgenommen?* (Bonn: F. Baaden, 1833), 54–56; Alfred von Kremer, *Geschichte der herrschenden Ideen des Islams: der Gottesbegriff, die Prophetie und Staatsidee* (Leipzig: F. A. Brockhaus, 1868), 226, n. 2; Siegmund Fraenkel, *De Vocabulis in antiquis Arabum carminibus et in Corano peregrinis* (Leiden: Brill, 1880), 23; Maier (Max) Grünbaum, "Ueber Schem hammephorasch als Nachbildung eines aramäischen Ausdrucks und über sprachliche Nachbildungen überhaupt," *ZDMG* 39 (1885): 543–616, 581–582; Ignaz Goldziher, "La notion de *Sakīnah* chez les Mohamétans," *Revue de l'Histoire des religions* 28 (1893): 1–13; idem, *Abhandlungen zur arabischen Philologie* (2 vols.; Leiden: E.J. Brill, 1896), 1.177–204; Otto Pautz, *Muhammeds Lehre von der Offenbarung* (Leipzig: J. C. Hinrichs'sche Buchhandlung, 1898), 251; Nöldeke, *Neue Beiträge zur semitischen Sprachwissenschaft*, 24–25; Horovitz, "Jewish Proper Names and Derivatives in the Koran," 208–209; Karl Ahrens, "Chrisliches im Qoran: Eine Nachlese," *ZDMG* 84

The Hebrew term *shekhinah* is a verbal noun meaning "dwelling, occupying" that derives from the verb *shakhan, yishkhon* ("to dwell"), just as the triconsonantal root *s-k-n* also means "to dwell, inhabit," as well as "to be calm" or "to be at rest." It is used to mean God's "indwelling," that is, His "presence" or "aura." The functional, idiomatic equivalent to the term in Arabic would probably be *ḥaḍrah* or *ḥuḍūr* ("presence") and not, for example, *sukūn* ("being quiet" or "being at rest"), even though both Hebrew and Arabic attach both general meanings, residence on the one hand and calm, rest, or quiet on the other, to the triconsonantal root combination *sh-k-n/s-k-n*. The history of the term *shekhinah* is complex.[37] A number of modern studies focus on *shekhinah* as representing the feminine aspect of the divine, something that became important in mysticism of the medieval kabbalah tradition and that has been emphasized in modern scholarship on account of its potential connections with feminist thought.[38] The consen-

---

(1930): 15–68, 21; Arthur Jeffery, *The Foreign Vocabulary of the Qur'ān*, 174; Reuven Firestone, "Shekhinah," *EQ*, s.v. (2004); Rubin, "Traditions in Transformation."

37. J. T. Marshall, "Shekinah," in J. Hastings (ed.), *A Dictionary of the Bible* (5 vols.; New York: Charles Scribner's Sons, 1898–1904), 4.489; Ludwig Blau and Kaufmann Kohler, "Shekinah," in Isidore Singer (ed.), *The Jewish Encyclopedia*, vol. 11 (New York: Funk & Wagnells Company, 1905), 259; Joshua Abelson, *The Immanence of God in Rabbinical Literature* (London: Macmillan 1912); Arnold Goldberg, *Untersuchungen über die Vorstellung von der Schekhinah in der frühen rabbinischen Literatur* (Berlin: Walter de Gruyter, 1969); Ephraim E. Urbach, *The Sages: Their Concepts and Beliefs*, trans. Israel Abrahams (Cambridge, MA: Harvard University Press, 1987), esp. ch. 3, 37–65; Gershom Scholem, "*Shekhinah*: The Feminine Element in Divinity," in Jonathan Chipman (ed.), *On the Mystical Shape of the Godhead: Basic Concepts in the Kabbalah*, trans. Joachim Neugroschel (New York: Schocken Books, 1991), 14–96, 293–300; J. Sievers, "'Where Two or Three ...': The Rabbinic Concept of Shekhinah and Matthew 18:20," in E. J. Fisher (ed.), *The Jewish roots of Christian Liturgy* (New York: Paulist Press, 1990), 47–61; Piero Capelli, "Figure e dimensioni della mediazione nell'ebraismo tardoantico e medievale: la voce dai cieli, la 'Šekinah' e la Torah orale," *Ricerche storico-bibliche* 29 (2017): 193–220.

38. Urbach, *The Sages*, esp. ch. 3; Peter Schäfer, *Mirror of His Beauty: Feminine Images of God from the Bible to the Early Kabbalah* (Princeton: Princeton University Press, 2002); Chani Smith, "The Symbol of the Shekhina: The Feminine Side of God," *European Judaism: A Journal for the New Europe* 19.1 (1985): 43–46; Rachel Elior, "Die Entwicklung der weiblichen Dimension Gottes in der mystischen Tradition des Judentums," in Michaela Feuerstein-Prasser und Felicitas Heimann-Jelinek (eds.), *Die weibliche Seite Gottes* (Hohenems: Bucher Verlag, 2017), 52–65; Moshe Idel, "Die Glieder der 'Schechina': Über den Aufstieg des Göttlich-Weiblichen in der Kabbala und seinen Niedergang im akademischen Diskurs der Moderne," in Eva S. Atlan et al. (eds.), *Die weibliche Seite Gottes: Kunst und Ritual* (Frankfurt: Jüdisches Museum Frankfurt; Bielefeld: Kerber, 2020), 80–114.

sus in biblical scholarship is that the term *shekhinah* first developed as a euphemism in the Targums, the Aramaic translations of the Hebrew Bible. It is generally understood that the term was used to replace the mention of God in passages that sound too anthropomorphic in the original Hebrew. When confronted with such anthropomorphic passages, the scholars who produced the Targums often referred to the *shekhinah*'s being located somewhere rather than referring to God directly. So, for example, Exod 34:6, "The Lord passed before him and proclaimed, 'The Lord, the Lord, a God merciful and gracious, slow to anger, and abounding in steadfast love and faithfulness,'" is rendered by Onqelos as "The Lord made his presence pass in front of him, and he proclaimed, 'O Lord! O Lord! Compassionate and gracious God, who keeps anger at a distance and abounds in doing true goodness.'"[39] Likewise, Exod 34:9, "And he said, 'If now I have found favor in your sight, O Lord, please let the Lord go in the midst of us, for it is a stiff-necked people, and pardon our iniquity and our sin, and take us for your inheritance,'" is rendered as follows: "And he said, 'If now I have found compassion before You, O Lord, let the Presence of the Lord now walk among us; although this is a stiff-necked people, forgive our iniquities and our sins, and make us Your possession ..."[40] In both of these examples, "the Lord"—i.e., Yahweh in the original Hebrew—has been replaced by "the presence (*shekhinah*) of the Lord" in order to avoid stating that God is simply walking among humans. According to Bernard Grossfeld, the translator of the Targum of Onqelos into English, the term *shekhinah* is used here instead of God because these verses appear to contradict a statement in Exod 33:20 that dictates that no man can survive seeing God directly.[41]

The interpretation of *shekhinah* as a euphemism designed to tone down the anthropomorphic implications of some verses in the earliest historical strata of the biblical text is certainly valid, but scholars in Biblical Studies, in my view, have exaggerated the attendant leap between biblical Hebrew and later use of the term *shekhinah*. It is true that the exact term *shekhinah* does not occur in the Hebrew Bible; the first historical attestations are in the Targums and rabbinic Hebrew. The form *peʿīlah* became much more frequent in later Hebrew than it was in the Hebrew Bible; it came to be a standard form of the verbal noun of verbs of the *qal* pattern in rabbinic

39. Bernard Grossfeld, *The Targum Onqelos to Exodus, Translated, with Apparatus and Notes* (Wilmington: Michael Glazier, 1988), 96.

40. Grossfeld, *The Targum Onqelos to Exodus*, 96.

41. Grossfeld, *The Targum Onqelos to Exodus*, 96–97, n. 3. Grossfeld points out that Targum of Pseudo-Jonathan uses the same periphrasis, while the Targum of Neophyti and the Fragmentary Targums (P, V) use "the Glory of His Divine Presence."

Hebrew.[42] Nevertheless, verbal nouns of this form already occurred in the Bible. An example is *hălîkôt* ("goings, ways, processions"; Ps 68:24, Prov 31:27, Hab 3:6), a plural of *hălîkâ*, which matches *shekhinah* in form. In addition, scholars seem to overlook the key role that cognates of *shekhinah* play in the Book of Exodus. Chief among these is *miškān* ("dwelling place"), the Hebrew term for the tabernacle, the mobile precursor of the temple, whose construction is described in great detail in Exod 25–31 and 35–40.[43] The term is obviously based on the conception that God is present in a specific locale; the tabernacle is called "the dwelling place" because God dwells there. This understanding of God's physical residence is stated explicitly in several passages using perfect verbs: "Then have them make a sanctuary for me, and I will dwell (*wəšākantî*) among them" (Exod 25:8); "Then I will dwell (*wəšākantî*) among the Israelites and be their God" (Exod 29:45); "And I will dwell (*wəšākantî*) among the sons of Israel" (1 Kgs 6:13). Other similar verses use the active participle: "You shall send away both male and female; you shall send them outside the camp so that they will not defile their camp where I dwell (*šōkēn*) in their midst" (Num 5:3); "You shall not defile the land in which you live, in the midst of which I dwell; for I the Lord am dwelling (*šōkēn*) in the midst of the sons of Israel" (Num 35:34). The "dweller" was originally the idol of the divinity, who inhabited the tabernacle and the temple generally, and the ark of the covenant specifically. A number of biblical passages, such as the report that the God of the Israelites repeatedly knocked over Dagon, the idol of the Philistines in their temple after they had captured the ark of the covenant, strongly suggest

42. Uri Mor, "The Verbal Noun of the *qal* Stem in Rabbinic Hebrew Traditions and *qĕṭēlâ*/*qĕṭîlâ* Alternations" *Journal of Jewish Studies* 66 (2015): 79–96. In modern Hebrew, this development became completely regularized.

43. The tabernacle is also termed *hāʾōhel*, "the tent" (e.g., Exod 26:9), *bêt hāʾōhel*, "the house of the tent" (e.g., 1 Chr 9:23), *ʾōhel môʿēd*, "the tent of meeting" (e.g., Exod 33:7), and *bêt YHWH*, "the house of Yahweh" (e.g., Exod 23:19). On the tabernacle in general, see A. R. S. Kennedy, "Tabernacle," in Hastings, *A Dictionary of the Bible*, 4.653–668; Frank M. Cross Jr., "The Tabernacle: A Study from an Archaeological and Historical Approach," *The Biblical Archaeologist* 10 (1947): 45–68; Richard E. Friedman, "The Tabernacle in the Temple," *Near Eastern Archaeology* 43 (1980): 241–248; Victor Hurowitz, "The Priestly Account of Building the Tabernacle," *JAOS* 105 (1985): 21–30; Craig R. Koester, *The Dwelling of God: The Tabernacle in the Old Testament, Intertestamental Jewish Literature, and the New Testament* (Washington, D.C.: The Catholic Biblical Association of America, 1989); Benjamin Sommer, "Conflicting Constructions of Divine Presence in the Priestly Tabernacle," *Biblical Interpretation* 9 (2001): 41–63; Michael M. Homan, "The Tabernacle and the Temple in Ancient Israel," *RC* 1 (January 2007): 38–49.

that He assumed the form of a similar idol (1 Sam 5). One could thus argue that the term *shekhinah* was implied already in the text of Exodus, and it is plausible that the instances of the term in later texts were merely recording an earlier, oral usage.[44]

Later strata of the Bible reveal that attempts were made to remove vestiges of idolatry from the religion of the Israelites but that facets of earlier beliefs continued to be relevant nevertheless. Direct references to an idol were for the most part removed—except that the incident of the Golden Calf in Exod 32 appears to be a back-handed admission that the Hebrews used to worship Yahweh as an idol in the form of a calf or cow—but the idea remained that God's power or presence could be located in a particular place. The divinity at certain times made His presence known, and then He could be sensed by those in the vicinity. Other terms used to describe God's nebulous presence in the Hebrew Bible are "cloud" (*ʿānān*) and "glory" (*kābôd*; 1 Kgs 8:10–13, 2 Chr 5:13–14 and 7:1–3). When the doctrine of God's transcendence was adopted in the Israelite religion and mentions of the physical idol were suppressed, the understanding came to be that the ark was associated with God's aura or presence, envisaged as invisible but nevertheless located or concentrated in a particular area. While it is clear that the qurʾānic term *sakīnah* cannot have derived directly from the Bible and must have come from later Jewish or Christian texts, the concept of God's presence is not only a post-biblical development.

The term *sakīnah* occurs six times in the qurʾānic text (Q 2:248, 9:26.40, 48:4.18.26). As seen above, the translators render this term regularly in English translations as "tranquility," "assurance," or "reassurance," and this is true not only in Q 2:248, but also in the other verses in which it occurs. However, the other instances do not occur in the midst of biblical narratives, so the connection with the Bible is attenuated. For example, Q 4:84 is translated as follows:

> He it is who hath sent down the Assurance in the hearts of the believers, that they may add faith to their faith; To Allah belong the hosts of the heavens and the earth, and Allah hath become knowing, wise. (Bell)

> [It is] He who sent down the reassurance into the hearts of the believers that they might add faith to their faith—to God belong the hosts of the heavens and the earth; God is Knowing and Wise. (Jones)

44. Indeed, one might even suggest that the term was used as a euphemism for the idol of Yahweh that was written out of descriptions of the ark of the covenant, the tabernacle.

Again, we see the use of "assurance" or "reassurance." It is not immediately clear what the connection between *sakīnah* in Q 2:248 and other similar verses would be with the biblical *shekhinah*, and this requires some careful consideration.

In Q 2:248, the *sakīnah* is used in a clearly biblical context, a scene that portrays a battle between the Israelites and the Philistines. It is associated with the ark of the covenant, as it is in the Bible. Furthermore, it is associated closely with battle, as it is in the Bible. In the books of the Hebrew Bible, one of the main functions of the ark of the covenant is to be marched out with the army of the tribes of Israel when they battle their enemies. The ark brings the very presence of God into their host and, on account of the deity's awesome power, both terrifies the enemy and infuses the army of Israel with the courage and determination to fight and to emerge victorious. 1 Samuel does not include a verse in which Saul utters the statement that appears in Q 2:248, but the ark of the covenant appears prominently in that book. The ark is first retrieved from Shiloh to help the army of Israel in a battle against the Philistines, who are terrified by its presence (1 Sam 4:3–8). Then, it is captured by the Philistines, who hold it for seven months but return it after being plagued by mice and hemorrhoids as a form of divine punishment (1 Sam 4:11–6:18). The return of the ark allows Israel to defeat the Philistines (1 Sam 7:10) and later facilitates another rout of the enemy (1 Sam 14:18–31).[45]

The situation described in Q 2:248 is typical of the contexts in which the ark of the covenant appears in the Bible in general and in the story of Saul in particular. In Q 2:248, the setting also involves the military conflict be-

45. The ark of the covenant is also termed *ʾărôn bərît YHWH*, "the ark of the covenant of Yahweh" (cf. 1 Kgs 6:19); *ʾărôn hā-ĕlōhîm*, "the ark of God" (1 and 2 Samuel); and *ʾarōn hāʿēdūt*, "the ark of testimony" (Exod 25:22). On the ark in general, see Gerhard von Rad, "The Tent and the Ark," in *The Problem of the Hexateuch and Other Essays* (Edinburgh: Oliver and Boyd, 1966), 103–124; T. E. Fretheim, "The Ark in Deuteronomy," *Catholic Biblical Quarterly* 30 (1968): 1–14; Johann Maier, *Das altisraelitische Ladeheiligtum* (Berlin: Töpelman, 1965); H. Davies, "The Ark of the Covenant," *Annual of the Swedish Theological Institute* 5 (1966–1967): 30–47; O. Eißfeldt, "Die Lade Jahwes in Geschichtserzählung, Sage und Lied," *Das Altertum* 14 (1968): 135–145; Joseph Gutmann, "The History of the Ark," *Zeitschrift für die alttestamentliche Wissenschaft* 83 (1971): 22–30; C. L. Seow, "The Designation of the Ark in Priestly Theology," *Hebrew Annual Review* 8 (1984): 185–198; George W. Coats, "The Ark of the Covenant in Joshua: A Probe into the History of a Tradition," *Hebrew Annual Review* 9 (1985): 137–157; John Day, "Whatever Happened to the Ark of the Covenant?" in John Day (ed.), *Temple and Worship in Biblical Israel* (London: T&T Clark, 2007): 250–270.

tween Israel and the Philistines. The verse describes the ark of the covenant as a sign of Saul's sovereignty (*mulk*) and does not mention a specific battle. Nevertheless, given that the figure of the king (*malik*) is associated with fighting in v. 247 and that the passage refers to Saul's campaign in v. 249 and ends with David's climactic victory over Goliath in vv. 250–251, it makes sense to interpret the prophet's statement as a promise of future victory. This being the case, one may assume that the *sakīnah* fulfills a much more warlike function than "tranquility" or "reassurance." Like the angels who, according to the Qur'ān, fought alongside the Muslims at the Battle of Badr (Q 3:123–125, 8:9), the *sakīnah* is a physical presence that will enable Saul's forces to overpower their enemies and grant them victory.

In general, scholars in Qur'ānic Studies have reached a consensus that while the term *sakīnah* is connected with the biblical *shekhinah* in Q 2:248, in the other verses in which it appears, its meaning has been conflated with or at least colored by one of the ordinary meanings of the root combination *s-k-n*, namely, *sukūn* ("quiet" or "calm"). Two translators, Bell and Arberry, have chosen to render the biblical allusion palpable in their renditions of Q 2:248. Although in the other instances Bell translates *sakīnah* as "assurance" (Q 9:26.40) or "the Assurance" (Q 48:4.18.26), he does not translate the term in Q 2:248, retaining the term in transliteration as "Sakīna." This is presumably due to the fact that this verse deals directly with the ark of the covenant in the time of Saul, and so *sakīnah* would have to take on a sense more appropriate to that context.

> Their prophet said to them: "The sign of his kingship will be that the Ark will come to you containing a Sakīna from your Lord, and a relic of what was left by the family of Moses and the family of Aaron, and the angels will bear it; surely in that is a sign for you if ye are believers."

In a note attached to this verse explaining the word *sakīnah*, Bell writes, "The Hebrew *shekhīna*; in the Qur'ān the word generally has the sense of 'assurance,' but as this is probably the first occasion of its use, it is doubtful if any such sense is attached to it here."[46] He thus recognizes that *sakīnah* is related to the Hebrew *shekhinah*, but he means to distinguish this verse from the other qur'ānic verses in which it appears. He does not indicate that the other uses of *sakīnah* in the Qur'ān are unrelated to this one, but he apparently believes that this "foreign" term was used here initially, with something closer to its original meaning, and was then adopted for other uses,

46. Bell, *The Qur'ān Translated*, 1.36, n. 2.

subsequently being assigned the meaning "assurance" on account of the term's association with cognates such as *sukūn* ("being at rest, quiescent").

Arberry goes further, but does not really translate, producing a version similar to Bell's rendition of Q 2:248:

> And their Prophet said to them, "The sign of his kingship is that the Ark will come to you, in it a Shechina from your Lord, and a remnant of what the folk of Moses and Aaron's folk left behind, the angels bearing it. Surely in that shall be a sign for you, if you are believers."

In all of the verses in which *sakīnah* occurs, Arberry renders the term as "Shechina," which certainly attempts to capture the connection with the Hebrew. However, one might ask what the sense of "Shechina" is, or whether that word in English conveys any clear sense, whether appropriate to the context or not. In one verse, Arberry presents the term Shechina, as usual, but also provides a gloss:

> It is He who sent down the Shechina (tranquility) into the hearts of the believers, that they might add faith to their faith – to God belong the hosts of the heavens and the earth; God is All-knowing, All-wise. (Q 48:4)

Here, his use of "tranquility" may be considered a debt to earlier translations, or to the generally understood connection of the root *s-k-n* with calm or silence.

The first question that arises is what translation of *sakīnah* would appropriately capture the invocation of biblical *shekhinah* in Q 2:248. A possible candidate is "God's overwhelming aura." The second question is whether those translations can be legitimately applied in the qurʾānic verses that do not involve the ark of the covenant or biblical history. The other five instances of *sakīnah* occur in two *sūrah*s, Sūrat al-Tawbah (Q 9) and Sūrat al-Fatḥ (Q 48), both of which have to do with military confrontation. In my view, the consensus is more or less correct: these latter instances of *sakīnah* are in fact distinct from Q 2:248, and they do appear to have been colored by association with the term *sukūn* ("calm"). In all cases, however, I would argue that the translations "tranquility," "calm," "assurance," or "reassurance," are insufficient because they do not capture the sense of overwhelming might that allows the forces to defeat their enemy attached to the term *sakīnah*.

Sūrat al-Tawbah is a particularly warlike *sūrah* which begins with an ultimatum to the pagan Meccans. The term *sakīnah* occurs in it twice, in the following verses:

> Then God sent His calm (*sakīnatahu*) down to His Messenger and the believers, and He sent down invisible forces (*junūdan lam tarawhā*). He punished the disbelievers—this is what the disbelievers deserve, but God turns in His mercy to whoever He will. God is most forgiving and merciful. (Q 9:26; Abdel Haleem)

> Even if you do not help the Prophet, God helped him when the disbelievers drove him out: when the two of them were in the cave, he [Muḥammad] said to his companion, "Do not worry, God is with us," and God sent His calm (*sakīnatahu*) down to him, aided him with forces invisible to you (*bi-junūdin lam tarawhā*), and spoiled the disbelievers' plan. God is almighty and wise. (Q 9:40; Abdel Haleem, with adjustments)

In both these verses the imagery is of a battle in which God grants victory to the Prophet and the believers over the disbelievers. The military implications of the term *sakīnah* are demonstrated by the fact that it is parallel to "forces" or "troops" (*junūd*) in both verses: *anzala junūdan lam tarawhā* ("He sent down troops that you did not see"; v. 26) and *ayyadahu bi-junūdin lam tarawhā* ("He supported him with troops that you did not see"; v. 40). Like the invisible troops, God's *sakīnah* is what made the believers' victory over their enemies possible. The translation "calm" is thus based mainly on the etymological meaning of the root *s-k-n* and does not entirely fit in the context.

Sūrat al-Fatḥ (Q 48) reports a victory over the pagan Meccans. It is generally understood to comment on the confrontation that occurred when the Prophet marched to Mecca with his followers with the intention of performing the pilgrimage but was barred by the Meccans. After a standoff, the two sides signed the treaty of al-Ḥudaybiyyah.[47] The term *sakīnah* occurs three times in the *sūrah*, in the following verses:

> It was He who made His tranquility (*sakīnatahu*) descend into the hearts of the believers, to add faith to their faith—the forces of the heavens and earth (*junūdu 'l-samāwāti wa'l-arḍi*) belong to Him; He is all knowing and all wise. (Q 48:4; Abdel Haleem)

> [18] God was pleased with the believers when they swore allegiance to you under the tree: He knew what was in their hearts and so He sent tranquility (*al-sakīnah*) down to them and rewarded them with a speedy triumph (*fatḥan qarībā*) [19] and with many future gains—God is mighty and wise. (Q 48:18–19; Abdel Haleem)

47. Al-Ṭabarī, *Jāmiʿ al-bayān ʿan taʾwīl āy al-Qurʾān*, ed. ʿAbd Allāh b. ʿAbd al-Muḥsin al-Turkī (27 vols.; Giza: Dār Hajar, 2001), 21.238–244.

> While the disbelievers had fury in their hearts—the fury of ignorance (*ḥamiyyata 'l-jāhiliyyah*)—God sent His tranquility (*sakīnatahu*) down on to His Messenger and the believers and made binding on them [their] promise to obey God, for that was more appropriate and fitting for them. God has full knowledge of all things. (Q 48:26; Abdel Haleem)

Again, military confrontation is prominent in these passages. As in the verses from Sūrat al-Tawbah, Q 48:4 pairs God's *sakīnah* with forces or troops (*junūd*), this time "the troops of the heavens and the earth." The forces of nature are apparently acting in concert with God's *sakīnah* to bring about the victory of the believers. Q 48:18 refers explicitly to a "swift victory" (*fatḥan qarībā*) as a consequence of God's sending down the *sakīnah*. There is a slight difference here regarding the location of the *sakīnah*. Verse 4 refers to its descending into the hearts of the believers, something that none of the other verses state. Clearly, in the Bible, the *shekhinah* is located outside the Hebrews, though it has a tremendous effect on their courage and inner resolve or determination, and this appears to be the case in most of the other verses that invoke God's *sakīnah* in the Qurʾān. The fact that it is in the Muslim believers' hearts here suggests that it is somehow conflated with the resolve to do battle with the enemy, and this is corroborated by the fact that the *sakīnah* counters, in effect, the fury of ignorance (*ḥamiyyata 'l-jāhiliyyah*) that appears in Q 48:26, which lies in the hearts of the disbelievers, propelling them to fight for their unjust cause.

One may compare *sakīnah* in such contexts with other passages in which God aids the prophet or believers in a confrontation or conflict. One of the most common terms that appears in such passages is the verb *thabbata, yuthabbitu* ("to make firm"): *thabbatnāka* ("We made you firm"; Q 17:74); *nuthabbitu bihi fuʾādaka* ("with which We make your heart firm"; Q 11:120, 25:32); *li-yarbiṭa ʿalā qulūbikum wa-yuthabbita bihi 'l-aqdāma* ("in order to bind your hearts and with which to fix your feet firmly"; Q 8:11; cf. Q 2:250, 3:147, 47:7). This act of making firm appears to be portraying in physical terms a figurative, emotional sense—it means to strengthen the resolve of the fighters. A noun that appears in such contexts and that may be interpreted as being closer to *sakīnah* in meaning is *ṣabr*, "patience, endurance." Just after Q 2:248, the text reads as follows:

> 249 ... But those who know that they were going to meet their Lord said, "How often a small force has defeated a large army with God's permission! God is with those who are steadfast (*wa'llāhu maʿa 'l-ṣābirīn*)."

> 250 And when they met Goliath and his warriors, they said, "Our Lord! Pour patience on us, make us stand firm, and help us against the disbelievers."

Here, the troops that have been fortified by the *sakīnah* are described as "steadfast" (*ṣābirīn*), having patience (*ṣabr*) poured upon them by God, and having their feet (*aqdām*) planted firmly by God. *Sakīnah* must be parallel and in harmony with these meanings.

Overall, *sakīnah* appears in two main contexts involving military confrontations between the forces of the believers and those of the pagan Meccans. In all cases, God's *sakīnah* aids them to gain victory over their opponents, and in this it is closely parallel to the biblical *shekhinah*. The contexts require a translation that captures the term's invocation of might, terror, and military prowess; "tranquility," "calm," "assurance," and "reassurance," are all too mild to convey the appropriate meaning. The translations examined here all appear inadequate in this case. "God's overwhelming, or awe-inspiring, aura" or a similar translation would better convey the appropriate meaning. If one considers *sakīnah* as parallel in meaning to *ṣabr* in these contexts, then one might suggest not translating them as "tranquility" and "patience," which are both too passive for the context of a military confrontation. *Ṣabr* might be rendered as "endurance, steadfastness, or the ability to withstand and resist," and *sakīnah* might be "resolve" or "determination."

"Jesus, the Messiah" (VI)

A survey of the presentation of Jesus in the Qur'ān reveals an overall strategy to agree with the Christian portrayal of Jesus to a large extent. Jesus's birth was miraculous. His mother, Mary, was a virgin (Q 3:35–37.42–50, 19:16–33). Jesus performed many miracles, including curing the sick, healing lepers, and bring the dead back to life (Q 3:49, 5:110). Jesus is termed "a word" (*kalimah*) from God (3:39.45, 4:171), something that recalls the opening of the Gospel of John. Jesus is associated with "the Holy Spirit" (*rūḥ al-qudus*; Q 2:87.253, 5:110), recalling the close association of the Holy Spirit with Jesus and the Trinity in Christian doctrine. God "raises him up" (Q 3:55), which recalls the Christian notion of Christ's resurrection. Of course, there are some differences of portrayal as well, reflecting real theological differences between Islam and Christianity: Jesus is not divine but rather a prophet; he cannot perform miracles of his own accord, for his actions depend on God's power and permission; and he did not die on the cross but was miraculously rescued by God at the last minute. However, the number and importance of the common features are striking, and they must be recognized as part of an intentional strategy of creating common ground with Christians. This has broad consequences for the translation of the qur'ānic material related to Jesus.

One qur'ānic term worth considering is that of *al-masīḥ*, "the Messiah," which is cognate with the Hebrew *hammāšîaḥ*, but which several authors in Qur'ānic Studies have argued derives more directly from the Syriac form, *mšīḥā*.[48] The Qur'ān applies the epithet *al-masīḥ* ("the Messiah") to Jesus eleven times (Q 3:45, 4:157.171.172, 5.17.72(twice).75, 9:30.31): three times as *al-masīḥ* "the Messiah" (Q 4:172, 5:72, 9:30), five times as *al-masīḥ ibn Maryam*, "the Messiah son of Mary" (Q 5:17.72(twice).75, 9:31), and three times as *al-masīḥ ʿīsā b. maryam*, "the Messiah Jesus son of Mary" (Q 3:45, 4:157.171). The term occurs in the Qur'ān only in connection with Jesus. A major impulse behind the use of this term in the Qur'ān is the intention to agree with Christian usage, and this view is corroborated by other examples such as those mentioned above.

In English translations of the Qur'ān, *al-masīḥ* is usually rendered as "the Messiah," mainly on the grounds that this is viewed as a literal equivalent. However, in my view, it would be preferable to render it as "Christ" instead. Of course, Christians believe that Jesus is the Messiah, and that is in fact the literal meaning of the term *al-masīḥ*—an obvious cognate and equivalent of the Hebrew *hammāšîaḥ* ("the Messiah"). However, the phrase would take on a different valence in English if the translations consistently rendered *al-masīḥ* as "Christ" and *al-masīḥ ʿīsā b. maryam* as "Jesus Christ, son of Mary." Christ is based on the literal Greek translation of the Hebrew *māšîaḥ* ("anointed"), referring to the practice of anointing the new king of Israel with holy oil in a ritual equivalent to coronation. Because of the fundamental status of Greek in Christian literature and technical terminology, "Jesus Christ" is used as an epithet by Christians speaking in English and the European language far more commonly than is "Jesus, the Messiah." (This difference falls away in Arabic, because, for Arab-speaking Christians, the two terms are identical, *al-masīḥ*.) As Parrinder points out, in Christian traditions the term "Christ" comes to have the character of a frozen epithet or proper noun, losing some of its connection with the promised Messiah of Jewish tradition, and the use of the term in the Qur'ān appears to re-

48. Siegmund Fraenkel, *De Vocabulis in antiquis Arabum carminibus et in Corano peregrinis* (Leiden: Brill, 1880), 24; Paul de Lagarde, *Übersicht über die im Aramäischen, Arabischen und Hebräischen übliche Bildung der Nomina* (Göttingen: Dieterichsche Verlagsbuchhandlung, 1889), 93–99; Horovitz, *Koranische Untersuchungen*, 129–130; Alphonse Mingana, "Syriac Influence on the Style of the Kuran," *Bulletin of the John Rylands Library* 11 (1927): 77–98, 85; Jeffery, *The Foreign Vocabulary of the Qur'ān*, 265–266.

flect this development.[49] Christians refer to themselves in English and the other European languages as Christians, and not as Messianists. Christian theological discourse generally refers to the body of Christ and not to the body of the Messiah, and the well-known port city in the state of Texas is *Corpus Christi*, not *Corpus Messiae*. Translating *al-masīḥ* as "Christ" would signal much more directly the intended strategy of agreement with formal Christian usage that lies behind it. Just as the term Christ in English usage loses a large part of its connection with the Jewish concept of the Messiah, so too does *al-masīḥ* in the Qur'ān appear to serve as an honorific title of Jesus, indicating his exalted and revered status in general and not evoking a restoration of the historical monarchy of Israel.

"The Table" (VII)

The fifth *sūrah* of the Qur'ān, al-Mā'idah, is often given the title "the Table" in English on the grounds that this is an accurate rendering of the literal meaning of the word. However, like the Arabic word *al-sufrah*, the term *al-mā'idah*, the context suggests, refers not to a piece of furniture but to the table along with the meal typically served upon it. Pickthall endeavors to capture this meaning without straying too far from the underlying Arabic by labeling the *sūrah* "The Table Spread," Abdel Haleem calls it "the Feast," and Michel Cuypers's work devoted to analysis of this *sūrah* terms it "the Banquet."[50] An additional issue, though, is that the *sūrah* derives its name from a scene in which God provides a banquet for Jesus's disciples, after they request, through Jesus, that they might be reassured in their belief (Q 5:111–115). This scene of Jesus and his disciples sharing an extraordinary banquet is a clear invocation of the scene of the Last Supper, which is described in the Gospels and becomes a central event in Christian tradition, serving as the basis for the Eucharist.[51] The question then becomes whether

49. Geoffrey Parrinder, *Jesus in the Qur'an* (Oxford: Oneworld, 1996), 30–33.
50. Michel Cuypers, *Le Festin: Une lecture de la sourate al-Mā'ida* (Paris: Lethielleux, 2007); idem, *The Banquet: A Reading of the Fifth Sura of the Qur'ān*, trans. Patricia Kelley (Miami: Convivium Press, 2009).
51. Several scholars have argued instead that this passage invokes John 6 or the agape meal. I am not entirely convinced, for the passage, in my view, suggests an invocation of the image of the Last Supper, which may have been known to the Prophet's contemporaries. It is also possible that the notions of the Last Supper and the agape meal have been conflated. Speyer, *Die biblischen Erzählungen*, 452; Wilhelm Rudolph, *Die Abhängigkeit des Qorans von Judentum und Christentum* (Stuttgart: Kohlhammer, 1922), 81–82; Paret, *Der Koran*, 133; Cuypers, *The Banquet*,

the translation of *al-mā'idah*, either in the passage in which it occurs or in the *sūrah*'s title, ought to signal the connection more forcefully.

This example is not as clear as some of the others presented above. One type of event has been given three quite different interpretations, depending on which religion one assumes as background. From the Jewish point of view, Jesus and his disciples are sharing a meal at the Passover *seder*, the annual commemoration of the liberation of the Hebrews from slavery in Egypt. From the Christian point of view, it is the Last Supper, which serves as the model for celebration of the mass, a reinterpretation of the Passover *seder* in which the meal represents Jesus's flesh and blood, which are sacrificed for the sins of believers. From the Islamic point of view, the banquet is a sign of God's unwavering support of his prophets and their faithful followers, yet another indication of Jesus's favored status, even among prophets. Perhaps the qur'ānic presentation is sufficiently and dramatically different to warrant not closely associating it with Christian views of the Last Supper.

I argue that the connection should be made obvious despite the theological differences between Christian and qur'ānic interpretations. It is clear that whatever theological work the scene at the end of Sūrat al-Mā'idah performs, it is intended to invoke the visual image of the Last Supper, which may have been well known to the audience. The disciples' request for the banquet to be *li-awwalinā wa-ākhirinā* ("for the first of us and the last of us"; Q 5:114) suggests the visual image of the disciples lined up in a row, as one sees in paintings of the Last Supper. Again, while this example involves the evocation of a well-known biblical scene, it differs from the others considered above in the extent to which reinterpretation is involved. In this case, to translate the term explicitly as the Last Supper would appear to invoke too strongly the Christian interpretation of the event that has been altered considerably in the Qur'ān. A translation that would capture the intended connection might include reference to Jesus's followers such as "the banquet of Jesus and his disciples." It is certainly not just any table, nor is it just any banquet. The qur'ānic presentation emphasizes the reassurance for the disciples represented by the miracle of the banquet, and not its finality and proximity to Christ's crucifixion.

417–418; A. J. Droge, *The Qur'ān: A New Annotated Translation* (Sheffield: Equinox, 2013), 74, n. 163; Gabriel S. Reynolds, *The Qur'ān and the Bible* (New Haven: Yale University Press, 2018), 217.

"The Book" and "The People of the Book" (VIII)

Much ink has been spilled over the qur'ānic term *kitāb*, which takes on a number of distinct meanings in the sacred text. Geo Widengren, Daniel Madigan, and Anne-Sylvie Boisliveau have discussed it thoroughly, along with other terms that the Qur'ān uses to describe itself.[52] Nicolai Sinai also treats aspects of the term *kitāb* in a study of qur'ānic self-referentiality.[53] Despite this attention, something seems to have escaped the translators of the Qur'ān: one of the prominent denotations of *al-kitāb* in the Qur'ān is simply "the Bible." Anne-Sylvie Boisliveau comes close to this translation in her study of the Qur'ān's references to itself when she concludes that the term *kitāb* designates the Qur'ān as an object linked clearly to Judaism and Christianity. It is a scripture that has been revealed "in the Judeo-Christian manner."[54] Translators seem to be unaware that, according to William Muir's 1856 study, *al-kitāb* refers to the Old Testament or to both the Old and New Testaments.[55]

The inherited tradition of Islamic Studies scholarship dictates that *ahl al-kitab* be rendered "people of the book" or "people of scripture." Similarly, the phrase *alladhīna ūtū 'l-kitāb* is regularly rendered as "those who have been given the book" or "those who have been given the scripture." Most translators have simply followed earlier translations in this regard. This usage is based on the idea that *al-kitāb* in the Qur'ān is throughout a general term referring to any member in the category of sacred text or scripture. This view may be justified by recourse to Arabic grammar, according to which the definite article *al-* serves not only to identify something that is known because it has been mentioned earlier in the conversation (in which case it is termed *lām al-ʿahd*, "the *al-* of familiarity"), but also to refer to an entire category (*lām li'stighrāq al-jins*, "the *al-* for encompassing the category"). Thus, in Arabic, one says *al-ḥubb*, "the love," just as the French say *l'amour*, to refer to "love" in general, while in English the definite article is

52. Geo Widengren, *The Ascension of the Apostle and the Heavenly Book* (Leipzig: Otto Harrassowitz, 1950); Daniel A. Madigan, *The Qur'ân's Self-Image: Writing and Authority in Islam's Scripture* (Princeton: Princeton University Press, 2001); idem, "The Limits of Self-Referentiality in the Qur'ān," in Stefan Wild (ed.), *Self-Referentiality in the Qur'ān* (Wiesbaden: Harrassowitz, 2006), 59–69.

53. Nicolai Sinai, "Qur'ānic Self-Referentiality as a Strategy of Self-Authorization," in Wild, *Self-Referentiality in the Qur'ān*, 103–134.

54. Anne-Sylvie Boisliveau, *Le Coran par lui-même: Vocabulaire et argumentation du discours coranique autoréférentiel* (Leiden: Brill, 2014), esp. 393–397.

55. William Muir, *The Testimony Borne by the Coran to the Jewish and Christian Scriptures* (Agra: Secundra Orphan Press, 1856).

not generally used in this fashion, but it is only deployed when a general term is specified in some fashion, as in "*the* love of Qays for Laylā" or "*the* love of a mother for her children." This usage is also upheld by the Islamic legal tradition, which has included several other religious communities under the protected category of *ahl al-kitāb*, such as Sabians and Zoroastrians. In short, translators have understood the usage of the term *al-kitāb* to refer to the general category of scripture, while I would argue that, in the Qurʾān, *al-kitāb* in many cases refers to a specific book. In grammatical terms, the definite article *al-* in this case is *lām al-ʿahd* and not *lām li'stighrāq al-jins*; it refers to a known and familiar scripture, and not to the general group of all scriptures.[56]

One hint that something might be amiss with these translations is the qurʾānic use of *ahl al-kitāb* and the alternative expression *alladhīna ūtū 'l-kitāb*. Muslims themselves are never described in the Qurʾān as *ahl al-kitāb* ("people of the book" or "people of the scripture"). Neither Muslim exegetes, nor later authors of texts in Islamic law, nor scholars writing in the European tradition of Qurʾānic Studies have argued that the term ever applies to them. However, if *al-kitāb* simply referred to the category of scripture, then this would be a startling fact. Clearly, Muslims have a scripture, and just as clearly, the qurʾānic text refers to the revelations delivered through the Prophet Muḥammad as belonging to a scripture. This is so even if one limits attention to explicit qurʾānic evidence and ignores the ubiquitous use of *al-kitāb* in later Islamic legal literature to refer either to the Qurʾān as a substantial scripture or to a specific prooftext from the Qurʾān. As seen above, Anne-Sylvie Boisliveau stresses that *kitāb* in the Qurʾān is meant to designate the Qurʾān as a scripture of the Judeo-Christian type. If *kitāb* is simply the generic label of "scripture," then why wouldn't Muslims be included in the category of *ahl al-kitāb*, along with Jews and Christians?

It is important to recognize that the term *ahl al-kitāb* excludes Muslims even when the term *al-kitāb* itself is used in a number of passages to refer unambiguously to the Qurʾān itself (e.g., Q 2:1, 13:1, 14:1). This suggests that the meaning of *al-kitāb* in the term *ahl al-kitāb* is distinct from its meaning when it refers to the Qurʾān. A solution suggests itself in the argument that *al-kitab* ("*the* Book") refers, in many passages, to a specific book. That this is so is corroborated by a passage that uses a parallel turn of phrase which unequivocally refers to a specific scripture, Q 5:47:

56. Mohsen Goudarzi also makes this point in his dissertation, "The Second Coming of the Book: Rethinking Qur'anic Scripturology and Prophetology" (Ph.D. diss., Harvard University, 2018), 20–22.

> *wa'l-yaḥkum ahlu 'l-injīli bi-mā anzala 'llāhu fīhi*
> Let the people of the Gospel judge according to what God has sent down therein.

Ahl al-injīl, "the people of the Gospel," here designates Christians through reference to their scripture, a specific sacred book. This suggests the possibility that *al-kitāb* as well refers to a specific book, namely, the Bible, and not just a member of the class of scripture in general.

If the term *ahl al-kitāb* refers to both Jews and Christians, and *al-kitāb* refers to a specific, known scripture, and not just to any scripture, it must refer to a sacred book that is shared by Jews and Christians. In some cases, *ahl al-kitāb* may be interpreted as referring to Jews alone, but in others it refers manifestly to both Jews and Christians. Moreover, there is little indication that *ahl al-kitāb* includes any other group besides Jews and Christians. A number of passages that include the term *ahl al-kitāb* refer explicitly either to Jews and Christians or to the Torah and the Gospel. The term *ahl al-kitāb* in Q 5:15 clearly refers both to the Israelites (*banū isrā'īl*) mentioned in Q 5:12–13 and to the Christians (*al-naṣārā*) mentioned in Q 5:14. Similarly the term *ahl al-kitāb* in Q 5:19 clearly includes both the Jews and the Christians mentioned in the previous verse, Q 5:18. Q 3:65 reads, "O people of the book! Why do you argue about Abraham, while the Torah and the Gospel were not revealed until long after him? Do you not understand?" This verse refers to the people of the book and to the Torah and the Gospel in the same verse. It suggests that Jews and Christians dispute over Abraham, each group arguing that they have a closer relationship to him or a better claim to his legacy. When the verse objects that neither the Torah nor the Gospel were revealed until long after Abraham's time, the point is that Abraham could have been neither a Jew nor a Christian, on the grounds that Judaism began only with the revelation of the Torah, and Christianity began only with the revelation of the Gospel. It is thus clear that *ahl al-kitāb* means Jews and Christians in this passage, and the book referred to by the term *ahl al-kitāb* corresponds both to the Torah and the Gospel. Arguably, then, *al-kitāb* means "the Bible," a sacred text that encompasses both Jewish and Christian scripture.

Sūrat al-Mā'idah (Q 5) provides yet more evidence that *al-kitāb* refers to a sacred text including both the Jewish and Christian scriptures. Q 5:65–66 report that God will admit *ahl al-kitāb* to paradise if they believe and fear God. If they observe the teachings of the Torah and the Gospel, they will enjoy providence from above and below. A similar conjunction occurs shortly after this statement in the same passage, in Q 5:68:

> Say, "O *ahl al-kitāb*! You have nothing to stand on unless you observe the Torah, the Gospel, and what has been revealed to you from your Lord."

Thus, in this passage, *ahl al-kitāb* are closely associated with both the Torah and the Gospel, which are both mentioned explicitly twice. In all of these cases, the use of the term *ahl al-kitāb* refers to Jews and Christians directly or to those whose sacred texts are the Torah and the Gospel, which evidently amounts to the same thing. These passages tend to justify the post-qurʾānic, historical definition of *ahl al-kitāb* as referring primarily to Jews and Christians, and not to a broader category consisting of any group endowed with a scripture. As argued above, the book mentioned in the designation *ahl al-kitāb* apparently includes both the Torah and the Gospel.

If the term *ahl al-kitāb* certainly refers to Jews and Christians, then this suggests that *al-kitāb* is not a generic reference to scripture but a reference to a specific scripture that Jews and Christians are understood to share. It is for this reason above all that I would suggest that *ahl al-kitāb* means "those who possess the Bible" and that *al-kitāb* in certain passages of the Qurʾān means simply "the Bible." This view was anticipated long ago by William Muir, who wrote a work in 1856 titled *The Testimony Borne by the Coran to the Jewish and Christian Scriptures.*[57] As a colonial official in India, he was struck by local Muslims' habit of disparaging the Bible and characterizing it as corrupt, so he wrote this work in order to present the qurʾānic view of the Jewish and Christian sacred texts and thereby correct his Muslim interlocutors with evidence from their own sacred text. He points out that the Qurʾān throughout exhibits veneration for these texts. The view commonly held by his interlocutors was that the "true" Torah and the "true" Gospel were essentially different from the texts in the possession of the Jews and Christians, but Muir argues that this view is mistaken because the Torah and the Gospel are described in the Qurʾān as what is *maʿahum* ("with them") or *ʿindahum* ("in their possession"). Qurʾānic usage does not restrict the terms Torah and Gospel to those texts as they were originally revealed by God.[58] In his view, the terms *al-kitāb* ("the book"), *kitāb allāh* ("the book of God"), *kalām allāh* ("God's speech"), *al-dhikr* ("the remembrance"), and so on, all refer to the Bible. In his analysis of the verse, "If thou are in doubt regarding that which We have sent down unto thee, then ask those who read the Book (revealed) before thee. Verily the truth hath come unto thee from thy Lord; be not therefore amongst those that doubt" (Q 10:94), he writes about the term *al-kitāb*: "Here, as in many other passages, the word is obviously

57. Muir, *Testimony*.
58. Muir, *Testimony*, 23, 100.

used in its widest sense, and intends the Scripture in use both amongst the Christians and Jews."[59] Muir stresses that, according to the Qurʾān, believers are required to believe in the whole of scripture and not simply part of it. The audience is asked, "Do you believe in part of the Book and reject part thereof?" (Q 2:85).[60] He means to argue that the Book refers to the Bible in the sense of the one body of scripture that is used both by Jews and by Christians.

Examination of the examples presented above suggests that it is not unreasonable to translate *al-kitāb* as "the Bible" in a number of qurʾānic passages. A clear example occurs in Sūrat al-Baqarah, Q 2:113:

> The Jews say, "The Christians have nothing to stand on" and the Christians say, "The Jews have nothing to stand on," although both recite the Book. ... Surely God will judge between them on the Day of Judgment regarding their dispute.

This verse refers explicitly to both Jews and Christians and states that they both read *al-kitāb* ("the Book"). It is possible to argue that the text means that the members of each group, the Jews on the one hand and the Christians on the other hand, read their own respective scripture. However, the probable meaning intended by the verse is that the book in question is the same book. The logic of the verse requires this: it is surprising that they disagree, because *they recite the same scripture.* Muir agrees with this interpretation of *al-kitāb* here, remarking, "These are the Scriptures of the Old and New Testaments, in current use among the Jews and Christians."[61] Another example occurs in Q 6:156: *an taqūlū innamā unzila ʾl-kitābu ʿalā ṭāʾifatayni min qablinā wa-in kunnā ʿan dirāsatihim la-ghāfilīn* ("Lest you say, 'The Book was only revealed to two communities before us, though we could not grasp what they recited'"). This verse reports that *al-kitāb*, again, apparently a single scripture, was revealed to two communities (*ṭāʾifatayn*), evidently Jews and Christians, and that they both read or studied that same scripture. The verse does not use the indefinite *kitāb* ("a book" or "a scripture"), one of which was revealed to each community. The point is that the pagan Arabs were arguing that they could not be held accountable to the one God and obligated to accept monotheism because they could not understand the biblical text, which was not in their own language. The revelation of the Qurʾān in Arabic served to invalidate that line of argument.

59. Muir, *Testimony*, 22.
60. Muir, *Testimony*, 50–51, 101.
61. Muir, *Testimony*, 54.

Both these verses suggest that *al-kitāb* refers to a scripture that is shared by the Jews and the Christians, and the most idiomatic way to convey this idea in English is to translate it as "the Bible." And, if this is the case, then *ahl al-kitāb* should be "the people of the Bible" or "those who possess the Bible," rather than "the people of the book" or "the people of scripture," and *alladhīna ūtū 'l-kitāb* should be "those who have been given the Bible."

Mohsen Goudarzi's 2018 dissertation focuses on qur'ānic scripturology and in particular on the term *al-kitāb*. He argues that *al-kitāb* is not a general referent to the category of scripture but rather a specific term identifying a particular scripture. He then argues that *al-kitāb* has exactly two major referents, the Torah and the Qur'ān.[62] I agree with Goudarzi that *al-kitāb* refers to a specific book, but while he limits the term exclusively to two referents, the Torah and the Qur'ān, I would argue that it also refers to the Bible. In some cases, this is conceived of as identical with the Torah, but in others, it must include Christian scripture as well. Goudarzi resolves this potential objection by arguing that, according to the Qur'ān, the Torah is presented as the scripture of the Christians as well, and by relegating the Gospel to a lower status than that of *al-kitāb*.[63] My suggestion, agreeing with the interpretation of Muir, is that the term takes on the sense of the Bible that is familiar from Christian usage, referring to the combination of the Old and New Testaments, while also conceding that the term may be used by Jews to refer to their sacred text.

Like the choice to render *allāh* as God, the qur'ānic personal names *ibrāhīm* and *mūsā* as Abraham and Moses, and *al-masīḥ* as "Christ," the choice to render *al-kitāb* as "the Bible" would give the reader of an English translation a stronger impression of the direct invocation of Jewish and Christian sacred texts that is in fact intended in the text of the Qur'ān. The use of "scripture" as the translation of the term *al-kitāb* weakens and diffuses that invocation by allowing it to refer to a broader and more nebulous category of sacred texts not necessarily connected with Jewish and Christian tradition.

Conclusion

Some connection between the Qur'ān and the Bible has always been obvious. However, the intimate relation between these sacred texts has often been played down in Islamic tradition in order to stress the uniqueness

62. Goudarzi, "The Second Coming of the Book."
63. Goudarzi, "The Second Coming of the Book," 184–240.

and superiority of Islam, stressing its status as a distinct religion from Judaism and Christianity. It has also often been attenuated by non-Muslim writers seeking to exclude Islam from the Judeo-Christian tradition. In yet other cases, translations that fail to capture adequately the Qur'ān's invocations of biblical tradition are simply the product of inertia in the history of qur'ānic translations, in which translators have simply fallen back on literal renditions or have relied heavily on earlier translations and have not undertaken independent investigations of key qur'ānic terms. In many cases, the translations have not kept up with developments in Qur'ānic Studies scholarship.

Several examples have been presented here of alienating renditions of qur'ānic phrases that I believe could be better rendered in a biblicizing manner in translations of the Qur'ān. In my view, current English translations of the Qur'ān obscure the fact that the Qur'ān refers to Jesus explicitly as "Jesus Christ" and refers explicitly to "the Bible" shared by Jews and Christians. In some cases, as with *safīnat nūḥ*, many of the existing translations already adopt the biblicizing form, referring to Noah's ark, and only a few translators have chosen to do otherwise. In other cases, however, such as those of *al-masīḥ*, *al-kitāb*, and *ahl al-kitāb*, the alienating translations are entirely dominant. Even specialists who focus on the Jewish and Christian connections of the Qur'ān rarely entertain the idea that *al-kitāb* in the Qur'ān could simply mean "the Bible"—*that* book in particular.

The extent to which "biblicizing" translations are correct is an issue that confronts every translator of the Qur'ān. When faced with a term that is related in some fashion with biblical language or with Jewish or Christian concepts, the translator must take into account how it is used in the qur'ānic text and what function it serves. Is it intended to call attention to the similarity between the Qur'ān and the earlier settings in which the term was used, or is the sense modified or reinterpreted? Is the former sense simply ignored altogether? The choice of a biblicizing vs. an alienating translation is not an automatic one. Both Wilfred Cantwell Smith and Walid Saleh have pointed out that simply knowing the origin of a word does not solve the puzzle of its later usage. However, in a number of cases biblicizing translations of particular qur'ānic terms have been regularly missed or passed over in favor of alienating translations, and these occur in contexts which suggest that the connections with Jewish and Christian material were meant to be understood.

Biblicizing translations may not always be appropriate. As explained above, the term *ḥanīf* is used in the Qur'ān in a way which suggests that it was not intended to invoke the meaning of the Syriac *ḥanpā* ("heretic"), which may nevertheless have been its etymological source. In his discussion of qur'ānic language, Nöldeke devotes a section to foreign terms that have been used in the Qur'ān in ways that are not true to their original meanings, including *furqān, sakīnah, zakāh, rajīm, burhān, millah,* and so on, which he gives the heading *Willkürlich und mißverständlich gebrauchte Fremdwörter im Koran* ("foreign words used in an arbitrary and misleading way in the Qur'ān").[64] He was concerned mainly with historical linguistics rather than theology, but some of these examples may not, in fact, be comparable to that of *ḥanīf,* for it is often the case that borrowed terms are modified or altered in some respects without losing the connection with the original term. Similarly, Mark Durie has argued that Islam cannot be construed as forming part of the Abrahamic tradition on account of fundamental differences between qur'ānic and Christian theology, despite their apparently shared vocabulary. For a number of terms from biblical tradition that appear in the Qur'ān, including *sakīnah* and *al-masīḥ,* he argues that while the cognate term figures in the qur'ānic corpus, the profound theological connection with Christian tradition does not.[65] Regarding the overall implications of the use of *al-masīḥ* in the Qur'ān, he writes, "There is no Christological 'subtext' in the Qur'an's allusive use of the name *al-masīḥ* to refer to ʿĪsā, for the Qur'ān has a 'Christ' without a Christology. ... *Al-Masīḥ* of the Qur'ān is to *mashiaḥ* of the Hebrew Bible and *christós* of the New Testament what 'juggernaut' is to Hindi *Jagannātha.*"[66] While it is true that there are fundamental differences between the portrayal of Christ in the Qur'ān and Christian Christology, Durie appears to overlook or downplay the fact that the qur'ānic use of the *al-masīḥ* is meant to recall Christians' use of the term "Christ," concentrating on implied theological differences instead. In my view, his argument, that such examples as this do not represent an organic inheritance of religious ideas but rather perfunctory borrowings that are not signs of a more profound affinity between the religious traditions, is overly rigid. Using the same types of evidence, one could make a similar argument that Christianity does not have a profound affinity with Judaism, or even that the religion of the Hebrews/Israelites/Jesus as evident from different strata from the Hebrew Bible are not indicative of any productive continuity.

It is important to point out here that differences in usage or theology often do not prove a lack of connection, with the consequence that if a biblical term occurs in the Qur'ān, the question is not whether it has the same exact

64. Nöldeke, *Neue Beiträge zur semitischen Sprachwissenschaft,* 23–30.

65. Mark Durie, *The Qur'an and Its Biblical Reflexes: Investigations into the Genesis of a Religion* (Lanham: Lexington Books, 2018), 160–164, 178–179.

66. Durie, *The Qur'an and Its Biblical Reflexes,* 163.

meaning or implications but whether its use is intended to invoke biblical precedent or not. For example, it has been observed that the Torah ark in a Jewish synagogue is meant to invoke the ark of the covenant and to conjure up God's presence, as if the Torah were an idol. The two arks are clearly different in their physical forms and literal definitions, but the analogy is nevertheless intended and important in the tradition.[67] Similarly, the term that devotees of the Islamic mystical traditions adopted for their chants or litanies, *dhikr* ("remembrance"), invokes qur'ānic uses of the term *dhikr* that clearly had very different meanings and referred instead to revelation, message, information, explanation, historical accounts, revealed books, or the Qur'ān.[68] Nevertheless, the use of the term *dhikr* allows Sufis to invoke and anchor their practice in the Qur'ān, and when reading the qur'ānic command *fa's'alū ahla 'l-dhikri in kuntum lā taʿlamūn* ("So ask the people of remembrance, if you do not know"; Q al-Naḥl 16:43) they can argue that this refers to Sufi masters, or as al-Qushayrī (d. 465) puts it, *al-ʿārifūn bi'llāh* ("those who know God").[69] Even if this reading is demonstrably anachronistic and arguably wrong, it cannot be dismissed as an ordinary misunderstanding, and one cannot say either that *dhikr* is simply an incorrect term for "Sufi chant" or argue that it does not invoke the Qur'ān. For present purposes, the main point is that, just as these terms are meant to conjure up connections with important terms and concepts in earlier religious history, many biblical terms in the Qur'ān are meant to do the same. Pointing out that the qur'ānic terms do not have the same exact referents or connotations does not explain away the intended invocation, just as pointing out that *dhikr* does not mean "Sufi chant" in the Qur'ān does not disprove that Sufis meant to invoke qur'ānic usage by adopting that term.

In *How to Read the Qur'an*, Carl W. Ernst stressed the unfamiliarity of Islam's sacred text to an anglophone audience in whose societies the Qur'ān, in contrast to the King James Bible, has not permeated the language for

---

67. Jeffrey H. Tigay, "The Torah Scroll and God's Presence," in M. L. Grossman (ed.), *Built by Wisdom, Established by Understanding: Essays on Biblical and Near Eastern Literature in Honor of Adele Berlin* (Bethesda: University Press of Maryland, 2013), 323–340; James W. Watts, "From Ark of the Covenant to Torah Scroll: Ritualizing Israel's Iconic Texts," in Nathan MacDonald (ed.), *Ritual Innovation in the Hebrew Bible and Early Judaism* (Berlin: de Gruyter, 2016), 21–34.

68. Elsaid M. Badawi and Muhammad Abdel Haleem, *Arabic-English Dictionary of Qur'ānic Usage* (Leiden: Brill, 2008), 330–331.

69. ʿAbd al-Karīm b. Hawāzin al-Qushayrī, *Tafsīr al-Qushayrī al-musammā Laṭā'if al-ishārāt*, ed. ʿAbd al-Laṭīf Ḥasan ʿAbd al-Raḥmān (3 vols.; Beirut: Dār al-Kutub al-ʿIlmiyyah, 1971), 2.158.

centuries. What I have attempted to show here is that this strangeness is in part the fault of alienating translations which fail to convey the biblical resonances that permeate the text of the Qurʾān. To translate the Qurʾān in ways that capture these resonances, or even to bring them into relief, is not to do violence to Islam's scripture but rather to render tangible to the reader of a translation something that, in many cases, was clearly an intended feature of the original text. This is not a foreign imposition, since the Qurʾān presents itself as a scripture in the biblical tradition and claims explicitly that it has been revealed to confirm earlier scriptures in that tradition, including the Torah and the Gospel. As a consequence, Jewish and Christian salvation history provided the necessary background for and models to be emulated by the nascent Islamic community.

While this investigation has not treated the many translations of the Qurʾān into other European languages, experience indicates that the situation is more or less the same in the existing French, German, and other translations: they, too, regularly engage in what I have described as alienating translations of biblical elements in the text. The only exception, in my view, are the Hebrew translations. Because Hebrew is both cognate with Arabic and also heavily imbued with biblical phraseology, even in its modern form, it is much more difficult to disguise or neglect the biblical valences of the terms and phrases like those that I have cited here. So, for example, translating *bayt* in reference to the Kaʿbah into *bet* in modern Hebrew is not like translating it as "house" in English, because Hebrew *bet* already shares with Arabic *bayt* the fundamental meaning of "temple," and appears prominently in the common terms for the temple in Jerusalem, *bêt hammiqdāš* and *bêt ĕlōhîm*.

JIQSA 6 (2021): 69–85

RESPONSE TO DEVIN STEWART'S 2019 PRESIDENTIAL ADDRESS

TODD LAWSON
University of Toronto, Canada

Abstract

Devin Stewart's discussion of English translation problems in some of the otherwise most successful or respected translations of the Qur'ān offers a timely opportunity to revisit issues that may be thought to have been sleeping for years and influencing, unbeknownst, the reading experience of those for whom the structure of the Book was already difficult enough, let alone the technical vocabulary. Some of the questions raised but not answered by Stewart, such as "Why on earth would anyone translate Noah's ark as Noah's ship?," are left for his reader to contemplate. It is difficult to resist the temptation to see such translation choices as reflecting perhaps culturally determined and perhaps unwitted desires to present the Qur'ān as a text revered by aliens rather than as another stage and text in the unfolding of a specifically and quite familiar Abrahamic religiosity that it so obviously is.

I. Introduction

Language, according to the Qur'ān, is the primary mode of a religious experience that attracts and nourishes the soul of the future or current believer. It is also the case that no matter how much an uninitiated anglophone student of Islam is impressed by the great achievements of Islam, its humanity, nobility, and the civilizational and cultural progress in human history it symbolizes, most English translations of the Qur'ān have sent people running in the opposite direction. Hodgson observed in clear terms this glaring and destructive cognitive or, more crucially formulated, cultural dissonance:

> The Qur'ân seems to most Western readers impossibly dull reading. To Muslims who read Arabic it has seemed the most beautiful composition in exis-

doi: http://dx.doi.org/10.5913/jiqsa.6.2021.a002

> tence—its literary inimitability forming a unique evidentiary miracle which every generation can verify anew for itself.[1]

Devin Stewart wishes to lessen or attenuate the dissonance. And his meditation on the problem is instructive, hopeful, and his points well-taken.

It seems reasonable, in translating the Qur'ān, to take five major factors into consideration: 1) its poetic, literary, and artistic character; 2) its normativity; 3) its function as a mode, method, and tool of worship and divine encounter; 4) its obvious function as the first book in Arabic, elucidating a theory of the unknowable, otherwise utterly transcendent, and therefore potentially remote God, "His" existence and connection with the world and each individual—at the level of both history and the jugular vein; and finally, 5) the Qur'ān's audience. Not one of these features is absolutely free-standing and independent of the other four. Indeed, that which is "Qur'ān" represents an instance in which all five elements are at work, and one in which none of them is Qur'ān without the other four. The great impact of the Qur'ān on its "original audience" seems to have been its undoubted literary-cum-poetic vitality carried by its innovative, perhaps even "modernist" or avant-garde, literary and compositional challenge, especially as it may have been heard abroad in the wider world. It was not like current poetry; Muhammad was not a poet. But this does not mean that the Qur'ān is not poetic. It was not like more familiar scriptures or holy books (or, in fact, any other existing literature) since it seemed to account for the current historical situation with its references to various religious communities, languages, and other books. It may have been one of the most intellectually and artistically exciting and challenging literary compositions of its time and place. As such, it transformed the imagination and the imaginary (*l'imaginaire*). So, later it became common to characterize the Qur'ān as neither poetry nor prose, and therefore the representative of a genre of literature of which it was the only member. The power of its expression, delivery, and performance have remained, through the centuries, a signal feature of its identity as "scripture"—more accurately and properly thought of as revelation: its deftly combined literary and religious appeal. Whether on account of the sheer vastness of its readership or its truly unparalleled "poeticity" and expressive effect, the Qur'ān, more than any other linguistic religious work today, is associated with verbal (of course, lawful) magic: *siḥr ḥalāl*. This feature is frequently adduced as a proof of its divine origin and inimitability. I think there is

1. Marshal G. S. Hodgson, "A Comparison of Islâm and Christianity as Framework for Religious Life," *Diogenes* 8.32 (1960): 49–74, 61.

near unanimous agreement here. But because much of this poeticity is simply and forever beyond the reach of translation we must not squander genuine opportunities to communicate accurately what the Qurʾān does say and how it says it.

The second feature that must be taken into consideration when translating the Qurʾān is its status as a normative, religious "law" or guidance about how best to live as a human being in addition to its overall or foundational *daʿwah* or kerygmatic dimension: its challenge to the audience to live godly lives, to control the appetites, to do good, and to form prosperous communities, and to instill in the mind of readers the absolutely non-negotiable doctrine of the unity of the human race, which is seen to reflect the unity of God, who in the Qurʾān is most frequently referred to as *allāh* amongst a vast plurality of other names and designations. This consideration entails treating the elements of such law and guidance not only for their illocutionary or normative function but also their literary, rhetorical, and poetic function: the spoonful of sugar that helps the medicine go down? Perhaps. This redounds to the Qurʾān's status as a *sui generis* literary event in addition to whatever else it might be. A law is a law and *also* a literary or poetic device: a marvelous sign of God's supreme artistry and authorship.

The third feature, extraordinarily connected with the second, is the teaching—also a law—of the deeply intimate interconnectedness of human experience on the planet, which includes a theory of history and "religion," suggesting a theory of language that takes shape through the periodic—however irregular such periodization may be—revelational, literally "apocalyptic," events of the type that the Qurʾān represents. All human communities have had such an experience in their history. And all these revelations have been couched in the language of their host community. Again: the focus is on shared experience. Stewart emphasizes, quite rightly, that such focus be preserved in translation and his special case is the way in which the Qurʾān in Arabic makes its kinship with the Bible a pillar of its message.

The fourth feature is in some ways the most difficult to convey either through translation or simple description. In Hodgson's words, it is that aspect of the Qurʾān through which its recitation and reading represents not a mere intellectual, homiletic, pedagogic, or nomothetic engagement in quest of information, instruction about the law, or even salvation, but precisely an anagogical engagement with "the Unseen" by means of worship, which entails an experience of reading the words of God that had first come alive—vibrated the air—through the voice of Muḥammad. The implication of the following quotation is that the Qur'ān is at bottom a prayer no matter how much information it may also contain:

> What one did with the Qur'ân was not to peruse it but to worship by means of it; not to passively receive it but, in reciting it, to reaffirm it for oneself: the event of revelation was renewed every time one of the faithful, in the act of worship, relived the Qur'ânic affirmations.[2]

The fifth factor entails the also impossible reading experiment of trying to channel the original, "pre-creational" audience in Mecca, where the embryo was conceived that would later be born as historical Islam in its highly variegated, cosmopolitan birthplace, conveniently designated as the Nile-to-Oxus region of the seventh–tenth centuries. Here the Qur'ān was heard by a philosophically and religiously sophisticated audience. Surely its prominence and, to use a perhaps inappropriate category, popularity, had something to do with the degree to which this "classical" audience saw itself, severally and universally, in the Qur'ān's wondrous signs (verses: *āyāt*), whether or not they all agreed with their meaning. Here and now, in the "New World," existing English translations of the Qur'ān have not made it a matter of course for the contemporary reader to experience such intimacy with the "text," and while it may be true, as Stewart said in his presentation, that the early Muslim community felt as if it were stepping into a Cecil B. DeMille film of the Bible when first hearing the Qur'ān, nothing in the experience of the contemporary English reader could be further from reality. The sometimes tortured syntax and strange usages committed on the part of even the frequently miraculous Arberry boggles the mind. It is as if "strangeness" not connection were a primary consideration of translation.

These five factors are, of course, in addition to what is the single most important consideration in translating the Qur'ān: the literary, poetic, normative, and "religious" profile of the target language and whatever this implies, including the culture and skill of the, in this case English, translator. Although it is doubtless impossible to delineate or describe with complete accuracy, one must attempt to use words in the target language that resonate accurately with regard to both lexical "meaning" and poetic/literary "musicality" and figuration: sound and sense and their reception. The perhaps somewhat heretical thought is: if we get the music right, everything else will fall into place. In the Qur'ān, possibly more than in any other translation "problem," the syzygy of meaning and form (i.e., sound) is most

2. Marshall G. S. Hodgson, *The Venture of Islam: Conscience and History in a World Civilization* (3 vols.; Chicago: University of Chicago Press, 1974), 1.104.

crucial. The revelation after all, was phonic, auditory. The "scripture," the written version of the oral composition, is a recording of the audio, as the Islamic tradition teaches.

II. The Words

If the road to hell is paved with good intentions, it may be that the road to paradise is paved with bad intentions. Thus, Mongomery Watt is singled out by Stewart as a leading culprit in the distancing of Islam from its original insistence on the close connection between the message of the Qur'ān and the Bible in its contemporary ecumene, and, by extension and circumstance, the one world in which we all now live and try to get along. Europe, at least in the modern sense, is that large part of the globe that managed to remain un-Muslim/non-Islamic, not part of the *Dār al-Islām* (now inevitably and irreversibly capitalized) during its rise and geographic spread up until the pre-modern period, to use a Eurocentric scheme of periodization. This is subconsciously, and sometimes consciously, understood as a great and heroic achievement. However, the historical *Kulturkampf* for which the current map of Europe functions as hologram indicates that whatever serious translation of the Qur'ān this or that faithful citizen of Europe managed to produce, it was not in the service of what from the Islamic side might be considered a pure, vertical quest for, and celebration and love of, qur'ānic truth. This is generally agreed upon and stated here now simply to introduce this section of our response.

Noah's Ship or Noah's Ark

The word "ark," Stewart says, should be used in those numerous passages to do with the flood where the Arabic word for Noah's large vessel is either *fulk* or *safīnah*. This is because "ark" is the familiar, mythic, and natural word with which the English reader thinks of the vessel by whose means Noah (*nūḥ* in the Qur'ān; thirty-tree occurrences) saved humanity. There is no argument against this perfectly sound suggestion. As it happens, most English translations also agree. Of the nearly sixty English translations listed on the useful website *Islam Awakened*, forty opt for "ark" in their translation of Q al-ʿAnkabūt 29:15. Nor does there appear to be any compelling reason to use the alternate words "boat," "ship," or "vessel." The word "ark" has been used in English for a very long time for this purpose, and conveniently elides, through paronomasia, both the "ark of the covenant" and Noah's Ark—two completely different Hebrew expressions. The English "ark" could not have more serious intent. By its use a transposition occurs in which the "ark of the covenant" becomes symbolized in Noah's Ark and vice versa. This conflation is a singular narratological moment in English translations of the Hebrew Bible. The God-sent disaster of the flood, the annihilation of most of humanity, and the salvation of Noah's retinue perfectly reflect both biblical and qur'ānic readings of respective doctrines of covenant and humanity's uneven response to its demands. For this reason alone it should appeal to translators of the Qur'ān in which the covenant, its fulfilment, and its violation are main topics of concern. (Note also that a floating ark, that of Moses, and the covenantal ark are also "punned" in the qur'ānic *tābūt* at Q 2:248 and 20:39). Not all such terminology is so richly charged with mutually enhancing significance, and therefore such opportunities should not be missed.

"Ark" is equated in the English reader's mind with a story of salvation and faithfulness to the covenant. If this word is not used to translate "Noah's boat," then the alchemy of typological figuration will be sadly vitiated. This is the same alchemy by which, for example, Jesus Christ is understood as the antitype of the both the marine Ark and the covenantal ark—the New Ark—in addition to his being seen as the antitype of the entire inventory of Hebrew Bible typological figures. Not to show that the Qur'ān is announcing an even newer covenant, or renewal of the original covenant, in such clear and unmistakable terms represents a missed opportunity. Whether or not one actually concurs with the Qur'ān's claims, such a lapse represents a clear translation error. And, not to emphasize such commonality is spiritually and intellectually miserly as well as wrong. Islam is largely about the inter-relatedness of humans through time and across linguistic borders. If such interrelatedness is disguised or hidden, it becomes less obvious as a major concern of the Qur'ān, a book which is already susceptible of much erroneous interpretation. By muting references to the Ark of Noah in English translation for a contemporary readership, poisonous interpretations at odds with the purpose of the Qur'ān and its concern for a common humanity are given artificial life support.

There is another instance of translators missing the boat. The Ark of our salvation today is surely the imagination by which we are able to transform an enemy into a friend and difference into similarity or commonality and deal with existential threats, whether political, biological, or ecological. The imagination, today as in the past, requires tools very much along the lines of the Qur'ān's theme of the oneness of humanity, which enabled and reflected such a lasting shift in consciousness. This is why resonance between a "poetics of relation" amongst the various types of humanity the Qur'ān speaks of and the literary poetics of the text are so important to observe. Stewart hints that the biblical story has a theme at variance with the qurʾānic story in that the Noah of the Bible and his Ark symbolize God's faithfulness and protection whereas the story as told in the Qurʾān wishes, primarily, to remind the reader that God is able and willing to punish violations of the covenant even in modern times, i.e., from the seventh century CE, the time of the Qurʾān's revelation. In the Bible such divine solicitude, love, and protection is represented by the beautiful "arc of colors"—the rainbow (French *arc-en-ciel*) shining above Mount Ararat after the flood recedes. By refusing to use the word "ark," translators efface this third element of the paronomastic triad of meaning and connection.

Several of the remaining eight words taken up by Stewart also connote or even denote the covenant through other associations. Perhaps it is, in the end, a disinclination—conscious or otherwise—to see Islam as a renewal of the Abrahamic covenant so dear to Judaism and Christianity that prevents some of our more talented English translators from using the word Ark instead of ship or boat (Arberry, Irving, Jones, Khalidi, Rodwell, *The Study Quran*)? Such could suggest that talent is not the only crucial factor determining the success of a Qurʾān translation. Thus, the appositeness of Stewart's use of the otherwise somewhat unexpected terms "tactics" and, more frequently, "strategy."

In some ways, it is more difficult to understand why "Muslim translations"—e.g., those thirty-five classed as "generally accepted translations of the meaning" on the above-mentioned website—avoid the word "ark." Ten translations, such as those in Pickthall, *The Study Quran*, and Shabbir Ahmed, use instead the obfuscating terms "ship," "boat," or "vessel." Why these translators would insist on avoiding the word "ark" in trying to reach an English audience is something of a mystery. Is it an example of self-censoring due to a kind of weird Stockholm Syndrome? However, the clear majority of English translations, Muslim or otherwise, do use the word "ark." It is supposed they not only have no difficulty in seeing Islam as a renewal of the ancient covenant but, in fact, draw much inspiration from this interpretation of history or understand such an interpretation to be an authentic and essential element of the Qurʾān's message. Not to highlight it explicitly through translation would be to distort such a message.

The Disasters or Sodom and Gomorrah

While the covenant is not evoked here through a direct reference, as in the "ark of the covenant" above, the biblical event surrounding Sodom and Gomorrah certainly contains references to breaking the covenant and ensuing punishment. By disguising Sodom and Gomorrah as "the disasters," the immediate covenantal and biblical connection is cauterized. It is a commonplace deserving of unwavering respect in translation and yet another salient typological moment in the scriptural conversation going on at this time in late antique and cosmopolite Islamdom. A qurʾānic improvisation may be seen in the characterization of the overthrow of Sodom and Gomorrah by the use of *jaʿalnā ʿāliyahā sāfilahā* at Q 11:82 and 15:74, which Stewart translates as "We made its uppermost part its lowermost part" or "We made its high part its low part." This captures, perhaps, the perversion (instead of subversion or inversion) implicated in the original biblical story. Islam represents a simultaneous break with and preservation-through-validation of such history. The words "Sodom and Gomorrah" should obviously be retained or inserted at the appropriate passages in any English translation.

The Burning Tree or the Burning Bush

Here we have the Abrahamic covenant once more exemplified in Moses's meeting with God at the burning bush, never tree. I have not much to add here except to say that while it is so that *shajarah* may also "correctly" be translated as "bush," even if it were not, "bush" should be used in English translation. What does *Islam Awakened* tell us? Amazingly, only ten of its fifty-eight English translations of the Qurʾān use "bush," one translation avoids the problem altogether by leaving *shajarah* completely untranslated (Moeinian), and one uses "voice from the woods" (Shafi).

The Chest of Tranquility or Divine (Military) Support: War Chest...?

The chest of tranquility implies, as Stewart observes, the ark of the covenant and God's glory, which must be portable because of the homelessness of the Hebrews. Already acknowledged as a perfect cognate for the Hebrew *shekhinah*, it signifies God's connection with humanity, an analogue of covenant, especially, in the case of the Qurʾān, the pre-existent covenant of the Day of *Alast* (Q 7:172). Stewart's criticism is that "tranquility" is simply not effective enough to communicate the qurʾānic, and biblical, account of God's presence and that this deficiency is particularly acute when the context is battle. And one agrees. If we consult the five dozen English translations at *Islam Awakened*, we find a wide variety of alternate translations, several along the lines of "promise of security" or "assurance," while nearly all point out the identity of the *tābūt* with the ark of the covenant. Tranquility for *sakīnah* in the six passages of the Qurʾān where it occurs may in fact be too weak. But sheer military power and triumph misrepresents the more numinous and therefore, in the context, more powerful and preferable ideas of divine presence, glory, or manifestation and its abiding—even though utterly transcendent—amongst the believers, whether they are at war or not. It is clear that in using such language the Qur'ān is connecting with biblical history and indicates that the early community felt strongly such a connection with biblical history and that God was indeed on the side of the communities of the Bible and is now on the side of the community of the Qur'ān. In this way, a proper translation of the word *sakīnah* would communicate the message of covenantal renewal from Old to New to Newer and capture something essential about the Qur'ān's view of what the uninitiated call "history."

God's House, the House, or the Temple

A temple is a place one enters in order to worship. The Kaʿbah is not entered for the purposes of general worship. It functions rather as an icon of the aniconism of Islam. This is why "temple" is not a good alternative in translating the Qur'ān. "House" (always capitalized) is the best choice in English translations. It is idiomatic: Christians and Muslims refer to their churches and temples as "houses of God." There is, because of the history of the Jews, a clear resonance with paganism in the use of the word "temple." Here the usage in English (since 1590) emblematizes a triumph of the Hebrews in extricating themselves from what the Qur'ān calls *shirk*, almost always translated as "polytheism," but which might better be thought of as paganism in the context of the eventual urban cosmopolitanism whose consolidation and regulation represents one of the greatest and enduring contributions of the venture of Islam. Again, in speaking of what we might think of as the soul of the Qur'ān and its workings, highlighted in the way in which the Qur'ān revolves simultaneously around the specific experience of Muḥammad and his community and also points toward a much wider arena of human life and experience where such commonality is also at the center, Hodgson observed:

> This intimate interweaving with the far-reaching experience it illuminates, perhaps even more than its single-mindedness and the monumentality of its formal impact, accounts for the enormous power of the Qur'ân as the charter and touchstone of a concrete historical community which has tried in its generations to express the universal.[3]

3. Hodgson, "A Comparison," 62.

In English, "temple" frequently connotes the High God, Babylonian and Egyptian royal and exclusive religion and, in popular culture, Indiana Jones. "House of God" is much more hospitable and welcoming and, in fact (therefore), more accurate both with regard to usage and etymology. The word "house" may derive from "hide" just as *bayt* means "tent." Finally, the House of God is a building for the worship of God, not the place where Islam's unknowable and infinitely transcendent God actually lives, apart from any place else. "Temple" as a place or occasion for con*templ*ation of this supreme mystery is, of course, perfectly apposite but this may be a rarified usage.

Jesus the Messiah / Jesus Christ

Jesus is subjected to interesting treatment in the Qur'ān. Much of it has to do with the freshness of the qur'ānic vision and *daʿwah*: to renew and extend the terms of the Abrahamic covenant throughout its world. In some sense, the Qur'ān wishes to broker a peace between Jews and Christians, especially—one might speculate—in the famous instance of the so-called denial of the crucifixion at Q 4:156. A steady reading of this verse of course confirms that it is not the crucifixion that is denied, it is the Jewish boastful claim to have crucified Jesus, son of Mary, the Messiah. In this qur'ānic moment (Q 4:156–157), Christians are asked to give up divine incarnation and Jews are asked to give up the finality of revelation. The word "Christ," because of its theopathic implications, would here run the risk of misrepresenting the Qur'ān's Jesus.

The Table / the Last Supper

Cuypers has convincingly demonstrated that the center of Sūrat al-Mā'idah (Q 5) is not the comparatively parochial event of Jesus and his beleaguered followers sharing a meal. Rather, the "table spread" here is an invitation to all humanity, represented in the *sūrah* that bears this name by the various religious groups of the Qur'ān. The hospitality here has more in common with the sacramental hospitality shown by Abraham, the so-called *philoxenia*.

The Book / the Bible

Leaving aside the "intention" of the author of the Qur'ān, it remains that such a word as *kitāb* may be understood as meaning the Holy Bible (*al-kitāb al-muqaddas*) and its constituents, the "Old Covenant" (*al-ʿahd al-qadīm*) and the "New Covenant" (*al-ʿahd al-jadīd*), while also leaving room for the conceptualization of the Qur'ān and the revelation it implies and represents as the Newest Covenant (*al-ʿahd al-ajadd*). In addition, *kitāb* and *ahl al-*

kitāb may be understood as referring to those who are able to read and write, an ability that Islamic tradition freely emphasizes was largely absent among the Qurʾān's first audience.

Allāh/God

A similar strategy is taken to an extreme, for example, when *allāh*, the Arabic term for the biblical God, is not translated as "God," but left in its Arabic form, transliterated, a practice that is quite common. Surely there is no more important or challenging word in the Qurʾān: the word الله, transliterated as Allāh, is guaranteed to alienate the "average" English reader, who cannot help pronounce it, silently or aloud, as a near homonym for "alley." The word is important not only because of what it means, but also for "how" it means. First, it denotes the ultimately unknowable unique source of the cosmos, all created things, revelation, laws and guidance and the education of humanity, history and the emotions and faculties of the human being including the human heart, mind and spirit. Secondly, the word *allāh* is incalculably powerful—didactically, heuristically, spiritually, pedagogically, and poetically, and also because of its sound in Arabic. It is rather naturally formed in the velar region of the throat, the channel of all qurʾānic revelation, which it thus highlights through the doubling of the liquid l-sounds and the final onomatopoeic breath-like aspirant soft aitch. Thus the word bespeaks by its very sound, and therefore emblematizes, the entire process of oral revelation—not the only kind the Qurʾān enshrines, but a major one, of course. It is also a beautiful sound—a sound or potential that is frequently exploited and sometimes overdone—in qurʾānic recitation in which the reverberant melisma is "long drawn out" as if to conjure the very presence of Allāh, who may be felt to actually inhabit the space indicated in the final syllable—even though this is technically, "rationally," and dogmatically acknowledged to be impossible in anything resembling a realistic conjuration. Thus, the word embodies numerous tensions and points to their resolution, which perhaps redounds also to its eschatological and apocalyptic programmatic musicality and verve.

Acknowledging the truth of Frost's dictum "poetry is that which is lost in translation," how can the English word "God" possibly compete? With its monosyllabic, "minimal pair" clippedness and its hard consonants bookending (truncating) whatever numinous and luminous "Allāh-meaning" might otherwise be encountered, it is a very queer choice. It might be more effective simply not to try to translate the word and to leave it completely out, as in the Jewish refusal to write the name of God. However, to insist on using "Allāh" rather than the usual, customary and idiomatic word

"God" in English translations of the Qur'ān is also to do a disservice to the message of "*the* Book" and the religiosity of Muslims. I think we have here a singular dilemma. This is so because to insist upon the word "Allāh" enhances precisely the opposite of the Qur'ān's intention, which is to educate, illumine, and enlighten humanity, especially that version of it abroad during the seventh century in the Nile-to-Oxus region of the globe, as to its essential commonality and relatedness despite—and this is key—*apparent* differences, multiplicity, variegation, chaotic fissiparousness, which late antique society had thrown up in the form of a relatively unregulated cosmopolitanism. The word "Allāh" still strikes the English ear as strange, foreign, "interplanetary." And its use, rather than cultivating a sense of oneness with the humans of Islam on the part of largely non-Muslim but also non-Arabic-speaking Muslim anglophones, tends to "Klingon-ize" those for whom the word represents the highest values and most noble aspects of what it means to be human *by virtue of what such humans worship as divine.* Historically, of course, the word "Allāh" symbolizes cosmopolitan enlightenment and imaginative acceptance of and engagement with a new historical and social reality.

Before proceeding to a conclusion, I would like to note another translation anomaly or dilemma not mentioned by Stewart but one that merits the kind of serious analysis and contemplation focused on the other words in his presidential address: *raḥmān* and *raḥīm*. The words *raḥmān* and *raḥīm* are nearly universally translated as "merciful and compassionate." Behold the strange alchemy of the handicapped imagination! While these words are perfectly expressive of the most laudable and life-affirming virtues and energies when thought of in terms, say, of the compassion of Mary, or Mother Theresa, or Noam Chomsky, their "semiology" is magically transformed to a nearly monstrous attribute when applied to Allāh. And even if such a transformation never takes place, the significance of these words—representing as they do one of the thematic pillars of the Qur'ān and Islam—is frequently and bewilderingly neglected and muted during "travel," when connotations of maternal, unconditional love (*agapē*) fall completely away.

III. Conclusion

You must have seen children playing with a string and a pebble. They tie a string to a pebble and they start swinging it over their head. And slowly they keep letting [out] the string, and it makes a bigger and bigger circle. Now, this pebble is the revolt from the tradition. It wants to move away. But the string is the tradition, the continuity, it is holding it. But if you break the string, the pebble will fall. If you remove the pebble, the string cannot go

> that far. This tension of tradition and revolt against the tradition are, in a way, contradictory. But as a matter of fact, it is a synthesis. You will always find the synthesis of tradition and revolt from the tradition, together in any good art.[4]

It is perhaps as it should be that several of the problematic vocabulary items above indicate covenant. Stewart mentions Islam's claim to superiority to previous religions. But in what does such a claim lie? Again, the theme of the covenant in the Qur'ān, despite strenuous attempts to attenuate its obvious universality, points to a thematic or literary/doctrinal gesture of balancing such claims to superiority with a benign hierarchical assertion of common humanity. The sociology of the Qur'ān functions somewhat as a *roman à clef* for its readership with the difference that the characters keep renewing themselves: Jews, Christians, *kāfirūn*, and so forth: so many human types. The population of Nile-to-Oxus late antique cosmopolitanism is made religiously, historically, and mythically meaningful through the Qur'ān. One word for this is enlightenment.

While there are of course many different approaches and methods suited to the scholarly, readerly, religio-literary understanding of the relation between the Qur'ān and the Bible, there is one without which all other approaches will remain impoverished with regard to their explanatory power of the Qur'ān's narratological élan. The Qur'ān without question sees itself as the fulfillment of biblical aspirations, promises, and fears. The Qur'ān also sees itself as a renewal, continuation and expansion of the terms of the biblical covenant. In this way, the Qur'ān, and its committed readership, function as a typological response to the biblical type in much the same way the so-called New Testament, and its believing readership, sees itself as the typological fulfilment of the so-called Old Testament myth, challenge, summons, and message. We hasten to add, as indicated above, that this is not the only choice available for an analysis of the—for lack of a better word—literary relation between the Qur'ān and the Bible. But this feature may be thought to stand for the "more than" in Northrop Frye's pronouncement: "The Bible is literature and more than literature."[5] By this, he means to

---

4. Javed Akhtar interviewed in *The Story of Film: An Odyssey*, episode 11, "The 1970s and Onwards, Innovation in Popular Culture," directed by Mark Cousins, aired September 2011, on More4, 32:57–34:00.

5. Northrop Frye, *The Great Code: The Bible and Literature* (New York: Harcourt Brace Jovanovich, 1982), xvi:

> "A literary approach to the Bible is not in itself illegitimate: no book could have had so specific a literary influence without itself possessing literary qualities. But the Bible is just as obviously 'more' than a work of literature ..."

emphasize that "mere" literature does not see itself as imparting a code for living, a moral and religious agenda—even though some literature clearly has what might be more safely thought of as an existential *daʿwah* or "political message." Frye seems here to tacitly agree with Nathaniel Hawthorne, who observed, in a letter to Melville, that no great work of literature has been made greater literature by the addition of a "message."

The opposite, as the Qurʾān itself stands as unimpeachable witness, is not the case. The literary artistry of the Qurʾān has breathed new life into familiar biblical themes and, yes, commonplaces—those things Professor Wansbrough celebrated as *topoi*. Thus, to give one example, the biblical covenant, a rather straightforward contract between God and the Jews and Christians, is honored, validated, highly esteemed, *and* imposed upon the readership. However, by this time—the seventh century CE—this readership has become a new creation having vastly expanded beyond the linguistic, religious, and ethnic borders of the original and even traditional covenantal range. (After all, the formulation *dār al-ʿahd*, "abode of the covenant," is frequently used as a synonym for *dār al-islām*, "abode of *islām*.") This Abrahamic (not Ibrāhīmic) covenant is presented by the Qurʾān in a new language and mode that unmistakably presents it not to a communal elite but proposes that this covenant is indeed the "property" and obligation of all humanity. While the idea of such an alliance, contract, or agreement is as old as time itself, the language and imagery with which it is certainly preached by the Qurʾān is fresh and, as a result of the passage of time and the unfoldment of the historical process (something of which the Qurʾān itself seems to be, in the context, newly aware), is now heard in a new setting that can perhaps best be described as late antique cosmopolitanism. Thus, the Qurʾān's insistence on a single humanity is, it would seem, perfectly timed.

Devin Stewart's discussion of translation problems points to much-needed improvements for the way in which the Qurʾān is rendered in English and raises a number of important questions precisely because the problems in translation he identifies seem to be at odds with the literary, social, and "religious" expectations of this late antique cosmopolitanism. The universal and universalizing message of the Qurʾān is, in fact, parochialized and cheapened by perverting its unmistakably and essentially universal *daʿwah* in translations which—whether this is the object or not—succeed in presenting its voice as one foreign to the human ear. His remarks on the exoticizing manner in which even the most well-known proper names—well-known to a primarily English-speaking, biblically-formed culture—are perversely or mischievously or lazily cast by translators, whether Eastern or Western, as

near transliterations of their Arabic cognates are very much to the point. Beginning with the proper name *allāh*, which very few anglophones bother to try to pronounce as indicated in this spelling, these names in their "translated" form may be thought to serve more to distance the target audience from the Qurʾān and Islam rather than offer an invitation to understanding and common human spiritual feeling. Who is Ibrāhīm? Who is ʿĪsā? Who is Mūsā? Who is Nūḥ? Who is Yūnus? Yūsuf? We, of course, have a right to be puzzled by such names as Hūd, Ṣāliḥ, and ʿĀd and Thamūd. And we are sort of okay with Isḥāq, Sulaymān, not forgetting Ādam. But if the translators wish to be true to the universalizing, cosmopolitan humanism of the Qurʾān and much of Islam's venture, then there needs to be some serious thought about the manner in which the Qurʾān's views on humanity and those figures whom it clearly conceives as the most important humans ever to have drawn breath—prophets and messengers from God—is presented to the uninitiated. Perhaps it is initiation that is at play here. In a real sense, to understand and concur with the Qurʾān's doctrine or teaching about the interconnectedness of humanity is really to be "of" the Qurʾān, at least as "lower-case *muslim*," to the extent that this striking and revolutionary late antique modernist world-view is seen for what it was, and is. To persist in the obfuscation is tantamount to deadening the persuasive and salubrious universalism the Qurʾān takes to be part of God's message to earthlings; and willfully to present to the English reader and scholar these common cultural heroes in such impenetrable and alien guise represents a process of "Klingonization" especially baleful at this moment in history. We should be seeking commonality not difference. We should be celebrating our human kinship. We should be teaching and studying the workings of our shared blessings and curses. Islam represents nearly a quarter of the population of the earth.

Not only does the Qurʾān enhance its timeless message by a new, in the context of religious history, Arabic literary poetics, it also repeats the ancient Abrahamic ethical values over the music of what would be interestingly described in a far-off future as the above-mentioned "poetics of relation."[6] Although Édouard Glissant meant perhaps something not precisely analogous to qurʾānic universalism, just the idea of a poetics of relation has profound qurʾānic resonance, for it could be argued that the literary poetics of the Qurʾān speaks to the predicament into which its voice proclaimed human unity: a chaos of religions. The Qurʾān wishes the reader to impose the qurʾānic map of a variegated community onto the human geography

6. Édouard Glissant, *Poetics of Relation* (Ann Arbor: University of Michigan Press, 1997).

of the time and place and transform such chaos into *communitas*: ponder its puzzles, just as the sometimes daunting pronouncements and connections, or apparent lack of them, puzzles its readership. The key is, of course, Q 7:172 and its many referents throughout the Qur᾿ān: in the beginning humans were united in the pure *muslim fiṭrah* state (in this context, *muslim* would seem to stand for a naturally observant human rather than yet another "trademark religion" vying for market share in the human welter of this same Late Antiquity) in their acknowledgement of, love for, and obedience to "their Lord." Here, "natural" is used in the sense in which the Qur᾿ān asserts that all created things are naturally in a state of praise to God (Q 17:44). The "nightmare of history" has destroyed or denatured (no pun intended) such primordial unity. The Qur᾿ān wishes people to wake up to such primal—later understood as ontic—unity, through recollection (*dhikr*). The originary state of natural unity is to be embodied and (typologically) reiterated through practice. Here, it is impossible not to think of Eliot's uncannily apposite lines near the end of his *Four Quartets*:

> We shall not cease from exploration
> And the end of all our exploring
> Will be to arrive where we started
> And know the place for the first time.[7]

I would, without hesitation, join my voice to Stewart's with regard to the dismaying manner in which translators of the Qur᾿ān have missed (purposely or otherwise) an opportunity to highlight the way in which this otherwise very foreign and "blockaded" book preaches the oneness of humanity with the same intensity that it preaches the oneness of God, the equally famous (sometimes infamous) Islamic desideratum of *tawḥīd*: "thinking in terms of oneness." Calling for a "biblicizing" translation limits in some ways the universal epic scope, the chronotope, of the Qur᾿ān. Biblicizing can give the wrong impression: we are not trying to biblicize the Qur᾿ān in this study of words and their translation. Rather, we are trying precisely to reveal the deep conversation that the Qur᾿ān carries on *with* the Bible. This is why we must be careful in the use of terms for method. Here, the expressions "strategy" and "tactic" also give a misleading impression. These terms make the composition of the Qur᾿ān sound too much like the result of planning an advertising campaign. While it is true that Islam has frequently, and especially in today's exquisitely multicultural and multireligious cosmopolitan world, embarrassingly been presented by proselytes as a "superior product,"

---

7. T. S. Eliot, *Four Quartets* (New York: Harcourt, Brace, 1943), 39.

it is wrong to assume that such literary imperialism is the driving vision of the original revelation even if the result of the Islamic "openings" led to what would later, in another conversation, be condemned as colonialism. Once again, we are all in the same boat, or, perhaps more accurately, we are all in the same flood (some of us have better boats than others): we have all committed the same sins, we have all done the same good deeds. More of the latter and less of the former is what is called for. Objectivity is a phantom. We need now to read such books as the Qurʾān for their gospel of universal salvation/survival and conviviality. However a word of the Qurʾān is translated, it must be heard as the word of God in the voice of Muḥammad—which blends with the voice (silent or aloud) of the reader. Moreover, it is a voice charged with powerful "trope" of deep connection through the periodic yet incessant, often fugue-like, literary energies of epic and apocalypse.[8] Thus, a key element in the challenge of translation is a deeper understanding of Muḥammad and his voice: his heroism, his wisdom, and his compassion. Otherwise the sound of the Qurʾān we hear will be false and its message deadened. Such a muted and distorted rendition of the Qurʾān's singular music becomes, then, like the alien noise leaking from headphones worn by someone else. Hodgson's insights on the nature of the Qurʾān and the problem of translation, especially when compared with the Bible, are more timely today than when originally formulated. We will end our discussion with them:

> [T]he Qur'ân reveals itself as a comprehensive cosmic challenge, monumentally delivered. It is at once more comprehensive in outline and more involved in the details of individual living than are its closest analogues, the Old Testament prophets, taken in themselves. ... It maintains an ultimate perspective on every point that arises, large or small. This it does even verse by verse in its sonorous endings recalling the power and the mercy of God and, more substantially, in the very mixture of passages exalted and prosaic. In Arabic, at least, the exalted passages manage to win out in such contests and give their tone to the whole. This can be seen in the Chapter of Light, which contains the most ethereal passage in the Qur'ân juxtaposed with what might seem some of its most sordid, dealing with matters of etiquette, with sexual decency, and in particular with an accusation of infidelity levied against a wife of the Prophet. The exalted effect is aided by an effective use of language, which lends an untranslatable dignity even to quite ordinary ideas, so that the phrases seem to take on a more general reference; much of real substance is lost when the thought is cast into less noble rhythms in another tongue.[9]

8. Todd Lawson, *The Quran: Epic and Apocalypse* (London: Oneworld, 2017).
9. Hodgson, "A Comparison," 61–62.

JIQSA 6 (2021): 87–105

DISSIMILATION OF *Ē* TO *Ā* IN THE QUR'ĀNIC CONSONANTAL TEXT

MARIJN VAN PUTTEN
Leiden University

Abstract

The *alifāt maqṣūrah* are kept strictly distinct in the Qur'ānic Consonantal Text. Depending on whether the final root consonant is a *yā'* or a *wāw*, they are spelled with ى and ا, respectively. As these two characters behave distinctly in qur'ānic rhyme, it is clear that they represent two distinct vowels in Qur'ānic Arabic, *ē* and *ā*, respectively. The current article shows that in a specific phonetic environment—namely, if *y* or *ī* stands in the vicinity of *ē*—it dissimilated towards *ā*. While representation of this dissimilation in the orthography of the Qur'ān has disappeared in modern print editions, careful examination across a large number of early qur'ānic manuscripts reveals that this original dissimilatory practice was reflected regularly in these manuscripts, and therefore also in the 'Uthmānic archetype.

Introduction

In 2017, I published an article on the development of the triphthongs in Qur'ānic and Classical Arabic.[1] On the basis of rhyme, orthography, etymology, and reading traditions, I argued that the *alif maqṣūrah bi-ṣūrat al-yā'*, such as in the verb هدى *hadā*, was not a vowel *ā*, but rather an etymologically and phonetically distinct vowel *ē* in Qur'ānic Arabic as reflected in the Qur'ānic Consonantal Text (QCT).[2] This can be deduced from the fact that

1. Marijn van Putten, "The Development of the Triphthongs in Quranic and Classical Arabic," *Arabian Epigraphic Notes* 3 (2017): 47–74.
2. In my transcriptions of the QCT, I will use consonantal dotting, even though it was employed quite sparingly in early qur'ānic manuscripts. It is often suggested that the original redaction of 'Uthmān's standard text had been completely without consonantal dotting and was just a bare consonantal skeleton, the *rasm*. Bursi has recently pointed out that there is rather little evidence for such a view. The very earliest manuscripts that we have all contain some amount of dotting—although it is indeed sometimes used sparingly. See Adam Bursi, "Connecting the Dots: Diacrit-

doi: http://dx.doi.org/10.5913/jiqsa.6.2021.a003

the letter in question exhibits orthographically distinct behavior and cannot rhyme with the *alif maqṣūrah bi-ṣūrat al-alif.* My claim stands in disagreement with Diem,[3] who drew the opposite conclusion, arguing that the *yāʾ* was a purely pseudo-etymological sign for ā, and that it not only was pronounced as ā in the Qurʾān but that it had always been pronounced as such in Arabic. Table 1 below summarizes the orthographic distinction, with a reconstruction of the original pronunciation in Qurʾānic Arabic, along with its etymological origin following my previous conclusions.

Table 1: The etymological origin of the two forms of *alif maqṣūrah.*

QCT	**Qurʾānic Arabic**	**Proto-Arabic**	
هدى	/hadē/	< *hadaya	"he guided"
هديه	/hadē-h/	< *hadaya-hu	"he guided him"
دعا	/daʿā/	< *daʿawa	"he called"
دعاه or دعه	/daʿā-h/	< *daʿawa-hu	"he called him"
الهدى	/al-hudē/	< *al-hudayu	"the guidance"
هديه	/hudē-h/	< *hudayu-hu	"his guidance"
سنا	/sanā/	< *sanawu	"a flash of"
عصاه or عصه	/ʿaṣā-h/	< *ʿaṣawu-hu	"his staff"
مزجيه	/muzjēh/	< *muzjayatin	"of little value"

My 2017 article lacks a satisfactory solution for the spelling هداى "my guidance" (Q al-Baqarah 2:38; Q Ṭā Hā 20:123), which seemingly spells *ē* with an *alif.*[4] Close examination of early qurʾānic manuscripts shows

ics, Scribal Culture, and the Qurʾān in the First/Seventh Century," *JIQSA* 3 (2018): 111–157; François Déroche, *La transmission écrite du Coran dans les débuts de l'Islam: Le Codex Parisino-Petropolitanus* (Leiden: Brill, 2009), 43–45. Whenever dots appear in early manuscripts, in the vast majority of cases the manuscripts agree with each other on the dotting, something we also observe in the high measure of agreement between the qurʾānic readings. For this reason, I believe it is justified in most cases to assert that we know what the intended dotting of any given word is. In this sense, my use of the QCT, which provides the most likely consonantal dotting, is distinct from the more broadly used term *rasm.* Differences in dotting, which occur occasionally among the canonical readers, do not affect the current study.

3. Werner Diem, "Untersuchungen zur frühen Geschichte der arabischen Orthographie I: Die Schreibung der Vokale," *Orientalia* 48 (1979): 207–257.

4. Van Putten, "Triphthongs," 61–62.

that this spelling is not unique to this word. There are several other cases where we find an *alif* (or a defective spelling with no representation of the *alif* at all, but where an *alif* is nonetheless clearly to be understood as present) while the Cairo Edition (henceforth CE) has the expected *yāʾ*, for example, Q al-Aʿrāf 7:143 ترانى in the Codex Parisino-Petropolitanus[5] (henceforth CPP) for CE *tarā-nī* ترينى. If the use of *alif* and *yāʾ* in early qurʾānic manuscripts were completely unpredictable, it would be a strong argument in favor of Diem's hypothesis that these two signs represent one and the same sound.[6] Indeed, such free variation has been a reason for Middle Arabists to suggest that the two *alifāt maqṣūrah* were not phonetically distinct.[7] However, this paper will examine the cases where the spelling with *alif* occurs, and will show that these deviations are not the result of free variation. Instead, early qurʾānic manuscripts display a high measure of orthographical agreement with each another, and the appearance of one spelling over the other is strictly phonetically conditioned. This phonetic conditioning is best explained as the result of a regular conditioned sound change that has taken place in Qurʾānic Arabic.[8]

The Material

Across multiple manuscripts we find a consistent absence of the expected final *yāʾ* in stems with *yāʾ* as their third root consonant that end in *alif maqṣūrah* in several cases throughout the Qurʾān. In its place we find an *alif*

5. Déroche, *Codex Parisino-Petropolitanus.*
6. Diem, "Die Schreibung der Vokale," § 45.
7. Simon Hopkins, *Studies in the Grammar of Early Arabic: Based upon Papyri Datable to before 300 A.H./912 A.D.* (Oxford: Oxford University Press, 1984), 14–16; Joshua Blau, *A Grammar of Christian Arabic: Based Mainly on the South-Palestinian Texts from the First Millennium* (Louvain: Secrétariat du CorpusCO, 1967), 81–83.
8. In a series of articles, I have argued that with careful examination of the orthography of the QCT, informed by rhyme, it is possible to derive information about the language of the Qurʾān independent of the later classicizing qurʾānic reading traditions. Besides Van Putten, "Triphthongs," see also idem, "The Feminine Ending *-at* as a Diptote in the Qurʾānic Consonantal Text and Its Implications for Proto-Arabic and Proto-Semitic," *Arabica* 64 (2017): 695–705; idem, "Inferring the Phonetics of Qurʾānic Arabic from the Quranic Consonantal Text," *International Journal of Arabic Linguistics* 5 (2019): 1–19; Marijn van Putten and Phillip W. Stokes, "Case in the Qurʾānic Consonantal Text," *WZKM* 108 (2018): 143–179; Marijn van Putten, "Hamzah in the Quranic Consonantal Text," *Orientalia* 87 (2018): 93–120. The current article is a continuation of this project. See now also Marijn van Putten, *Quranic Arabic: From Its Hijazi Origins to Its Classical Reading Traditions* (Leiden: Brill, 2022).

or a defective spelling. The modern standard text, however, has corrected the *alif* spelling and has replaced it with a *yāʾ* in the majority of these cases. This is somewhat surprising, as the original spelling was closer to Classical Arabic orthography. Therefore, in this case the CE moves *away* from classical orthography towards a non-standard orthography. The absence of the *yāʾ* in these examples is so consistent across manuscripts that there can be little doubt that the *yāʾ*-less form is original, and should be assumed to have been part of the ʿUthmānic archetype.[9] Early qurʾānic manuscripts have been accessed through the *Corpus Coranicum* website (www.corpus-coranicum.de) unless stated otherwise. A key to the abbreviations used for these manuscripts is provided at the end of this article.

The conditioning of the spelling is clear: whenever the first-person singular suffixes of the direct object *-nī* or of the possessive *-ya* follow the final *yāʾ* root letter, the vowel is written with *alif* or is not expressed in writing. Table 2 below provides the attestations in the manuscripts. "A" means that the form is written with an *alif* (e.g., اوصانى); "Ø" denotes a defective spelling (اوصنى); and "Y" denotes a spelling with a *yāʾ* (اوصينى). The leftmost column displays the location and spelling as attested in the CE.

Table 2: The spelling of words with *alif maqṣūrah* that have *yāʾ* as their third root consonant followed by *-nī* or *-ya*

	W	SM	GK	BL	CPP	Q	SU	S	Bb	331	T	Top	CA1	CM
Q 6:80 هدين	A	A	Y		A			A	A			A		Y
Q 6:161 هدينى	Ø[10]	Ø	A		A[11]		Ø	A				A		Y

9. It is clear from consistent agreement in the position and appearance of specific orthographic idiosyncrasies that all early qurʾānic manuscripts of the ʿUthmānic Text Type (which are all manuscripts found so far, except for the lower text of the Sanʿāʾ Palimpsest) go back to a single written archetype, which I call here the ʿUthmānic archetype. For a discussion, see Marijn van Putten, "'The Grace of God' as Evidence for a Written Uthmanic Archetype: The Importance of Shared Orthographic Idiosyncrasies," *BSOAS* 82 (2019): 271–288; Nicolai Sinai, "When Did the Consonantal Skeleton of the Quran Reach Closure? Part I," *BSOAS* 77 (2014): 273–292; idem, "When Did the Consonantal Skeleton of the Quran Reach Closure? Part II," *BSOAS* 77 (2014): 509–521; idem, "Beyond the Cairo Edition: On the Study of Early Quranic Codices," *JAOS* 140 (2020): 189–204.

10. A later hand has added an *alif*.

11. Déroche read this as هدانى. Having checked the digitized photographs on the

	W	SM	GK	BL	CPP	Q	SU	S	Bb	331	T	Top	CA1	CM
Q 39:57 هدينى	A	A	Y									A		Y
Q 7:143 ترينى	A	A	A	A	A							A		A
Q 7:143 ترينى	A	A	A	A	A							A		A
Q 12:36 ارينى	A	A	A	A								A		A
Q 12:36 ارينى	A	A	A	A								A		A
Q 11:28 اتينى	A	A	A	A		A			A			A	Ø	A
Q 11:63 اتينى		Y?	A	A				A	Y			A	Ø	Ø
Q 19:30 اتينى		Y	A	A				A			A	A		Y
Q 27:36 اتين	Y	Y	Y	Y	Y						Y	Y		Y
Q 18:63 انسينيه	A[12]	A[13]										Ø		Ø
Q 19:31 اوصنى	A	Y	Ø	Ø				Ø			A[14]	Ø		Y
Q 14:36 عصانى	A	Ø	A	Ø	Ø	Ø				Y		A	Ø	Ø
Q 2:38 هداى	Ø		A					Ø				A		A
Q 20:123 هداى	Ø[15]	A	A	A			Ø[16]	A			Ø	A		A
Q 12:23 مثواى	Ø	Ø	A	Ø								Ø		A

The fact that this use of *alif* or defective spelling is typical for words of this type *only* when they are followed by first-person object suffix *-nī* or possessive suffix *-ya* can be demonstrated by comparing the verbs *hadē*

Gallica website (gallica.bnf.fr), it is clear the reading هداى is correct. See Déroche, *Codex Parisino-Petropolitanus*, ٨٠١.

12. Dot apparently on the wrong denticle: انسنه rather than انسنه.
13. Dot apparently on the wrong denticle: اسنه rather than انسنه.
14. A denticle appears to have been removed here.
15. Re-inked, *alif* was added.
16. *Alif* added later.

("to lead") in the perfect and *yarē* ("to see") in the imperfect when they are followed by other object suffixes. In such cases, the vowel is spelled almost invariably with *yāʾ* across all early qurʾānic manuscripts, as we can see in table 3 below.

Table 3: The spelling *hadē* and *yarē* followed by suffixes other than the object suffix *-nī* or possessive suffix *-ya*.

	W	SM	GK	BL	CPP	Q	SU	S	Ba	331	T	Top	CA1	CM
Q 3:152 اريكم	Y		Y		Y							Y		
Q 4:105 اريك	Y		Y		Y	Y		Y				Y		Y
Q 6:74 اريك	Y	Y	Y		Y	Y		Y				Y		Y
Q 7:27 يريكم	Y	Y	Y		Y			Y				Y		Y
Q 7:60 نريك	Y	Y	Y	Y	Y			Y				Y		Y
Q 7:66 نريك	Y	Y	Y	Y	Y			Y				Y		Y
Q 7:198 تريهم	Y	Y	Y	Y	Y					Y		Y		Y
Q 9:127 يريكم	Y	Y	Y		Y	Y						Y	Y	Y
Q 11:27 نريك	Y	Y	A	Y	Y	Y			Y			Y	Y	Y
Q 11:27 نريك	Y	Y	A	Y	Y				Y			A	Y	Y
Q 11:29 اريكم	Y	Y	A	Y	Y				Y			Y	Y	Y
Q 11:84 اريكم	Y	Y	Y	Y				Y	Y			Y	Y	Y
Q 11:91 نريك	Y	Y	Y	Y					Y			Y		Y
Q 12:30 نريها	Y	Y	Y	Y								Y		Y
Q 12:36 نريك	Y	Y	A	A								Y		Y
Q 12:78 نريك	A	Y	A	A								Y		Y

	W	SM	GK	BL	CPP	Q	SU	S	Ba	331	T	Top	CA1	CM
Q 24:40 يريها		Y	Y	Y	Y						Y	Y		Y
Q 26:218 يريك	Y	Y		A	A						Y	Y		Y
Q 39:21 تريه	Y	Y	Y	Y								Y		Y
Q 42:45 تريهم	Y	Y	Y	Y	Y			Y				Y	Y	Y
Q 46:23 اريكم	Y	Y	Y							Y		Y		Y
Q 48:29 تريهم	Y	Y	Y							Y		Y		Y
Q 57:20 تريه	Y	Y			A		Y[17]			Y		Y	Y	Y
Q 70:7 نريه	Y	Y	Y		Y							Y		Y
Q 79:20 اريه	Y	Y										Y		Y
Q 2:185 هديكم	A	Y						Y		A		A		Y
Q 2:198 هديكم	A	Y										A		Y
Q 6:71 هدينا	Y	Y	Y		Y	Y	Y	Y				A		Y
Q 6:149 هديكم	Y	Y	Y		Y			Y				Y		Y
Q 7:43 هدينا	A	Y	Ø	Y	Ø			Ø				A		Y
Q 7:43 هدينا	A	Y	Ø	Y	Ø			Ø				A		Y
Q 9:115 هديهم	Y	Y	Y		Y							Y	Y	Y
Q 14:12 هدينا	Y	Ø	Y	Y	Y					Y		Y		Y

17. A *yāʾ* has been deleted and an *alif* added.

	W	SM	GK	BL	CPP	Q	SU	S	Ba	331	T	Top	CA1	CM
Q 14:21 هدينا	A[18]	ø	Y	Y	Y					Y		Y	Y[19]	Y
Q 16:9 هديكم	Y	Y	Y	Y				Y		Y		Y		Y
Q 16:121 هديه	Y	Y	Y	Y			Y			Y		Y		Y
Q 22:37 هديكم	A	A	A	A					A		Y	Y		Y
Q 39:18 هديهم	A	Y	Y	A								A		Y
Q 49:17 هديكم	Y	Y	Y							Y		Y	Y	Y

The spelling of the two cases of *hadē-nā* in Q al-Aʿrāf 7:43 seems to be attested more commonly with the *alif* or defective spelling. This is likewise the case for Q al-Ḥajj 22:37 *hadē-kum*. As both phrases are otherwise consistently spelled with *yāʾ*, it is difficult to decide what to make of this pattern.

Interpretation

What can be seen in the tables above is that it is indeed very typical for early qurʾānic manuscripts to lack the *alif maqṣūrah bi-ṣūrat al-yāʾ* in final-*yāʾ* roots when the nouns and verbs formed from such roots are followed by the first-person singular pronominal suffixes. This regular treatment needs an explanation. At first blush, it might be tempting to explain the absence of the expected spelling of *hudā-ya* and *mathwā-ya*, **هديى and **مثويى, to result from avoiding a sequence of two consecutive *yāʾ*s. But while the CE does indeed avoid the sequence of two *yāʾ*s in word-final position, such an orthographic principle is not operative in the QCT. Thus, in the CE *yuḥyī* and *yastaḥyī* are spelled يحى and يستحى,[20] but this is an idiosyncrasy of the CE that cannot be reconstructed for the ʿUthmānic archetype, as early qurʾānic manuscripts invariably write both *yāʾ*s. The spelling of the CE is based on the account of Abū ʿAmr ʿUthmān b. Saʿīd al-Dānī (d. 444/1053),[21]

18. The *alif* appears to be a later addition.
19. Corrected, from هدا (without the suffix pronoun?) seemingly by the same hand and ductus as the text itself.
20. Diem, "Die Schreibung Der Vokale," § 39.
21. Abū ʿAmr al-Dānī, *al-Muqniʿ fī rasm maṣāḥif al-amṣār maʿa kitāb al-naqṭ*, ed.

who says that such forms are only written with one *yā'*, but this seems to have no basis in actual manuscript evidence. Therefore, there is no obvious orthographic reason why words ending /ē-ya/ would be written with اى or just ى over the expected spelling with two *yā'*s.[22]

The use of *alif* is even more difficult to explain as the result of some hitherto unrecognized orthographic principle when it occurs before the suffix ـنى, where a principle of double *yā'* avoidance cannot be invoked. The spelling is clearly conditioned, but this conditioning cannot easily be explained as an orthographic principle. Hence, it would rather seem that spellings of the type هدانى and هداى are best considered to represent a phonetic reality. Therefore, they were likely pronounced /hadā-nī/ and /hudā-y/ respectively. As this same /ā/ does not regularly show up before other suffixes,[23] it seems that we are dealing with a phonetically conditioned dissimmilatory sound shift which shifts *ē* to *ā* in the vicinity of *ī* or *y*. The archetypal spellings—such as Q Maryam 19:30 اتانى, Q al-Baqarah 2:38 هداى, and Q Maryam 19:31 اوصانى—must therefore be understood as representing /atā-nī/, /hudā-y/, and /awṣā-nī/, respectively.

An outstanding issue is the question of how the shortened form of the object pronoun *-n(i)* plays into the dissimilation at hand.[24] Here the QCT gives two conflicting answers: for Q al-Anʿām 6:80, the spelling هدان /hadā-n/ seems to suggest that the dissimilation is applied here too, whereas Q al-Naml 27:36 اتين /ātē-n/ predominantly has spellings in manuscripts that point to the dissimilation not applying. It seems possible that in this context the dissimilation may have been optional. As these are the only two cases, it is impossible to be more precise.

Muḥammad al-Sāḍiq Qamḥāwī (Cairo: Maktabat al-Kulliyyāt al-Azhariyyah, 1978), 56.

22. See, for example, يحيى at Q 9:116, 10:56 (mistranscribed as يحى), 40:68, 42:9, 44:8; نحيى at Q 15:23, 50:43 in Éléonore Cellard, *Codex Amrensis 1* (Leiden: Brill, 2018); and يحيى at Q 3:156, 7:158, 9:116, 10:56, 23:80, 44:8 (mistranscribed as يحى), 57:2; نحيى at Q 15:23; يستحيى at Q 7:127 (mistranscribed as يستحى), 28:4 in Déroche, *Codex Parisino-Petropolitanus*. A cursory look on the *Corpus Coranicum* website will convince the reader that this is the regular spelling in other manuscripts too.

23. See, for example, Q al-Nāziʿāt 79:27–32, 42–46; Q al-Shams 91. Both rhyme on *-ē-hā* and are consistently spelled ىها, e.g., *ḍuḥē-hā*, *talē-hā*. For a further discussion of this phonemic distinction evidenced by rhyme, see Van Putten, "Triphthongs," 57–58.

24. The QCT shows fairly consistent shortening of word-final *ī* in pausal position; see Van Putten and Stokes, "Case in the Qurʔānic Consonantal Text," 156–158.

Final *-*yayV* Sequences

In light of the proposed dissimilation, we may reconsider the spelling of a sequence that is historically from *-*yayV*, such as الدنيا < **al-dunyayu* ("the world"), العليا < **al-ʿulyayu* ("the highest") etc.[25] Words of this type are generally spelled with a final *alif.* Diem explains these spellings as an attempt to avoid a sequence of two word-final *yāʾ*s.[26] As has been pointed out above, the avoidance of two word-final *yāʾ*s in the Qurʾān is an artifact of the *rasm* of the CE, which was based on traditional *rasm* literature, rather than being grounded in ancient manuscripts. As such, this cannot be the solution. Rabin already suggested that this spelling was the result of a dissimilation of the original *-*yē* to -*yā*,[27] which would mean that the dissimilation proposed in the previous section is bidirectional: original *ē* becomes *ā* not only when followed by *ī* or *y* but also when preceded by *y*.

As I have observed previously,[28] with regard to the issue at hand the information provided by qurʾānic rhyme and by the orthography of the QCT diverges somewhat: الدنيا "the world" (Q 20:72, 53:29, 79:38 87:16), احيا "he gives life" (Q 53:44), and سقيها "her drinking" (Q 91:13) all stand in -*ē(-hā)* rhymes, which suggests that they were pronounced as something close to [ad-dunyē], [ʾaḥyē], and [suqyē-hā], respectively. With only six examples of this kind, it is difficult to decide what to make of this. The phenomenon may simply be a case of poetic license, or it may indicate that these verses stem from an earlier text in a dialect that lacked this dissimilation. Finally, it is possible that the sequence /yā/ had a vowel that was phonetically not quite identical to the /ā/ found in other cases but was rather a little closer to [ǣ], thus facilitating rhyme. Any explanation will remain *ad hoc*, but it is attractive to consider the orthographic practice found here to be part of the same dissimilation that we see when *ī* and *y* follow *ē*.

As I have pointed out, the verb *ḥayya* ("to live") in the prefix conjugation is not infrequently spelled with a final *yāʾ*.[29] In the CE, like in early qurʾānic manuscripts, the third-person masculine forms are always spelled as such. As shown in table 4, for the two cases of the first-person plural form, the

25. On the reconstruction of the feminine ending as *-*ay*-, see Marijn van Putten, "The Feminine Endings *-Ay and *-Āy in Semitic and Berber," *BSOAS* 81 (2018): 205–225.

26. Diem, "Die Schreibung der Vokale," § 46.

27. Chaim Rabin, *Ancient West-Arabian* (London: Taylor's Foreign Press, 1951), 115ff.

28. Van Putten, "Triphthongs."

29. Ibid., 59.

data is somewhat ambiguous. Q al-Mu'minūn 23:37 is usually spelled with *yā'* (نحيى) but two fairly early manuscripts have the Classical Arabic spelling with *alif*. Meanwhile, Q al-Jāthiyah 45:24 has a majority spelling with *alif* (نحيا), but other manuscripts, generally considered to be earlier, spell it with *yā'*. It is difficult to reconstruct what spelling the ʿUthmānic archetype may have used.

Table 4: The spelling of prefix conjugation forms of *ḥayya*.

	W	SM	GK	BL	CPP	S	Bb	331	T	Top	CA1	CM
Q 23:37 ونحيا	A	Y	Y	Y	Y				A	Y		A
Q 45:24 ونحيا	A	A	Y		Y			A		A	A	A
Q 8:42 يحيى	Y	Y	Y	Y				Y		Y	Y	Y
Q 20:74 يحيى	Y	Y	Y	Y			Y		Y	Y		Y
Q 87:13 يحيى	Y	Y	Y							Y		Y

In the perfect third-person masculine of the causative verb *aḥyā*, the spelling in the CE is either with *alif* or defective. While occasional manuscripts have spellings with *yā'*, the overwhelming trend is towards the dissimilated spelling with *alif* or defective spellings (see table 5).

Table 5: The spelling of *aḥyā*.

	W	SM	GK	BL	CPP	S	Ba	331	T	Top	CA1	CM
Q 5:32 احيا	Y		A	Y	Y					A		A
Q 2:164 فاحيا	A		A			A		A		A		A
Q 16:65 فاحيا	A	A	Y	A		Y				A		
Q 29:63 فاحيا		A	Y	A					A	A		A
Q 45:5 فاحيا	A	A	Y		Y					A	A	A

	W	SM	GK	BL	CPP	S	Ba	331	T	Top	CA1	CM
Q 53:44 واحيا	A	A	A					Y		Y		A
Q 5:32 احياها	Ø		Ø		Ø					A		Ø
Q 41:39 احياها	Ø	Ø	Ø	Ø	Ø	Ø				A	Y	Ø
Q 22:66 احياكم	A	Ø	A	Ø			Ø		A	A		A
Q 2:28 فاحيكم			A			A				A		A
Q 2:243 احيهم	A		A					A		A		A

Though it is difficult to present an exact explanation for the asymmetry, it is clear that for Qurʾānic Arabic we should probably reconstruct the base stem as having *ḥayy*/*yaḥyē* without the *yē* > *yā* dissimilation, whereas the causative stem should be reconstructed as *aḥyā*/*yuḥyī* with the *yē* > *yā* dissimilation.

Traces of the Dissimilation in the Reading Traditions

The most common reading tradition today is that of ʿĀṣim in the transmission of Ḥafṣ, and this is the reading used by the CE. However, Warsh and Qālūn, the transmitters of Nāfiʿ, are still followed by millions in the Maghreb today. Besides ʿĀṣim and Nāfiʿ there are five more canonical readings with two canonical transmitters each.[30] While such readings are often ignored, they are just as much part of the accepted canon as Ḥafṣ is. The canonical reading traditions are in many ways dependent on the written form. After all, they all follow the same ʿUthmānic *rasm*, and thus derive much of their pronunciation from the written form of the text, rather than the other way around.

The fact that the orthographic variation between final *yāʾ* and *alif* is phonetically conditioned is already a strong indication that these spellings must reflect a linguistic reality in the language of the QCT. This leads us

30. Ḥamzah, al-Kisāʾī, Abū ʿAmr, Ibn ʿĀmir, and Ibn Kathīr. The earliest extant work on the reading traditions, that of Ibn Mujāhid (d. 324/936), described these seven readings and quickly came to be considered canonical. Three more readings, those

to wonder to what extent the qurʾānic reading traditions may preserve a memory of the dissimilation as found in early qurʾānic manuscripts. I shall now go on to argue that several of the reading traditions do indeed preserve an echo of the dissimilation reconstructed above.

There are three canonical reading traditions among the seven that consistently read the *alif maqṣūrah bi-ṣūrat al-yāʾ* with *imālah* and thereby distinguish it from the *alif maqṣūrah bi-ṣūrat al-alif.* The two Kufans, Ḥamzah and al-Kisāʾī,[31] read nouns and verbs with a root final *yāʾ* with *imālah,* e.g., هدى *hadē* ("he led"), هديهم *hadē-hum* ("he led them"), الهدى *al-hudē* ("the guidance"), الموتى *al-mawtē* ("the dead"), but دعا *daʿā* ("he called"), سنا *sanā* ("flash"), عصاه *ʿaṣā-hu* ("his stick").[32] Warsh, a transmitter of the Medinan reader Nāfiʿ, follows much the same pattern, but pronounces the vowel in between the *ā* and the *ē*, i.e., *ǣ* (variously called *imālah bayna bayn, imālah bayn al-lafẓayn* or *taqlīl*).[33] As this distinction between *ē/ǣ* versus *ā* would not be predictable from an underlying form that had *ā* for both, we must conclude that in these reading traditions the distinction was fully phonemic. The distribution that we find in these reading traditions is, in fact, identical to the phonemic distinction that is reconstructible on the basis of the orthography and rhyme of the QCT.[34]

Several exceptions to these rules are mentioned in al-Dānī's account of *imālah.*[35] Here we find that the absence of *imālah* in fact very often coincides with cases where the suffixes *-ya* or *-nī* follow (and thus where manuscripts generally do not write the *yāʾ*). Al-Kisāʾī in all these cases of *-nī/-ni/ya* has

---

of Abū Jaʿfar, Yaʿqūb, and Khalaf, came to be accepted into the canon after the work of Ibn al-Jazarī (d. 833/1429); these are of little consequence to the discussion here, and will not be discussed further.

31. The Kufan reader Khalaf, among the ten, also a transmitter of Ḥamzah's reading, likewise has *imālah* in this position, but does not add any new information to the transmissions of Ḥamzah and al-Kisāʾī, so I do not include him in the discussion here.

32. Abū ʿAmr al-Dānī, *al-Taysīr fī 'l-qirāʾāt al-sabʿ*, ed. Otto Pretzl (Beirut: Dār al-Kitāb al-ʿArabī, 1984), 46.

33. This is the most commonly adhered to transmission of Warsh today, following the transmission path of al-Azraq, and presented as the only option by al-Dānī in his *Taysīr* (ibid., 47–48). But there is another option within the transmission path of al-Azraq, which only applies *imālah bayna bayn* when the word occurs at the end of a verse; see, for example, Abū 'l-Khayr b. al-Jazarī, *Nashr al-qirāʾāt al-ʿashr*, ed. Ayman Rushdī Suwayd (Beirut: Dār al-Ghawthānī, 2018), § 2017, § 2022. The eastern transmission path of al-Aṣbahānī from Warsh does not transmit *imālah* at all.

34. Van Putten, "Triphthongs."

35. Al-Dānī, *al-Taysīr*, 48–49.

the *imālah* variant, but one of his transmitters, Abū 'l-Ḥārith, lacks *imālah* before *-ya* whereas his other transmitter, al-Dūrī, does not. Table 6 below provides the readings of the different forms. The leftmost column displays the QCT as it can be reconstructed for the ʿUthmānic archetype. While the correspondence is not perfect—presumably the result of not entirely complete transmission—it is clear that Ḥamzah's reading follows the dissimilation visible in the QCT quite closely.

Table 6: The recitation of *alif maqṣūrah bi-ṣūrat al-yāʾ* when followed by *-nī* or *-ya*.

QCT	Ḥamzah	Abū 'l-Ḥārith	Al-Dūrī	Warsh
هدان (Q 6:80)	***hadā-ni***	*hadē-ni*	*hadē-ni*	*hadǣ-ni*
هدانی (Q 6:161, 39:57)	*hadē-nī*	*hadē-nī*	*hadē-nī*	*hadǣ-nī*
عصانی (Q 14:36)	***ʿaṣā-nī***	*ʿaṣē-nī*	*ʿaṣē-nī*	*ʿaṣǣ-nī*
انسانیه (Q 18:63)	***ansā-nī-hi***	*ansē-nī-hi*	*ansē-nī-hi*	*ansǣ-nī-hi*
اتانی (Q 19:30)	***ātā-nī***	*ātē-niya*	*ātē-niya*	*ātǣ-niya*
اتین (Q 27:36)[36]	***ātā-ni***	*ātē-ni*	*ātē-ni*	*ātǣ-niya*
اتانی (Q 11:28.63)	*ātē-nī*	*ātē-nī*	*ātē-nī*	*ātǣ-nī*
اوصانی (Q 19:31)	***awṣā-nī***	*awṣē-nī*	*awṣē-nī*	*awsǣ-nī*
مثوای (Q 12:23)	***mathwā-ya***	***mathwā-ya***	*mathwē-ya*	*mathwǣ-ya*
هدای (Q 2:38, 20:123)	***hudā-ya***	***hudā-ya***	*hudē-ya*	*hudǣ-ya*

36. Note that while Ḥamzah reads this with *ā*, manuscript evidence actually seems to suggest that this verse is an exception to the dissimilation rule and is written with *yāʾ*.

Among the nouns and verbs that have the original **-yayV* sequence, we find once again that Ḥamzah follows the QCT (see table 7). Thus, the prefix conjugation of the base stem *ḥayya* ("to live") has *ē* for all the readers with this type of *imālah*, including Ḥamzah (meaning that he reads *yaḥyē* and *naḥyē*), whereas the causative *aḥyā* has *ā*. While three nouns (one of them extremely common, namely *al-dunyē*) are read with a final *-yē*, most other nouns lack the *imālah* in Ḥamzah's reading, following the spelling in the QCT. Once again, while the match is not perfect, and in fact readings with *yē* are overwhelmingly in the majority due to *al-dunyē* being read as such in all its 115 attestations, there is a clear relation between the *-yā* sequence being read as *-yā* rather than *-yē* following the dissimilation as found in the QCT.

Table 7: The recitation of words with an historical **-yayV* sequence.

	Ḥamzah	Abū 'l-Ḥārith	Al-Dūrī	Warsh
فاحيا (Q 2:164, 16:65, 29:63, 45:5)	***fa-aḥyā***	*fa-aḥyē*	*fa-aḥyē*	*fa-aḥyǣ*
واحيا (Q 53:44)	*wa-aḥyē*	*wa-aḥyē*	*wa-aḥyē*	*wa-aḥyǣ*
احياكم (Q 22:66)	***aḥyā-kum***	*aḥyē-kum*	*aḥyē-kum*	*aḥyǣ-kum*
احياها (Q 5:32, 41:39)	***aḥyā-hā***	*aḥyē-hā*	*aḥyē-hā*	*aḥyǣ-hā*
خطيكم (Q 2:58, 29:12)	***khaṭāyā-kum***	*khaṭāyē-kum*	*khaṭāyē-kum*	*khaṭāyǣ-kum*
خطيهم (Q 29:12)	***khaṭāyā-hum***	*khaṭāyē-hum*	*khaṭāyē-hum*	*khaṭāyǣ-hum*
خطينا (Q 20:73, 26:51)	***khaṭāyā-nā***	*khaṭāyē-nā*	*khaṭāyē-nā*	*khaṭāyǣ-nā*
الريا (Q 12:43, 17:60, 37:105, 48:27)	***al-ruʾyā***	*al-ruʾyē*	*al-ruʾyē*	*al-ruʾyǣ*
رياك (Q 12:5)	***ruʾyā-ka***	***ruʾyā-ka***	*ruʾyē-ka*	*ruʾyǣ-ka*
ريى (Q 12:43, 100)	***ruʾyā-ya***	*ruʾyē-ya*	*ruʾyē-ya*	*ruʾyǣ-ya*

محياى (Q 6:162)	***maḥyā-ya***	***maḥyā-ya***	*maḥyē-ya*	*maḥyǣ-ya*
محياهم (Q 45:21)	***maḥyā-hum***	*maḥyē-hum*	*maḥyē-hum*	*maḥyǣ-hum*
الدنيا (*passim*)	*al-dunyē*	*al-dunyē*	*al-dunyē*	*al-dunyǣ*
العليا (Q 9:41)	*al-ʿulyē*	*al-ʿulyē*	*al-ʿulyē*	*al-ʿulyǣ*
الحوايا (Q 6:146)	*al-ḥawāyē*	*al-ḥawāyē*	*al-ḥawāyē*	*al-ḥawāyǣ*

Conclusion

In this article we have seen that, far from showing free alternation between the spellings with *yāʾ* and *alif*, the QCT follows a strict structure in its spelling. As I have previously shown,[37] stems with *alif maqṣūrah* that have *yāʾ* as the third root consonant spell the final vowel with *yāʾ* for /ē/ and stems with *alif maqṣūrah* that have *wāw* as the third root consonant spell the final vowel with *alif* for /ā/. This is a phonemic distinction that is moreover maintained in the qurʾānic reading traditions of Ḥamzah, al-Kisāʾī, and Warsh *ʿan* Nāfiʿ. Early qurʾānic manuscripts reveal that there are two specific environments where the distinction between /ā/ and /ē/ is neutralized: first, when a suffix *-nī* or *-ya* follows, and secondly, when a *y* precedes. This can most easily be understood as a phonetic dissimilation, where /ē/ is regularly shifted to /ā/ in the vicinity of /ī/ or /y/. The linguistic reality of this dissimilation is further reflected in the qurʾānic reading of Ḥamzah, which largely agrees in reading these vowels as /ā/ rather than /ē/ in these environments.

It is hoped that this article demonstrates the importance of not relying solely on the modern standard text for informing us about the linguistic facts of Qurʾānic Arabic. Early qurʾānic manuscripts may show consistent and significant deviations from the standard text, and further corroboration of the linguistic analysis may be provided by a careful examination of reading traditions other than the ubiquitous reading of Ḥafṣ *ʿan* ʿĀṣim.

37. Van Putten, "Triphthongs."

Abbreviations of Qurʾān Manuscripts

The manuscripts were accessed through the *Corpus Coranicum* website (www.corpuscoranicum.de) or, for the manuscripts held at the Bibliothèque nationale de France (BnF), the Gallica website (gallica.bnf.fr). Information on these manuscripts is based on the *Corpus Coranicum* website unless explicitly stated otherwise. If other sources were used to access these manuscripts this has been stated as well.

W = Berlin, Staatsbibliothek Wetzstein II 1913 + BnF Arabe 6087
216 folios; ^{14}C: 662–765 2σ (95.4%); Kufic B.Ia.[38]

SM = Gotthelf-Bergsträßer-Archiv, Saray Medina 1a (= Istanbul, Topkapı Sarayı Müzesi: M 1)
308 folios; late first/early second century; mixed (part Ḥijāzī III, part O.I, part close to Kufic B.Ib or Ḥijāzī).

GK = Cairo, al-Maktabah al-Markaziyyah li'l-Makhṭūṭāt al-Islāmiyyah: Großer Korankodex
1087 folios; not before 700; Kufic B.Ib or B.II.

BL = British Library Or. 2165 + BnF Arabe 328e + Dār al-Āthār al-Islāmiyyah, Kuwait 1 LNS 19 CAab (bifolio)
128 folios; second half of the first/seventh century[39]; Ḥijāzī II.[40] British Library folios were accessed through the British Library website.[41]

CPP = Codex Parisino-Petropolitanus[42]
98 folios; c. third quarter of the first/seventh century;[43] Ḥijāzī I.[44]

Q = Cairo, Dār al-Kutub MS 247 (= Ms. Qāf 47) + Staatsbibliothek, Berlin Ms. Or. Fol. 4313
36 folios; ^{14}C: 606–652, 2σ (95.4%); unclassified (similar to Arabe 330g).

SU = Codex Ṣanʿāʾ I, upper text = Sanʿāʾ, Dār al-Makhṭūṭāt, DAM 01-27.01 + Ḥamdūn 2004[45] + auctioned folios Christie's 2008, Bonhams 2000, Sotheby's 1992, and Sotheby's 1993.

---

38. François Déroche, *Les manuscrits du Coran: Aux origines de la calligraphie coranique* (Paris: Bibliothèque nationale, 1983), 67, no. 16.
39. Yasin Dutton, "Some Notes on the British Library's 'Oldest Qur'an Manuscript' (Or. 2165)," *JQS* 6.1 (2004): 43–71.
40. Déroche, *Manuscrits du Coran*, 62, no. 7.
41. http://www.bl.uk/manuscripts/FullDisplay.aspx?ref=Or_2165.
42. Déroche, *Codex Parisino-Petropolitanus.*
43. Ibid., 177.
44. Déroche, *Manuscrits du Coran*, 59, nos. 2, 3.
45. R. Gh. Ḥamdūn, "*al-Makhṭūṭāt al-qurʾāniyyah fī Ṣanʿāʾ mundhu al-qarn al-awwal al-hijrī wa-ḥifẓ al-Qurʾān al-karīm bi'l-ṣuṭūr*" (MA thesis, Al-Yemenia University, Sanʿāʾ, 2004).

75 folios; ^{14}C: 578–669 CE, 2σ (95.4%)/606–649, σ2 (95.4%) (Coranica); Ḥijāzī I. Photographs of the upper text of DAM 01-27.01 were accessed through the Islamic Awareness website.[46] Hilali has cast some doubts as to whether the folios of Ḥamdūn's thesis belong to the Sanʿāʾ palimpsest.[47] From the gaps in the Ḥamdūn thesis, it is clear that the auctioned folios were taken from the manuscript before Ḥamdūn wrote the thesis. As Hilali does seem to accept that the auctioned folios belong to this manuscript,[48] it strikes me as overly critical to exclude or even suspend judgement as to whether the folios of Ḥamdūn's thesis belong to the same manuscript. Cellard has now convincingly shown that both the lower and upper text of the Sanʿāʾ Palimpsest once formed complete *muṣḥafs*.[49] I do not discuss the lower text of the Sanʿāʾ Palimpsest in this paper as I am sufficiently convinced by the arguments that it represents a non-ʿUthmānic Text Type,[50] and therefore cannot be used in discussing the archetypal orthography of the ʿUthmānic text.

S = Berlin, Staatsbibliothek Kodex Samarkand (facsimile print)
353 folios; dated to about 700–850. A style similar to Kufic D.

Ba = Birmingham Mingana Islamic Arabic 1572a + BnF Arabe 328c[51]
16 folios; ^{14}C: 568–645 CE, 2σ (95.4%); Ḥijāzī I.[52]

Bb = Birmingham Mingana Islamic Arabic 1572b
6 folios; before 750 (?); Ḥijāzī I.

331 = BnF Arabe 331 + Leiden, University Library Leiden Or. 14.545b + Or. 14.545c
58 folios; ^{14}C: 652–763, 2σ (95.4%); Kufic B.Ia.[53]

T = Tübingen, Universitätsbibliothek Ma VI 165
77 folios; ^{14}C: 649–675, 2σ (95.4%); Kufic B.Ia.

Top = Istanbul, Topkapı Sarayı Müzesi H.S. 44/32[54]

---

46. https://www.islamic-awareness.org/quran/text/mss/soth.html.
47. Asma Hilali, *The Sanaa Palimpsest: The Transmission of the Qur'an in the First Centuries AH* (Oxford: Oxford University Press, 2017), 15.
48. Ibid., 18.
49. Éléonore Cellard, "The Ṣanʿāʾ Palimpsest: Materializing the Codices," *JNES* 80 (2021): 1–30.
50. Behnam Sadeghi and Uwe Bergmann, "The Codex of a Companion of the Prophet and the Qurʾān of the Prophet," *Arabica* 57 (2010): 343–436; Behnam Sadeghi and Mohsen Goudarzi, "Ṣanʿāʾ 1 and the Origins of the Qurʾān," *Der Islam* 87 (2011): 1–129; Sinai, "Beyond the Cairo Edition."
51. The connection of these folios was identified by A. Fedeli, "Early Qurʾānic Manuscripts, Their Text, and the Alphonse Mingana Papers Held in the Department of Special Collections of the University of Birmingham" (Ph.D. diss., University of Birmingham, 2015).
52. Déroche, *Manuscrits du Coran*, 60, no. 4.
53. Ibid., 67, no. 14.
54. Tayyar Altıkulaç, *Al-Muṣḥaf al-sharīf: Attributed to ʿUthmān Bin ʿAffān (The*

408 folios; Umayyad era (661-750); Kufic C.I.

CA1 = Codex Amrensis 1[55]
75 folios; late Ḥijāzī[56]/Ḥijāzī I[57]; first half second/eighth century?[58]

Copy at The Topkapi Palace Museum) (Istanbul: Organization of the Islamic Conference Research Centre for Islamic History, 2007).

55. Cellard, *Codex Amrensis 1.*

56. Ibid., 7.

57. Déroche, *Manuscrits du Coran*, 59, no. 1.

58. Cellard, *Codex Amrensis 1*, 15.

JIQSA 6 (2021): 107–136

THE PRE-ISLAMIC DIVINE NAME *ʿSY* AND THE BACKGROUND OF THE QUR'ĀNIC JESUS

AHMAD AL-JALLAD AND ALI AL-MANASER
Ohio State University, USA
The Hashemite University, Jordan

Abstract

This paper presents a newly discovered Safaitic inscription bearing the divine name *ʿsy*. It is argued that this theonym corresponds to Qurʾānic Arabic عيسى <ʿysy>, and reflects the earliest attestation of this form of Jesus's name, likely dating to the fourth century CE, during the initial spread of Christianity to Arabia.

Part I: The Inscription (Ahmad Al-Jallad)

The Arabic name of Jesus عيسى <ʿysy> has perplexed scholars since the beginning of source-critical studies of the Qurʾān. It cannot be derived directly from any Northwest Semitic source, neither the Hebrew ישוע /yēšûaʿ/, nor the Syriac ܝܫܘܥ in either its West /yešūʿ/ or East /ʾišōʿ/ vocalizations, nor can it be explained by appealing to Greek Ἰησοῦς or its Ethiopic form ኢየሱስ /ʾīyasūs/.[1] The name had seemed to appear for the first time in the Qurʾān, where its identification as Jesus is unambiguous.[2] Early Christian Arabic, however, makes use of the expected Arabic reflex of ישוע, namely, *yasūʿ*.[3] Its irregular shape has lent itself to several explanations, ranging from taboo deformation by Muḥammad to various avenues of corruption through the oral or written transmission of the name from Aramaic to Arabic.[4] A major

1. For an up-to-date and detailed discussion of these problems, see Manfred Kropp and Guillaume Dye, "Le nom de Jésus (ʿĪsā) dans le Coran, et quelques autres noms bibliques: Remarques sur l'onomastique coranique," in Guillaume Dye and Fabien Nobilio (eds.), *Figures bibliques en Islam* (Brussels-Fernelmont: EME, 2011), 171–198.
2. See Carlos Segovia, *The Qur'anic Jesus: A New Interpretation* (Berlin: De Gruyter, 2019), ch. 2, for a comprehensive list and discussion of the occurrences of Jesus in the Qurʾān.
3. I will come back to this form in section 3.
4. The classic discussion is Arthur Jeffery, *The Foreign Vocabulary of the Qur'ān*

doi: http://dx.doi.org/10.5913/jiqsa.6.2021.a004

limitation in the discussion of the background of qur'ānic عيسى has been the paucity of evidence. The name had not appeared in any text before the Qur'ān and therefore there was little to help arbitrate between the various theories of its origin.

This article presents a new Safaitic inscription containing the first occurrence of a theonym *ʿsy*, which in Safaitic orthography corresponds to Qur'ānic Arabic عيسى.[5] The present discovery could therefore document our first pre-qur'ānic attestation of this name, likely as the name of Jesus. This edition will provide a reading of the inscription and an interpretation couched in its Safaitic and Roman/Byzantine Near Eastern context.

1. Discovery

The present inscription was discovered during the summer campaign of the 2019 Badia Survey season from the Jordanian basalt desert (*ḥarrah*).[6] The text comes from a large collection of inscriptions—more than 100—surrounding a small cairn on the side of a footpath connecting Wādī al-Khuḍarī to a dry watering hole, called Naqʿat al-Khuḍarī.[7] The large number of inscriptions, many of which mention the watering hole itself (*'aḍayat*),[8] suggest that this was an important stopping point on the road connecting the settled areas of the Ḥawrān to Lake Burquʿ, and then east to Palmyra

(Baroda: Oriental Institute, 1938), 218–220, which is expanded in Kropp and Dye, "Le nom de Jésus." The reader is referred to those works for further bibliography.

5. Word-internal long vowels are not represented orthographically in Safaitic or other Ancient North Arabian alphabets; see Michael C. A. Macdonald, "Ancient North Arabian," in Roger Wood (ed.), *The Cambridge Encyclopedia of the World's Ancient Languages* (Cambridge: Cambridge University Press, 2004), 488–533, 495, 502; Ahmad Al-Jallad, "Safaitic," in John Huehnergard and Na'ama Pat-El (eds.), *The Semitic Languages*, 2nd ed. (Abingdon: Routledge, 2019), 342–366, 345.

6. The Badia Epigraphic Survey project aims to document in a comprehensive manner the inscriptions and archaeological sites of the Jordanian Ḥarrah. The summer 2019 campaign was led by Ahmad Al-Jallad (Ohio State University) and Ali al-Manaser (Jordanian Department of Antiquities) and carried out within the framework of the "Missing Link" project co-directed by Zuhayr al-Qadi (al-Ḥuṣn research center, Abu Dhabi).

7. See Ali al-Manaser's contribution in part 2 for a detailed description of the site.

8. On the linguistic affiliation of the inscriptions and discussion of the various opinions on the matter, see Ahmad Al-Jallad, "What is Ancient North Arabian?," in Daniel Birnstiel and Na'ama Pat-El (eds.), *Re-engaging Comparative Semitic and Arabic Studies* (Wiesbaden: Harrassowitz, 2018), 1–45.

and into North Arabia.[9] While most of the inscriptions documented at the site are Safaitic, at least one Greek text suggests that locals and outsiders alike would have made use of the precious resource.[10]

Before entering the main subject of this essay, a few remarks on Safaitic are in order. Safaitic is a modern conventional label given to the northern-most variety of the South Semitic script family. It is a sister of the Ancient South Arabian alphabet rather than a descendent of it.[11] The inscriptions are concentrated in the Syro-Jordanian basalt desert, extending into North Arabia, but isolated examples can be found much further away.[12] The inscriptions express a continuum of Old Arabic dialects, most closely related to Classical and Qurʾānic Arabic, and to the shadowy vernacular of the Nabataeans.

The corpus covers a wide range of textual genres, including, but not limited to, funerary texts, religious invocations, commemorative inscriptions, and isolated personal names.[13] The writing tradition is highly formulaic, which aids in the interpretation of *hapax legomena* and rare grammatical constructions. In terms of chronology, scholars have very cautiously suggested a range between the first century BCE to the fourth century CE. These dates are not based on any archaeological evidence; rather, they are defined by the contents of a minority of Safaitic inscriptions. A small number of texts are dated using the formula *snt* ("year") followed by the description of a prominent event. While many are dated to local happenings now lost to history, those that are recognizable tend to anchor in events that transpired in the Nabataean and Roman periods. Such texts therefore became the basis for the conventional first century BCE starting date of the Safaitic corpus. However, the recent archaeological excavations in the Jebel

9. For other inscriptions published from this site, see Ahmad Al-Jallad, "ʿArab, ʾAʿrāb, and Arabic in Ancient North Arabia: The First Attestation of (ʾ)ʿrb as a Group Name in Safaitic," *Arabian Archaeology and Epigraphy* 31 (2020): 1–14.

10. On this text, see note 35.

11. Michael C. A. Macdonald, "Safaitic," *EI²*, s.v. (1995); Ahmad Al-Jallad, *An Outline of the Grammar of the Safaitic Inscriptions* (Leiden: Brill, 2015), ch. 1; Ahmad Al-Jallad and Karolina Jaworksa, *A Dictionary of the Safaitic Inscriptions* (Leiden: Brill, 2021), 5–8.

12. For a map of the distribution of the Safaitic inscriptions based on the OCIANA corpus (*Online Corpus of the Inscriptions of Ancient North Arabia*, http://krcfm.orient.ox.ac.uk/fmi/webd/ociana), see Al-Jallad and Jaworska, *Dictionary*, 3. See Michael C. A. Macdonald, "The Distribution of Safaitic Inscriptions in Jordan," *Studies in the History and Archaeology of Jordan* 4 (1992): 303–307.

13. See Al-Jallad and Jaworska, *Dictionary*, 8–20, on Safaitic text genres and writing formula.

Qurma region led by P. Akkermans have made a good case for pushing back the *terminus post quem* to at least the third century BCE.[14] The end of the writing tradition is based on silence—the known inscriptions do not seem to refer to Christianity or, leaving aside inscriptions that have references we do not understand, any event post-dating the third century CE. The present inscription will no doubt contribute to the discussion on the chronology of Safaitic, but unfortunately brings us no closer to solid dates.

2. The Inscription

The text is carved on an unworked piece of basalt, approximately forty centimeters at its widest (fig. 1). The letter shapes correspond best to the "common" category of Clark's rough classification of Safaitic hands.[15] This may be significant, as most of the Safaitic inscriptions at this site are carved in the "fine" script, which may suggest that our author's text dates to a different period. The inscription is carved in a winding style, resembling a snake (fig. 2). This manner of orientation is not uncommon and simply reflects an aesthetic choice of the author, partly motivated by his desire to avoid carving over a pre-existing text on the rock. Four sets of seven parallel lines and one sequence of twelve parallel lines accompany the inscription; the latter symbol is quite rare and this may be its first attestation. The meaning of these symbols is unclear; most scholars have assumed that they serve an apotropaic function.[16] Another short Safaitic inscription shares the rock

14. See Peter Akkermans, "Living on the Edge or Forced into the Margins? Hunter-Herders in Jordan's Northeastern Badlands in the Hellenistic and Roman Periods," *Journal of Eastern Mediterranean Archaeology & Heritage Studies* 7 (2019): 412–431.

15. Vincent A. Clark, "A Study of New Safaitic Inscriptions from Jordan" (Ph.D. diss., University of Melbourne, 1970), 70–71. It should be said however that this classification is extremely preliminary and much more work is needed to distill legitimate sub-varieties of the script from idiosyncratic variation in the handwriting of individual authors. On the "square" variety of the Safaitic script, see Michael C. A. Macdonald, "On the Uses of Writing in Ancient Arabia and the Role of Palaeography in Studying Them," *Arabian Epigraphic Notes* 1 (2015): 1–45. On the "Safaitic-Hismaic" script type, see Jérôme Norris, "A Survey of the Ancient North Arabian Inscriptions from the Dūmat al-Jandal Area (Saudi Arabia)," in Michael C. A. Macdonald (ed.), *Languages, Scripts and Their Uses in Ancient North Arabia: Supplement to Volume 48 of the Proceedings of the Seminar for Arabian Studies* (Oxford: Archaeopress, 2018), 71–93.

16. See Nathalie Brusgaard, *Carving Interactions: Rock Art in the Nomadic Landscape of the Black Desert, North-Eastern Jordan* (Oxford: Archaeopress, 2019), 117, for further examples.

Figure 1: The *ʿsy* inscription (by the Badia Survey team).

Figure 2: Tracing of *ʿsy* inscription (by A. Al-Jallad).

face with the primary text but appears to be unrelated and to pre-date the main text. It is edited in Appendix 1 following this article.

Reading: *l whbʾl bn gyz bn ʾʿbs bn ʾḥbb bn rfʾt bn ʿbṭ bn ḫl bn qṭṭ bn ḏnbn w-wgm ʿl-ḫl-h h-ʾślly h ʿsy nṣr-h m-kfr-k*

Division into formulaic segments:
Genealogy: *l whb'l bn gyz bn ''bs bn 'ḥbb bn rf't bn 'bṭ bn ḫl bn qṭṭ bn ḏnbn*
Narrative: *w-wgm 'l-ḫl-h h-'ślly*
Invocation: *h 'sy nṣr-h m-kfr-k*

Interpretation:
"By Whb'l son of Gyz son of ''bs son of 'ḥrr son of Rf't son of 'bṭ son of Ḫl son of Qṭṭ son of Ḏnbn and he grieved for his maternal uncle, the 'śll-ite; O 'sy help him against those who deny you"

2.1 Commentary

2.1.1 The Genealogy and Narrative

The genealogy contains names that have all been attested previously in Safaitic and have good Arabic etymologies.[17] However, this exact genealogy is not known from other inscriptions. No part of it repeats in the thousands of attested genealogical chains in the corpus, suggesting perhaps that our author does not come from a line that was active in the production of Safaitic inscriptions. But members of Wahb'el's[18] maternal line, the tribe of 'śll, have produced a fair number of texts. The following is a comprehensive list of inscriptions—containing relevant genealogical information—by 'śll-ites and those that mention the tribe in the OCIANA corpus (*Online Corpus of the Inscriptions of Ancient North Arabia*, http://krcfm.orient.ox.ac.uk/fmi/webd/ociana). It is possible that many more men from this lineage carved inscriptions but did not mention explicitly their tribal affiliation.

17. The OCIANA database contains the most up-to-date onomasticon, replacing G. Lankester Harding, *An Index and Concordance of Pre-Islamic Arabian Names and Inscriptions* (Toronto: Toronto University Press, 1971).
18. The name of our author, *whb'l*, appears in Greek transcription as Ουαβηλος, indicating the pronunciation *wahb'el*; see Heinz Wuthnow, *Die semitischen Menschennamen in griechischen Inschriften und Papyri des vorderen Orients* (Leipzig: Dieterich'sche Verlagsbuchhandlung, 1930), 91.

Table 1: References to the line of ʾśll in the Safaitic inscriptions.

Reference	Location	Identification	Translation
BS 1240	NE Jordan; 32.463073; 37.237803	*l tm ḏ-ʾl ʾśll*	"By Taym of the lineage of ʾśll"
Al-Mafraq Museum 59	Mafraq Museum (original provenance unknown)	*…w ʿdy b-ʾśll*	"…and he raided (the tribe of) ʾśll"
MWH 2[19]	Wādī al-Ḥashād, NE Jordan	*l ʾnʿm bn ẓʿn ḏ-ʾl ʾśll*	"By ʾnʿm son of Ẓʿn of the lineage of ʾśll"
HSNS 5[20]	Wādī Umm Khnayṣrī, NE Jordan	*…w ḥl dr snt mlk grfṣ bn hrdṣ w wgd ʾṯr ʾḫwl-h ʾl ʾśll tm w grmʾ w ʾḥwḏ w zbd f ngʿ w h dśry w lt ġnmt l-ḏ d{ʿ}y w lm yḫbl sfr*	"and he encamped here the year of king Agrippa son of Herod and he found the traces of his maternal uncles of the lineage of ʾśll, Tm, Grmʾ, and ʾḥwḏ, and grieved in pain, so O Allāt and Dusares, may he who reads (this inscription) have spoil and let the inscription not be effaced"

19. MWH = Inscriptions recorded by Ali al-Manaser on his survey in Wādī Ḥashād in 2004 and published on OCIANA.
20. HSNS = Rafe M.A. Harahsheh & Yunus M. Al-Shdeifat, "*Nuqūsh ṣafawiyyah muʾarrakhah ilā ḥukm aghrībā al-thānī* (19/50 – 92/93 m)," *Majallat Muʾtah li'l-Buḥūth wa'l-Dirāsāt* 21.6 (2006): 111–129.

Reference	Location	Identification	Translation
RWQ 65[21]	Wādī Salmā, NE Jordan	*l ʾwsn bn wdm bn rbʾl bn ʾswr bn sẖr bn ʾksr bn br bn ḥs bn ydʿ ʾl ʾśll*	"By ʾwsn son of Wdm son of Rbʾl son of ʾswr son of Sẖr son of ʾksr son of Br son of Ḥs son of Ydʿ, the lineage of ʾśll"
HaNSC[22]	Tell al-Jaʿbariyyah, Wādī al-ʿAbd, NE Jordan.	*l bk bn nṣrʾ {bn} hrml h-ʾślly*	"By Bk son of Nṣrʾ son of Hrml the ʾśll-ite"
Is.H 205[23]	ʿĪsāwī, Rīf Dimashq, Syria	*l dd bn ʾśyb h-ʾślly*	"By Dd son of ʾśyb the ʾśll-ite"
Is.L 325	ʿĪsāwī, Rīf Dimashq, Syria	*l hsrk bn śdd bn nkf bn mlḥ bn ḥnn h-ʾślly*	"By Hsrk son of Śdd son of Nkf son of Mlḥ son of Ḥnn the ʾśll-ite"
RaIM 3074.1[24]	Iraq Museum	*l mʿz bn slm bn sny bn ḥnʾl bn slm bn sny ḏ-ʾl ʾśll*	"By Mʿz son of Slm son of Ḥnʾl son of Slm son of Sny of the lineage of ʾśll"
KRS 2824	NE Jordan	*l ʿzhm bn śmtʾl h-dr h-ʾślly*	"By ʿzhm son of Śmtʾl, in this place, the ʾśll-ite."
KRS 1508	NE Jordan	*...snt ḥrb ḥb{q} w ʾśll*	"... the year Ḥbq and ʾśll made war"

21. RWQ = Mahmud M. Al-Rousan, "*Nuqūsh ṣafawiyyah min Wādī Qaṣṣāb bi'l-Urdunn: Dirāsah maydāniyyah taḥlīliyyah muqāranah*" (Ph.D. diss., King Saʿūd University, 2004).

22. HaNSC = Rafe M.A. Harahsheh, "*Nuqūsh ṣafāʾiyyah mukhtārah min al-bādiyah al-urdunniyyah*," *Journal of Epigraphy and Rock Drawings* 1 (2007): 29–52.

23. Inscriptions from ʿĪsāwī, Syria collected by the Safaitic Epigraphic Survey Programme (SESP) and published on OCIANA.

24. Iraq Museum (Inv. # 3074), published on OCIANA.

Reference	Location	Identification	Translation
KRS 68	NE Jordan	*l ʾnʿm {b}{n} {w}rl bn dmy ḏ-ʾl ʾśll*	"By ʾnʿm son of Wrl son of Dmy of the lineage of ʾśll"
SIJ 658[25]	Jāwā, NE Jordan	*l ġny ḏ-ʾl ʾśll*	"By Ġny of the lineage of ʾśll"
SIJ 630	Jāwā, NE Jordan	*l f{ḏ}g b[n] gryt ḏ-ʾl {ʾ}śll*	"By Fḏg son of Gryt of the lineage of ʾśll"
SIJ 43	Jāthūm, NE Jordan	*l {q}dm bn bny ḏ-ʾl ʾśll*	"By Qdm son of Bny of the lineage of ʾśll"
C 2962[26]	Zalaf, Rīf Dimashq, Syria	*l w{s}ṭ bn ḍb bn ʾgmḥ h-ʾślly*	"By Wsṭ son of Ḍb son of ʾgmh the ʾśll-ite"
HCH 33[27]	Amman Museum (Cairn of Hāniʾ, NE Jordan).	*l gḥś bn tmlh bn tm ḏ- ʾl ʾśll*	"By Gḥś son of Tmlh son of Tm of the lineage of ʾśll"

HSNS 5 records a grieving formula very similar to our inscription: its author finds the traces (*wgd ʾṯr)* of his maternal uncles of the lineage of ʾśll (*ʾḫwl-h ḏ ʾl ʾśll*) and so he grieves in pain (*ngʿ*).[28] The texts dates to the reign of "Agrippa son of Herod."[29] This particular choice of dating could be understood as an expression of cultural affiliation with the settled world.[30] Indeed,

25. SIJ = Fredrick V. Winnett, *Safaitic Inscriptions from Jordan* (Toronto: University of Toronto Press, 1957).
26. C = Gonzague Ryckmans, *Corpus Inscriptionum Semiticarum: Pars Quinta, Inscriptiones Saracenicae Continens: Tomus I, Fasciculus I, Inscriptiones Safaiticae* (Paris: E Reipublicae Typographeo, 1950–1951).
27. HCH = G. Lankaster Harding, "The Cairn of Haniʾ," *Annual of the Department of Antiquities of Jordan* 2 (1953): 8–56, plates 1–7.
28. The recording of expressions of grief and longing at the finding of the traces of lost/absent loved ones is an established writing genre; see Al-Jallad and Jaworska, *Dictionary,* 15.
29. As argued by the editors, this is likely the final ruler of the Herodian dynasty, Agrippa II, d. 92 or 100 CE.
30. The use of the Greek script and language by the nomads could be taken as

the inscription's author hails from the lineage of Ḍayf, a large confederation with clear ties to the Roman military and whose members have furnished occasional Greek inscriptions.[31] Roman military camps were set up deep in the desert. Jāthūm, which attests the presence of ʾśll-ites (SIJ 43, 630), for example, could have acted as a nexus of contact between Arabian nomads and the Roman military. A rather long and well-preserved Greek inscription carved by a musician and barber serving a Roman captain confirms the presence of a Roman military encampment at the site.[32] This inscription calls the place *siwāy ʾabgar*, "the cairn of Abgar," indicating that they cooperated with local nomads to navigate through the region and had learned the local toponymy. Similar cooperation is attested in a new inscription published by Z. Al-Salameen et al., where a Safaitic-writing nomad records himself serving as a guide (*ḫfr*) for the Palmyrenes through the Ḥarrah.[33]

---

a marker of this affiliation as well; see, for example, Ahmad Al-Jallad and Ali al-Manaser, "New Epigraphica from Jordan II: Three Safaitic-Greek Partial Bilingual Inscriptions," *Arabian Epigraphic Notes* 2 (2016): 55–66.

31. A Ḍayfite named Shaʿar produced a Greek text at a site near Wādī Rushaydah in S. Syria; see Michael C. A. Macdonald, Muna Al Muʾazzin, and Laïla Nehmé, "*Les inscriptions safaïtiques de Syrie, cent quarante ans après leur découverte*," *Comptes rendus des séances de l'Académie des Inscriptions & Belles-Lettres* (1996): 435–494, 480–484, number 1. The same man carved a nearly identical text in the upper part of Ghadīr al-Ghuṣayn in NE Jordan, which was discovered by William and Fidelity Lancaster but was never formally published; it appears on OCIANA as MG 1. On the ties between the tribe of Ḍayf and the Roman military (and settled areas), see Ahmad Al-Jallad and Chams Bernard, "New Safaitic and Greek Inscriptions from the Jordanian Ḥarrah Relating to Auxiliary Roman Military Units," *ZDMG* (2021): 61–72; Ahmad Al-Jallad, Zeyad Al-Salameen, Yunus Shdeifat, and Rafe Harahsheh, "Gaius the Roman and the Kawnites: Inscriptional Evidence for Roman Auxiliary Units Raised from the Nomads of the Ḥarrah," in Peter Akkermans (ed.), *Landscapes of Survival* (Oxford: Archaeopress, 2021): 353–359. More broadly on this phenomenon, see Michael C. A. Macdonald, "Romans Go Home? Rome and Other 'Outsiders' as Viewed from the Syro-Arabian Desert," in Jitse H. F. Dijkstra and Greg Fisher (eds.), *Inside and Out: Interactions between Rome and the Peoples on the Arabian and Egyptian Frontiers in Late Antiquity* (Leuven: Peeters, 2014), 145–163.

32. See Lucetta Mowry, "A Greek Inscription at Jathum in Transjordan," *BASOR* 132 (1931): 34–41. Other Greek graffiti may have been carved by soldiers stationed there.

33. Zeyad Al-Salameen, Rafe Harahsheh, and Younis Al-Shdaifat, "The Palmyrenes in a New Safaitic Inscription," *Syria* 96 (2019): 387–394. The editors of the inscription, however, have misread and misinterpreted an important section of it. They read: *l mʿn bn ṣyd bn ḥd ḏ ʾl mslq w-qyf mʿ-ʾl tdmr ʿl-fnyt ḫfr l-hm w-wgd sfr ḫl-h mḥwr*, "By Mʿn son of Ṣyd son of Ḥd of the tribe of Mslq and he followed the trace (sic) with the Palmyrenes in Fnyt, [and] protected them, and he found the inscription of his maternal uncle Mḥwr." What Al-Salameen et al. read as *qyf* is, however, clearly *qyẓ*,

These facts allow us to sketch two possible explanations for our author's unique lineage and his connection to the tribe of ʾśll, which will come into play later once we attempt to establish a historical context for the unique invocation contained in our inscription. Perhaps like Lobayʾat,[34] the author of HSNS 5, Wahbʾel, whose father had married a woman of the ʾśll tribe, hails from a local tribe with some connection to the Roman world. Such contacts allow for the possibility of cultural diffusion from settled areas to the desert.

But if the uniqueness of the long genealogy is significant, then perhaps it could suggest that Wahbʾel hails from a settled tribe, and was only moving through the area. Indeed, a Greek inscription carved at the same site by a man named Ααρικος Βαδαρου—the first name of which is not clearly attested in the Safaitic onomasticon—could reflect the same phenomenon.[35] Outsiders passing through the Ḥarrah have produced Safaitic texts from time to time: a man named Taymallāh of the people of Bostra carved at text at Ruʿaylah, several kilometers deeper in the basalt desert.[36] Several texts were carved by people who identified as Nabataeans,[37] and a so-far unique text records the presence of a man named Gaius "of the people of Rome."[38] In addition to this, settled tribesmen have left their mark in the desert. Al-Salameen et al. published a fascinating inscription by a man from the tribe

---

which means "to spend the dry season." The term *ḫfr* is also better understood as "to guide" rather than "to protect" in this particular context, as it would be rather odd indeed for a single man to protect an entire group of people. The narrative should be re-read and interpreted as follows: *w-**qyẓ** mʿ-ʾl tdmr ʿl-fnyt ḫfr l-hm*, "and he spent the dry season with the people of Palmyra on the edge of Fnyt (the edge of the basalt desert near Burquʿ), acting as a guide for them."

34. The genealogy of the author of HSNS 5 is: *lbʾt bn ḫṭst bn flṭt bn bhś bn ʾḏnt bn ʾslm bn zkr bn rfʾt bn wśyt bn ḍf bn ʿg(d) bn tʿwḏ*, where *ḍf* is the eponymous ancestor of the tribe Ḍayf. The vocalization of the name *lbʾt* is assured by its appearance as Λοβαιαθου in Greek transcription in the bilingual text J1 in Michael C. A. Macdonald et al., "Les inscriptions safaïtiques de Syrie."

35. See Ahmad Al-Jallad and Ali al-Manaser, "Old Arabic Minutiae II: Greek-Safaitic Bilinguals and Language Contact in the Ḥarrah," *Arabica* (forthcoming).

36. This simple text states *l-tmlh bn ʾnhk ḏ ʾl bṣry*, "By Taymallāh son of ʾAnhak of the people of Bostra," and was found at Wādī al-Ruʿaylah on the way to Jubbat al-Ruʿaylah in NE Jordan. It will appear in Al-Jallad and al-Manaser, "Old Arabic Minutiae II."

37. For example, CSNS 661; see Michael C. A. Macdonald, *Literacy and Identity in Pre-Islamic Arabia* (Farnham: Ashgate, 2009), II, 307, n. 28; 350, n. 302; 2009 IV, 185, n. 23, 186, on this phenomenon.

38. This text appears to belong to a Roman soldier, although it was likely carved by a local; see Ahmad Al-Jallad et al., "Gaius the Roman and the Kawnites."

of Kawkab, which apparently had both settled and nomadic sections. Our author, ʿAzīz son of Ṣayyād, wrote that he was spending the season of the later rains in the desert although his residence was in the Ḥawrānī town of Ṣalḫad.[39] Thus, Wahbʾel may fit into this category of writer, a man with links to the desert, clearly capable of writing Safaitic, but whose social group resided beyond the Ḥarrah.

It should be noted, however, that all Safaitic texts carved by settled peoples so far contain rather short genealogies. The long genealogy of the present inscription could therefore suggest that the author hailed from a nomadic tribe. But this is not decisive. The short genealogies of the inscriptions by settled peoples so far may simply reflect a bias of the writing tradition. Most inscriptions contain short genealogies: 15,608 inscriptions in the OCIANA Safaitic corpus contain only two-generation genealogies while a mere sixty-two contain ten generations, and the number shrinks as the generations increase. It is possible, then, that the short genealogies in the small number of texts produced by settled folk simply reflect this tendency rather than reduced genealogical knowledge on the part of town dwellers of Arabian extraction.

Thus, both possibilities—namely, that Wahbʾel was a local nomad with ties to the Roman world, like the author of HSNS 5, or a settled person of Arabian extraction—can be well supported. But the unique genealogy and contents of this text could be the result of another factor—chronology. In order to treat this matter, we should now turn to the discussion of the inscription's unique invocation.

2.1.2 The Invocation

Safaitic inscriptions may terminate in an invocation to the gods. These prayers are often semantically connected to the narrative.[40] Invocations for the improvement of the condition of a mourner, for example, often follow expressions of grief and loss of loved ones. The author of Ms 30 expresses grief for the dead (*wgm*) and then calls upon Allāt to relieve his condition (*h*

---

39. The text is: *l ʿzz bn ṣyd bn qdm ḏ ʾl kkb w yʿmr b-ṣlḫd w-dṯʾ snt mlk rbʾl* "By ʿzz son of Ṣyd son of Qdm of the lineage of Kawkab and he resides in Ṣalḫad but spent the season of the later rains (here) in the year of king Rabbʾel"; see Ziyad Al-Salameen, Yunus Shdeifat, and Rafe Harahsheh, "Nabataean Echoes in al-Ḥarrah: New Evidence in Light of Recent Field Work," *Palestine Exploration Quarterly* 150 (2018): 60–79. On this phenomenon, see Michael C. A. Macdonald, *Literacy and Identity in Pre-Islamic Arabia*, II, and on the tribe of *kkb*, 357.

40. See Al-Jallad and Jaworksa, *Dictionary*, 16.

lt rwḥ);[41] similarly *ʾglḥ*, author of KRS 270, grieves for an unnamed loved one (*ḥbb*) and calls on the god Roḍay for relief (*h rḍy rwḥ*). KRS 1188 expresses grief for the loss of the author's companions and the camels, presumably taken off in a raid (*wgm ʿl-ʾśyʿ-h w h-ʾbl*), and invokes Allāt to grant relief to those who remain alive (*rwḥ l-ḏ sʾr*) and then the god Yayṯeʿ for security from enemies (*slm m-śnʾ*). The author of HaNSB 163 asks Yayṯeʿ for relief from the enemy tribe Ḍayf (*h yṯʿ rwḥ m-ḍf*).[42]

The present invocation falls into this thematic and structural category, but its contents have not been previously attested. After grieving for the demise of his maternal uncle, Wahbʾel calls upon a new deity, *ʿsy*. Its identity as such is assured by the formulaic context—it follows the vocative particle *h* and precedes an invocation. In its consonantal form, the theonym is compatible with qurʾānic عيسى, which was pronounced as *ʿīsē* in Old Ḥigāzī and *ʿīsā* in normative Classical Arabic.[43] The graphic connection between Safaitic *ʿsy* and qurʾānic *ʿysy* is bolstered by the contents of the invocation that follows, which suggest a monotheistic context: *nṣr-h m-kfr-h*.

The collocation of *nṣr* and *kfr* is remarkable and reminiscent of qurʾānic and Syriac diction, as we shall see later. While *nṣr*, "to help, aid," is previously known in Safaitic prayers,[44] *kfr* as a verb or substantive appears for the first time. In a recent paper, Juan Cole has treated in a comprehensive manner this root's entire spectrum of meaning in Qurʾānic Arabic, restricting the sense of "deny, disbelieve" to the idiomatic expression *kafara bi-*.[45]

---

41. Ms = Safaitic inscriptions from NE Jordan published on OCIANA; this text comes from Shiʿb Ghuṣayn.

42. See Cassandra Bennet, "Geographic and Religious Trends in the Pre-Islamic Religious Beliefs of the North Arabian Nomadic and Semi-nomadic Tribes," *Proceedings of the Seminar for Arabian Studies* 44 (2014): 43–52, for a list of popular Safaitic deities and associated invocations. A comprehensive study of divine names and titles remains a desideratum.

43. Safaitic orthography does not represent internal long vowels with *matres lectionis*. The pronunciation *ʿīsē* obtains in several qurʾānic reading traditions, such as that of al-Kisāʾī. The so-called *alif maqṣūrah* (*bi-ṣūrat al-yāʾ*) derives from an original word-final diphthong/triphthong that yielded a different reflex in Old Ḥigāzī, /ē/, and in what would become normative Classical Arabic, /ā/. On the outcome of the Proto-Arabic triphthongs, see Marijn van Putten, "The Development of the Triphthongs in Qur'anic and Classical Arabic," *Arabian Epigraphic Notes* 3 (2017): 47–74. The correspondence between qurʾānic *alif maqṣūrah* and Safaitic final *y* is abundantly illustrated: بنى = Safaitic *bny*, "he built"; أتى = Safaitic *ʾty*, "he came"; فتى = Safaitic *fty*, "youth."

44. Al-Jallad and Jaworska, *Dictionary*, 107b.

45. Other meanings discussed by Cole are "peasant," "pagan," "libertine," "rebel," and

Outside the canonical Qurʾān, *kafara* can take a direct object, as in the *duʿāʾ qunūt al-witr*, which originates in the controversial lost *sūrah* of the Qurʾān, Sūrat al-Khalʿ:[46]

lā nakfuruka wa-nuʾminu bika
We do not deny you but we believe in you.

In Classical Arabic, the L-stem *kāfara* can take a direct object, meaning "to deny, to disacknowledge," e.g., *idhā aqarra ʿinda ʾl-qāḍī bi-shayʾin thumma kāfara* ("when he confesses a thing in the presence of a judge but then denies [it]").[47] The earliest attestation of this form occurs in a line of al-Farazdaq (d. c. 110/728), *kāfaranī in lam ughithhu* ("he would have denied me [my right] if I had not helped him").[48] While the L-stem is not attested in the qurʾānic reading traditions, the consonantal text would not consistently distinguish between it and the G-stem; both would appear as كفر. It is therefore possible that the L-stem underlies some of the occurrences of كفر in the *rasm.*

The sense of denial and rejection is a metaphorical derivative of the more basic meaning of the root, "to cover, conceal."[49] This meaning—which always takes a direct object—is attested in the earliest layers of Classical Arabic, for example, in a line of the *muʿallaqah* attributed to Labīd b. Rabīʿah (d. 40/660–661): *fī laylatin kafara ʾl-nujūma ghamāmuhā* ("on a night whose clouds have concealed the stars"). Since the sense of "to deny, renounce" is also expressed by the Syriac G-stem *kpar,* where it takes an object introduced by *b-* as in the Qurʾān, the construction found in Sūrat al-Khalʿ may reflect the original Arabic syntax of this verb, while the construction *kafara bi-* could betray the impact of Syriac.[50]

"blasphemer"; see Juan Cole, "Infidel or Paganus? The Polysemy of *kafara* in the Qur'an," *JAOS* 140 (2020): 615–635, and the bibliography there for further literature.

46. Sūrat al-Khalʿ was supposedly part of the codex of Ubayy. Sean Anthony treats this issue in his characteristically brilliant manner, arguing that while the *sūrah* and its counterpart Sūrat al-Ḥafd were ultimately excluded from the qurʾānic canon, their use in *qunūt-* and *witr-*prayers ensured their preservation; see Sean Anthony, "Two Lost Sūrahs of the Qurʾān: Sūrat al-Khalʿ and Sūrat al-Ḥafd between Textual and Ritual Canon (1st-3rd/7th-9th centuries)," *JSAI* 46 (2019): 67–112.

47. Edward W. Lane, *An Arabic-English Lexicon, Derived from the Best and Most Copious Eastern Sources* (London: Williams & Norgate, 1863–1893), 2621a.

48. See the *Doha Historical Dictionary of Arabic* (https://www.dohadictionary.org/; accessed December 17, 2021).

49. Lane, *Lexicon,* 2620a–b.

50. For example: ܘܟܦܪ ܒܗܝܡܢܘܬܐ ܢܨܪܝܬܐ, "(if) he denies the Nazarene faith"; from *The*

The second relevant family of meanings signaled by this root is "to atone, to forgive," which, like "to deny," ultimately derives from a more basic meaning "to cover."[51] This sense is expressed by the D-stem in Arabic, e.g., *kaffara 'llāhu ʿanhu 'l-dhanba* ("Allāh has forgiven his sins").[52] Lane records the expression *kaffara lahu*, meaning "to give obeisance to him," used to refer to the lowering (i.e., covering) of one's head as a symbol of submission to a superior.[53] The Hebrew D-stem *kipper* conveys the same meaning, "to pardon (< to cover), to seek atonement," where the sin or guilty party is the logical direct object of the verb, usually introduced by *ʿal*, and the pardoning agent is introduced by *min*, "from."[54] Thus, Lev 5:26: *wə-kipper ʿālāyw hak-kōhēn lipnê YHWH*, "and the priest shall make atonement for him before YHWH." This meaning is also attested in a Late Sabaic monotheistic inscription, *(ykf)rn ḥ(b)-hmw*, "may he (God) forgive their sins."[55]

The various options the lexicographical sources provide must be judged against Safaitic syntax and formulaic language. The sense of "atonement, forgiveness," and even "obedience," seems unlikely, as they require prepositional objects while the Safaitic attestation takes a pronominal direct object *-k*, the antecedent of which is the divine name. Further, when the verb is used with the meaning of "atonement, forgiveness," across all languages, its direct object is the "sin"—which can be implied—for which one seeks atonement *from* a deity. In the case of the meaning of obedience, the subject covers an implied object (the head, face) for the ruler or deity, which is introduced by a preposition.

As shown by table 2, the syntactic construction *nṣr-h m-kfr-k* follows an established invocational pattern in Safaitic.

Julian Romance (Com. JulSok 181[87]:15). See the *Comprehensive Aramaic Lexicon* (http://cal.huc.edu/; accessed December 17, 2021) and Jeffery, *Foreign Vocabulary*, 250.

51. In Syriac, *kpr* can also produce verbs meaning "to erase" and "to blaspheme," but neither of these meanings is plausible in the present context.

52. Lane, *Lexicon*, 2620b.

53. Lane, *Lexicon*, 2621a.

54. Wilhelm Gesenius, *Hebrew and Chaldee Lexicon*, trans. S. P. Tregelles (London: Samuel Bagster and Sons, 1846), 411.

55. CIH 539; see *Sabäisches Wörterbuch* (http://sabaweb.uni-jena.de/sabaweb; accessed December 17, 2020).

Table 2: The formulaic structure of the invocation.

Siglum	Vocative	Imperative	Direct object	Prepositional phrase	Translation
C 4148	*h yṯʿ*	*slm*	*ʾgdy*	*mn-sqm*	"O Yayṯeʿ, keep my kids safe from illness"
WH 2163	*h rḍw*	*sʿd*	*-h*	*m-śnʾ*	"O Roṣaw, help him against enemies"
C 3744	*h yṯʿ*	*sʿd*	*-h*	*m-bʾs*	"O Yayṯeʿ, help him against misfortune"
C 1548	*h rḍw*	*flṭ*	*-h*	*m-śnʾ*	"O Roṣaw, deliver him from enemies"
KRS 372	----	*nqm*	*-h*	*m-mrm-h*[56]	"Allow him to take vengeance upon the one who struck him with arrows"

The syntax of our invocation becomes clear in light of these parallels. The verb *nṣr* corresponds to other verbs of aid and deliverance, such as *sʿd*, "help," and *flṭ*, "deliver," while the phrase following *m-* signifies what the author is seeking protection/deliverance from. It therefore seems best to take *kfr* as a G-stem participle meaning "to deny," taking a pronominal direct object. Safaitic orthography does not allow us to distinguish between singular and plural forms in this situation, thus it may be translated as either.

While the preceding interpretation seems secure, we must exercise due diligence and consider all *possible* understandings of this brief clause. There is a second path of interpretation that would read the invocation through another syntactic lens. The *m-* preposition could introduce the instrument of divine aid. Returning to the primary meaning of *kfr*, namely "to cover," we could understand the word as an abstract noun "protection," paralleling

56. The form *mrm-h* is likely the participle of the L-stem *rāmā* "to shoot arrows at someone"; the OCIANA edition translated it as "he took vengeance on those who accused {him}," but this ignores the fact that the *nqm* takes an object introduced by *m-*.

the development of the meaning of *gnn*.[57] There are two drawbacks to this explanation: the first is that while Safaitic frequently invokes the deities for protection, it is almost always using terms derived from *wqy*.[58] Indeed, in no case in which the root *kpr* is attested does it come to mean something like "protection." The second drawback is that the instrumental is almost always introduced by *b*-. The use of the preposition *m*- (= *min*) is difficult to reconcile with this proposed meaning. Finally, it is possible to understand *kfr* as "forgiveness," with the partitive use of *m*-, rendering "help us by means of your forgiveness."[59]

Weighing these options, I would suggest that the understanding *nṣr-h m-kfr-k* as "help him against those who deny you" appears to be most likely. Indeed, once we take *kfr* in this way, the choice of *nṣr* as the verb of aid seems to be deliberate, perhaps the result of word play signaling a connection with Christianity and Christians, cf. Syriac *nāṣrāyūtā* and Qurʾān *nṣry* /naṣārē/. Indeed, the same lexical pair appears in Q Āl ʿImrān 3:147 and al-Baqarah 2:250, producing an invocation with a meaning quite like the one suggested here:

> *wa'nṣurnā ʿalā 'l-qawmi 'l-kāfirīn*
> And grant us victory over the disbelieving host.

3. The Identity of *ʿsy*

If my interpretation of the invocation is correct, then this would strongly suggest that *ʿsy* corresponds to qurʾānic *ʿysy* and that we are dealing with an invocation addressed to Jesus. This brings us to the problem of the etymology of the Arabic name of Jesus. Its attestation in Safaitic would rule out explanations of imperfect transmission to Muḥammad, either orally or through textual corruption, which appear to be the most popular in the literature. Indeed, the name would have been Arabicized early, perhaps at the dawn of the spread of Christianity in North Arabia.

57. Safaitic *gnn* can mean "to protect"; see Al-Jallad and Jaworksa, *Dictionary*, 72, cf. Classical Arabic *jannahu* "he veiled him," "he protected him," Lane, *Lexicon*, 462a.
58. Al-Jallad and Jaworska, *Dictionary*, 140–141.
59. A comparable prayer is attested in KRS 68 with the preposition *b*- introducing the instrument and *m*- the object from which the author seeks deliverance: *h śʿhqm ... b-ẖfrt-k fltn m-mt*, "O Śʿhqm ... by means of your protection/guidance there is deliverance from death"; this interpretation was first offered in Ahmad Al-Jallad, *An Outline of the Grammar of the Safaitic Inscriptions* (Leiden, Brill: 2015), and repeated in Ahmad Al-Jallad and Karolina Jaworska, *Dictionary*, 69.

The problem of *ʿsy*/*ʿysy* is that it does not reflect the outcome of normal phonological processes of borrowing. A putative *yešūʿ* should have come into the QCT as *yswʿ* or, if via Syriac *ʾišoʿ*, as *ʾswʿ*. Recently, Guillaume Dye and Manfred Kropp have discussed this issue in great detail and attempted to explain the development of Arabic *ʿīsā* from a form of Aramaic.[60] They posit an East Syrian source, similar to Mandaic, which had lost *ʿayn*, producing *yešūʿ* > *ʾišūʿ* > *ʾišū*/*ʾišō*. They then argue that once this form was transmitted to Arabic, it gained an *ʿayn* in initial position, a rare yet attested phenomenon.[61] This would produce *ʿīšū*/*ʿīšō*, which was then changed to *ʿīsā* by an ad-hoc lowering of the final vowel. While ingenious, the explanatory power of this account depends on the existence of this unattested Aramaic antecedent at a rather early historical period and on the status of final *y* as a *mater lectionis.* While Kropp and Dye suggest that the final *y* should not be taken as a representation of final *ē* or *ay*, and is therefore available to represent other qualities of final long vowels, advances in the study of early Arabic orthography and the writing system of the Qurʾān in fact require that it reflect an i-class vowel.[62] There are to date no examples of etymological *ā or *ū written with a final *y* in early Arabic.

We should also remember that the pronunciation *ʿīsā* itself is a result of what Sohaib Saeed has termed "Ḥafṣonormativity," that is, the assumption that the pronunciation of Arabic as reflected in the reading tradition of Ḥafṣ *ʿan* ʿĀṣim reflects the earliest and most authentic vocalization of the Qurʾānic Consonantal Text (QCT), relegating other pronunciations to scholarly arcana. While Ḥafṣ *ʿan* ʿĀṣim reads عيسى as *ʿīsā*, the equally canonical tradition of al-Dūrī *ʿan* al-Kisāʾī reads it as *ʿīsē*. There is no objective reason to treat Ḥafṣ's pronunciation as original, and the assumption that it is, is entirely anachronistic. In fact, the earliest material we have to inform the pronunciation of the name عيسى is the transcription of the Arabic name موسى <mwsy> in Greek. In a document dated to 716 CE from Aphrodites Kome, a man name موسى بن نصير appears in Greek transcription as Μουση υἱ(οῦ) Νοσα[ειρ] = Mūsē son of Noṣayr, confirming that the pronunciation of the *alif maqṣūrah* was /ē/.[63] Indeed, in this layer of early Arabic material, what is termed the *alif maqṣūrah* (*bi-ṣūrat al-yāʾ*) is consistently represent-

60. Kropp and Dye, "Le nom de Jésus," 171–198. This article contains an up-to-date and thorough discussion of previous suggestions and their weaknesses. The reader is referred there for previous opinions.

61. Kropp and Dye, "Le nom de Jésus," 188.

62. See note 43 on Arabic triphthongs.

63. Harold I. Bell, *The Aphrodito Papyri: With an Appendix of Coptic Papyri* (London: British Museum, 1911), p.lond 4 1434–1435.

ed with e-class vowels in Greek transcription, ε and η.[64] Considering these facts, it then appears certain that the earliest pronunciation of عسى in the Umayyad period and the pronunciation underlying the qurʾānic *rasm* was *ʿīsē*, in agreement with the reading tradition of al-Kisāʾī. This is even more difficult to reconcile with a source along the lines of *ʾišō*/*ʾišū*.

Given that the name عسى eludes a satisfactory derivation from an Aramaic source, and now in light of the appearance of *ʿsy* in Safaitic, I would like to suggest a new way of thinking about this problem. If Christianity spread to Arabic speakers during the period in which Safaitic inscriptions were composed, then the pre-Classical Arabic lexicon and methods of rendering foreign divine names into the Arabic of this period should inform our interpretation of the form *ʿ(y)sy*. But before entering into the details of etymology, we should note that the *alif maqṣūrah* corresponds to Safaitic *y*, which signifies a final diphthong in nominal forms and a triphthong in verbs: Safaitic *fty* /fatay/, "youth" = qurʾānic فتى /fatē/; Safaitic *bny* /banaya/, "he built" = qurʾānic بنى /banē/.

The Safaitic pantheon contained both local Arabian gods, such as *rḍw*/*rḍy*, and gods whose cult centers lay beyond the Ḥarrah. In most cases, the names of these foreign gods were simply taken over without modification. For example, the storm god Baʿal-Šamīn—whose local cult center was at the town of Sīʿ in southern Syria—is rendered into Safaitic as *bʿlsmn*, preserving its Aramaic form.[65] However, in a few cases, authors translated the divine name into Arabic, producing *bʿlsmy* /baʿal-samāy/, where Aramaic *šamēn*/*šamīn* was replaced with Arabic *samāy*.[66] And in one case, the entire name was replaced by a Safaitic epithet *mālek has-samāy*.[67] Another intriguing example is the possible attestation of the Greek divine title εἷς θεός in Safaitic as *ʾḥd*, reflecting a direct translation of the epithet.[68] While these examples are certainly a minority situation, they do represent a living strategy of localizing foreign gods.

---

64. See Ahmad Al-Jallad, "The Arabic of the Islamic Conquests: Notes on Phonology and Morphology Based on the Greek Transcriptions from the First Islamic Century," *BSOAS* 80 (2017): 419–439, 431.

65. On the town of Sīʿ and Baʿal-Šamīn's temple there, see Michael C. A. Macdonald, "References to Sīʿ in the Safaitic Inscriptions," in J. Dentzer-Feydy, J.-M. Dentzer, and P.-M. Blanc (eds.), *Hauran II: Les installations de Sīʿ 8: Du sanctuaire à l'établissement viticole* (Beirut: IFPO), 278–279.

66. For example, C 88; RWQ 281.

67. KRS 1944.

68. Ahmad Al-Jallad, "The 'One' God in a Safaitic Inscription" *Eretz-Israel* 34 (2021): 37–48. Cf. Q 112:1.

The second option—which does not preclude the first—is the equation of pre-existing names with foreign ones through phonosemantic matching.[69] We can see this process active in the Qurʾān. The name *yaḥyē*, for example, is not a direct port of *yôḥānān* or any of its derivatives, but is rather a pre-existing Arabic name—attested in Safaitic as *yḥyy* (C 614) and *yḥy* (RWQ 115)—that was *equated* with John.[70] Indeed, this equation was employed by Arabian Jews as well. The Jewish Nabataean funerary inscription JSNab 386 (dated 306 CE), from al-ʿUlā, was set up by a man named *yḥyʾ bn šmʿwn*, where *yḥyʾ* substitutes for the common Hebrew name *ywḥnn* (= *yôḥānān*).[71] The two names derive from different roots, which demonstrates that phonetic proximity, rather than etymology, was the main driving force connecting them.

It may, then, be possible that the foreign name *yešūʿ* was equated with a pre-existing Safaitic name, regarded perhaps as its local equivalent. The name *ʿsy* is attested some seven times in the Safaitic corpus as an anthroponym, suggesting that it pre-existed its application to Jesus. In fact, a man named *qdm* son of *ʿsy* records an invocation to Rḍw in Is.H 144:[72] *l qdm bn ʿsy w h rḍw ʾws-h*, "By Qdm son of *ʿsy*; O Roṣaw grant him a boon." This proves that the personal name *ʿsy* was used in a pagan context.

So if *ʿīsē* pre-existed the introduction of Christianity, what did the name mean? Traditional exegetes have devoted much time to this subject and their opinions are discussed by Jeffery and, more recently, by Robinson.[73] Most have assumed that it derives from the root *ʿ-y-s*, which denotes the semantic sphere of "off-whiteness" in Arabic, e.g., *ʿīsatun* and *ʿayasun*, "reddish whiteness" in a camel's color; and *rajulun aʿyasu*, "a man with white hair."

---

69. Phonosemantic matching is similar to calquing, but, in addition to semantic approximation, attempts to match the sound of the word in the source language with a pre-existing word in the target language; see Ghilʿad Zuckermann, *Language Contact and Lexical Enrichment in Israeli Hebrew* (London: Palgrave Macmillan, 2003), § 1.2.4.

70. This issue is discussed as early as Arthur Jeffery, who takes note of the pre-Islamic epigraphic evidence and states: "It would thus seem that Muḥammad was using a form of the name already naturalized among the northern Arabs, though there appears to be no trace of the name in the early literature," though he seems to still regard it as a mutation of *yôḥānān*; see Jeffery, *Foreign Vocabulary*, 290–291.

71. JSNab = Antonin Jaussen and Raphaël Savignac, *Mission archéologique en Arabie* (5 vols; Paris: Leroux/Geuthner, 1909–1920).

72. IS.H = Safaitic inscriptions from ʿĪsāwī, Syria, collected by the SESP project and published on OCIANA.

73. Jeffery, *Foreign Vocabulary*, 218–220; Neal Robinson, "Jesus," *EQ*, s.v. (2003).

Anthroponyms derived from color terms are common, e.g., *ʾswd*, "black."[74] The form, however, is irregular. One would expect something like *ʾʿys* along the lines of *ʾswd*. Rather, if we assume that the vocalization represented in the qurʾānic reading traditions reflects the word's original derivation, then it should be construed as an abstract noun based on the feminine *fiʿlē* (فعلى) pattern. The discord between morphological and natural gender in Arabic anthroponyms is well attested and not surprising, so: *usāmah*, *muʿāwiyah*, *rabīʿah*, all names of men. While the abstract noun *ʿīsay* "whiteness" is not attested in classical sources, its appearance in Safaitic predates this material by nearly a millennium. Thus, such a rare word could have easily fallen into disuse by the time the lexica were compiled. It is also possible to regard the word as a hypocoristic formation based on the noun *ʿīsatun*, "reddish white," where the final feminine ending is replaced with the *-ay* termination; compare with names such as *ʿbdy*, a hypocoristic of *ʿbd*, or *zbdy* from *zbd*.

The above discussion also holds if we assume that the root *ʿ-y-s* in early Arabic had a meaning closer to Gəʿəz *ʿesa* < (*ʿayisa), "to grow soft" and *taʿesa*, "to be patient";[75] both of these meanings would serve as suitable personal names.

One may also consider a derivation from the root *ʿsy*, which opens new interpretive possibilities but creates several morphological problems in its wake. This root gives rise to the verb *ʿasā* in Arabic, which functions as a modal auxiliary, indicating a wish or hope.[76] In Sabaic, however, the verb *ʿsy* means "to purchase, acquire, make (a sacrifice)" and is sometimes interpreted as "to do, make";[77] in Gəʿəz, we find *ʿasaya*, *ʿassaya*, *ʿaśaya* "to repay, reward, recompense."[78]

If we assume a name derived from this root, it challenges a straightforward connection with *ʿīsay*, as it would assume an unattested noun pattern,

---

74. This name is attested seventy-five times in the OCIANA corpus.
75. Wolf Leslau, *Comparative Dictionary of Geʿez (Classical Ethiopic): Geʿez-English, English-Geʿez, with an Index of the Semitic Roots* (Wiesbaden: Harrassowitz, 1987), 80.
76. The modal function of this word is also attested in Safaitic: WH 2840 *w tẓr ḏ ʿs ytf*, "and he kept watch for him whom he hopes to return." This translation replaces the one suggested in Al-Jallad and Jaworska, *Dictionary*, 55: "… him who might return."
77. *Sabäisches Wörterbuch* (http://sabaweb.uni-jena.de/sabaweb; accessed December 17, 2020).
78. Leslau, *Dictionary*, 75. On the relationship of this root with Hebrew *ʿāśā*, see Frithiof Rundgren, "Zur arabischen Wortkunde," in Carl Brockelmann and Manfred Fleischhammer (eds.), *Studia Orientalia in memoriam Caroli Brockelmann*. (Halle: Martin-Luther Universität, 1968), 161–166, 161–162.

fiʿal. This gives us two options. First, we could assume that the Safaitic form reflects a putative name *ʿasīy* (< *ʿasiyyun), "purchased." Names of this sort are typologically common, cf. *zabīd, taym, kareyy, ʾagīr*, and so on. But to connect this with later *ʿīsay*, we must assume metathesis of the vowels as it was transferred across communities in Arabia, so *ʿasīy* > *ʿīsay*. This is possible but unprovable.

The consonantal spelling *ʿsy* could reflect a participial form *ʿāsey*, meaning "purchaser," but this would not be compatible with the qurʾānic form *ʿysy* and its vocalization in later reading traditions. Perhaps, then, the root *ʿsy* was applied to the *fayʿal* pattern, which is an adjectival/agentive pattern: thus, we have *ḍayghamun*, "gnawing," from *ḍaghama*, "to bite without tearing"; *ṣayrafun*, "money exchanger," from *ṣarafa*, "to exchange money"; *bayʾasun*, "harsh and powerful" (applied to a man), that is, "causing affliction," or *buʾsun*; *ṣayqalun*, "polisher" (of swords), from *ṣaqala*, "to polish," and so on. If this is correct, then *ʿsy* should be understood as meaning literally "purchaser" or "redeemer." This would make the name the equivalent of the Classical Arabic anthroponym *fādī*, from the root *fdy*, "to ransom."[79] Thus, a form like *ʿaysay* would appear in Safaitic orthography as *ʿsy* as medial diphthongs were not normally indicated.[80]

The path from *ʿaysay* to the pronunciation in the qurʾānic reading traditions is explained through two steps, one regular and the second *ad hoc* yet linguistically sound. First, the final *ay* collapses to *ē* in Old Ḥigāzī, producing *ʿaysē*, as discussed above. The second change involves the shift of the medial diphthong to *ī* as a result of dissimilation. While this is admittedly an *ad-hoc* process, the repetition of two diphthongs would have certainly provided the impetus for such a change; the dissimilation of *ay* to *ī* could have preceded or followed the collapse of final *ay* to *ē*. We should note, however, that the qurʾānic *rasm* does not require this dissimilation—indeed, the pronunciation *ʿaysē* could have been current in the compositional dialect of the Qurʾān.

Phonosemantic matching could have motivated Arabic speakers to equate the name of Jesus with this pre-existing anthroponym. In fact, *ʿsy* could also have been felt to be a suitable equivalent—and not a translation—

79. Note that the name *fdy* is also attested in Safaitic, eighty times in the OCIANA corpus (accessed May 25, 2021).

80. While the root *ʿsy* has not appeared as a verb in Safaitic, its presence in the onomasticon confirms its existence in the northern dialects. The rigid formulaic structure of the Safaitic inscriptions give us a frustratingly narrow view of the language's lexicon, so the absence of a word in the inscriptions is not necessarily evidence for its absence in the language.

of the Greek title *sōtēr*[81] and its Syriac equivalent *pārōqā*.[82] The focus on the redemptive aspect of salvation in the Arabic name may be deliberate—the pagan gods were frequently invoked for deliverance and salvation, yet they never pay or sacrifice anything in order to save the faithful. This would have been a unique quality of Christian salvation and such an epithet could have served to distinguish Christ as a redeeming savior from the old gods. Indeed, Christ's sacrifice as redemption is expressed in several of Paul's letters and is a universal aspect of Christian theology.[83]

3.1 ʿsy*, the Creator, a Pagan Epithet?*

Is it possible that the divine title *ʿsy* should be understood as "creator" (cf. Hebrew *ʿāśâ* "to make"), a divine epithet applied to the creator deity of the local pantheon? Or could it have been the title of the Jewish God? The sound correspondence between Arabic *s* = s1 and Hebrew *ś* = s2, however, is irregular; the true cognate of Hebrew *ʿāśâ* would be عشى, which would appear in Safaitic as *ʿśy*. While the Sabaic cognate *ʿsy* has been interpreted to mean "to do, make," this seems always to occur in a sacrificial context, i.e., "to make (a sacrifice)"; the basic meaning of the verb is "to purchase, acquire."[84] Moreover, the use of *kfr*, "to deny," with the deity himself as the direct object in the invocation, challenges a pagan or even Jewish interpretation, and indicates, rather, that we are couched within a Christian context.

81. The title was employed in pagan times and was popular among the post-Alexandrian dynasties. The title was applied to YHWH in the Septuagint and was one of the earliest popular epithets applied to Christ, as in the final word in the abbreviation ΙΧΘΥΣ used by early Christians as their secret symbol.

82. The Syriac root *prq* has attracted considerable discussion in qurʾānic studies, especially its connection to the difficult word *furqānun* and the title *fārūqun*. For the most recent opinions on the matter, see Fred M. Donner, "Qurʾānic *Furqān*," *JSS* 52 (2007): 279–300; Uri Rubin, "On the Arabian Origins of the Qurʾān: The Case of *al-Furqān*," *JSS* 54 (2009): 421–433; Walid A. Saleh, "A Piecemeal Qurʾān: *Furqān* and Its Meaning in Classical Islam and in Modern Qurʾānic Studies," *JSAI* 42 (2015): 31–71.

83. For example, Rom 3:24: "being justified freely by his grace through the redemption that is in Christ Jesus," where the Greek uses ἀπολυτρώσεως (genitive) for redemption. In the New Testament this is expressed by the verbs ἀπολύω, "to grant acquittal, set free, release"; λύτρωσις, "redemption" in the sense of "ransoming," "releasing"; ἀγοράζω, literally "to acquire at the forum," used for "redeem" in the Book of Revelation; and ἐξαγοράζω, literally "to acquire outside the forum," which Paul uses to mean "redeem" in his epistles. See also 1 Cor 1:30; Rev 1:5; 1 Thess 1:10; Heb 9:12; Eph 1:7; Tit 2:14; Rom 8:23.

84. See the detailed lemma in the *Sabäisches Wörterbuch*, http://sabaweb.uni-jena.de/.

If we accept the understanding of *ʿsy* as "redeemer," could it have nevertheless applied to a pagan deity? Deliverance and salvation are major themes in Safaitic invocations to the ancient gods, so it is easy to imagine how one or several of these divinities may have taken such a title. But as we have noted before, the very essence of redemption is to make a payment in order to release or save someone—none of the verbs of deliverance used in pagan Safaitic invocations have this implication, [85] let alone its fundamental meaning. The conception of redemption therefore seems to be alien to divine activity in the pagan Safaitic context. Given the great number of philological issues and coincidences that the pagan interpretation produces, I believe we are rather secure in understanding the present text as a monotheistic invocation, and more precisely as an invocation of Jesus himself.

4. Concluding Remarks: Dating and Context

If the identification of *ʿsy* as Christ is correct, then this inscription constitutes the earliest Arabic witness to Christianity discovered so far—pre-fifth century CE. Its precise dating, however, remains uncertain, as does the social background of its author. Recalling the discussion in section 2, Wahbʾel could have been a local nomad, with possible links to settled areas, or a settled person of Arabian background passing through the region. The task here is to attempt to explain how a Christian invocation has appeared in a Safaitic context.

Early literary sources record several accounts of Christian holy men and ascetics venturing out into the deserts to convert its nomadic inhabitants.[86] Perhaps one of the most famous descriptions belongs to Jerome (347–419 CE), who recounts an encounter between St. Hilarion and the Arabs in Elusa, southwest of the Dead Sea.[87] He describes the "Saracens" as devoted

---

85. The commonest roots for these are *ḫlṣ, flṭ, flt, ngw*; Al-Jallad and Jaworksa, *Dictionary*, s.v.

86. For an excellent summary of this material, see Greg Fisher and Walter Ward, "Arabs and Christianity before the Sixth Century: Miracles, Conversion, and Raiding," in Greg Fisher (ed.), *Arabs and Empires before Islam* (Oxford: Oxford University Press, 2015), 287–296. See also the essays in Johannes Hahn and Volker Menze (eds.), *The Wandering Holy Man: The Life of Barsauma, Christian Asceticism, and Religious Conflict in Late Antique Palestine* (Berkley: University of California Press, 2020).

87. For a critical discussion of this story in the context of similar processes and topoi, see Konstatin Klein, "How to Get Rid of Venus: Some Remarks on Jerome's *Vita Hilarionis* and the Conversion of Elusa in the Negev," in Arietta Papaconstantinou,

to the cult of the Morning Star. Stories of St. Hilarion's miracle working caused the nomads to flock to him to receive blessings, at which point he invited them to abandon idols and worship God alone.[88] Stories such as these became a topos in conversion literature; nevertheless, Fisher sees little reason to doubt their basis in real activities. While we possess no accounts describing such ventures in the Ḥarrah, it is topologically comparable to the Negev, a semi-arid region on the edge of the Roman Empire, and so it would stand to reason that its nomadic population was eventually missionized as well. Considering the military connections between the nomads of the Ḥarrah and the Roman empire, Christianization would have further served to consolidate alliances and Roman political power in these border areas.[89]

Greek inscriptions left by men with Greek names litter the remote parts of these deserts and could have possibly been carved by ascetics venturing into the basalt for the purpose of proselytization. There is, so far, one Greek inscription that contains Christian devotional language, discovered near Qaṣr Burquʿ.[90]

Jerome describes Elusa as a "semi-barbarous town"; Fisher speculates on the connotations of this phrase: mixed pagan and Christian or perhaps mixed settled and nomadic. The second option could imply the first, as Christianity took longer to penetrate the deserts. As we have previously discussed, the villages of the Ḥawrān were home to settled sections of nomad tribes who maintained ties with their nomadic kinsmen. Jerome's description could have easily applied to such places as well. Our man Wahbʾel could therefore have received Christianity through either channel, being a sedentary person with nomadic roots or a nomad at the end of the period of Safaitic documentation, perhaps in the fourth century CE. The fact that

Niel McLynn, and Daniel L. Schwartz (eds.), *Conversion in Late Antiquity: Christianity, Islam, and Beyond: Papers from the Andrew W. Mellon Foundation Sawyer Seminar, University of Oxford, 2009–2010* (Farnham: Ashgate, 2015), 241–266.

88. Fisher and Ward, "Arabs and Christianity," 287–289.

89. See note 31. Jerome reports that the Saracens bowed their heads and shouted "barech" meaning "bless" in "Syrian" = (Aramaic). Does this mean that Jerome's Saracens were Aramaic speakers or that they used Aramaic with the foreign miracle worker? Irfân Shahîd suggests that Jerome mistook Arabic *bārik* for Syriac *barek*, which is indeed possible; Irfân Shahîd, *Byzantium and the Arabs in the Fourth Century* (Washington DC: Dumbarton Oaks, 1984), 294. See Klein, *Venus*, n. 15, for further discussion. In general, it is perhaps misguided to treat such quotations as authentic documentation of nomadic speech rather than literary devices to set the scene.

90. This text was discovered on the 2018 season of the Badia Surveys and remains unpublished. See Al-Jallad and al-Manaser, "Old Arabic Minutiae II," for further examples.

Jesus is invoked in a manner similar to the pagan gods could suggest that Wahb'el himself was a convert and modified his writing tradition to accommodate his new faith. Klein suggests that the type of conversion described by Jerome was merely the grafting of the new upon the old, and that may be what we are witnessing here.[91]

But this would not be sustainable. It seems that Safaitic writing, which was clearly very closely tied to traditional religious expression, was abandoned in the wake of the spread of Christianity. And so this precious text may be a rare witness to the transition from Arabian paganism to Christianity among the nomads of the fourth century CE.

It is then in such an environment that we may posit the transformation of *yešūʿ* to *ʿaysay* and ultimately *ʿīsē*, through one of the avenues discussed in section 3. Epithets and localization were normal processes in the formation of divine names among the pre-Islamic Arabs. Even theonyms such as *al-ʿuzzay*, *ḏū-śaray* (Dusares), and even the monotheistic deity of South Arabia, *raḥmānān*, are titles that eventually became proper names.[92] It is therefore possible that when Christ was introduced to the Arabs, they chose to refer to him by a pre-existing anthroponym, the semantics of which would have allowed it to double as a divine epithet, *ʿaysay*, "redeemer." Thus, it would have been in this northern edge of Arabia that Jesus became *ʿīsē*, and from there the name would have spread with Arabic vernacular proselytization, until finally appearing in writing when Arabic became a language of scripture.

The simultaneous existence of *yasūʿ* in Arabic would suggest a second process of importation, but this time directly adapting the West Syriac *yešūʿ* to Arabic. The earliest securely dated attestation of *yasūʿ* comes from Sin.Ar 72, an Arabic translation of the Gospels dated by the copyist to 897 CE.[93] The form of the name *yasūʿ*, however, suggests a much earlier date of borrowing. Had the Aramaic form been adapted to Arabic in the ninth century CE, we would expect it to be pronounced *yashūʿ*, with Arabic ش rendering Syriac ܫ. The use of س and the pronunciation *yasūʿ* reflects the ancient strategy of consistently rendering pre-Islamic Aramaic /š/ into Arabic with /s/. Thus,

91. Klein, *Venus*, 256.

92. See John F. Healey, *The Religion of the Nabataeans: A Conspectus* (Leiden: Brill, 2001), ch. 4, for a discussion.

93. See Aziz S. Atiya, *The Arabic Manuscripts of Mt. Sinai: A Handlist of the Arabic Manuscripts and Scrolls Microfilmed at the Library of the Monastery of St. Catherine, Mt. Sinai* (Baltimore: Johns Hopkins, 1955). I thank Phillip Stokes for this reference. I have excluded mentions of *yasūʿ* in poetry attributed to the pre-Islamic period as it is impossible to determine the authenticity of these occurrences.

while we cannot be sure of the antiquity of *yasūʿ*, it appears to belong to the same stratum of loans as the Aramaic vocabulary of the Qurʾān in contrast to later practice.[94]

We may now conclude with a few words on who was meant by the term *kfr*. We see in other comparable invocations that the gods are invoked in order to deliver the mourner from his own grief and from enemies, often those who murdered his beloved. Wahbʾel's maternal uncle could have been killed by a rival nomadic group who in this early period remained practitioners of traditional Arabian religion. His invocation refers to them with Christian polemical language, as those who have denied Christ.

Part II: The Site (Ali al-Manaser)

Al-Khuḍari is one of the largest areas in the Jordanian Black Desert, the Ḥarrah (fig. 3). The area comprises Wādī al-Khuḍarī, Wādī Ḥashād al-Khuḍarī, Sūḥ al-Khuḍarī, Marabb al-Khuḍarī, Maṭabb al-Khuḍarī, Naqʿat al-Khuḍarī, and Ābār al-Khuḍarī. Sūḥ al-Khuḍarī is an open and level area in which it is possible to engage in agriculture. It is distinguished from the Marabb by its size only. The area called Ḥashād is a relatively flat area characterized by basalt gravel. This term is applied to many areas in the Ḥarrah, each qualified by the larger region in which they are located—e.g., Ḥashād Salmā, Ḥashād al-ʿŌsajī, and Ḥashād al-Swēʿid. As for the region called Maṭabb, it describes the boundary of the Ḥarrah and the sand/mud desert, the *ḥamād*.

The present inscription was discovered at one of the tributaries of Wādī al-Khuḍarī, near Naqʿat al-Khuḍarī, "the pond of al-Khuḍarī," which leads to the area of Ābār al-Khuḍarī, "the wells of al-Khuḍarī," which continues to be used by Bedouin today in the summer. The area of Naqʿat al-Khuḍarī is located between the larger area of al-Khuḍarī and Tell al-Hfēf, which leads to the of the area of al-Ṣqērāt, an area in which there is an abundance of inscriptions. The nearby Tell al-Hfēf, which faces the cairn at which the present inscription was discovered, was surveyed in 2017, resulting in the documentation of more than 1,000 Safaitic inscriptions.

This region has enjoyed significant epigraphic attention in the past, especially the area of Tulūl al-Ghuṣayn, al-Shbēkah, Jāwā, and Qaṣr Burquʿ. The discoveries at these sites point towards continuous human habitation from the Neolithic to present times.

94. For a thorough discussion of this issue and previous opinions, see Ahmad Al-Jallad, "The Month ʾdr in Safaitic and the Status of Spirantisation in 'Arabian' Aramaic," *Aramaic Studies* 18 (2020): 147–170.

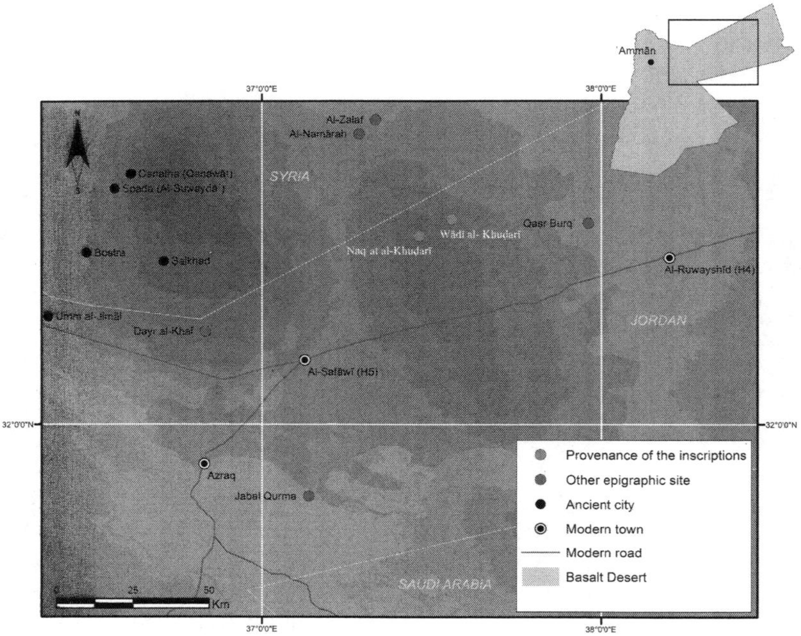

Figure 3: Map of the area (by Ali al-Manaser) in which the inscription was discovered.

Appendix 1: The Second Inscription

Reading: *l {f}ld bn nfl bn {g}ḏ*
Interpretation: By {Fld} son of Nfl son of Gḏ

Fld is attested once in WH 2725. The *f* of this name, however, seems to be smaller than the clear *f* of the following anthroponym. There could be several further undulations towards the bottom of the glyph, which could permit reading it as an *ś*. A name *śld*, however, is not attested in the OCIANA corpus. Both roots are unattested in Classical Arabic. *Nfl* corresponds to the Classical Arabic name *nawfalun*, and occurs in eighteen Safaitic texts. Finally, *{g}ḏ* is not yet attested in the Safaitic onomasticon but the root is attested in Classical Arabic, *gadhdha*, "he broke." The name *ʿḏ*, however, is fairly common; but the first glyph in the present inscription is clearly oblong, making its reading as an *ʿ* quite impossible.

Appendix 2: On Littmann's Identification of Jesus in an Ancient North Arabian Inscription

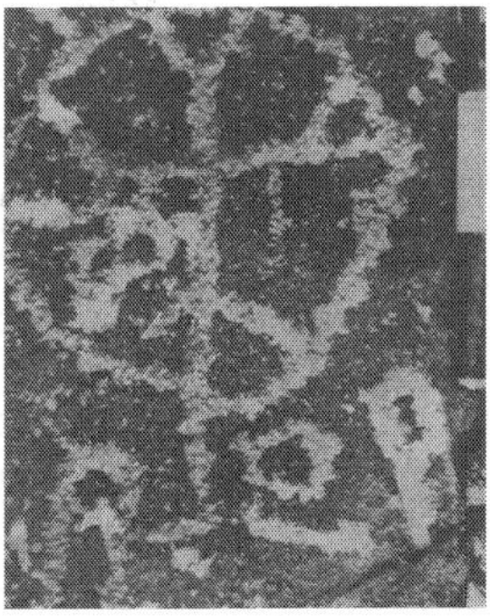

Figure 4: Photo of G. L. Harding of the alleged "Jesus" inscription, published in Enno Littmann, "Jesus in a pre-Islamic Arabic inscription," *MW* 40 (1950): 16–18.

In 1950, the great E. Littmann produced an edition of a short Hismaic inscription alleged to carry the name of Jesus underneath a cross (fig. 4). Three glyphs appear under the Christian mark, which Littmann identified as a *y*, *ś*, and ʿ. This reading, however, should be doubted.

Once we inspect the photograph closely, it becomes clear that what Littmann took as a *y* is in fact simply a circle. The alleged shaft is a secondary marking, carved later and in a lighter fashion than the circle to which it appears to attach. Another similar, secondary mark attaches to the left side of the leftmost glyph as well. So, if we were to take these glyphs as an Ancient North Arabian inscription,

Figure 5: The o | o carved on a wall of Qaṣr Kharrānah, Jordan (photograph by A. Al-Jallad).

specifically a Hismaic one, then they should read as *ʿ-ś-ʿ*, which is not compatible with the name *yešūʿ*. But I would question whether these marks are to be understood as letters at all. Rather, they should more likely be interpreted as tribal symbols, a *wasm*, which the nomads use to mark their animals and property and can often be found carved on rock faces. The o | o design is quite common in Jordan, and remains in use even today. The same design was carved into the walls of Qaṣr Kharrānah, one of the Umayyad desert castles near al-Azraq (fig. 4). Thus, it seems that the o | o of Littmann's inscription can be securely understood as a *wasm*, a tribal mark rather than an Ancient North Arabian inscription. As such it is most likely not contemporary with the Christian symbol it sits beneath, but carved centuries later by a passerby.

JIQSA 6 (2021): 137–166

THE NARRATIVES OF "THE COMPANIONS OF THE CAVE," MOSES AND HIS SERVANT, AND DHŪ 'L-QARNAYN IN SŪRAT AL-KAHF: LATE ANTIQUE LORE WITHIN THE PURVIEW OF THE QUR'ĀN

SIDNEY GRIFFITH
The Catholic University of America, USA

Abstract

The Qur'ān's accounts of the Companions of the Cave and the travels of Dhū 'l-Qarnayn strongly resonate with popular late antique Syriac Christian stories, namely, accounts of the so-called Sleepers of Ephesus and of Alexander the Great. Yet there is no evidence in the Qur'ān's telling of these stories that it directly relied upon the specific form in which these stories have been preserved in Syriac. Rather, it is likely that oral versions of these narratives preceded their surviving written accounts and that the Qur'ān recalled aspects of these oral versions for its own purposes. Differences between the qur'ānic accounts of the Companions of the Cave and Dhū 'l-Qarnayn, on the one hand, and their Syriac parallels, on the other, serve to highlight how the qur'ānic telling of the stories under consideration is in line with and stresses the Qur'ān's particular theological concerns. Similarly, the echoes between the story of Moses and his servant in Sūrat al-Kahf and motifs associated with Alexander should not be taken to mean that the Qur'ān is purposely creating a Moses-Alexander equivalence. Rather, the Islamic scripture may be read as utilizing familiar motifs in order to craft a new episode in the life of the biblical Moses, an episode that reports how Moses came to be prepared for his subsequent prophetic mission.

I. Introduction

Unlike the Qur'ān's many reminiscences of the stories of the biblical patriarchs and prophets, found in both Meccan and Medinan *sūrah*s, in Sūrat al-Kahf the Arabic scripture somewhat unexpectedly also calls the attention of its audience to several stories not connected to the biblical or para-biblical tradition, which were nevertheless widely popular in Late Antiquity.

doi: http://dx.doi.org/10.5913/jiqsa.6.2021.a005

Outside of the Qurʾān, these stories are found only in extra-biblical Jewish and Christian texts. The Qurʾān recalls features of the Christian story of the Seven Sleepers of Ephesus, echoes of Jewish and Christian stories of the exploits of a "Two-Horned" hero, most likely an evocation of the saga of Alexander the Great, and the extra-biblical story of the adventures of the patriarch Moses with his servant and with "one of Our servants" (v. 65), as the Qurʾān calls him; this account also recalls elements of the tales of Alexander the Great. Probably because this story of Moses is not to be found in the Bible, nor in rabbinic texts, Heinrich Speyer gave it short shrift in his ground-breaking book, *Die biblischen Erzählungen im Qoran.*[1]

While the stories of the so-called "Sleepers of Ephesus" and of the exploits of Alexander the Great appear in numerous texts in all the languages of late antique Christianity and in contemporaneous Jewish lore as well, the Qurʾān's narratives involving them seem to many scholars to relate the most closely in the telling to Syriac narratives current in the first half of the seventh century CE,[2] and in particular to several metrical homilies (*mēmrē*) in Syriac attributed to the fifth/sixth century "Jacobite" Christian writer, Jacob of Sarug (c. 451–521 CE),[3] and as well to several Syriac versions of the ever popular "Legend of Alexander." That Syriac homiletic texts and prose narratives should be among the closest contemporary, late antique literary locations in which rehearsals of the stories comparable to the Qurʾān's recollection of the same narratives is to be found is not surprising. It has become increasingly clear in numerous recent scholarly studies of partic-

---

1. See Heinrich Speyer, *Die biblischen Erzählungen im Qoran* (Gräfenhainichen: C. Schulze and Co., 1931), 238–239.
2. While the story of the "Sleepers of Ephesus" is uniquely Christian in the form in which the Qurʾān recalls it, there is a tradition of "long sleepers" in Jewish tradition as well. See Pieter W. van der Horst, "Pious Long-Sleepers in Greek, Jewish and Christian Antiquity" (paper presentation, Thirteenth International Orion Symposium, Jerusalem, February 22–24, 2011). Both Jews and Christians recalled the story of Alexander the Great in various ways in their late antique traditions. For Alexander in Jewish tradition, see Jonathan Goldstein, "Alexander and the Jews," *Proceedings of the American Academy for Jewish Research* 59 (1993), 59–101; Ory Amitay, *From Alexander to Jesus* (Berkeley, CA: University of California Press, 2010). For Alexander in Christian tradition, see the appropriate articles in Z. David Zuwihha (ed.), *A Companion to Alexander Literature in the Middle Ages* (Leiden: Brill, 2011); Christian Thrue Djurslev, *Alexander the Great in Early Christian Tradition: Classical Reception and Patristic Literature* (London: J. B. Tauris, 2018).
3. On whom see Sebastian P. Brock, "Yaʿqūb of Serūgh," in Sebastian P. Brock et al. (eds.), *Gorgias Encyclopedic Dictionary of the Syriac Heritage* (Piscataway, NJ: Gorgias Press, 2011), 433–435.

ular narratives that the biblical and Christian lore with which the Arabic Qurʾān is most familiar is most often seen to have a striking resonance with the texts and traditions of contemporary and neighboring Syriac-speaking Christian communities. The congruence of storyline and sometimes even of vocabulary, as we shall see, often strongly suggests that both Arabic-speaking non-Christians and Arabic-speaking Christians within the Qurʾān's purview inherited their knowledge of Christian tradition, in all likelihood for the most part orally, from Syriac-speaking interlocutors and co-religionists. But here is not the place to explore this likely hypothesis further.[4] Rather, the point to be made now is that it is reasonable, albeit not exclusively as we shall see, to approach the study of the Qurʾān's accounts of the "Companions of the Cave" (*aṣḥāb al-kahf*) and Dhū 'l-Qarnayn in reference to the telling of their stories in Syriac homiletic and historical texts, both in terms of privileging the most likely channel of the currency of their stories in the late antique, Arabic-speaking milieu of the Qurʾān's origins and in the effort, hermeneutically speaking, at the same time to discern more specifically the Arabic scripture's didactic purpose in recalling and retelling the stories in a scriptural counter-discourse in accord with the Qurʾān's requirements of its own over-arching paradigm of prophetic revelation.

II. The Character and Structure of Sūrat al-Kahf

Sūrat al-Kahf is commonly taken in earlier, Western scholarship to have been first proclaimed in the middle Meccan period of Muḥammad's career as God's Messenger and Prophet.[5] It is the period during which, in other more or less contemporary *sūrahs*, such as Sūrat al-Shuʿarāʾ and Sūrat Maryām,

4. See in this connection, Sidney H. Griffith, "*Al-Naṣārā* in the Qur'ān: A Hermeneutical Reflection," in Gabriel Said Reynolds (ed.), *New Perspectives on the Qur'ān: The Qur'ān in Its Historical Context 2* (Abingdon: Routledge, 2011), 301–322; idem, "What Does Mecca Have to Do with Urhōy? Syriac Christianity, Islamic Origins, and the Qur'ān," in Maria Doerfler, Emanuel Fiano, and Kyle Smith (eds.), *Syriac Encounters: Papers from the Sixth North American Syriac Symposium, Duke University, 26-29 June 2011* (Leuven: Peeters, 2015), 369–399; idem, "The Qur'ān's 'Nazarenes' and Other Late Antique Christians: Arabic-Speaking 'Gospel People' in Qur'ānic Perspective," in S.H. Griffith and S. Grebenstein (eds.), *Christsein in der islamischen Welt: Festschrift für Martin Tamcke zum 60. Geburtstag* (Wiesbaden: Harrassowitz, 2015), 81–106.

5. See *GdQ* 1.117–143. The position is not incompatible with the calculations of "mean verse length" in Nicolai Sinai, *The Qur'ān: A Historical-Critical Introduction* (Edinburgh: Edinburgh University Press, 2017), 120.

one of the so-called *raḥmān sūrahs*,[6] one finds the Qur'ān's earliest, more inclusive listings of biblical and non-biblical messengers and prophets, and reminiscences of their stories, some of whom, like Noah, Abraham, and Moses, were already mentioned by name in the early Meccan period. It is notable too that these same middle Meccan *sūrahs*, and Sūrat Maryām in particular, where Jesus and his mother Mary are first mentioned, are also the earliest places in the Qur'ān in which one finds an appreciable number of reminiscences of the stories of biblical personalities that feature a high quotient of narrative coincidence with traditional, Christian lore about them, most particularly in late antique Syriac homiletic and exegetical texts.[7]

Within the parameters of its broad outline, which some recent scholarship analyzes as a ring composition,[8] Sūrat al-Kahf includes reminiscences of several seemingly popular stories, which, given the mode of their introduction to the Qur'ān's audience, as I shall argue, must have been already current and widely known in late antique Arabia's store of religious lore. They are the story of the Sleepers of Ephesus, as it is called in Christian tradition (vv. 9–26); the parable of two men and their gardens (vv. 32–44); the otherwise unattested story of Moses in conversation with an unknown servant and travelling companion (vv. 60–82); and finally a recollection of the ever popular exploits of the late antique stories of Alexander the Great (vv. 83–98). The reminiscences are embedded in the *sūrah*'s overall mode of direct address to Muḥammad in the context of his relations with his audience and interlocutors. In the introductory verses to the *sūrah* (vv. 1–8) the emphasis is on God's address to His servant, Muḥammad, to whom He has sent down the scripture (*al-kitāb*), reminding him of his mission to warn and to announce good news to the believers; in particular, he is to warn "those who say, 'God has taken a son (*walad*),'" about which neither they nor their fathers, the text says, have any real knowledge, albeit that they have much to say about it. What is more, God's servant is not grievously to

6. See Angelika Neuwirth, *Der Koran als Text der Spätantike: Ein europäischer Zugang* (Berlin: Verlag der Weltreligionen im Insel Verlag, 2010), 472–474.

7. See in particular the detailed analysis of Sūrat Maryam, with extensive bibliographical references, in Angelika Neuwirth, *Der Koran*, vol. 2/1, *Frümittelmekkanische Suren: Handkommentar mit Übersetzung* (Berlin: Verlag der Weltreligionen im Insel Verlag, 2017), 584–658.

8. See in particular George Archer, *A Place Between Two Places: The Qur'ānic Barzakh* (Piscataway, NJ: Gorgias Press, 2017), esp. 107–192. Regarding the proposal of a ring structure for the *sūrah*, with vv. 50–51 as the center point, Archer notes (p. 108, n. 1) his agreement in the main with the view of Muḥammad ʿĀdil al-Qalqīlī, *al-Handasah al-ilāhiyyah fī Sūrat al-Kahf* (Amman: Dār ʿAmmār, 1986).

trouble himself about the effects of their non-belief in "this message" (*hādhā 'l-ḥadīth*, v. 6), that is to say, this occasion of his proclamation of the Qur'ān. The concluding verses of the *sūrah* (vv. 100–110) are similarly addressed to the Messenger, and they speak of the recompense due to those who "disbelieve the signs (*āyāt*) of their Lord" (v. 105) and those who "take My signs and My messengers as a joke" (v. 106). The Messenger is instructed: "Say, I am only a man like you; it has been revealed to me that your God is a single God. Whoever hopes to meet His Lord should do good works and he must not associate anything with the worship of his Lord" (vv. 109–110). That is also the import of the reminiscences of the stories of God's notable servants of the past included in the body of the *sūrah*, the recollections of the stories of the Companions of the Cave, of Moses's travels, and of Dhū 'l-Qarnayn in particular.[9] Similar passages addressed to the Messenger, assuring him in his vocation and instructing him in the scriptural message he is to deliver, appear at intervals between the narratives in the *sūrah*: between the story of the "Companions of the Cave" and the parable of two men and their gardens (vv. 27–31); and between the parable and the stories of Moses with his travelling companion and the reminiscence of the "Two-Horned One." The *sūrah* outline may then be displayed as follows:

Opening Address to the Messenger: vv. 1–8.
  The Companions of the Cave: vv. 9–26.
Intervening Instructions to the Messenger: vv. 27–31.
  Parable of Two Men and their Gardens: vv. 32–44.
Intervening Instructions; Adam and Iblīs: vv. 45–59.
  Moses and Dhū 'l-Qarnayn: vv. 60–82; 83–101.
Closing Peroration: vv. 102–110.

III. The Qur'ānic Account of the Companions of the Cave

The beginning of the Qur'ān's reminiscence of the story of the Companions of the Cave (vv. 9–26) opens with the Speaker's rhetorical question addressed to the Messenger: "Do you [singular] reckon the Companions

9. For an overall discussion of the structure of Sūrat al-Kahf, with an emphasis on form critical analysis, see the bibliographically rich discussion in Hannelies Koloska, *Offenbarung, Ästhetik und Koranexegesse: Zwei Studien zu Sure 18 (al-Kahf)* (Wiesbaden: Harrassowitz, 2015), 21–51. See also the discussion of earlier models and the alternative, form-critical proposal of Marianna Klar, "Re-Examining Textual Boundaries: Towards a Form-Critical Sūrat al-Kahf," in Majid Daneshgar and Walid Saleh (eds.), *Islamic Studies Today: Essays in Honor of Andrew Rippin* (Leiden: Brill, 2017), 215–238.

of the Cave and the inscription[10] are marvelous among Our signs?" (v. 9). One may then distinguish two phases in the following narrative. In the first phase (vv. 10–20), the Speaker directly addresses the Messenger in the second person singular, in familiar qur'ānic phraseology, and He recalls the central elements of the traditional story of the young companions' sojourn in the cave. In the second phase (vv. 21–26), the Speaker addresses several points of interest that had arisen in tradition about the details of the story, particularly regarding the number of companions and their dog, and the length of time they were thought to have stayed in the cave; He issues instructions to the Messenger about how to deal with the discrepancies.

The first phase of the narrative proceeds in two stages. The Speaker first recounts the central scenario of the story (vv. 10–12), recalling how the companions first took refuge in the cave, calling on God's mercy and asking for guidance, and how God put them to sleep for a number of years, until He would wake them up, in order to know which of two groups know best about how to reckon the length of their sleep. Secondly, the Speaker presents the story of the youthful companions in accord with the familiar narrative pattern and vocabulary of the Qur'ān's usual portrait of righteous individuals of the past who believed in their Lord (v. 13), who called on none other than God (v. 14), whose people had taken on other gods without any show of power (v. 15). So too the companions, the Speaker says, after their refusal to worship any other than God, exhorted one another to take refuge in the cave, where their Lord's mercy would unfold for them and God would provide a way out of their predicament (v. 16). The Speaker then discloses to the Messenger the miracle of the sun's movements over the cave's opening while the companions were inside, specifying that this too was one of God's signs (*āyāt*, v. 17). The Speaker assures the Messenger that if he had come upon the scene he would have fled in terror (v. 18). Finally, the Speaker recalls the drama of the sleepers' awakening and their dialogue with one another about how long they were asleep, and about the adventure of their envoy into the nearby city, centuries after their having taken refuge in the cave.

In the second and concluding phase of the narrative, the Speaker addresses points of controversy, which had arisen about some details of the

10. There has been considerable discussion among both the traditional commentators and modern scholars about the meaning of the *hapax legomenon* in qur'ānic lexicography, *al-raqīm*. See Gabriel Said Reynolds, *The Qur'ān and Its Biblical Subtext* (Abingdon: Routledge, 2010), 168, n. 567, and 171–173. See the most common understandings listed in Elsaid M. Badawi and Muhammad Abdel Haleem, *Arabic-English Dictionary of Qur'anic Usage* (Leiden: Brill, 2008), 377–378.

traditional story, and he instructs the Messenger about how to deal with them. He mentions that opinion was divided about how many companions there were. The Speaker says about the companions, "We alerted [people] to them so that they would know that God's promise is true; there is no doubt about the hour, albeit that [people] dispute among themselves about their (i.e., the companions') experience" (v. 21). The Qurʾān then recalls that some people wanted to put up a building over them; those who prevailed opted for a place of worship (*masjid*, v. 21). Regarding the differing estimates about the number of companions, the Speaker instructs, "Say, 'My Lord knows best ...' Do not engage in dispute about them ... Do not ask anyone's considered opinion about them" (v. 22). In the next two verses, the Speaker reminds the Messenger not ever to say about something on his own recognizance, "I will do that tomorrow" (v. 23). Should he forget to mention his Lord, he is to remember, "and say, 'Perhaps my Lord will guide me ...'" (v. 24). Then, depending on how one understands the Arabic text, either the Speaker makes the declarative statement about the companions that "they stayed in their cave three hundred years; nine are to be added," or He reports declaratively that this is an estimate commonly given (v. 25). In the end, the Speaker tells the Messenger, "Say, 'God knows best how long they stayed ...' They had no protector apart from Him, and He has not taken any other being as an associate in His governance" (v. 26).

IV. The Companions of the Cave and the Sleepers of Ephesus

Scholars have long called attention to the Syriac telling of the late antique, Christian legend of the Seven Sleepers of Ephesus as providing the principal point of reference in their search for historical evidence of the currency of the story of the Sleepers in the proximate milieu of the Arabic Qurʾān's origins with its reminiscence of "the Companions of the Cave and the inscription" in Sūrat al-Kahf.[11] The earliest texts in which the Christian story of the Seven Sleepers actually survives from antiquity are in fact in Syriac, albeit that it may well have been first told in Greek.[12] And the earliest Syriac texts

11. See the review of scholarship in Sidney H. Griffith, "Christian Lore and the Arabic Qur'ān: The 'Companions of the Cave' in *Sūrat al-Kahf* and in Syriac Christian Tradition," in Gabriel Said Reynolds (ed.), *The Qur'ān in Its Historical Context* (Abingdon: Routledge, 2008), 109–137. See also François Jourdan, *La tradition des Sept Dormants: Une rencontre entre chrétiens et musulmans* (Paris: Maisonneuve and Larose, 2001).

12. See A. Allgeier, "Untersuchungen zur syrischen Überlieferung der Siebenschläferlegende," *Oriens Christianus* 4 (1915): 10–59; idem, *Die westsyrische Über-*

which feature the story of the "youths (*ṭlāyē*) of Ephesus," as the "Companions of the Cave" or the "Seven Sleepers" are always called in Syriac, are two recensions of a liturgical homily (*mēmrā*) attributed to Jacob of Sarug, a "Syrian Orthodox" or "Jacobite" writer, the text of whose homilies were popular in Late Antiquity; there is every reason to think that they were still being copied and performed in Syriac, in Christian liturgies in the seventh and eighth centuries CE.[13]

Reading the Qur'ān's narrative of the "Companions of the Cave" in Sūrat al-Kahf in tandem with the story of the "Youths of Ephesus" in Jacob of Sarug's Syriac *mēmrā* reveals a number of striking coincidences of words, phrases, narrative details, and topical outline between the two texts, the earlier Syriac homily and the later qur'ānic narrative.[14] The reader nevertheless readily recognizes that while Sūrat al-Kahf does not retell the story in all its original narrative details, it does recall particular moments in the transmission of the legend and it does so in its own distinctive qur'ānic idiom; particularly noticeable is the paradigmatic, formulaic phraseology of the Qur'ān's reminiscence of the earlier messengers and prophets in *sūrahs* such as Sūrat al-Shuʿarā', Sūrat Hūd, and Sūrat al-Aʿrāf.[15] Accordingly, the Speaker calls the Messenger's attention to the Companions of the Cave and to the inscription, asking, "Do you reckon that the Companions of the Cave and the inscription are marvelous among Our signs (*āyāt*)?" (v. 9). The question assumes the Messenger's familiarity with details of the traditional story and the Speaker goes on without further elaboration to address issues

lieferung der Siebenschläferlegende (Leipzig: W. Drugulin, 1915); idem, "Die älteste Gestalt der Siebenschläferlegende," *Oriens Christianus* 6 (1916): 1–43, and *Oriens Christianus* 7 and 8 (1918): 33–87.

13. The texts are published in I. Guidi, *Testi Orientali Inediti sopra I Sette Dormienti di Efeso* (Roma: Tipografia dell R. Accademia dei Lincei, 1885), 18–29. One of the recensions is also published in H. Gismondi, *Linguae Syriacae Grammatica et Chrestomathia cum Glossario*, 4th ed. (Rome: C. De Luigi, 1913), 45–53. On the copying and manuscript circulation of Jacob's homily on "The Youths of Ephesus," see A. Vööbus, *Handschriftliche Überlieferung der Mēmrē des Jaʿqōb von Serūg*, CSCO vols. 344 and 345, 421 and 422 (Louvain: Secrétariat du CSCO, 1973 and 1980), vol. 344, esp. 51–52.

14. See pertinent, parallel passages quoted in English translation in Gabriel Said Reynolds, *The Qur'ān and the Bible: Text and Commentary* (New Haven: Yale University Press, 2018), 450–458.

15. See in this connection Sidney H. Griffith, "The Sunna of Our Messengers: The Qur'ān's Paradigm for Messengers and Prophets; A Reading of *Sūrat ash-Shuʿarā'*," in Angelika Neuwirth and Michael Sells (eds.), *Qur'ānic Studies Today* (Abingdon: Routledge, 2016), 208–227.

of interpretation and differing opinions about the length of time the Companions spent in the cave. He says, "We are going to tell you their story truthfully" (v. 13).

The centerpiece of the qur'ānic narrative of the Companions of the Cave according to most commentators is found in verses 17–18, which give voice to the Arabic scripture's original contributions to the telling, features of the account not found anywhere else in writing in any other late antique texts that have survived. Addressing the Messenger, the Speaker says:

> 17 You could see the sun when it rose declining away from their cave to the right, and when it set, turning away from them to the left, while they were in an open part of it. That is one of God's signs (*āyāt*). Whomever God guides is guided aright; whomever He leads astray, you will never find a patron for him, to guide him aright.
> 18 You would reckon them to be awake while they were asleep. We would turn them to the right and to the left. Their dog would stretch out his paws at the threshold. Were you to come upon them you would turn away from them in flight; you would be full of fear of them.

The vivid details in this passage highlight the notice that here indeed was "one of God's signs (*āyāt*)," an affirmation that is typical of the Qur'ān's recollections of narratives of God's messengers and prophets, albeit that the text does not explicitly include the Companions of the Cave among their number. Rather, the story is presented as yet another instance of the Qur'ān's insistence on the revelatory power of historical reminiscence for those endowed with the wit to understand its message correctly. The verses leading up to the narrative suggest that the Qur'ān's telling of the story is in fact intended as a corrective to the understanding of it current among the local Christians, whom the Arabic scripture most likely has in mind when in an earlier verse it speaks of its role to warn "those who say, 'God has taken a son'" (v. 4). This expression, which occurs in a number of other places in the Qur'ān, in passages addressing "Scripture People," echoes language reminiscent of Syriac usage in late antique Christological texts, just as the Qur'ān's immediately following reminiscence of the story of the "Companions of the Cave" closely recalls the telling of the story of the "Youths of Ephesus" in Jacob of Sarug's Syriac homily on the same event. The Syriac dialect of Aramaic was the dominant, liturgical language of the Christian communities who lived within the purview of the Arabic scripture in the milieu of its origins in the first half of the seventh century. So it is not surprising that the Qur'ān's recollections of Christian lore should reflect the discursive patterns and even the vocabulary of the idiom in which it originally circulated among the Christian near-neighbors of the Arabic-speaking peoples of Late Antiquity. The same phenomenon is noticeable in the Qurʾān's reminiscence of the story of Dhū 'l-Qarnayn later in Sūrat al-Kahf.

V. The Qurʾānic Account of Dhū 'l-Qarnayn

The Qurʾān's reminiscence of the story of Dhū 'l-Qarnayn (vv. 83–101) comes as the final historical narrative in the *sūrah*'s evocation of several exemplary instances of God's intervention in past human affairs, including the story of the biblical Moses's apocryphal adventures with his travelling companions, a young disciple and a mysterious stranger (vv. 60–82). One might even structurally pair the memory of Dhū 'l-Qarnayn with the story of the Companions of the Cave to set up the *sūrah*'s reminiscences of the two stories of largely Christian hagiographical background as the opening and closing narratives of the whole of Sūrat al-Kahf. As in the instance of the story of the Companions, so here too the Speaker introduces the reminiscence addressing the Messenger and instructing him to share the memory of the "Two-Horned One" with his interlocutors, "They will ask you [singular] about Dhū 'l-Qarnayn. Say, 'I will recount a memory (*dhikr*) of him for you'" (v. 83). And the Speaker goes on to tell the Messenger, "We have made a place for him on the earth and in everything We have given him a way forward (*sabab*)" (v. 84).[16] Muslim commentators have for the most part

16. Interpreters have for the most part understood the term *sabab* to mean a "way" or a "means" of accomplishing something. It occurs four times in this pericope, three of them marking Dhū 'l-Qarnayn's progress on his journey. See Arne A. Ambros, *A Concise Dictionary of Koranic Arabic* (Wiesbaden: Reichert Verlag, 2004), 126–127. See also Koloska, *Offenbarung, Ästhetik und Koranexegese*, 146 and n. 524, rejecting the suggestion that in the present instance the term recalls "sky-cords" or "heaven's ropes," as suggested in Kevin van Bladel, "Heavenly Cords and Prophetic Authority in the Qur'ān and its Late Antique Context," *BSOAS* 70 (2007): 223–247. More plausible is the suggestion of Tommaso Tesei that the *asbāb* in the reminiscence of the story of Dhū 'l-Qarnayn refer to the "sky-ways" along which Alexander travelled according to the "Legend of Alexander." See Tommaso Tesei, "The Prophecy of Ḏū-l-Qarnayn (Q 18:83–102) and the Origins of the Qurʾānic Corpus," in Angelo Arioli (ed.), *Miscellanea Arabica 2013–2014* (Rome: Aracne, 2014), 273–290. It is interesting to note in passing that in the present context, early and late Muslim commentators have associated the term *sabab* (pl. *asbāb*) with *ṭarīq* (pl. *ṭuruq*), i.e., "road" and "way," including knowledge of the earth's ways and roads. See *Tafsīr Muqātil ibn Sulaymān*, ed. Aḥmad Farīd (3 vols.; Beirut: Dār al-Kutub al-ʿIlmiyyah, 1424/2003), 2.299; *Tafsīr al-Jalālayn li'l-imāmayn al-jalīlayn* (Saudi Arabia: Dār al-Salām, 1422/2002), 314.

identified Dhū 'l-Qarnayn with the historical Alexander the Great (356–323 BCE) of Hellenistic times, whom late antique Christians had adopted as the legendary hero who by divine providence had historically prepared the way for the dawn of the Christian era.[17] And as we shall see below, in its outline and in some details the Qur'ān's reminiscence of the "Two Horned One" is in fact broadly congruent with the narrative of the "Legend of Alexander" as it circulated especially among Syriac-speaking Christians contemporaneous with the Qur'ān in its origins.[18] Nevertheless, Islamic tradition and some modern scholars too have also proposed other figures as candidates for the role of Dhū 'l-Qarnayn in Sūrat al-Kahf, most notably the biblical patriarch Moses, a suggestion to be discussed below.

The story of Dhū 'l-Qarnayn proceeds in three narrative steps, each one introduced with the recurrent, formulaic phrase, "He followed a way forward until, when he arrived ..." (*atbaʿa sababan ḥattā idhā balagha ...*; vv. 85–86; 89–90; 92–93). The "Two Horned One" is first of all said to have followed the course of the sun westward to its setting "in a muddied spring" (v. 86), settling by the side of which he is further said to have found a people. In answer to God's question to him, he avers that he will punish the wrongdoers among them and reward the believers who do good deeds. Then the text says he followed a way forward until he came to the place of the sun's rising, where he found a people "for whom We had not provided any covering under it" (v. 90). Here the Speaker says only, "We have full knowledge (*khubr*) of what concerned him" (v. 91). Finally, the text says that Dhū 'l-Qarnayn followed a way forward until he came to an otherwise unidentified place where there were double ramparts, behind which he found "a people who were scarcely able to understand [his] speech" (v. 93). They urged him to build a rampart (*saddan*) between themselves and Gog and Magog, who were despoiling the land. The final portion of the narrative describes how Dhū 'l-Qarnayn complied with the request and with God's help built a wall (*radman*) against the marauders (vv. 95–98). The final verses invoke the familiar qur'ānic warning of the end-time, concluding with a remark that resumes the mention of the "memory" (*dhikr*) of the "Two-Horned One" that the Speaker had initially bidden the Messenger to recount to his in-

17. See especially H. J. Gleixner, "Das Alexanderbild der Byzantiner" (Ph.D. diss., University of Munich, 1961); Stephen Gero, "The Alexander Legend in Byzantium: Some Literary Gleanings," *Dumbarton Oaks Papers* 46 (1992): 83–87.

18. See the detailed analysis by Kevin van Bladel, "The *Alexander Legend* in the Qur'ān 18:83–102," in Reynolds, *The Qur'ān in Its Historical Context*, 175–203. See also pertinent, parallel passages in English translation in Reynolds, *The Qur'ān and the Bible*, 467–471.

terlocutors. Proposing to leave Gehenna wide open on "that day" for the unbelievers, the Speaker describes them as "those whose eyes were in the dark about My memory (*ʿan dhikrī*) and they were unable to hear" (v. 101).

Unlike Sūrat al-Kahf's reminiscence of the story of the "Companions of the Cave," which for the most part is phrased in a readily recognizable qurʾānic idiom, there is only a scant echo in the recollection of Dhū 'l-Qarnayn's exploits of the Qurʾān's typical language of prophetism and messengership, save for the wording of his promise to punish the wrongdoers and reward the believers who do good deeds among those whom he came upon in his journey, who were living by the muddy spring at the place of the sun's setting (vv. 87–88). Rather, the emphasis in the narrative is only briefly on Dhū 'l-Qarnayn's journeys west and east and the peoples he encounters there, and more pointedly on the episode of his building the wall against the incursions of Gog and Magog in the mountainous region where he finds people who did not readily understand his speech (vv. 93–101). This narrative sequence of the Two-Horned One's journeys to the ends of the earth and of his building the wall against Gog and Magog is the feature of Sūrat al-Kahf's reminiscence of Dhū 'l-Qarnayn that for most scholars, strongly, if succinctly, mirrors in outline and narrative sequence the telling of the story of Alexander the Great's exploits as it circulated in writing among the Syriac-speaking Christians of the Qurʾān's late antique origins. As scholars have pointed out, this narrative sequence is particularly evident in the prose texts of the Syriac "Legend of Alexander" and in the so-called Syriac *Alexanderlied*, composed on the model of a Syriac *mēmrā* written in the style of the above-mentioned Jacob of Sarug.[19] Tommaso Tesei suc-

19. For recent scholarly discussions of the late antique narratives of the legend of Alexander the Great and the congruence between the Qurʾān's narrative and that found in contemporary Syriac texts, see, Stephen Gero, "The Legend of Alexander the Great in the Christian Orient," *Bulletin of the John Rylands University Library of Manchester* 75 (1993): 3–9; see in particular: G. J. Reinink, *Das syrische Alexanderlied: Die drei Rezensionen*, CSCO vols. 454 and 455 (Louvain: Peeters, 1983); idem, "Die Entstehung der syrischen Alexanderlegende als politisch-religiöse Propagandaschrift für Herakleios' Kirkenpolitik," in C. Laga, J. A. Munitiz, and L. van Rompai (eds.), *After Chalcedon: Studies in Theology and Church History Offered to Professor Albert van Roey for his Seventieth Birthday* (Leuven: Peeters, 1985), 263–281; idem, "Alexander the Great in Seventh-Century Syriac 'Apocalyptic' Texts," *Byzantinorossica* 2 (2003), 150–178; Kevin van Bladel, "The Syriac Sources of the Early Arabic Narratives of Alexander," in H. P. Ray and D. T. Potts (eds.), *Memory as History: The Legacy of Alexander in Asia* (New Delhi: Aryan Books International, 2007), 54–75; idem, "The *Alexander Legend* in the Qur'ān 18:83–102"; Tesei, "The Prophecy of Ḏū-l-Qarnayn (Q 18:83–102) and the Origins of the Qur'ānic Corpus"; Koloska, *Of-*

cinctly states the conclusion: "Not only [do] the two Syriac sources and the Qur'ānic pericope evocate the same stories, but they also share the order in which previous traditions are organized in the narration. It is also noticeable that the three sources reflect how previous materials have been reworked."[20] They are re-worked to reflect the concerns of their authors and just as in the two Syriac texts, this is clearly also the case with the Speaker's reminiscence of the story in the Qur'ān, as we shall see.

The coincidence of storyline and narrative details has made it evident to most commentators, both ancient and modern, that the Qur'ān's Dhū 'l-Qarnayn, the "Two-Horned One," is indeed none other than Alexander the Great, Late Antiquity's religiously appropriated, imperial hero par excellence. As Kevin van Bladel has put it, "The details of the Arabic account are all matched only by this Syriac *Alexander Legend*,"[21] albeit that Alexander is not named in the Qur'ān, nor is the epithet "Two-Horned One" to be found applied to him in the "Legend of Alexander."

While most scholars both early and late, both Muslims and non-Muslims, have concurred with the identification of Dhū 'l-Qarnayn, the "Two-Horned One," as Alexander the Great, there have over the centuries been dissenters from this view.[22] Perhaps the most interesting counter-proposal has been the suggestion tentatively put forward by some Muslim and some Western scholars that the biblical Moses is the "Two-Horned One" envisioned here.[23] After all, the passage concerning Dhū 'l-Qarnayn immediately follows the account of Moses's travels with his servant and with "one of Our servants" in Sūrat al-Kahf, vv. 60–82. The suggestion of Moses as Dhū 'l-Qarnayn was no doubt prompted in the west by the Latin Vulgate translation of Exodus 34:29–30, recording the moment when Moses came down from Mount Sinai having received the tablets of the Law: "Cumque descenderet Moyses de monte Sinai, tenebat duas tabulas testimonii, et ignorabat quod cornuta esset facies sua ex consortio sermonis Domini. Videntes autem Aaron et filii Israel cornutam Moysi faciem, timuerunt prope accedere." The phrase, "cor-

fenbarung, Ästhetik und Koranexegese, 144–159; Archer, *A Place between Two Places*, 142–161.

20. Tesei, "The Prophecy of Ḏū-l-Qarnayn," 277.

21. Van Bladel, "The *Alexander Legend* in the Qur'ān," 181.

22. See the discussion in Koloska, *Offenbarung, Ästhetik und Koranexegese*, 153–159. For a selection of commentaries by Muslim exegetes in English translation, see Brannon M. Wheeler, *Prophets in the Quran: An Introduction to the Quran and Muslim Exegesis* (London: Continuum, 2002), 227–237.

23. See, e.g., Abraham Geiger, *Was hat Muhammed aus dem Judenthume aufgenommen* (Bonn: F. Baaden, 1831), 168.

nuta esset facies sua," a seeming misunderstanding of the original Hebrew on the part of St. Jerome (347–420), was interpreted to mean that Moses's countenance was horned, an understanding shared by the western medieval Jewish commentator, Solomon ben Isaac Rashi (1040–1105), and dramatically portrayed by Michelangelo Buonrotti (1475–1564) in his portraits of Moses in fresco and statue.[24] As tempting as the identification of Moses as the Qur'ān's Dhū 'l-Qarnayn might initially seem to be, the exploits of the "Horned One" described in the Qur'ān's pericope are undoubtedly more in accord with those of Alexander the Great, even if it may be thought in some quarters that the epic hero shares an epithet with the biblical Moses.

An interesting modern example of Islamic exegesis of the Dhū 'l-Qarnayn pericope that challenges the identification with Alexander the Great is the opinion of Muhammad Asad, who in the commentary on his translation of Sūrat al-Kahf makes the following remark.

> It is precisely the Qur'anic stress on his faith in God that makes it impossible to identify Dhu 'l-Qarnayn, as most of the commentators do, with Alexander the Great ... or with one or another of the pre-Islamic, Himyaritic kings of Yemen. All those historic personages were pagans and worshipped a plurality of deities as a matter of course, whereas our Dhu 'l-Qarnayn is depicted as a firm believer in the One God: indeed, it is this aspect of his personality that provides the innermost reason of the Qur'anic allegory. We must, therefore, conclude that the latter has nothing to do with history or even legend, and that its sole purport is a parabolic discourse on faith and ethics, with specific reference to the problem of worldly power ...[25]

While the literary historian will not readily accept Asad's essentially theological interpretation of Dhū 'l-Qarnayn's identity, his exegetical reasoning nevertheless does call attention to an important aspect of qur'ānic interreligious rhetoric to be brought up below, in the discussion of the Qur'ān's counter-discourse to the concurrent narratives circulating among the "Scripture People" that also feature the "Companions of the Cave," of Dhū 'l-Qarnayn, and of Moses's travels with an unnamed companion. More immediately, the question that now calls for attention has to do with the literary and historical relationship between the seventh century Arabic and Syriac texts, the Arabic Qur'ān, the Syriac "Legend of Alexander," and the

24. See Brannon M. Wheeler, *Moses in the Qur'ān and Islamic Exegesis* (Abingdon: RoutledgeCurzon, 2002), esp. 26–34; idem, "Moses," in Andrew Rippin (ed.), *The Blackwell Companion to the Qur'ān* (Oxford: Blackwell, 2006), 248–265.

25. Muhammad Asad, *The Message of the Qur'ān: Translated and Explained* (Gibraltar: Dar al-Andalus, 1980), 452, n. 81.

Syriac *mēmrē* of Jacob of Sarug, in which the congruent accounts of the "Companions of the Cave" and of Dhū 'l-Qarnayn are included.

VI. Dhū 'l-Qarnayn and Alexander the Great: Dating the *Sūrah*

The textual evidence of the Arabic Qur'ān, taken together with the evidence of multiple texts in Syriac circulating in the first third of the seventh century, testify to the currency of the Christian stories of the "Companions of the Cave" and of Dhū 'l-Qarnayn among the Syriac and Arabic-speaking peoples of the Levant in the milieu of the Qur'ān's origins. The Syriac *mēmrē* on the "Youths of Ephesus" composed by Jacob of Sarug, in which the storyline of the account and notable narrative details are, as we have seen, congruent with the Arabic Qur'ān's reminiscence of the "Companions of the Cave and the inscription," circulated widely in the Syriac-speaking, Christian communities, especially the "Jacobites," of the sixth and seventh centuries.[26] Similarly, the Syriac "Legend of Alexander," which was most likely composed around the year 628 CE, and the Syriac *Alexanderlied*, which was composed somewhat subsequently and in response to the political agenda of the "Legend," seems likewise to have circulated widely within the Syriac-speaking communities from the first third of the seventh century onward. As Gerrit Reinink has put it, "[t]he Syriac Alexander Legend and the Syriac Alexander Poem had formulated different responses to the events of the first decades of the seventh century."[27] And here too the storyline and notable narrative details are seen to be congruent with Sūrat al-Kahf's reminiscence of the story of Dhū 'l-Qarnayn.[28] The immediately evident difference between the Syriac narratives and the Arabic Qur'ān's reminiscences of the same stories is that unlike the Syriac narratives, the Qur'ān's reminiscences are more on the order of highly abbreviated references to well-known stories than they are narrative translations of them into another language. In its recollections of the stories, the Qur'ān can be seen simply to put its own construction of meaning on the memory (*dhikr*) of the familiar characters in the narrative, according to its own distinctive hermeneutic of religious significance. It remains, then, briefly to describe this hermeneutic of memory and narrative

26. See Griffith, "Christian Lore and the Arabic Qur'ān," esp. 120–129.

27. Reinink, "Alexander the Great in Seventh-Century Syriac 'Apocalyptic' Texts," 168.

28. See Van Bladel, "The *Alexander Legend* in the Qur'ān," and Tesei, "The Prophecy of Ḏū-l-Qarnayn."

recall, and to explore the relationship, if any, between the Syriac and Arabic texts, circulating simultaneously in the seventh century, in which the tales of the main characters are recollected.

There is no evidence in the Arabic Qurʾān that any portion of either the Syriac story of the "Youths of Ephesus" or the Syriac "Legend of Alexander" and the *Alexanderlied* had been translated from Syriac into Arabic; the narrative idiom in the Arabic scripture is characteristically qurʾānic. Nor is there any evidence of any textual relationship in writing between the Qurʾān and the Syriac texts; the Syriac texts are not as such "sources" for the Qurʾān, nor are they aptly described as textual "influences" on the Arabic Scripture. Rather, they are texts in a non-Arabic language that transmit stories that the Qurʾān recollects orally in its own language. On the face of it, the Qurʾān recalls two stories, which also circulated among contemporary Christians, which in outline and content are known to have circulated in writing in the first third of the seventh century in Syriac. The Qurʾān's contemporaneous reminiscence of them within its own frame of reference is their first appearance in any form in Arabic. As in the case of other instances of the Qurʾān's seemingly eccentric reminiscences of Jewish or Christian lore, the transmission from Syriac or from any other late antique language into Arabic is most likely to have occurred orally and not textually, that is, not in writing. After all, the Qurʾān itself is widely taken to be the first Arabic book.

In the instance of the Qurʾān's reminiscence of the story of Dhū 'l-Qarnayn, as we have seen, scholars have proposed that both the Syriac "Legend of Alexander" and the *Alexanderlied* were first composed in writing only sometime after the year 628 CE. On this basis, some scholars have then concluded that due to the congruence in outline and some narrative detail of the Qurʾān's brief reminiscence of the "Two-Horned One" with the storyline in the much longer and more detailed Syriac texts that the Arabic Qurʾān's reminiscence of the story could only have come about sometime after the year 630 CE. The scholarly reasoning would seem to be that the oral tradition in either Syriac or Arabic could only postdate the first appearance of the narrative in writing in Syriac, in the congruent form in which it is found in the Qurʾān.[29] The problem with this line of reasoning is that from a historiographical perspective and anthropologically speaking the more plausible sequence would have been that the story line and the

29. See in particular the argument put forward in Tommaso Tesei, "The Chronological Problems of the Qur'ān: The Case of the Story of Ḏū l-Qarnayn (Q 18:83–102)," *Rivista degli Studi Orientali Nuova Serie* 84 (2011): 457–464.

major features of such a popular narrative as that of the "Two-Horned One" in Late Antiquity would have first circulated orally and would have only subsequently been incorporated into written compositions intended to play a role in the ongoing political scene in the Levant in the middle years of the seventh century CE.[30] Given this hypothesis, it seems further more likely that such was the case with both the Syriac "Legend of Alexander" and the *Alexanderlied*; their stories most likely circulated orally in broad outline and narrative detail prior to their being composed in writing for any particular political or religious purpose. Their simple storyline featuring Alexander's journeys westward and then eastward, culminating with the barrier against God and Magog,[31] which is at the heart of the Qur'ān's brief reminiscence of the story of Dhū 'l-Qarnayn, would most likely have already have been current orally well before the composition of either of the Syriac texts in writing. In other words, the written compositions more probably made use of an already popular storyline in oral circulation in order to commend the verity of their several political and religious agendas. Therefore, there is no compelling reason to posit the year 630 CE as the necessary date *post quem* for the Qur'ān's reminiscence of the story of the exploits of Alexander the Great. Given the wealth of pre-existing Alexander stories in Late Antiquity, one might more reasonably suppose that the basic storyline that the Qur'ān shares with both the Syriac "Legend of Alexander" and the *Alexanderlied* could just as plausibly have been in circulation orally in both Syriac and Arabic in the "middle Meccan" period of the Qur'ān's origins as at any later time in the seventh century.

According to Islamic tradition and modern historical-critical scholarship as well, in its origins the Qur'ān was primarily an oral composition, even an oral "scripture" (*kitāb*), well before it progressed from "memory" (*dhikr*) to the status of a written "book" (*muṣḥaf*).[32] This oral process of the Qur'ān's

30. Here is not the place to develop this line reasoning in detail. See Walter J. Ong, *Orality and Literacy: The Technologizing of the Word* (Abingdon: Routledge, 2000 [originally published Methuen, 1982]), esp. 136–152. See now the important study by Andrew G. Bannister, *An Oral-Formulaic Study of the Qur'ān* (Lanham: Lexington Books, 2014), who emphasizes the fact that "a new paradigm, an *oral paradigm*, is needed in qur'anic studies" (p. 274).

31. For the record, it is interesting to note in passing that whereas the Qur'ān speaks of Alexander building a "rampart" or "barrier" (*saddan*) (v. 94), or a "wall" (*radman*) (v. 95), the Syriac texts constantly speak rather of a "gate," "door," or "entrance" (*tar'ā*).

32. See in particular the work of Gregor Schoeler, *Écrire et transmettre dans les débuts de l'Islam* (Paris: Presses Universitaires de France, 2002); idem, *The Oral and the Written in Early Islam* (Abingdon: Routledge, 2006); idem, "Writing and Publish-

coming to be makes it methodologically implausible to suppose that the composer of the Qur'ān's text in its origins would have in the process been inclined to consult any pre-existing, written text in any of the non-Arabic, late antique languages available in the milieu of the Arabic-speaking peoples of the seventh century CE. Rather, the evidence of the Qur'ān itself, which does not literally quote any one of the Syriac narratives of the "Youths of Ephesus" or any part of either the "Legend of Alexander" or the *Alexanderlied*, assuming that their stories are already well-known to its Arabic-speaking audience, strongly suggests that the transmission of the stories in Arabic came about orally and not textually. That the Qur'ān recalled the stories in its own idiom and in accord with its own distinctive paradigm of prophetic discourse, in large part meant in this instance that it re-construed the message of the already currently popular and widely known late antique lore of the "Scripture People," circulating in the Arabic-speaking milieu of the Qur'ān's origins.[33]

VII. Retelling Para-Biblical Lore in the Qur'ān

The Qur'ān's earliest reminiscence of distinctly Christian biblical and para-biblical lore comes first in the middle Meccan *sūrah*s, Sūrat al-Kahf and Sūrat Maryam, *sūrah*s that modern structuralist commentators list among those they call "chapter pairs." They note that in the instance of Sūrat al-Kahf and Sūrat Maryam, "at their outer ends they are tied by strong rejection of the Christian claim that God has a son (18:4–5 and 19:88–95)."[34] Within this broader context, the recollection in particular of the "Companions of the Cave" and of the "Two-Horned One" in Sūrat al-Kahf readily remind one of the Christian stories of the "Youths of Ephesus" and of the saga of Alexander the Great, both stories probably circulating orally in Arabic within the

ing: On the Use and Function of Writing in Early Islam," in Gregor Schoeler (ed.), *The Oral and the Written in Early Islam* (Abingdon: Routledge, 2006), 62–86. See too François Déroche, *La transmission écrit du Coran dans les débuts de l'Islam* (Leiden: Brill, 2009); Angelika Neuwirth, "The 'Discovery of Writing' in the Qur'ān: Tracing an Epistemic Revolution in Arab Late Antiquity," *JSAI* 42 (2015): 1–29.

33. On this point see Sidney H. Griffith, "Script, Text, and the Bible in Arabic: The Evidence of the Qur'ān," in the series *Late Antique and Medieval Islamic Near East* (Chicago: The Oriental Institute of the University of Chicago, forthoming)

34. Raymond Farrin, *Structure and Qur'anic Interpretation: A Study of Symmetry and Coherence in Islam's Holy Text* (Ashland: White Cloud Press, 2014), 102. It is important to note that in both cases the word here translated "son" is not *ibn* but *walad*, more properly simply "offspring" or "child."

Qurʾān's purview and circulating in writing in Syriac in *mēmrē* attributed to Jacob of Sarug and in the "Legend of Alexander" and the *Alexanderlied*, respectively. As we have seen, the storylines in both instances, in the Syriac texts and in the Arabic Qurʾān, are broadly congruent, while they are significantly different in narrative detail. The differences record the Qurʾān's re-construal, or re-direction of the meaning, of the two popular stories that it presumes were already familiar to its audience, both of which on the evidence of the Qurʾān itself were no doubt circulating orally in Arabic at the time of the Qurʾān's origins.

In the reminiscence of the story of the "Companions of the Cave," the first obvious difference is in the Qurʾān's initial reference to the story; there is no explicit reference to the "Youths of Ephesus"; there is simply the question addressed to the Messenger, "Do you reckon that the Companions of the Cave and the inscription are marvelous among our signs (*āyāt*)?" In context, the question arises in connection with the Speaker's concern about the Messenger's fretting over the behavior of those in his audience who would, to their peril, not accept what he had been preaching to them (v. 6). The Speaker then recalls for him the time "when the youths (*fityah*) took refuge in the cave" (v. 10). He recalls that they said a prayer, "O Lord, bring us mercy from Your presence and put our affairs aright for us" (v. 10). After briefly telling the Messenger how He had put the youths asleep for a number of years and having then awakened them, the Speaker says that He did this in order to know which of two factions were the best in computing how long the youths remained in the cave (vv. 11–12). The remark highlights the inter-communal, even polemical context of the Speaker's reminiscence of the popular story. He says to the Messenger (vv. 13–14):

> 13 We are going to recount their story to you truthfully. They were youths who believed in their Lord, and We gave them increased guidance.
> 14 They said, "Our Lord, Lord of the heavens and of the earth, we will never call upon any other than Him as a god; otherwise we would say something outrageous."

As the Speaker then evokes a verbal icon of the shifting sun and its shadows along with the disposition of the sleeping youths in the cave, with their dog at the entrance, He says, "That is one of God's signs (*āyāt*). Whomever God guides is rightly guided; whomever He leads astray, you [Messenger] will never find a patron for him, to guide him aright" (v. 17). The Speaker recalls accounts of peoples' reactions to the youths' experiences in an oral style of narrative discourse that readily shifts forms of address, person, and number, and displaces attention from the youths themselves to those who on encountering their situation are said to have reacted in various ways. The Speaker remarks that "those who prevailed in their affair said, 'Let us provide a place of prayer (*masjid*) over them'" (v. 21).[35] The Speaker then turns to recalling the controversy over the number of the companions, plus their dog,[36] as an unknowing and frivolous concern. He abruptly announces that the youths' stay in the cave was for 309 years (v. 25). In closing, the Speaker's instruction to the Messenger is (v. 26): "Say, 'God knows best how long they stayed. His is the mystery of the heavens and the earth; He is the one who best sees and hears. They had no protector apart from Him, and He has not taken any other being as an associate in His governance.'"

One notices that the Speaker recalls the story of the youths in the cave in a familiar, qur'ānic idiom, most obviously perhaps in the notice that the sun's movements relative to the sleeping youths' disposition in the mouth of the cave were among "God's signs (*āyāt*)" (v. 17), a remark that echoes the Speaker's initial question to the Messenger, "Do you reckon that the Companions of the Cave and the inscription are marvelous among Our signs (*āyāt*)?" (v. 9). There is no more revelatory a phenomenon ever mentioned in the Qur'ān than one of God's *āyāt*, which may be a natural event, a miracle, a person or persons, most notably, the careers of God's messengers and prophets, and conversion stories of those who have foresworn polytheism for monotheism, such as Sūrat al-Kahf's reminiscence of the story of the "Companions of the Cave."[37] The Qur'ān's reminiscence of their story is told in a discourse that is counter to that of the story's recollection recorded elsewhere—in this instance most notably in the Syriac accounts of the "Youths of Ephesus." The historical, geographical, and overtly Christian frame of reference, so much a feature of the Syriac tradition, is left out altogether in favor of highlighting recognizably qur'ānic themes.

The same is the case in the Qur'ān's reminiscence of the "Two-Horned One" in Sūrat al-Kahf (vv. 83–101). The Speaker tells the Messenger that people will ask him about Dhū 'l-Qarnayn, and He instructs him to say,

35. This notice seems obviously to counter the Christian account of the construction of a *martyrium*.

36. Only the Qur'ān mentions the dog; the Christian, Syriac account speaks of an angelic "watcher" (*'īrā*) stationed at the cave's entrance. See Griffith, "Christian Lore and the Arabic Qur'ān," 127–128. See George Archer, "The Hellhound of the Qur'ān: A Dog at the Gate of the Underworld," *JQS* 18.3 (2016): 1–33.

37. Non-Muslim scholars in particular have not paid sufficient attention to the overwhelmingly important qur'ānic *theologoumenon* expressed in the designation of a phenomenon as being God's *āyah* (pl. *āyāt*). See Binyamin Abrahamov, "Signs," *EQ*, s.v. (2006).

"I will recount a memory (*dhikr*) of him for you [plural]" (v. 83).[38] And the Speaker goes on to say in the very next verse, "We have made a place for him on the earth and in everything We have given him a way forward" (v. 84). The text then proceeds to recall the three opportunities in particular, which in the Qur'ān's narrative the "Two-Horned One" is said to have followed up on. Significantly, in the verses that come immediately after the account of Dhū 'l-Qarnayn's construction of the barrier against Gog and Magog, just as in the Christian Syriac accounts, the Speaker's thoughts turn to the turmoil of the end-time. His concern is with the trumpet blast that in the qur'ānic view will announce the gathering of all humankind for judgment and with the fate of the unbelievers, "whose eyes are in the dark about My way of remembering (*dhikrī*) and who are unable to hear" (v. 101). The Speaker asks, "Have those who have disbelieved reckoned that they would take My servants instead of Me as patrons? We have prepared Hell as an abode for the unbelievers" (v. 102). His words recall the familiar qur'ānic themes of the one God, of "the Day," of the resurrection and the judgment. His way of remembrance leaves out entirely the Christian, Syriac, typological and apocalyptic vision of Alexander, in both the "Legend of Alexander" and in the *Alexanderlied*, which envision the eschatological return of the kingdom of the Romans, to rule the world from Jerusalem at the second coming of Christ, and replaces it with the Qur'ān's vision of the *yawm al-dīn*. In this way the Qur'ān has almost literally provided what in another context Emran El-Badawi has called a process of "dogmatic re-articulation."[39] It describes the process whereby the Qur'ān systematically re-appropriates, re-writes and re-interprets, or replaces Jewish or Christian expressions of belief that are at variance with its own strict monotheism and its rejection in particular of the Christian Christology of Late Antiquity, which speaks of Jesus of Nazareth as the Son of God.

---

38. To interpret the multifaceted term *dhikr*, to mean a "way of remembering" seems justified in the context. For the variety of its meanings, see Arne A. Ambros, *A Concise Dictionary of Koranic Arabic*, 104; Badawi and Haleem, *Arabic-English Dictionary*, 330–331. Note Asad's translation, "I will convey unto you something by which he ought to be remembered." See Asad, *The Message of the Qur'ān*, 451.

39. See Emran Iqbal El-Badawi, *The Qur'ān and the Aramaic Gospel Traditions* (Abingdon: Routledge, 2014), esp. 5–10. While the present writer rejects the author's application of his methodological concept of "dogmatic re-articulation" to passages allegedly quoted in the Qur'ān from the Gospels in Aramaic, the concept itself nevertheless provides a fruitful hermeneutical principle for understanding the fuller import of the Qur'ān's distinctive reminiscences of scriptural and non-scriptural Jewish and Christian lore. See Sidney H. Griffith, "Review of Emran I. El-Badawi, *The Qur'ān and the Aramaic Gospel Traditions*," *Ilahiyat Studies* 5 (2014): 115–121.

VIII. The Qurʾānic Account of Moses's Journey

Recalling that some scholars have suggested that the epithet Dhū 'l-Qarnayn in Sūrat al-Kahf actually refers to the biblical patriarch Moses and not to Alexander the Great, or, alternatively, that it refers to both of them, we note that scholars have also argued that just a few verses earlier in the same *sūrah*, in verses often taken together as a unit of discourse with the Dhū 'l-Qarnayn pericope, the Qurʾān has seemingly substituted Moses for Alexander the Great in a story that recalls another event in Late Antiquity's widespread lore of the Macedonian king. The passage in Sūrat al-Kahf (vv. 60–64) speaks of a journey that Moses and his servant undertook in search of the place in the world where the two seas meet. When they arrived at a certain point in the journey, at a location called simply "the rock" (*al-ṣakhrah*) in the Qurʾān (v. 63),[40] they realized that they had forgotten a fish they had caught, intended for their meal; the Qurʾān says that it had miraculously escaped back into the sea (vv. 61 and 63). Many scholars have proposed that this snippet of the larger Moses story in Sūrat al-Kahf (vv. 60–82) is in fact a qurʾānic echo of an incident in the widely reported, earlier tale of Alexander the Great, his cook, and a salted fish, which is said to have been mysteriously revived at one point in their journey together, in the waters of the fountain of life, a story repeated, among other late antique literary places, most proximately to the Qurʾān in the aforementioned Syriac *Alexanderlied* attributed to Jacob of Sarug.[41] This narrative echo has in turn reminded scholars of the Alexander tradition's own perceived echo of comparable episodes in the ancient Mesopotamian epic of Gilgamesh, and in the story of a revivified, salted fish in the Babylonian Talmud.[42] The suggestion is that the Speaker in the Qurʾān, as Jacob of Sarug had done earlier, "borrowed" these same motifs, found also in earlier narratives, and for His own reasons integrated them into His narratives of Moses's travels with his

40. Tommaso Tesei has suggested that the "rock" refers to the sacred rock of Jerusalem, the *even shetiyya*, now sheltered under the Dome of the Rock. See Tommaso Tesei, "Some Cosmological Notions from Late Antiquity in Q 18:60–65: The Quran in Light of Its Cultural Context," *JAOS* 135 (2015): 29–31.

41. See Reinink, *Das syrische Alexanderlied*, Syriac text, ll. 170–197 (pp. 46–53).

42. See the discussion in Armand Abel, "Ḏū 'l Qarnayn, Prophète de l'Universalité," *Annuaire de l'Institut de Philologie et d'Histoire Orientales et Slaves* 11 (1951): 5–18; Brannon M. Wheeler, "Moses or Alexander? Early Islamic Exegesis of Qur'ān 18:60–65; Van Bladel, "The Syriac Sources of the Early Arabic Narratives of Alexander," esp., 58–60; Tesei, "Some Cosmological Notions from Late Antiquity," 19–31.

unnamed servant, often identified in later Islamic Qurʾān exegesis as the biblical Joshua, son of Nun.[43]

There are significant hermeneutical problems with scholarly hypotheses that suppose that the story of Moses's journey with his servant to the meeting point of the two waters (*majmaʿ al-baḥrayn*) (v. 60),[44] where the fish they had forgotten along the way is said to have "taken its way into the sea" (vv. 61 and 63), actually constitutes a qurʾānic "reference" to the somewhat similar story of Alexander the Great's journey with his cook to "a spring in which there was living water," which, on his orders, his cook "approached to wash the [dried] fish in the water and it came alive and fled."[45] To speak of a "reference" to, or a "borrowing" on the Qurʾān's part from the story of Alexander, or to suppose that the story of Alexander was somehow a "source" for the Qurʾān's story of Moses's journey to the meeting of the two seas, suggests an intentional authorial or editorial choice to echo, or to draw on motifs from earlier narratives in the process of composing the Qurʾān, almost as if it were a library project, put together in a scholarly study. The problem is not only that the Moses story is not the Alexander story, which it resembles only in its recollection of a common narrative motif, but that the Qurʾān in its origins is not a textual but an oral composition, only latterly edited and set down in writing. That much said, the fact remains that the wide familiarity in Late Antiquity with episodes in the Alexander legend could not but have come to the mind of the Qurʾān's Speaker, who seems to have intended to invest the biblical Moses in the garb not only of the Jewish and Christian, biblical "lawgiver" but also in the corrective guise of a qurʾānic "messenger" and "warner," even a qurʾānic epic hero.

As it happens, Zishan Ahmad Ghaffar has discerned yet another instance of the echo of the Alexander epic in the Qurʾān, in Q al-Naml 27:15–44, in the Qurʾān's recollection of the biblical narrative of Solomon and the Queen of Sheba (1 Kgs 10:1–13). Ghaffar calls attention to narrative elements and motifs also found elsewhere, in Jacob of Sarug's aforementioned *Alexanderlied*, which in Ghaffar's view seem to have given form to the Qurʾān's presentation of the biblical Solomon as a believing ruler in contrast to what he calls the *Herrschergestalt* of the epic ruler, Alexander, presented in the *Alexanderlied*.[46] Not insignificantly, as Ghaffar argues, pseudo-Jacob of Sarug's own purpose in composing the *Alexanderlied* was in all likelihood

43. See, e.g., Muqātil ibn Sulaymān, *Tafsīr*, 2.294.
44. On the significance of the gathering place of the heavenly and earthly bodies of water, see Tesei, "Some Cosmological Notions," 19–29.
45. Reinink, *Das syrische Alexanderlied*, Syriac text, ll. 182–183 (p. 48).
46. See Zishan Ahmad Ghaffar, *Der Koran in seinem religions- und weltgeschichtli-*

to support the political and religious program of the Byzantine Emperor Heraclius (r. 610–641), even creating an "Alexander-Heraclius typology" in the process, as G. J. Reinink had proposed.[47] In other words, at the time of the Qurʾān's origins, the Alexander traditions were already widespread in the late antique intellectual milieu, commending lines of thought clearly critiqued in the Qurʾān, in reminiscences of the locally circulating, popular, and familiar stories.

It is interesting to note that following the story in Sūrat al-Kahf of Moses's journey to the meeting of the two seas in the company of his servant and the episode of the dried fish, which is reminiscent of an event also recounted in the late antique Alexander legend (vv. 60–64), the *sūrah* proceeds with an account of Moses's journey with "one of Our Servants" (v. 65), whom Moses begs to accompany. The interesting thing here is that just as in Dhū 'l-Qarnayn's qurʾānic journey (vv. 83–101), the preceding, non-canonical account of Moses's journey with "one of Our Servants" (vv. 65–82) similarly features three stages,[48] which recount three learning moments for Moses, along with the Qurʾān's interpretation of each moment (vv. 78–82). In the Qurʾān's account of Moses's travels with "one of Our Servants," unlike that of Dhū 'l-Qarnayn's three-stage journey, Moses is presented as the disciple, not the master. While scholars have not so far found any scriptural or traditional accounts of Moses's adventures with "one of Our Servants" in any late antique Jewish or Christian telling, the Qurʾān's account does accent Moses's humanity in accord with qurʾānic prophetology, thereby seemingly countering any tendency there might have been among the contemporary "Scripture People" or others to elevate Moses's stature beyond the merely human.[49] In the end, broadly speaking, it seems not unreasonable to suppose that the very popular legend of the epic hero

---

chen Kontext: Eschatologie und Apokalyptik in den mittelmekkanischen Suren (Leiden: Ferdinand Schöningh, 2019), 75–110.

47. See the article cited above by G. J. Reinink, "Die Entstehung der syrischen Alexanderlegende als politisch-religiöse Propagandaschrift für Herakleios' Kirchenpolitik," esp. 280.

48. Marianna Klar makes this connection in a private communication and calls attention to the repetition of vocabulary in the two narratives. See her article, "Qurʾānic Exempla and Late Antique Narratives," in Mustafa Shah and Muhammad Abdel Haleem (eds.), *The Oxford Handbook of Qur'anic Studies* (Oxford: Oxford University Press), 128–139. See also the remarks of Reyhan Durmaz, "Stories, Saints, and Sanctity between Christianity and Islam in the Middle Ages" (Ph.D. diss., Brown University, 2019), esp. 149–169.

49. Here following ideas discussed by Patricia Crone, "Angels versus Humans as Messengers of God: The View of the Qurʾānic Pagans," in Philippa Townsend and

Alexander in its broad outlines of travel, suggested the narrative framework for the Qur'ān's counter-narrative of both the travels of Moses and Dhū 'l-Qarnayn, in both instances emphasizing their purely human stature and their providential mission, in accord with the requirements of the Qur'ān's own "*sunnah* of Our Messengers."

But a question has arisen in recent scholarship about the identity of the Mūsā whose story is recounted in Sūrat al-Kahf, vv. 60–82. Is he meant to be the biblical patriarch Mūsā or another, otherwise now unrecognized Mūsā, whose story was nevertheless well enough known in the late antique milieu of the Qur'ān's origins to be distinctly familiar to the Arabic scripture's original audience? Recalling the fact that in this *sūrah*, the Speaker effectively presents Mūsā as the befuddled disciple of "one of Our servants, to whom We had given a mercy from Us and taught him knowledge from Us" (v. 65, in the translation of Alan Jones), some scholars have cautioned that this Mūsā should not immediately be assumed to have been the biblical Moses. They reason that since his servile behavior and obsequious manner described here is unlike that described in the traditional lore of the biblical figure, his name might rather have been meant to be taken in this instance as a code name for someone else. He who is called Moses in this passage, these scholars suggest, might more aptly be identified as Alexander the Great, who was an ideal political figure from the past whose memory was cherished by the Byzantine emperor Heraclius, the contemporary of Muḥammad. What is more, they argue, nothing of what is recorded about Mūsā in Sūrah 18 actually relates to the familiar, biblical Moses, but it does accord well with the standard, late antique Alexander lore. As for the "one of Our servants" who tutors Mūsā, he might most plausibly be thought to have been an angel, they suggest. Furthermore, these scholars point out that Mūsā is obviously portrayed as inferior in rank to the "servant of God"; he is rebuked by him and he is finally sent away—all of this amounting to conduct unbecoming a biblical or qur'ānic prophet and messenger. Mūsā therefore should reasonably be considered, so the argument goes, a pseudonym or by-name, most plausibly for Alexander the Great / Dhū 'l-Qarnayn, they suggest, the story of whose travels immediately precedes the story of Mūsā in the *sūrah*, and in the text the recollection of the story of Mūsā also structurally mirrors the preceding Alexander narrative, thereby providing an immediate point of reference for the Mūsā pericope

Moulie Vidas (eds.), *Revelation, Literature, and Community in Late Antiquity* (Tübingen: Mohr Siebeck, 2011), 315–336.

in Q 18.[50] But why would this not totally implausible exegesis be the case? Why would the Qurʾān want to invest the biblical figure, or his namesake, in the likeness of Alexander? Why would the Qurʾān seemingly invent an otherwise unknown Moses, or subtly accord Alexander the Great the name of a well-known Prophet and Messenger of God?

Contrary to the Mūsā = Alexander hypothesis, it seems unlikely on the face of it to the present writer that the Mūsā named in v. 60 of Sūrat al-Kahf would be anyone other than the well-known biblical patriarch, named some 135 times elsewhere in the Qurʾān. Just because there is no counterpart or precedent for what is said of Mūsā in the present pericope in any known contemporary or earlier Jewish or Christian "source" or "subtext" does not of itself preclude his identity here as the biblical patriarch. Nor does the fact that the storyline seems to feature behavior unbefitting for one of the Qurʾān's most prominent messengers of God mean that he could not be the prophet Moses, with the Qurʾān having its own reasons for relating his early experience as a disciple of an unexpected master here. Why could it not be the case that the Qurʾān, being a self-proclaimed inspired scripture, has here disclosed a hitherto unknown revelation about the early career of the biblical Moses, before the beginning of his apostolic mission, together with his brother Aaron, to Pharaoh in Egypt and what follows thereafter in the earlier scriptural narratives? The newly revealed episode, in which Moses is putatively tutored by an angel, "one of Our servants," might then plausibly be interpreted to have been intended as a preparatory teaching moment, a prolegomenon to the account of his eventual commission as one of God's most prominent prophets and messengers. One might well imagine that the encounter happened in the course of Moses's biblically well-known sojourn to Midian and his wanderings there before his prophetic "call" (Exod 2:15–25). It was there too that "an angel of the Lord appeared to him in fire flaming out of a bush" (Exod 3:2; cf. Q al-Qaṣaṣ 28:29–30). The inclusion of the recognizable "echo" of Alexander lore in the telling of the story in Q 18:60–64, the journey to where the waters meet and the episode of the escaped fish, could then be understood most readily as the Qurʾān's use of narrative motifs already familiar in the immediate cultural lore of its origins, namely, the motif of the journey experiences of heroes from Gilgamesh to Alexander. From this point of view, this narrative could more likely be characterized as a qurʾānic *praeparatio prophetica* for Moses's

50. See this line of reasoning adumbrated in Ghaffar, *Der Koran in seinem religions- und weltgeschichtlichen Kontext.* See also the studies by Angelika Neuwirth and Dirk Hartwig, "Mūsā und sein Bursche," and "Mūsā und der Gottesdiener," in their forthcoming commentary on Sūrat al-Kahf.

scriptural mission, not unlike the role of the Qur'ān's non-biblical narrative of Abraham's engagement with his father in preparation for his mission as God's prophet and messenger (Q al-Anʿām 6:74–87).

To paraphrase what Andrew Bannister has said about his analysis of another qur'ānic theme—namely, the seven qur'ānic tellings of the Adam/Iblīs story, one of which actually comes in Sūrat al-Kahf (vv. 45–59)[51]—it is clear that the Qur'ān "does not simply lift," as Bannister says, the tale of the "Youths of Ephesus," or the story of Moses's travels, or those of Dhū 'l-Qarnayn and Alexander the Great's adventures, "verbatim" from pre-existing, late antique traditions that predate the Qur'ān's recollections of them. Rather, one might say that the Qur'ān's Speaker fishes from a "common pool of oral tradition," "shaping" the well-known stories found there for His own purposes, with the result that each of the accounts is as qur'ānic as it once was biblical, para-biblical, hagiographical, or epical.[52] The "common pool of oral tradition" of which Bannister speaks includes a collection of narrative motifs and modes of expression, common in the late antique religious narratives, which the Qur'ān had within its purview at its origins. It recollects earlier stories only in the terms of its own distinctive narrative idiom, thereby investing the popular lore with its own interpretive construction of meaning. The Qur'ān sets aright what it regards as wrong or misleading understandings of tradition by others within its milieu. The traditional stories would have furnished the only narrative idiom readily available to the Speaker of the oral Qur'ān, who chose to promulgate a distinctive message of warning and proclamation to the Arabic-speaking peoples in the first third of the seventh century CE.

In the case of the Moses pericope in Sūrat al-Kahf, scholars have noticed, as explained above, that the elements of the Alexander Legend recollected in the *sūrah* reflect narrative patterns of the legend also found in near-contemporary compositions in Syriac attributed to Jacob of Sarug. It has been argued in particular that the Syriac *Alexanderlied* attributed to Jacob reflects the contemporary use of the legend in support of the religio-political agenda of the Byzantine emperor Heraclius, whose reign was coeval with the years of the Qur'ān's origins.[53] The contemporary political relevance of the Alexander Legend suggests to some scholars in turn that the prom-

---

51. See Tommaso Tesei, "The Fall of Iblīs and its Enochic Background," in T. Kadari, V. Tohar, M. Poorthuis, and A. Houtman (eds.), *Stories and Traditions in Transformation* (Leiden: Brill, 2016), 66–81; Marianna Klar, "An Exploration of the Qur'anic Fall of Iblīs in the Wider Context of *Sūrat al Kahf*," unpublished typescript.

52. Bannister, *The Oral-Formulaic Study of the Qur'an*, 271.

53. See the references in n. 19 above.

inence of Alexander motifs in the Moses pericope in Sūrat al-Kahf reflects the Qur'ān's own awareness of the political situation in the Romano-Persian milieu of its origins.[54] While this is a plausible historical interpretation, it is unclear why it would also plausibly suggest that there must have been a Mūsā other than the biblical Moses as the recipient of the tutelage of "one of Our Servants" in the narrative. Rather, the Qur'ān employs the Alexander motifs in order to highlight the epic stature of God's Messenger Moses in contemporary terms as leader of the people on their journey out of servitude, recipient of the Torah, and hero on the order of both Alexander of old and perhaps even the emperor Heraclius.

IX. Concluding Remarks

Sūrat al-Kahf, together with its companion, Sūrat Maryam, is noticeably distinctive in that already in the middle Meccan period it calls the attention of the Arabic Qur'ān's original audience to recognizably Jewish and Christian themes, recalling popular biblical, para-biblical, and hagiographical narratives and recasting them in notably qur'ānic terms that reflect in particular the Arabic scripture's signature idiom of prophecy and messengership. Whereas Sūrat Maryam deftly weaves its reminiscences of the Gospel narratives of Zachary, John the Baptist, Jesus and his mother Mary, as they circulated in the Christian lore of Late Antiquity, into the Qur'ān's distinctive, interpretive, narrative framework of the sequence of God's messengers and prophets, Sūrat al-Kahf recalls the non-scriptural stories of three sets of persons whose renown was widespread among late antique Scripture People, and presents them as distinctly qur'ānic personae. Interestingly, with the exception of Moses, no personal names are given in the *sūrah*. We hear the story of the "Companions of the Cave," the "youths who believed in their Lord" (vv. 10 and 13); they are not called the "Youths of Ephesus," as in Christian tradition, nor are their names mentioned, as they are in Christian and later Islamic traditions. We hear the story of "two men" and their God-given gardens (v. 32), but there is no hint of a textual echo of the Gospel parables, which modern scholars are reminded of. We hear a non-biblical story of Moses and of his journey to the meeting of the two seas, like Alexander the Great after him, during which a presumably dead fish escapes alive into the water (vv. 60–64). As we have seen, it reminds modern scholars of a similar story told in the late antique lore of the Macedonian king, but there is no hint in the telling of a textual relationship

54. See the references in n. 50 above.

between the stories. Then there is the story of Moses's travels with "one of Our servants" (vv. 65–82), which some modern scholars again want to connect with the lore of Alexander the Great,[55] albeit that there is no evident textual relationship between the two stories, nor is there any mention of al-Khiḍr, whom later Islamic tradition identifies as the "servant of God" accompanied by Moses. Finally, we hear the story of the "Two-Horned One," which is plausibly seen as a reminiscence of the travels and exploits of Alexander the Great, but again, without mention of his name.

What the reader of the popular stories reminisced in Sūrat al-Kahf does readily notice is that none of the dramatis personae, with the exception of Moses, is known as a messenger or prophet in the Qur᾽ān, albeit that the language of the *sūrah* is replete with the repetitive, even formulaic vocabulary of the Qur᾽ān's distinctive "prophetology," terms such as "scripture" (*al-kitāb*), "warning" (verb: *andhara*), "announcing" (verb: *bashshara*), "We will tell you their story" (*naḥnu naquṣṣu ʿalayka naba'ahum*), "remembrance" (*dhikrā*), "God's signs" (*āyāt allāh*), and more. In the central framing passage there is even the following verse: "We do not dispatch messengers except as warners and announcers; they also debate with those who falsely disbelieve, thereby weakening the truth and taking My signs and what I put forth in warning as a mockery" (v. 56). Clearly, the Qur᾽ān intends that the aura of prophetism and messengership should hover over the "believing youths," "Our servant," and Dhū 'l-Qarnayn, even if they are not scriptural personalities. Perhaps the purpose was on the one hand to divest the recollection of these well-known personae of their Christian associations, the better to commend the qur᾽ānic message, and, on the other hand, to demythologize, as it were, tales that might otherwise, in the Qur᾽ān's estimation, readily invite infidel magical or ritual observances, such as reverence for martyrs' bones in the case of the "Companions of the Cave," or the virtual deification of the hero Alexander the Great in the story of the "Two-Horned One."

When all is said and done, it has become clear that the narratives of the "Companions of the Cave," of Moses's travels, and of Dhū 'l-Qarnayn in Sūrat al-Kahf can only be passably well understood relative to their places within the *sūrah*'s overall rhetorical design. It is furthermore also the case that for hermeneutical reasons, the message of Sūrat al-Kahf is itself best understood when it is read as a sequel to that of its companion, Sūrat Maryam, which precedes it according to both the Nöldeke and Egyptian chronologies of the *sūrah*s, albeit that their order in the canonical *muṣḥaf* is the reverse. Together the two *sūrah*s present the Qur᾽ān's Meccan, correc-

55. See Reynolds, *The Qur'ān and the Bible*, 465.

tive response to the popular kerygma of Christianity in the Arabic-speaking milieu of its origins. In its Medinan phase, the Qurʾān turns its attention more polemically to the rebuttal of the doctrinal and practical claims of those among the "Israelites" (*banī isrā'il*) whom it now calls "Jews" and "Nazarenes" (*an-naṣārā*).[56]

56. See in this connection, Sidney H. Griffith, "*Al-Naṣārā* in the Qur'ān: A Hermeneutical Reflection"; idem, "The Qur'ān's 'Nazarenes' and Other Late Antique Christians."

JIQSA 6 (2021): 167–224

THE TWO SONS OF ADAM: RABBINIC RESONANCES AND SCRIPTURAL VIRTUOSITY IN SŪRAT AL-MĀʾIDAH*

MICHAEL PREGILL
Chapman University, USA

Abstract

The qurʾānic Cain and Abel narrative in Q Māʾidah 5, which features a well-known ethical maxim about the value of human life, exhibits a conspicuous connection to a Jewish precursor. As has been observed since the time of Abraham Geiger, the coincidence of the narrative and the maxim in Mishnah tractate Sanhedrin and its parallels in classical rabbinic literature appears to demonstrate the Qurʾān's direct dependence on a Jewish source. In this article, I will pursue a more nuanced approach to the relationship between Sūrat al-Māʾidah and rabbinic tradition. On the one hand, I will propose a new interpretation of the famous motif of the raven that Cain imitated in burying his brother, which has persistently—but incorrectly—been understood to be drawn from a midrashic precursor. On the other, I will show that Sūrat al-Māʾidah does not intersect with tractate Sanhedrin solely at the point of this individual tradition; rather, investigation of the larger context of both the qurʾānic passage and the apparent source of the Jewish maxim in the Mishnah indicates that the two are linked through a much larger web of intertwined textual allusions. This coincidence possibly has implications for our understanding of the circumstances of the *sūrah*'s revelation as well as of the Jewish presence in the Medinan milieu, especially on the basis of the Qurʾān's legitimation of violence in response to the alleged Jewish crime of spreading corruption in the land (*fasād fī ʾl-arḍ*).

Over the last decade, research into the literary and religious background to the Qurʾān has shifted strongly towards a focus on Eastern Christian scriptural and parascriptural traditions, reviving the pioneering work on Syriac comparanda by scholars such as Tor Andræ and Alphonse Mingana over a century ago.[1] This trend stands in sharp contrast to the emphasis on Jewish

* I presented early discussions of some of the material in this article in two conference papers, one at the panel "Prophets and Prophethood between Bible and Quran"

doi: http://dx.doi.org/10.5913/jiqsa.6.2021.a006

precursors and parallels that formerly prevailed among those inclined to investigate the late antique sources of the Qurʾān, an approach that dominated the field from the time of Abraham Geiger's germinal work in the 1830s until the emergence of major debates over method in the 1970s and 1980s.[2] As Devin Stewart has noted regarding what we might call the "Syriac turn" in the field, although the arguments of those whom he dubs the "New Biblicists" tend to be subtler and more refined than those of their predecessors who focused on Jewish comparanda, those arguments are functionally quite similar to those of older scholarship rather than representing a wholly new approach.[3] Nevertheless, a conspicuous difference marking contemporary arguments is that most scholars working today strive to avoid the wild reductionism of the past, especially what I have elsewhere termed the "influence paradigm" that was once pervasive in work on the Qurʾān and Islamic origins.[4]

Judging by current trends in scholarship, it might seem somewhat retrograde to attempt to revisit Geiger's claim that the qurʾānic corpus was strongly informed by dialogue with Jewish informants, or predominantly shaped in a Jewish matrix. However, despite the enormous contribution that scholars working on Syriac Christian parallels to the Qurʾān have made to the field in recent years, the basic phenomenon Geiger observed in the Qurʾān cannot be denied. We certainly cannot endorse a return to Geiger's methodology, in which Muḥammad's Jewish companions and informants are presented as the main vectors of "influence" upon him; nor should we revert to a perspective that reduces the Qurʾān's engagement with older

---

at the Society of Biblical Literature International Meeting at the University of St. Andrews in 2013 and another at the panel "Violence and Belief in the Qur'anic Milieu" at the International Qur'anic Studies Association Annual Meeting in Atlanta in 2015. I thank the panel attendees and my fellow presenters for their insightful questions and comments.

1. For concise overviews of the issues, see Emran Elbadawi [*sic*], "The Impact of Aramaic (Especially Syriac) on the Qurʾān," *RC* 8 (2014): 220–228 and Devin Stewart, "Reflections on the State of the Art in Western Qurʾanic Studies," in Carol Bakhos and Michael Cook (eds.), *Islam and Its Past: Jahiliyya, Late Antiquity, and the Qur'an* (Oxford: Oxford University Press, 2017), 4–68, 20–28.

2. For Geiger's understanding of the origins of the Qurʾān and Muḥammad's attitude towards the Jews and the scriptural knowledge he received from them, see *Judaism and Islám: A Prize Essay*, trans. F. M. Young (Madras: M.D.C.S.P.C.K. Press, 1898), 4–17.

3. Stewart, "Reflections on the State of the Art," 23.

4. See my "The Hebrew Bible and the Quran: The Problem of the Jewish 'Influence' on Islam," *RC* 1 (2007): 643–659.

scriptural and parascriptural tradition to a dynamic of passive reception and half-garbled regurgitation. But it is abundantly clear that at least some passages of the Qur'ān demonstrate a close relationship with specific precursors drawn from rabbinic literature, and that relationship may reasonably be construed as reflecting the direct impact of rabbinic literary material upon the qur'ānic milieu.

As has long been noted, qur'ānic discourse appears to have been shaped to a significant degree by direct engagement with Jewish interlocutors; although the Qur'ān's engagement with Christians and Christianity is significant as well, qur'ānic material seemingly oriented towards Jews and Judaism is much more prominent in the corpus.[5] Barring some unforeseen discovery of seismic importance for our understanding of the origins of the Qur'ān, uncovering the exact historical processes of transmission and reception that shaped the corpus and led to the genesis of the Islamic community in late antique Arabia will probably remain beyond our reach. However, acknowledging the discernible relationships between textual corpora does not mean that we must blithely indulge the problematic proposition of Geiger and others among the scholarly *salaf* of the Euro-American academic tradition: that rabbinic scholars in Medina simply schooled Muḥammad, who unknowingly wrote down (or struggled to memorize, but often misremembered) what he heard in adapting Jewish teachings for his pagan Arab audience in order to convince them of his prophetic bona fides.

In what follows here, I will present a case study that has perennially attracted much scholarly attention, the qur'ānic account of Cain and Abel, and suggest a different approach to both the interpretation of the tradition and the Qur'ān's broader revelatory context, particularly as it pertains to the question of Jewish "influence" on formative Islam.[6] As has often been acknowledged, the Qur'ān here exhibits a particularly conspicuous connection to a Jewish precursor, insofar as the passage in which the Cain and Abel narrative is found also contains what seems at first glance to be a direct quotation of rabbinic tradition. This is a famous maxim about the value of human life, still frequently quoted today, that is preserved in the

5. This is to say nothing of those passages in the Qur'ān that appear to address both groups together under the rubric of *ahl al-kitāb*, and possibly *banū isrā'īl* as well. For the permutations of these overlapping signifiers and their complex associations, see Michael E. Pregill, "The People of Scripture (*Ahl al-Kitāb*)," in George Archer, Maria M. Dakake, and Daniel A. Madigan (eds.), *The Routledge Companion to the Qur'an* (Abingdon: Routledge, 2021), 121–134.

6. I will refer to the brothers by their biblical names throughout this article, although—like their mother Eve—they are actually anonymous in the Qur'ān.

Mishnah as well as both Talmuds. In contrast to older approaches, I will argue that the Qurʾān does not intersect with rabbinic tradition here solely at the point of this individual tradition. Rather, investigation of the larger context of both the qurʾānic passage in Sūrat al-Māʾidah and the apparent source of the Jewish maxim in the mishnaic tractate Sanhedrin indicates that the two passages are linked through a much larger web of interwoven textual allusions.

Overall, the passage in Sūrat al-Māʾidah in which the Cain and Abel story appears stands in close proximity to a textual precursor that is recognizably rabbinic in origin. It portrays the fratricidal episode from Genesis, read in a very specific way, with a readily identifiable parallel in a major rabbinic text; it then proceeds to adumbrate an ethical maxim, famously paralleled in the same part of that rabbinic text; and finally, it explicitly signals its relationship with the rabbinic precursor in noting a precedent for the maxim in God's previous revelation to the Jews—implying that God is, essentially, just repeating Himself here in the Qurʾān in rehearsing the rule for a new audience.

Scholars have of late tended to see the biblical-parabiblical substrate in qurʾānic discourse as originating through processes of oral diffusion and strategic adaptation—an assimilation and appropriation of shared material circulating in a common cultural milieu, rather than a relationship of "dependence," "borrowing," or the like. However, in the case at hand, a direct connection between the texts seems like the most plausible explanation for their resemblances. It is equally noteworthy that this qurʾānic passage also appears to contain exegetical flourishes of a clear Christian ambience as well; this is more in keeping with those contemporary approaches to the Qurʾān's cultural horizon that favor Syriac precursors, and must be taken into account in considering both the compositional background and intended rhetorical and ideological function of the qurʾānic passage. Finally—a point I will revisit in the conclusion—it is plausible that this appropriation and restructuring should be located in the historical context of the early community's conflict with the Jews of Medina.

Understanding the full reasoning behind Sūrat al-Māʾidah's evocation of a mishnaic intertext—both the Cain and Abel story and the maxim it is cited to explain—demands that we appreciate the very particular way the *sūrah* addresses questions of the Qurʾān's own legitimacy, the primacy of the prophetic community it is bringing into being, and the deficiencies of the rival communities that it seeks to subordinate, delegitimize, and either assimilate or demolish. What sets Sūrat al-Māʾidah apart in the qurʾānic corpus is its particular emphasis on themes of violence and bloodshed in relation to questions of authority, specifically the way it uses the question of the proper, authorized use of punitive violence to draw distinctions between a set of intertwined binaries: the old and the new revelations; legitimate and illegitimate types of bloodshed, particularly those sanctioned or mandated by God and those that are counter to His will; and the community of rightly-guided believers who follow the Qur'ān and the older communities who have misinterpreted their revelations, concealed what they know to be their true significance, and broken their pledges to God. Understanding how qur'ānic arguments were constructed out of not only the narrative traditions but the larger scriptural logics of rival communities to address such situations makes a substantial contribution to our conception of the Qur'ān's originality, reflected in its deft, strategic appropriation and recasting of its scriptural and parascriptural predecessors.

"I Could Not Even Be Like This Raven ...": Jewish and Christian Textual Artifacts in the Qur'ān

Scholars have repeatedly observed the conspicuous points of connection between the Qur'ān's depiction of the fatal encounter between the brothers referred to only as "the two sons of Adam" (Q 5:27) and Jewish tradition.[7] These points of connection have—in keeping with the long-prevalent "influence paradigm" inspired by Geiger—usually been interpreted as signaling the Qur'ān's clear relationship of dependence on midrashic traditions and teachings. As we shall see, this evaluation is only partially correct, and demands much more nuance and precision than have usually been offered in such appraisals.

The core of the qur'ānic story appears in Q 5:27–31:

> 27 Recount to them truthfully the story of the two sons of Adam. When they brought offerings, that of one of them was accepted, but that of the other was

7. See, e.g., Susannah Heschel's trenchant comments on the passage and the impression it made on Geiger and his contemporaries at the beginning of her "The Philological Uncanny: Nineteenth-Century Jewish Readings of the Qur'an," *JQS* 20.3 (2018): 191–211. Classic older treatments of the Qur'ān's presentation of the story are found in Abraham Geiger, *Judaism and Islám*, 80–81; William St. Clair Tisdall, *The Original Sources of the Qur'ân* (London: Society for Promoting Christian Knowledge and New York: E. S. Gorham, 1905), 62–66; and Heinrich Speyer, *Die biblischen Erzählungen im Qoran* (Gräfenhainichen: C. Schultze & Co., 1931, actually published 1937–1939), 84–88. Heribert Busse's 2001 treatment of the episode is not unusual for its focus on later Muslim interpretation of the story rather than that of the Qur'ān itself ("Cain and Abel," *EQ*, s.v., 2001).

> not. The latter said: "Oh, I'm going to kill you!" The other replied: "God only accepts offerings from those who truly fear Him. 28 If you raise your hand against me to kill me, I won't raise my hand against you to kill you. It's only God, the Lord of the Worlds, that I fear! 29 I would rather you bear responsibility for my sins as well as your own, so that you join the inhabitants of the Fire; that is the recompense of wrongdoers."
>
> 30 Despite this, the first brother was still driven to kill the other, and he did so, and thus joined the ranks of the losers. 31 Then God sent a raven to scratch in the ground, to show him how he should cover up the shameful corpse of his brother. He said: "Woe to me! Could I not even be like this raven, to cover up the shameful corpse of my brother?" And he became one of those who regret.[8]

Arguably, as some translators and commentators have recognized, this account is thematically linked to the verses that follow, and so Q 5:27–34 should be read as a single pericope. Conversely, reading the account of the two brothers in isolation from what follows obscures the story's real significance. We will return to this point momentarily.

There have been a number of important contributions to our understanding of aspects of Sūrat al-Māʾidah in recent years. Above all, we must take into account Michel Cuypers's magisterial 2007 study *Le Festin* (published in English in 2009 as *The Banquet*), a thorough structural analysis of the chapter as a whole. The work represents the culmination of Cuypers's extensive research into qurʾānic *sūrah*s as compositional unities over a number of decades, and he makes numerous significant remarks about the Cain and Abel pericope and its place in the chapter.[9] Also noteworthy is a 2011 article by Gabriel Said Reynolds on the culminating episode of the *sūrah*, the descent of the eponymous *māʾidah* (commonly translated as "table," but actually "feast") called down from on high by Jesus for his apostles (vv. 112–115). Many have been content to interpret this scene as an overly literal distortion of the gospel depiction of the Last Supper. In contrast, Reynolds points to the *sūrah*'s engagement of a topos from the Hebrew Bible that seems to have been filtered through a Christian intermediary in Ethiopic, but reoriented in order to communicate an anti-Christian message—essentially appropriating and subverting an older Christian appropriation and subversion of Jewish tradition.[10] This twinned dynamic of appropriation and

8. All translations from primary sources are the author's unless otherwise noted.

9. Michel Cuypers, *The Banquet: A Reading of the Fifth Sura of the Qur'an* (Miami: Convivium Press, 2009). The main discussion of the Cain and Abel pericope appears on 191–219.

10. Gabriel Said Reynolds, "On the Qur'ān's *Māʾida* Passage and the Wanderings of

subversion is especially relevant for understanding how the *sūrah* draws upon older sources on the Cain and Abel story, but ultimately reorients the narrative in the service of a new message.

The aforementioned publications reflect two possible approaches to material in Sūrat al-Māʾidah, mirroring two dominant approaches to the qurʾānic corpus in general. On the one hand, we have a very thorough, sophisticated literature of relatively recent vintage on the compositional structure of the *sūrah* as a whole, epitomized by the monograph of Cuypers.[11] On the other hand, we have a more traditional scholarly literature that has focused on the origins and background of the *sūrah*'s presentations and reinterpretations of well-known biblical episodes and topoi, particularly in the light of its messaging concerning Jews and Christians; the Reynolds piece on the eponymous table (or feast) may be considered an especially productive contribution to this branch of the scholarly literature. Typically, structuralist approaches to qurʾānic *sūrah*s tend very strongly to focus on the text as we have it, avoiding the question of sources in favor of more holistic methods of reading and literary analysis. Conversely, scholars more concerned with precursors and parallels—emphasizing specific traditions as the end-result of particular trajectories of narrative and exegetical development—have usually tended to speculate about the background of an individual story without much regard for the larger context of the *sūrah* in which it is embedded, or the purpose that story might serve in the *sūrah*'s overarching literary design.

However, the Cain and Abel pericope demonstrates that structural-literary analysis and source criticism can and should go hand-in-hand. Investigation of the Qurʾān's methods of engagement with its precursors can be considerably enriched through understanding the internal literary context in which such traditions are embedded. In turn, the attempt to investigate the larger literary design of *sūrah*s can be enriched by understanding how and why the Qurʾān seems to repurpose older traditions. In this connection, it is worth noting that the intertextual resonances of the treatment of Cain and Abel in the chapter represent one of the very few examples in

---

the Israelites," in Carlos A. Segovia and Basil Lourié (eds.), *The Coming of the Comforter: When, Where, and to Whom? Studies on the Rise of Islam in Memory of John Wansbrough* (Piscataway: Gorgias Press, 2011), 91–108.

11. See also Neal Robinson, "Hands Outstretched: Towards a Re-reading of *Sūrat al-Māʾida*," *JQS* 3.1 (2001): 1–19, an important forerunner to the structuralist treatment of Cuypers.

Cuypers's work where he actually ventures to discuss the Qurʾān's use of older source material.[12]

At the outset, we must address one of the most famous, and yet persistently misunderstood, aspects of the story, one that has continually invited speculation concerning the purported Jewish background to the Qurʾān. This is the detail of the raven sent by God "to scratch in the ground, to show [Cain] how he should cover up the shameful corpse of his brother" (v. 31). Traditions that mention a raven—or, for that matter, a *pair* of ravens, or some other bird entirely—in connection with the Cain and Abel episode are found in two major Jewish sources that are roughly contemporary with the Qurʾān, Midrash Tanḥuma and Pirqe de-Rabbi Eliʿezer.

The passage from chapter 21 of Pirqe de-Rabbi Eliʿezer is likely the better-known Jewish version of this story:

> Adam and his helpmate were sitting and weeping and sorrowing (*mitʾabbelîm*) over Abel, and they did not know what to do with his body, for they did not know what burial is. Then they saw a raven, one of its fellow ravens dead by its side. It took its fellow and dug in the earth, then buried the body in the ground before their eyes.[13]

Notably, here the instruction is offered to Adam and Eve, who proceed to follow suit by burying Abel. Moreover, the second raven is here already dead, with the cause of its demise left unknown.

In contrast, the parallel from the Tanḥuma is more explicit, and somewhat more disturbing. In one respect it is closer to the qurʾānic account, in that the episode is more overtly fratricidal; however, oddly, here the birds involved are no longer identified as corvids.

> When Cain slew Abel, his body remained splayed out there on the ground, for Cain did not know what to do with him. Then the Holy One, blessed be He, chose a pair of clean birds and induced one to kill the other. Then it dug in the earth with its talons and buried the body. From this, Cain learned how he should bury Abel.

---

12. Cuypers focuses on Matt 23:33–38, Jesus's famous attack on the Pharisees as a "brood of vipers" who shed the blood of their prophets. He also notes that structural analysis can assist in the recognition and understanding of intertextual allusions (*The Banquet*, 218–219), but sees the repurposing of Jewish intertexts as ultimately less relevant here than the *sūrah*'s extended engagement with Christianity.

13. *Pirke de-Rabbi Elieser*, ed. and trans. Dagmar Börner-Klein (Berlin: De Gruyter, 2004), 233. The word for "mourning," *mitʾabbel*, is suggestive of "Abel" (*hevel*) and perhaps implies that the word was coined in reference to him—since, of course, Abel's was the first death, and Adam and Eve the first bereaved.

The passage concludes by noting that on account of this event, birds killed for food merit having their spilled blood covered over with earth—a token of respect not afforded to unclean animals.[14] Due to the impulse to connect this episode etiologically to the custom of *kissûy ha-dam* or "covering blood," the author of this tradition has specifically designated the birds as pure (*ṭahôr*); this passage from the Tanḥuma thus effaces the connection to ravens entirely, since corvids are halakhically unfit either for consumption or sacrifice.[15]

Geiger cites the Pirqe de-Rabbi Eliʿezer account as the primary influence on the qurʾānic narrative. However, beginning in the first half of the twentieth century, a number of scholars recognized that this account actually dates to the early Islamic period.[16] At this point in the history of scholarship on the narrative, it became fashionable to assert that the Tanḥuma is the source of the account of the qurʾānic raven instead, a claim that persisted in the literature for a number of decades.[17]

Given that the two midrashic versions of the raven story appear in sources that were redacted after the rise of Islam, one might justifiably be skeptical of claims that these traditions furnish the influences upon which the qurʾānic version draws.[18] Even more stupendously anachronistic arguments

---

14. *Midrash Tanḥuma* (Vilna, 1831; repr. Jerusalem: Levin-Epstein, 1964), 10. The details surrounding the covering of the blood of a slain animal are somewhat complex, but Lev 17:13 unambiguously legislates the practice for a beast of the field or a wild bird slain for food.

15. Corvids are established as impure, presumably because they are predatory and carnivorous, in Lev 11:15.

16. Thus Victor Aptowitzer, *Kain und Abel in der Aggada: Der Apokryphen, der Hellenistichen, Christlichen und Mohammedanischen Literatur* (Vienna and Leipzig: Löwit, 1922), 54.

17. This view was popularized by the treatment in the widely cited work of David Sidersky, *Les origines des légendes musulmanes dans le Coran et dans les vies des prophètes* (Paris: Geuthner, 1933), 18; it has recently been revived in the treatment of the episode in Meir Bar-Asher, "Les Judaïsme et le Coran," in Mohammad Ali Amir-Moezzi and Guillaume Dye (eds.), *Le Coran des Historiens* (3 vols.; Paris: Cerf, 2019), 1.293–329, 1.309–310. Bar-Asher's repetition of Sidersky's claim is unsurprising given the conservatism of his approach to the subject.

18. Scholars now commonly recognize that Pirqe de-Rabbi Eliʿezer was redacted after the rise of Islam and cannot be trusted as a source of securely pre-Islamic narrative material. Although the traditional printed version of the Tanḥuma undoubtedly preserves some unique older material, this text was also redacted well after the rise of Islam, and like Pirqe de-Rabbi Eliʿezer, arguably much of its contents bears the stamp of later aggadic developments in direct or indirect response to Muslim tradition. The episode with Cain and the birds is lacking from the so-called Buber

appear in the scholarly literature as well. Thus, in a short notice published in 1981, Hans Peter Rüger acknowledges that the Pirqe de-Rabbi Eliʿezer tradition is only peripherally related to the Sūrat al-Māʾidah story, but then argues that both the Qurʾān and Pirqe de-Rabbi Eliʿezer are here indebted to an ancient Jewish tradition that is no longer extant except as preserved in a medieval witness. Without any obvious justification, he identifies the interpretation of the Cain and Abel episode preserved in the Bible commentary of Jacob ben Asher (known as the Baʿal ha-Ṭurim, d. 1343) as the ultimate source of the versions of both Pirqe de-Rabbi Eliʿezer and the Qurʾān. This hypothesis was refuted some years later by Christfried Böttrich.[19]

In my recent book on the qurʾānic Golden Calf episode—another example of a narrative in the Qurʾān purportedly derived from a Jewish precursor—I have demonstrated that similar claims of dependence have long been predicated on traditions drawn from these works, especially Pirqe de-Rabbi Eliʿezer. However, the relevant narratives preserved in these works likely do not precede the Qurʾān, but rather are modeled on the interpretations of the qurʾānic episode found in early Muslim commentary or *tafsīr*.[20] In the case at hand, one may likewise justifiably be suspicious of claims that the qurʾānic story is based upon these aggadic accounts, let alone a lost midrashic tradition that is now only extant in a demonstrably late source.[21]

Admittedly, the Qurʾān relates the Cain and Abel story in characteristically vague fashion, with much detail seemingly elided; this makes it hard to speak with total confidence about what it includes and what it omits from its possible precursors. However, one cannot help but notice that the

---

recension of the Tanḥuma, which has often been understood as the older version of the work.

19. H. P. Rüger, "Das Begräbnis Abels: Zur Vorlage von Sure 5,31," *Biblische Notizen* 14 (1981): 37–45, 44. Böttrich follows Sidersky in seeing the Tanḥuma narrative as the ultimate source of the qurʾānic raven story (*"Die Vögel des Himmels haben ihn begraben": Überlieferungen zu Abels Bestattung und zur Ätiologie des Grabes* [Göttingen: Vandenhoeck & Ruprecht, 1995], 34–40; cf. 46–50 for his criticism of Rüger's preference for the Jacob ben Asher tradition).

20. See Michael E. Pregill, *The Golden Calf between Bible and Qur'an: Scripture, Polemic, and Exegesis from Late Antiquity to Islam* (Oxford: Oxford University Press, 2020), 303–317.

21. On the propensity for some scholars to point to lost midrashic traditions as the sources of the Qurʾān, see ibid., 297–303; this approach seems to have been particularly fashionable in the early to mid-twentieth century among scholars who recognized the anachronism of many of Geiger's arguments, but who wished to maintain the thesis of a pervasive Jewish influence on the Qurʾān. Rüger's argument appears to be a late example of this tendency.

fundamental point of the story in Sūrah 5 is that Cain was ignorant of how to bury his brother and had to be taught how to do so through God's providential sending of the raven, who scratched at the ground and so indicated through analogy how Cain should dispose of the body of his brother. This depiction is congruous with a motif that is ubiquitous in the Qur'ān: the signs of nature providentially demonstrate essential moral and theological truths (and, apparently, practical lessons for upright behavior) to the perceptive individual who is sensitive to them. This reading of the basic thematic point of the story is underscored by an interesting linguistic element of the Arabic text: v. 31 punningly states that God sends (*baʿatha*) the bird so it can scratch (*yabḥathu*) in the ground and teach Cain what to do.

In contrast, the Jewish parallels noted above seem essentially like secondary elaborations on the basic scenario presented in the Qur'ān. In the qur'ānic account, the bird merely scratches in the dirt, from which Cain is to learn the proper action through inference. Here the solitary bird is not burying anything, and there is certainly no fratricide involved on the part of the animal. The Pirqe de-Rabbi Eliʿezer version appears to reflect the first stage of development of the basic narrative: here it is Adam and Eve who learn the raven's lesson; presumably the identity of the protagonists has been shifted in order to avoid valorizing the murderous, cursed son by depicting his remorse and his engaging in the virtuous act of burial. More importantly, a second, deceased bird has been introduced, making the lesson Adam and Eve were to learn from the corvid more transparent. In the Tanḥuma version, even more changes have been introduced into the basic narrative template: the first bird has now explicitly been made a fratricide, like Cain himself, with God not only teaching him the custom of burial by means of the bird's actions but actually driving the message home for Cain by having its act of killing mirror Cain's exactly. Further, as noted above, the birds in this account are no longer ravens at all; their species is unknown, but they are rendered clean birds rather than corvids so that the story can serve as a prooftext for a halakhic practice.

Overall, it is rather unlikely that the more straightforward narrative of the Qur'ān represents a simplification of either of these midrashic accounts, with two birds reduced to one, or the act of burial (and killing, in the case of the Tanḥuma) becoming a mere scratching in the ground. This is especially the case given that the qur'ānic version is cogent on its own terms, much more so than we would expect to be the case if the narrative elements presented here had been drawn out of an originally much more complex narrative and streamlined. Rather, it is more plausible that the midrashic versions both represent reinterpretations of the more basic script provided in the qur'ānic story.[22] However, the important differences between the Jewish and qur'ānic accounts—and the way in which the former seem to build on the foundation of the latter and not vice versa—have usually been overlooked in scholarship.

More precisely, these midrashic accounts may actually be Hebraizations or Judaizations of the narrative as known from Islamic traditions on the episode that themselves elaborate upon the qur'ānic account. In the Muslim commentary tradition, we see a number of imaginative developments of the qur'ānic story; we may thus readily conclude that these, rather than the Qur'ān itself, are the sources of the late midrashic parallels in Pirqe de-Rabbi Eliʿezer and Midrash Tanḥuma. This is especially likely because we find some of the same narrative developments in commentaries on the qur'ānic account that we observe in the midrashic versions. In particular, in traditions preserved in works of qur'ānic exegesis (*tafsīr*) and collections of "tales of the prophets" (*qiṣaṣ al-anbiyā'*), the single raven often becomes a pair, with one becoming a fratricide just like Cain.[23] As a representative example, we might consider the account in the famous *tafsīr* of al-Bayḍāwī (d. 685/1286):

> "Then God sent a raven to scratch in the ground, to show him how he should cover up the shameful corpse of his brother" (Q 5:31). It is related that when [Cain] killed [his brother], he was perplexed about the situation and didn't know what to do with him, given that this was the first death in human history. So God sent a pair of ravens, and they fought, and one of them killed the other. Then it commenced digging with its beak and talons, and cast the body of the other into the hole it had dug.[24]

---

22. Witztum emphasizes that the raven's activity in the qur'ānic story is limited to digging rather than burial per se, and so similarly concludes that the midrashic accounts typically adduced as the precursors to that version are most likely dependent upon it. See Joseph Witztum, "The Syriac Milieu of the Quran: The Recasting of Biblical Narratives" (Ph.D. diss., Princeton University, 2011), 119–121.

23. For a comprehensive treatment of the understanding of the episode in Islamic tradition, see the classic work of Waltraud Bork-Qaysieh, *Die Geschichte von Kain und Abel (Hābil wa-Qābil) in der sunnitsch-islamischen Überlieferung* (Berlin: Klaus Schwarz Verlag, 1993). Bork-Qaysieh's study is unfortunately limited to Sunnī tradition, but ranges from the classical to the modern period, and encompasses material from a stunningly wide variety of sources. See also the more recent discussion in Robert C. Gregg, *Shared Stories, Rival Tellings: Early Encounters of Jews, Christians, and Muslims* (Oxford: Oxford University Press, 2015), 75–108, a subtle and sensitive consideration of Muslim approaches to the story compared with those found in Jewish and Christian tradition.

24. Nāṣir al-Dīn Abū 'l-Khayr ʿAbd Allāh b. ʿUmar al-Bayḍāwī, *Anwār al-tanzīl al-*

The sight of the raven's act with its companion's body thus triggers Cain's conscience and he undertakes to do likewise with Abel's body.

In approaches to the intersections of midrash and *tafsīr* on this story in the scholarly literature, a conspicuous anachronism once again prevails. Thus, Norman Stillman claims that the qurʾānic version of the story is an "epitome" of that found in the Tanḥuma, while the version found in the *tafsīr* of Bayḍāwī accurately preserves the original aggadic tradition, albeit in Arabic translation.[25] However, it is more likely that the versions of both Bayḍāwī and the Tanḥuma echo an older Muslim precursor that elaborates on the qurʾānic episode rather than hearkening back to some pre-Islamic Jewish precursor that originally informed Sūrat al-Māʾidah.

Overall, the fission of one raven at the scene into two, as well as the depiction of the first bird killing its counterpart just as Cain had, appears to be a post-qurʾānic narrative development, and the traditions from Pirqe de-Rabbi Eliʿezer and the Tanḥuma most likely drew upon Muslim exegesis of the Qurʾān that featured this development. Suffice to say, these Jewish traditions should not be considered potential sources of the qurʾānic story. If we disqualify these late aggadic traditions as the sources of the qurʾānic narrative, however, no single textual precursor presents itself as a wholly credible alternative. In the absence of evidence to the contrary, then, we might conclude that the inclusion of the raven in the retelling of the Cain and Abel story here in Sūrat al-Māʾidah is original to the Qurʾān.

But why a raven specifically? We might conjecture that the qurʾānic author is playing on certain time-honored associations of the raven in order to endow the story with subtle symbolic resonances. The raven seems to have a bad reputation in the folklore of many cultures, probably based upon its

---

maʿrūf bi-Tafsīr al-Bayḍāwī (5 vols.; Beirut: Dār Iḥyāʾ al-Turāth al-ʿArabī, [n.d.]), 2.124, *ad* 5:31. As Witztum notes, occasionally Muslim commentators did recognize the simple, unadorned sense of the qurʾānic reference to the single raven scratching in the ground; see "The Syriac Milieu of the Quran," 119–121, citing the common-sense readings of Abū Muslim al-Iṣfahānī (d. 322/934) and al-Qurṭubī (d. 671/1273), in contrast to the "fanciful" readings of other exegetes, far more prevalent in *tafsīr* and related genres.

25. Norman Stillman, "The Story of Cain and Abel in the Qurʾan and the Muslim Commentators: Some Observations," *JSS* 19 (1974): 231–239, 236–237. For another demonstration of the complex relationship between Pirqe de-Rabbi Eliʿezer, the Tanḥuma, and Muslim tradition, see Michael E. Pregill, "Some Reflections on Borrowing, Influence, and the Entwining of Jewish and Islamic Traditions; or, What an Image of a Calf Might Do," in Majid Daneshgar and Walid A. Saleh (eds.), *Islamic Studies Today: Essays in Honor of Andrew Rippin* (Leiden: Brill, 2016), 164–197, 184–191.

readily observable behavior of predation on smaller birds, especially hatchlings in the nest, as well as its penchant of scavenging in garbage and especially picking at carrion and corpses. In many ancient mythologies, ravens are symbols of desolation and isolation, and even a harbinger of death; as is widely known, in English a congregation of crows, another member of the genus *corvus*, is termed a "murder." In European myth and folklore, ravens may be associated with intelligence and wisdom, as with the famous ravens Huginn and Muninn who attend the Norse god Odin/Wotan, but they may also carry more sinister associations, for example, as the symbol of the Celtic war goddess Morrigan/Mór-Ríoghain. Closer to the cultural ambit of the Qur'ān, the famed British antiquarian Reginald Campbell Thompson noted a number of traditions associating ravens with demonic forces in his classic *The Demons and Evil Spirits of Babylonia*, including some drawn from Arab and Syriac Christian lore, although admittedly (as is common in such encyclopedic treatments of the nineteenth century) the provenance and chronology of Thompson's material is generally vague and uncertain.[26]

However, in the qur'ānic story the raven is not a diabolical presence; there is no hint of a demonic aspect to it here. Rather, the connection to the story of Cain and Abel plays upon an association with desolation and death that is readily inferred as an aspect of the bird's identity in Arab culture, though again it is difficult to establish this for the pre-Islamic period. In Arabic, *ghurāb* seems to be a loanword from Latin *corvus*, but Arab lexicographers derived the term from the root *gh-r-b*, which has a basic meaning of "estrangement"; this perhaps contributed to the bird becoming a symbol of desolation and alienation (a role played by owls in later Persian art and literature).[27] It is not difficult to see how these themes linked the bird to Cain, though we have no evidence that this thematic connection is authentically pre-Islamic; if it were, then we might argue that the association of the raven with Cain would have seemed natural to the Qur'ān's audience.[28]

---

26. R. Campbell Thompson, *The Demons and Evil Spirits of Babylonia*, vol. 1: *Evil Spirits* (London: Luzac, 1903), XLI, L–LI. It seems that demons taking the form of ravens is something of a trope in some Syriac sources, though this appears somewhat remote from our concerns here. Notably, in a well-known case discussed by Sebastian Brock, the early Jewish source Jubilees depicts Mastemah (i.e., Satan) sending ravens to plague Abraham, but in later Syriac versions of this story the ravens are presented as minions of God instead. See Sebastian Brock, "Abraham and the Ravens: A Syriac Counterpart to Jubilees 11–12 and Its Implications," *Journal for the Study of Judaism* 9 (1978): 135–152.

27. Ch. Pellat, "Ghurāb," *EI*², s.v. (1965).

28. Thus Pellat. For an example of the appearance of the raven as sign of the de-

However, there is another possibility. Although the Qurʾān's depiction of Cain's learning how to bury his brother by imitating a raven is likely prior to those Jewish traditions that develop this image, the specific choice of a raven here may allude to genuinely older late antique traditions that depict the raven as cursed. These traditions are not explicitly tied to the episode of the primordial fratricide, but nevertheless suggest a subtle connection between the bird and Cain, who would be cursed by God for killing his brother. David Goldenberg has discussed a number of these traditions in connection with the theme of the raven being cursed in the time of Noah, and this curse then being reflected in the raven's plumage being turned black. In one early tradition, Philo Iudaeus posits that the raven was originally black; Noah's sending the raven away from the Ark is construed allegorically, as a symbol of the necessity of casting evil out of the mind. Thus, the animal's cursed nature is, as it were, inherent, and reflected in its black plumage from the start.[29] However, in the famous *Metamorphoses* of the Roman poet Ovid (an older contemporary of Philo), the raven is originally white and cursed to be black in retribution for its tattling and so bringing the wrath of Apollo upon an unfaithful lover.[30] Philo's precedent notwithstanding, the conception of the raven's acquiring its black plumage (or some other distinctive physical alteration) as a curse would later become quite widespread among authors glossing the biblical story of the flood.

The critical question, naturally, is how widespread this conception was before the rise of Islam. Already in the early centuries of the Common Era a brief reference to Noah blessing the dove and cursing the raven is found in the Mandaean Ginza Rabba, though the content of the curse is not specified.[31] A more substantial description of the cursing of the raven, one that specifically recounts that Noah cursed the originally white bird by making

---

parture of the beloved (and thus symbolic of desolation) in a putatively pre-Islamic poem, see Omar Edaibat's partial translation of the *qaṣīdah* of al-Nābighah in Harry Munt et al., "Arabic and Persian Sources for Pre-Islamic Arabia," in Greg Fisher (ed.), *Arabs and Empires before Islam* (Oxford: Oxford University Press, 2015), 434–500, 481–482.

29. David M. Goldenberg, *The Curse of Ham: Race and Slavery in Early Judaism, Christianity, and Islam* (Princeton, NJ: Princeton University Press, 2003), 51, citing Philo's *Questions on Genesis* 2.35–36. On the biblical and early Jewish depiction of Noah's raven, see also David Marcus, "The Mission of the Raven (Gen. 8:7)," *Journal of the Ancient Near Eastern Society* 29 (2002): 71–80.

30. The story of Coronis (*Metamorphoses* 2.531–632).

31. Goldenberg, *The Curse of Ham*, 287, citing *Ginzā: Der Schatz oder Das Grosse Buch der Mandäer*, ed. and trans. Mark Lidzbarski (Göttingen: Vandenhoeck & Ruprecht and Leipzig: Hinrichs, 1925), 410 (the *Right Ginza*, Book 18 [381, 3]).

it black, is found in a tradition ascribed to Ephrem the Syrian (d. 373). However, this tradition is only preserved in a late source, a unique Leiden manuscript that probably dates to the thirteenth century. The text is a *catena* or commentary on scripture that compiles quotations from various ancient authorities; it is in Arabic, presumably having been translated at some point from Syriac, and was published by Paul de Lagarde over one hundred and fifty years ago.[32]

The pertinent passage in the tradition attributed to Ephrem in the Leiden *catena*, which elaborates upon the scene with Noah and the raven in Gen 8:7, describes how Noah sent the raven forth from the ark to scout out dry land; at that time, the bird's plumage was pure white. Failing to find dry land at first, after a time the raven spotted the remains of animals and people who had been drowned in the deluge floating in the water, and it began feeding on these remains (not an implausible behavior to anyone who has observed the animal's attraction to carrion). Distracted by this unseemly feast, the raven forgot all about its mission. By the time the raven remembered to return to Noah, the waters had already receded from the earth, and when Noah learned how the raven had abandoned its mission, he cursed it to be black as a sign of its impure status among all the birds.[33]

As Goldenberg notes, there is some question of whether this statement is authentically attributable to Ephrem, as with the associated tradition found in the Leiden *catena* that depicts the curse of blackness on Ham and Canaan. None of these statements are found in the extant corpus of works attributed to Ephrem that are generally believed to be genuine.[34] However, it is not unreasonable to conclude that the tradition on the raven represented here may reflect a genuinely pre-Islamic conception. Goldenberg avers that the tradition of the curse of blackness imposed on Ham and his descendants is attested no later than the fourth century CE, though the dating of the text upon which he relies for this, the Samaritan Tibat Marqe, is somewhat problematic.[35] That said, an associated rabbinic tradition attested in multiple

---

32. Scaliger Arab. 230 in the collection of the University of Leiden; published in volume 2 of Paul de Lagarde, *Materialien zur Kritik und Geschichte des Pentateuchs* (2 vols.; Leipzig: Teubner, 1867).

33. De Lagarde, *Materialien*, 2.79. Goldenberg's interest in this tradition in the Leiden *catena* is due to its foreshadowing of the curse of blackness imposed on Ham and his son Canaan for uncovering the nakedness of Noah, depicted later on in the text (2.87).

34. Goldenberg, *The Curse of Ham*, 99–100.

35. Ibid., 100. Here Goldenberg refers to the Tibat Marqe tradition as "one of the earliest" stories about the curse of blackness upon one of Noah's descendants (whether

sources connects Noah's son Ham with the dog and the raven, all of whom were cursed because they engaged in coitus with their partners on the Ark against Noah's wishes. In this case, though, it seems the curse on the raven, like the curse on the dog, pertains to an aspect of its physiology linked to copulation, not to the animal's appearance (as is the case with Ham).[36] Nevertheless, here too the raven is said to be cursed, as in the Ginza.

The Qurʾān does not directly refer to Cain as cursed, of course—although it does note that by killing Abel he became one of the losers, *min al-khāsirīn*, a common qurʾānic phrase that designates someone joining the ranks of the damned on account of some grave sin. But a general perception among late antique communities of the raven as cursed could have suggested an analogy with Cain, with the qurʾānic author capitalizing upon this symbolic resonance by introducing the bird to the narrative of the fratricide. Put another way, the presence of the raven in the qurʾānic story may be a reflex of two originally separate ideas: the raven as a cursed animal and Cain as a cursed man. Neither is explicitly cursed in the Qurʾān, but the conjunction of the raven and Cain in the Sūrat al-Māʾidah story may reflect both of these genuinely pre-Islamic conceptions.

Again, one may reasonably question whether the tradition in the Leiden *catena* is actually pre-Islamic. However, I am not suggesting that this tradition is the direct source of the scene with the raven in the Qurʾān, only that

---

it is Ham, Kush, or Canaan). However, elsewhere in his book Goldenberg notes (following Ben-Ḥayyim, the editor of Tibat Marqe) that the later sections of Tibat Marqe seem to have been reworked extensively in the sixth through ninth centuries, although (again following Ben-Ḥayyim) "these linguistically later texts are likely to contain older concepts and traditions drawn from early sources" (382, under the glossary entry for Marqe). One must admit that although the *floruit* of the Samaritan commentator Marqe himself is dated from the third to the late fourth century CE, the tradition on the curse of blackness in Tibat Marqe cited by Goldenberg here is drawn from a section of the work that appears to represent the later stratum of the Marqe (or pseudo-Marqe) tradition, though Goldenberg fails to acknowledge this. In his later revisiting of the theme of the curse of blackness, Goldenberg once again cites the Tibat Marqe tradition and presents it as plausible evidence of the early (third–fourth century) circulation of the motif, again failing to note the problematic chronology. See David M. Goldenberg, *Black and Slave: The Origins and History of the Curse of Ham* (Berlin: De Gruyter, 2017), 45.

36. Goldenberg, *Black and Slave*, 103, citing y. Taʿan. 1:6, 64d, b. Sanh. 108b, and Tanḥ. (Buber), Noaḥ 12:9 (the parallel tradition at Gen. Rab. 36:7 mentions Ham and the dog, but not the raven). See also Goldenberg's discussion of this rabbinic tradition as it was misunderstood by later commentators and modern scholars alike in *Black and Slave*, 253–256.

the narrative in Sūrat al-Māʾidah reflects a general notion of the raven as a cursed animal that may have been current in the late antique milieu. Positing this motif as part of the more diffuse cultural background to the qurʾānic story is arguably more cogent than claiming that story's direct dependence on Jewish traditions that are evidently posterior to the *tafsīr* tradition, let alone to the Qurʾān.

The possible link between the qurʾānic raven and the Syriac milieu specifically is bolstered by another aspect of the tradition that may have been informed by Christian precursors. In his brief treatment of the story and its interpretation, Stillman, like others before him, correctly discounts the Pirqe de-Rabbi Eliʿezer account as late and so unlikely to be the source of the narrative element of the raven in the Qurʾān. Unfortunately, as already noted, Stillman mistakenly points to the depiction of the episode in Midrash Tanḥuma as the putative source instead.[37] Nevertheless, Stillman was quite prescient in surmising that the amount of Jewish material taken over into the Qurʾān had been exaggerated by scholars, and that there were no doubt significant traces of Eastern Christian literary traditions to be found in the Qurʾān as well. He thus conjectures that the distinctive element of Abel's passivity in the qurʾānic story, with his lack of resistance to Cain strongly underscored (v. 28: "If you raise your hand against me to kill me, I won't raise my hand against you to kill you"), may reflect Christian approaches to the story.[38] In Christian exegesis, Abel is important as a prefiguration or type of Jesus, and while he is not exactly a willing victim here in the qurʾānic story, his refusal to resist violence with violence is certainly reminiscent of the well-known Christian admonition to turn the other cheek.[39]

Stillman was ultimately unable to furnish a Christian prototype for the Qurʾān's depiction of its Christ-like Abel. However, almost forty years later, Joseph Witztum confirmed the ultimate basis of this portrayal in Syriac sources. Witztum's chapter on the Cain and Abel narrative in his 2011 dissertation is perhaps the most important contemporary treatment of the episode; here, he links narrative elements such as Abel's passivity and Cain's

---

37. Stillman, "Some Observations," 236. Thus Cuypers as well (*The Banquet*, 200).
38. Stillman, "Some Observations." This attitude is already anticipated by Geiger, who prefaces his massive discourse on the Jewish material on the Qurʾān by noting that only through a thorough exploration of the Christian sources could one definitively determine that Muḥammad had relied on one tradition and not the other in any particular case (*Judaism and Islám*, 29).
39. On the Christian depiction of Abel as willing victim and protomartyr, see John Byron, *Cain and Abel in Text and Tradition: Jewish and Christian Interpretations of the First Sibling Rivalry* (Leiden: Brill, 2011), esp. 190–196.

wickedness in vv. 27–30 to similar portrayals in such texts as the *Homily on Cain and Abel* by Isaac of Antioch and Symmachus's *Life of Abel.* In these sources, the episode has been rewritten in various ways that clearly seem to anticipate its portrayal in the Qur'ān.

In particular, in contrast to many of the Jewish traditions on the episode in which Cain and Abel engage in disputation, in these late antique Christian versions Cain simply announces his intention to kill Abel and Abel states in turn that he will not resist, though Cain will be damned for his act.[40] As Witztum notes, the qur'ānic account not only resembles these versions thematically but linguistically as well, with verbal roots and other aspects of the phraseology found in the Syriac versions paralleled in the Arabic of the Qur'ān.[41] These aspects of the text make it very likely that the qur'ānic account reflects more than casual familiarity with this Syriac tradition, which is especially noteworthy given that, as we shall demonstrate, that account is mainly shaped by a broader engagement with a rabbinic precursor.

"We Ordained for Israel in Their Scripture": A Shared Mishnaic-Qur'ānic Ethical Maxim

The overwhelming amount of attention scholars have placed on the motif of the raven as evidence of Jewish influence on the Sūrat al-Mā'idah account of the two sons of Adam has often distracted them from investigating the larger significance of the passage in which it appears. If one posits that there is a fundamental coherence to Sūrat al-Mā'idah, or at least important thematic continuities and symmetries undergirding it, then we should try to ascertain how the appropriation and redeployment of older scriptural or parascriptural materials such as we see in the Cain and Abel pericope advance the larger message and agenda of the *sūrah* as a whole. I would sug-

40. A disputation scene between the brothers is found in the Tanḥuma account as well as the roughly contemporary Targum Pseudo-Jonathan, but is not found in the narrative in Pirqe de-Rabbi Eliʿezer. Targum Pseudo-Jonathan and related witnesses to the Palestinian targum tradition exhibit a curious growth of material pertaining to Abel's words to Cain in Gen 4:8; it seems clear that this is a Jewish response to Christian elaborations on the theme that began in Late Antiquity and continued into the medieval period. See the concise discussion of Rimon Kasher, "The Palestinian Targums to Genesis 4:8: A New Approach to an Old Controversy," in Isaac Kalimi and Peter J. Haas (eds.), *Biblical Interpretation in Judaism and Christianity* (New York: T&T Clark, 2006), 33–43.
41. Witztum, "The Syriac Milieu of the Quran," 125–144.

gest that understanding the overarching thematic structure and design of the chapter not only illuminates the meaning of the qurʾānic interpretation of this episode, but allows us to discern something of the specific purpose behind the author's evocation of Jewish and Christian precursors. Arguably, such evocation is deliberate, enhancing the larger message the author wishes to project through a conspicuous display of virtuosity in navigating and synthesizing a specific set of scriptural intertexts.

The next set of verses in the *sūrah* appear to be essential to the larger meaning and function of the Cain and Abel pericope.[42] I would thus suggest that vv. 27–37 constitute a coherent whole, and that the gist of the underlying argument that informs the qurʾānic presentation of Cain and Abel in vv. 27–31 cannot be grasped without considering the following vv. 32–37 as well. From the initial invocation of the story of the two sons to the passage's final exhortation to the believers to strive in the path of God, vv. 27–37 are conceptually united as well as being deeply linked to broader themes in the *sūrah* as a whole.

While v. 32 is well known, and much commented-upon, because it seems to confirm a Jewish background to the pericope, neither it nor the preceding verses on the first homicide should be isolated from the further development of the central themes of the passage in vv. 33–34 following:

> [32] On account of that (*min ajli dhālika*) [i.e., Cain's act], We ordained for Israel in their scripture (*katabnā ʿalā banī isrāʾīl*) that whoever slays a single soul, it is as if he had slain all humanity, except if it is in retaliation for homicide or spreading corruption in the land. And whoever preserves a single soul, it is as if he had preserved all humanity. Our messengers have come to them with clear signs, but even after that, many of them committed excesses in the land.
> [33] The recompense of those who wage war against God and His messenger and spread corruption in the land is that they will be killed, or crucified, or mutilated with alternating hands and feet chopped off, or be exiled from the

42. Scholars have seldom agreed on the exact parameters of the pericope and how the Cain and Abel account relates to the surrounding verses. Many scholars and translators seem to identify 5:27–32 as a discrete passage, seeing the episode of the brothers as ending with the maxim about the slaying or saving of a single soul (cf., e.g., Busse, "Cain and Abel," 1.270; Robinson, "Hands Outstretched"). Cuypers divides v. 32 in half, seeing the clause that begins "Our messengers have come to them ..." as the start of a new section (*The Banquet*, 200–203). At the very least, vv. 33–34 must be recognized as thematically continuous with vv. 27–32, as these two verses represent a crucial addition that helps to illuminate the subtext of the Cain and Abel story.

land. Their lot is humiliation in this world, and a tremendous punishment in the next,
[34] unless they repent before you overpower them. Know that God is forgiving and merciful.

Verses 35–37 then serve as a conclusion to the passage. Here a contrast is drawn between the unbelievers, who are promised an inescapable, terrible punishment in the afterlife, and the believers, who will prosper if they obey the injunction to strive in the path of God (*jāhidū fī sabīlihi*), which here most likely means engaging in violence against the community's opponents.

The principle adumbrated in v. 32—whoever slays or saves a single person, it is as if they had done the same to all humanity—has for many modern commentators provided the linchpin for the argument about Jewish influence on this passage, since a direct parallel to it is found in the Mishnah, the foundation document of rabbinic Judaism, which reached its final form in the early third century CE. There, the maxim is given as "the one who causes a single soul to perish, scripture imputes it to him as if he had caused an entire world to perish, but the one who preserves a single soul, scripture imputes it to him as if he had preserved an entire world."[43]

There has occasionally been some discussion of the fact that this mishnaic maxim is given in divergent forms in the two Talmuds. While the line is attested in the form given here in the Palestinian Talmud, the version in most manuscripts and the standard printed edition of the Babylonian Talmud has a crucial addition, and so specifies that the rule refers to the one who kills or saves a single soul *in Israel*.[44] The question of why what appears

43. M. Sanh. 4:5, emending the standard text slightly to omit what is universally acknowledged to be a later addition (see next note). The maxim is often given in the more famous formulation "whoever saves a single life saves the world entire," or some variation on this; it is also very often decontextualized from its origins in rabbinic tradition, similar to Hillel's statement from Avot, "If not now, when?" (often misattributed to Goethe and so de-judaized completely). By referring to this dictum as a "maxim" or "rule," I attempt to bridge the gap between its presentation in rabbinic tradition, where it is not strictly halakhic, and the Qur'ān, which implies that it is law by using the language of prescription (*kataba ʿalā*, on which see below).
44. Y. Sanh. 4:11, 22b; b. Sanh. 37a. For the Yerushalmi, I have followed the text as represented in *The Jerusalem Talmud, Fourth Order: Neziqin, Tractates Sanhedrin, Makkot, and Horaiot*, ed. and trans. Heinrich W. Guggenheimer (Berlin: De Gruyter, 2010), 164; for the Bavli, I rely on the standard printed edition. Confusingly, most modern printed editions of the Mishnah, as well as very many translations, correct the text to conform to the Bavli, and so the more particularistic statement is commonly believed to be original there (see, e.g., my own mistaken comment in Mehdi

to be a universalizing sentiment seems to have been altered in the Bavli tradition to make it more restricted and particular is significant, though not particularly germane for our concerns here. While some might cite this instance as evidence that the Qurʾān may be closer to Palestinian rabbinic tradition than Babylonian—a logical enough inference even based simply on political geography—even this is not particularly germane for the present argument.[45] For our purposes here, it is immaterial whether the Qurʾān is engaging this rabbinic discourse through the medium of the Mishnah or the Palestinian Talmud (though I will take the former largely for granted). It is the basic fact of such engagement, which appears to be extensive and profound, that I would emphasize here.

There has also been some uncertainty regarding the way the Qurʾān presents its quotation of the Mishnah here, with God stating that He had ordained this principle for Israel in their scripture (*katabnā ʿalā banī isrāʾīl*)—literally, that he had "written" or "prescribed" it for them, which is to say, that He revealed it to them in the Torah.[46] It may at first appear that there is some confusion between the canonical Bible and the Mishnah here, but in Late Antiquity, rabbinic Jews would have considered the Mishnah genuine revelation, communicated orally rather than in writing as the canonical scriptures were. Regarding the seeming slippage in terminology, the most one can say is that there is a certain irony in the Qurʾān here deploying a

---

Azaiez et al. [eds.], *The Qur'an Seminar Commentary* [Berlin: De Gruyter, 2016], 109, and compare the correct evaluation of Holger Zellentin on 110). See the authoritative discussion of E. E. Urbach, "'*Kol ha-meqayyem nefesh aḥat': Gilgûlaw shel nôṣaḥ, tehapûkhôt ṣenzûrah we-ʿesqê madpîsîm*," *Tarbiẕ* 40 (1971): 268–284.

45. Yahuda asserts the Qurʾān's proximity to Palestinian Jewish tradition based on the similarity of the qurʾānic depiction of the conversation between Cain and Abel to that found in Targum Pseudo-Jonathan, getting the chronology of narrative development wrong. See A. S. Yahuda, "A Contribution to Qurʾān and Ḥadīth Interpretation," in S. Löwinger and J. Somogyi (eds.), *Ignace Goldziher Memorial Volume, Part I* (Budapest: Globus Nyomdai Müintézet, 1948), 280–308, 292–293.

46. The phrase *katabnā ʿalā* is also used to note God's prescription of the *lex talionis* in Q 5:45 (echoing Exod 21:23–25 and Lev 24:19–21); and compare Q 2:178, where retaliation is similarly "prescribed" for the believers (*kutiba ʿalaykum*). The quotation of Ps 21:105 in Q 37:29 is marked by *katabnā* as well; there has been some significant scholarly commentary on this verse (see, e.g., Walid Saleh, "The Psalms in the Qur'an and in the Islamic Religious Imagination," in William P. Brown [ed.], *The Oxford Handbook of the Psalms* [Oxford: Oxford University Press, 2014], 281–296). Madigan notes that *kataba ʿalā* carries a general sense of legal obligation or prescription of punishment for a transgression; see Daniel Madigan, *The Qur'ân's Self-Image: Writing and Authority in Islam's Scripture* (Princeton: Princeton University Press, 2001), 108–113.

term that connotes revelation but literally indicates writing when the Mishnah was primarily transmitted through the medium of orality in antiquity—as the Qurʾān itself was when it was first revealed, and for decades after, though it too is *kitāb* in its own self-fashioning and presentation.[47] It is also perhaps significant that the Qurʾān here seems to recognize and enfranchise rabbinic claims about the authority of the oral Torah as genuine revelation.

In any event, what is indisputable is that the Qurʾān presents the institution of the maxim or rule as a direct consequence of Cain's act.[48] Overall, what we have in this pericope is a concatenation of a biblical story (Cain and Abel), a classic rabbinic dictum (the rule about killing), and then narrative flourishes of possibly more contemporary vintage (the raven, Abel depicted as an obedient victim) that have at least remote, and possibly more proximate, Christian roots in particular. One could argue that this simply vindicates a diffusionist model of qurʾānic composition: perhaps it was simply the case that these diverse elements were floating around in the environment when the Qurʾān was revealed, and they were knitted together by the qurʾānic author or editors into the form we now see in Sūrat al-Māʾidah.

However, the Qurʾān's linkage of the Cain and Abel story and the rule about killing is absolutely not coincidental, for the mishnaic passage likewise alludes to the fratricide and uses it as the pretext for adumbrating the rule: "So we have found in the case of Cain, who slew his brother ... therefore was man created alone in the world initially, to teach you that the one who causes a single soul to perish ..." The mishnaic passage also openly invokes scriptural authority for the rule, as it is scripture that imputes blame or assigns credit to one who slays or saves a life.[49] In Geiger's view, the citation of the rule about killing is a *non sequitur* after the depiction of the Cain and Abel story in the qurʾānic passage, and so he concludes that we can only make sense of that passage if we posit the Qurʾān's direct dependence on

---

47. For a classic discussion of early Muslims' awareness of rabbinic claims about the oral Torah, see Michael Cook, "The Opponents of the Writing of Tradition in Early Islam," *Arabica* 44 (1997): 437–523, 498–507.

48. The specific phrase *min ajli dhālika* used in v. 32 ("on account of that ...") is unique in the Qurʾān. As Lane notes, one of the basic meanings of the root *ʾ-j-l* is "to commit a crime"; the infinitive form *ajl* seems to connote causation or consequence, especially a negative one. See Edward William Lane, *An Arabic-English Lexicon* (8 vols.; London: Williams and Norgate, 1863–1893), 1.24–25.

49. This, perhaps, is the underlying logic behind the Qurʾān's implication that both Jews and Christians should know the rule; the Bibles of both communities indict Cain for the murder of Abel, so Jews and Christians alike should understand the consequences of unjustified killing.

the Mishnah here. For him, this is irrefutable proof of Muḥammad's reliance on Jewish informants; otherwise the qur'ānic passage is simply incoherent.[50] This position is rather puzzling, not least of all because the underlying logic that unites the two elements in the qur'ānic passage—the depiction of the first murder occasioning a strident condemnation of this crime as equivalent to killing all humanity—is not particularly difficult to discern.

I cannot accept the premise of the qur'ānic passage's incoherence, for its message is entirely cogent both in itself and in the larger context of the *sūrah*.[51] However, I would agree with Geiger that the coincidence between the Qur'ān and the Mishnah here is too much to ignore. If one carefully compares the qur'ānic and mishnaic passages, it is difficult to avoid the conclusion that the former not only presupposes the latter, betraying its familiarity with that textual precursor in several ways, but is engaging in a deliberate rescripting of the rabbinic text.[52] Moreover, consideration of *how* the mishnaic passage is being rescripted, and to what end, may, in the final analysis, allow us to advance a hypothesis about the context in which this passage was composed. While the connection between the maxims of Q 5:32 and m. Sanh. 4:5 has been observed consistently since the time of Geiger, there has been virtually no scholarly interest in examining the larger literary setting in the Mishnah in which the original rule is located and how this might relate to the repurposing of this material in Sūrah 5—that is, discerning the larger textual logics at work both in the Mishnah and in the Qur'ān, especially how each text relates the rule about murder to the primordial fratricide.

50. Geiger, *Judaism and Islám*, 80–81. St. Clair Tisdall makes the same point in *Original Sources*, 65–66, which is unsurprising since he, like Geiger, often emphasizes Muḥammad's confusion and the resulting incoherence of the Qur'ān.

51. For an especially convincing and sensitive reading of the qur'ānic story on its own terms, see John Kaltner, *Ishmael Instructs Isaac: An Introduction to the Qur'an for Bible Readers* (Collegeville: Liturgical Press, 1999), 40–46. Kaltner argues that the Sūrat al-Mā'idah narrative is steeped in irony. On the one hand, Cain needs the bird to instruct him how to dig, although he himself is a tiller, which demonstrates his initial cluelessness, both practical and moral. On the other, Cain's repentance is providential, triggered by his observation of the bird, and although he does come to an awareness of his proper role regarding his brother—contrary to his statement in the biblical original (Gen 4:9), he *is* his brother's keeper after all—in the end, he remains ignorant of God's role in the affair, and thus of his dependence on the Creator.

52. My use of the language of writing here and throughout this article is not meant to foreclose upon the possibility that the reception of older material and the composition of the qur'ānic corpus were oral processes. "Rescripting" may be taken metaphorically, as pointing to a process of oral reformulation.

Considering the larger literary context in which the parallel passages appear in both the Qurʾān and the Mishnah demonstrates that the two passages are linked through a much larger network of intertextual allusions. The overarching theme of tractate Sanhedrin is judgment, in particular the constitution of courts that may administer the law legitimately in accordance with the precepts of Torah. It is certainly relevant to our interests here that the procedures concerning capital cases brought before the Sanhedrin predominate in the tractate, and chapter 4 is entirely concerned with the special considerations such proceedings entail.[53] Thus, the mention of Cain's killing of Abel is prompted here by a reference to the grave admonitions that are to be issued to witnesses in such cases; it is in this context that the Mishnah articulates its famous maxim about the value of human life:

> In capital cases the witness is accountable for the blood of the accused and the blood of the descendants he would have had for all eternity. So we have found in the case of Cain, who slew his brother—as it is written, "The voice of your brother's blood (*dāmîm*) [lit. bloods] cries out to me ..." (Gen 4:10). It says "your brother's bloods" and not "your brother's blood," for it refers to both [Abel's] blood and the blood of his descendants ...
>
> Therefore was man created alone in the world at first, to teach you that the one who causes a single soul to perish, scripture imputes it to him as if he had caused an entire world to perish; the one who preserves a single soul, scripture imputes it to him as if he had preserved an entire world.[54]

The idiomatic reference to the "bloods" of Cain's brother (*dəmê ʾāḥîkā*) crying out to God is glossed as meaning that because God established humanity by creating a single person, when one of Adam's sons killed the other, it was not only the life of Abel himself that demanded retribution. Rather, those of his countless unborn descendants did so as well, for all of their lives—their "bloods"—were extinguished when Abel was slain.[55]

---

53. For our purposes here, it is irrelevant whether the historical Sanhedrin—if there ever really was such an institution, at least as the rabbis imagined it—ever had the power to try capital cases. Beth Berkowitz argues elegantly for a reading of this mishnaic tractate in symbolic and ritualized terms; in her view, as a composition the tractate tells us more about the rabbinic construction of authority than about actual historical circumstances (see *Execution and Invention: Death Penalty Discourse in Early Rabbinic and Christian Cultures* [Oxford: Oxford University Press, 2006], ch. 2).
54. M. Sanh. 4:5.
55. Reuven Firestone is the latest in a series of commentators to point out that whereas the Mishnah here invokes the precedent set by Cain on the basis of the specific phrasing of the Genesis prooftext, that phrasing has no parallel in the Qurʾān

This exegesis then leads to the citation of the maxim: the taking of a single life is like taking the lives of all humanity, while the sparing of one life is comparable to sparing the lives of all. For this reason was humanity created from a single soul, and thus did Cain's murder of his brother cause all his unborn progeny to cry for justice, because one life is tantamount to many lives—perhaps the lives of all beings in the world. Thus, judges and witnesses in capital cases, in which a human life is at stake, must take their responsibilities very seriously indeed.

The passage in the Mishnah goes on to give other reasons for God's creation of humanity through the original (and originally unique) protoplast Adam. Notably, the literature on the qurʾānic parallel seldom if ever takes the continuation of the passage into account, presumably deeming it irrelevant for our understanding of the qurʾānic "reception" of the mishnaic material:

> [Humanity was also created from a single soul] for the sake of maintaining peace among God's creatures, so that one person should not say to his fellow, "My father was greater than yours"; and also so sectarians (*mînîn*) should not say, "There are many powers in heaven." It also teaches God's greatness, for while a man may stamp many coins with one press, they will all come out the same, while the King of All Kings, blessed be He, stamps all people with one press and yet they all come out different. Thus, anyone may justifiably say, "For my sake was the world created."[56]

The subtexts of this passage are complex. The overarching theme is one of equality and singularity: people all have the same origin and are all created equal by God, and so all lives have the same value, the diversity of individuals notwithstanding. But the implied *us* of the passage is of course not a universal humanity, but rather the idealized Jewish subject that rabbinic texts address—or rather construct—as their audience.[57]

While Adam is naturally recognized as the ancestor of all humanity, gentiles and Israel alike, the reference to "sectarians" (*mînîn* or *mînîm*) here indicates that particular sorts of communal concerns are at hand. It is not farfetched to imagine that the lesson communicated here is that one *Jew*

---

or Arabic, making the Qurʾān's dependence on the mishnaic precursor even more conspicuous; see Azaiez et al. (eds.), *The Qur'an Seminar Commentary*, 108.

56. M. Sanh. 4:5 continued.

57. Rabbinic tradition recognizes a concept of gentile moral capacity and accountability, most famously expressed in the idea of the Noachian commandments that the Creator expects all people to observe. Nevertheless, it is highly probable that the rule is here related for the benefit of Jews, not a generic humanity.

should not say to another that he is greater: all members of the flock of Israel are equal, while perhaps implicitly being greater than gentiles. The equality of people may be discerned from their common descent from a single ancestor; in turn, we should also conclude that the Creator is unitary as well from this. However, some, specifically designated as *mînîm* or "sectarians" (whoever such heretics may be, whether Gnostics, Christians, or others) countenance the possibility of multiple divine powers or aspects or hypostases. Ironically, given that the point of the passage is to denounce the communal strife caused by sectarians, the theological speculation of said sectarians is asserted to place them beyond the bounds of belonging to the community of Israel. By denying that unity above, they disrupt unity below, and so must be excluded from it.

The famous utterance attributed to the *mînîm*—namely, that there are "two powers in heaven"—has been widely discussed. In the past, it was understood either to confirm the existence of Gnosticism in first-century Jewish circles as a distinct communal formation, or else to point to an early and normative distinction between Jews and Christians based on dichotomous theologies.[58] In contrast, contemporary scholarship has tended to recognize the invocation of the term *mînîm* as signaling a discursive turn towards issues of communal integrity and identity in rabbinic literary sources, regardless of whether these "sectarians" are conceived as—or actually represent—heretics, Christians, Gnostics, or just straw men.[59]

This is to say that beyond its superficially egalitarian message, this passage is about ethnopolitics and communal boundaries. Embedded in a larger discussion about judicial authority and the legitimacy of punitive violence, we find a subtle and concentrated reflection upon communal stability and the claims that potentially disrupt it. As God is one and creates all as one,

58. The literature debating the meaning of the "two powers" tradition is substantial. For recent contributions, see Adiel Schremer, "Midrash, Theology, and History: Two Powers in Heaven Revisited," *Journal for the Study of Judaism* 39 (2007): 1–25, and compare the introductory comments in Andrei A. Orlov, *The Glory of the Invisible God: Two Powers in Heaven Traditions and Early Christology* (London: T&T Clark, 2019) and the bibliography therein.

59. The rabbinic construction of orthodoxy and the polemic against *mînîm* has been debated extensively; see, e.g., Daniel Boyarin, *Border Lines: The Partition of Judaeo-Christianity* (Philadelphia: University of Pennsylvania Press, 2004); Christine E. Hayes, "The 'Other' in Rabbinic Literature," in Charlotte Elisheva Fonrobert and Martin S. Jaffee (eds.), *The Cambridge Companion to the Talmud and Rabbinic Literature* (Cambridge: Cambridge University Press, 2007), 243–269; and Adiel Schremer, *Brothers Estranged: Heresy, Christianity, and Jewish Identity in Late Antiquity* (Oxford: Oxford University Press, 2010).

people—that is, the people Israel—should also maintain the oneness of God and humanity, and avoid contentious particularist claims that could cause strife, whether it is exalting themselves above others or denying the singularity of the divine creator. If there really is a universalizing sentiment here—with the equality of all humanity writ large at stake—it is hard to reconcile this with the broader implications of the passage, which is quite finely attuned to the familiar communal concerns that often abide in rabbinic sources.[60]

Corruption in the Land: The Primordial Fratricide as Admonition to the Jews

Numerous modern commentators on the Cain and Abel passage in Sūrat al-Māʾidah have concluded that the overarching point of the Qurʾān's reinterpretation of the story is to align its prophet and community with Abel, the righteous victim of aggression, while vilifying their Jewish opponents as latter-day embodiments of Cain. The dual integration of Jewish and Christian subtexts in the passage thus serves the primary agenda of a hermeneutic reorientation of the biblical account.[61] I agree with the fundamentals of this characterization, but would go much further than this. First, it is the

60. Thus, we might conclude that the addition of the Bavli that restricts the application of the rule—"the one who causes a single soul to perish *in Israel*..."—is perhaps not so much changing the valence of an originally universalizing statement as it is merely making explicit a particularist sentiment that was always implicit. This is the view of Urbach, who emphasizes that in the original context in tractate Sanhedrin, the Mishnah is addressing the situation in which Jews are bearing witness against other Jews accused of capital crimes ("'*Kol ha-meqayyem*'," 269).

61. See, e.g., Robinson, who observes the very strong symmetry between vv. 27–31 and 51–53, which establish a vigorous and direct parallel between Cain and the Jews as potentially fratricidal if taken as allies ("Hands Outstretched," 12–13); and compare Witztum, "The Syriac Milieu of the Quran," 145–152, where Cain is understood as a "literary proxy" for the Jews (147). In contrast to the qurʾānic use of these figures, the story of the wicked Cain's aggression against his righteous brother Abel was invoked in discussions of intra-communal violence in early Muslim discourse, and the original context of the qurʾānic allegory was mostly forgotten. As van Ess has demonstrated, some early commentators presented the image of Abel's passive acquiescence as a model for the behavior of upright Muslims during the outbreak of civil war in the community, refusing to fight other Muslims and atoning for their sins through passive acceptance of death at the hands of others. See Josef van Ess, "Unfertige Studien 6: Der Brudermord des Kain aus theologischer Sicht," *Asiatische Studien/Études Asiatiques* 73 (2019): 447–488.

Qurʾān's engagement with the Mishnah in particular that is most significant; as I have already shown, that engagement is rather more profound, extensive, and deliberate than has sometimes been recognized. Moreover, the revisiting and reorientation of mishnaic motifs here is entirely purposeful: the passage not only casts the qurʾānic prophet's Jewish opponents as heirs of Cain, but appropriates and restructures the logic of the larger mishnaic passage to present the claim that the shedding of Jewish blood is licit according to principles adumbrated *in their own scripture*, which Israel recognizes (or should recognize) as the foundation of their law.

This is not to say that the appropriation of Christian narrative currents in this passage is unimportant, or that we should disregard Sūrat al-Māʾidah's particular anti-Christian (or broadly anti-"Israelite," that is, targeting both Jews and Christians) messaging, in which its anti-Jewish rhetoric is embedded. Here, the analysis of Cuypers may be especially germane, for he locates our passage in the larger structural context of vv. 27–40, a unit within the *sūrah* to which he assigns the rubric "the punishment of the rebel children of Israel." Cuypers divides the *sūrah* into two halves, with the major theme of the first half (vv. 1–71) being the establishment of a new covenant through the revelation of the Qurʾān. The initial sections of the chapter draw a sharp contrast between "you who believe" (*alladhīna āmanū*), for whom a quasi-Israelite code of behavior mainly centering on purity is legislated, and other, deficient monotheists who are critiqued for their shortcomings. They are variously identified in the first part of the *sūrah* as Israel (*banī isrāʾīl*, vv. 12, 32), the People of Scripture (*alladhīna ūtū ʾl-kitāb* or simply *ahl al-kitāb*, vv. 5, 15, 19), Jews and Christians (*yahūd* and *naṣārā*, vv. 14, 18), and "the people of the Gospel" (*ahl al-injīl*, v. 47).[62]

According to Cuypers, the *sūrah* reaches an initial crescendo in vv. 48–50, in which the qurʾānic prophet's authority as judge is asserted not only over his followers, but seemingly over Jews and Christians as well, before the transition to the second half of the *sūrah* (72–120), in which Christians are summoned to enter the new covenant with the believers. If one follows Cuypers's line of reasoning about the structure of the first part of the *sūrah*, the Cain and Abel passage appears in the center of this sequence of verses, which would seem to highlight its importance for the underlying argument of this portion of the text. This is not accidental, for Cuypers avers that

62. The locution *ahl al-injīl* is unique to Q 5:47, and its obvious counterpart, *ahl al-tawrāh*, does not appear in the Qurʾān at all, though it is common in later Muslim discourse on the Bible and Jews. Nevertheless, repeated mention is made in Sūrat al-Māʾidah to the Torah specifically (and its recipients' refusal to follow it), sometimes juxtaposed with the Gospel and revelation to Israel in general (e.g., Q 5:66–67).

Muḥammad's authority as arbiter and judge rests on the license to engage in the legitimate violence of retaliation, which is granted in v. 45.[63]

Although his structuralist approach has met with sharp critique, Cuypers's analysis at the very least encourages us to consider the function of the Cain and Abel pericope within the larger message of Sūrat al-Māʾidah.[64] Here the Qurʾān positions both its own authority and that of its prophet above that of the older revelations and communities to which it is the successor. Arguably this is one of the most strongly supersessionist *sūrahs* in the Qurʾān: here the claims of Jews and Christians to special chosen status are contested—especially since they have misinterpreted and failed to fulfill their covenants (e.g., v. 14)—while the chosen status of the *ummah* is asserted, on the very basis of their anticipated (or current?) fulfillment of their covenantal obligations. This is implied by the very first line of the *sūrah*: *yā-ayyuhā 'llādhīna āmanū awfū bi'l-ʿuqūdi*, "O you who believe, fulfill the stipulations."[65] As in older Christian discourse vis-à-vis the Bible and the Jews, the supersessionist impulse is here manifest in twin gestures of delegitimation (as in vv. 17–18, which state that Jews and Christians are not real monotheists and falsely assert their elect status) and appropriation (as in vv. 44–45, in which the biblical *lex talionis* is reiterated and expanded, and thus valorized as an aspect of Qurʾān rather than Torah or Gospel).[66]

---

63. See Cuypers, *The Banquet*, 242–253. It is important to note that vv. 48–50 have sometimes been seen as maladroit in the *sūrah*, but Cuypers argues quite convincingly that this segment, the effective center of the chapter, should be understood as key to deciphering the meaning of the whole. Given that the legitimation of violence, the theme of the qurʾānic presentation of Cain and Abel, is crucial to the establishment of the qurʾānic prophet's authority, we can see quite clearly here that structural analysis makes a critical contribution to our interpretation of the purpose behind the Qurʾān's appropriation and deployment of mishnaic material.

64. For such a critique, see Nicolai Sinai, "Review Essay: Going Around in Circles," *JQS* 19.2 (2017): 106–147; see also his brief comments regarding the structure of Sūrat al-Māʾidah in "Towards a Redactional History of the Medinan Qur'an: A Case Study of Sūrat al-Nisāʾ (Q 4) and Sūrat al-Māʾidah (Q 5)," in Marianna Klar (ed.), *Structural Dividers in the Qur'an* (Abingdon: Routledge, 2021), 365–402, 383–386.

65. Compare also v. 7, the believers said "we hear and obey," in contrast to the Jews' distortion of what they were commanded to utter (v. 13 and 41, as elsewhere in the Qurʾān) and the failure of both the Jews and the Christians to uphold their pledges (vv. 12–14, and likewise similarly expressed elsewhere).

66. It cannot be accidental that the next verses (46–50) refer first to Jesus being sent to Israel with the Gospel to confirm the Torah, then to the qurʾānic prophet's mission to confirm what came before him and establish God's law for both his followers and the remnants of older prophetic communities.

It should be acknowledged that the Qurʾān here recognizes the authenticity of the older manifestations of *kitāb* that the forerunner communities possessed, but positions itself as the new primary embodiment of divine law, which its community will and must follow—in contrast to those older communities who failed to follow the law as mediated through the older instantiations of *kitāb* that were bestowed upon them.[67] Essentially—so the *sūrah* implies—if Jews and Christians will not judge according to the precepts of Torah and Gospel (vv. 66, 68), the *ummah* will. It is specifically in relation to this question of the failure to uphold the divinely mandated law that the *sūrah* seems to address the Jews in particular, especially pertaining to the question of legitimate or illegitimate bloodshed. I do not mean to suggest that this is the only organizing theme of significance in the *sūrah*, or that other approaches to its interpretation are incorrect. However, focusing on themes of violence and bloodshed helps us to tie together some of what seem like disparate or incongruous elements within the chapter.

Blood and the spilling of blood are concerns that recur throughout the *sūrah*; arguably, they are the underlying theme that ties its opening passage, the legislative jumble of vv. 1–5, together—when to fight, what to eat, when to hunt, even whom to marry.[68] But the activity tied to bloodshed that is arguably of greatest concern in Sūrat al-Māʾidah is fighting. In contrast to the rules issued here about when blood can legitimately be shed by believ-

---

67. For a classic discussion of *kitāb* as connoting God's ongoing revelatory process to humanity more than "scripture" per se, see Madigan, *The Qurʾân's Self-Image.*

68. Given the reference to licit foodstuffs at the beginning of the *sūrah* and that to the table or feast demanded of Jesus by his disciples towards the end (vv. 112–115), it is a natural exegetical imperative to try to draw them together. Thus, in his translation of the Qurʾān, Abdel Haleem highlights the theme of food in his introduction to this chapter (M. A. S. Abdel Haleem, *The Qur'an: A New Translation*, corrected ed. [Oxford: Oxford University Press, 2016], 67). Likewise, Freidenreich's nimble reading of food prohibition and permission in Sūrat al-Māʾidah convincingly demonstrates the importance of this theme to the erection and negotiation of communal boundaries in the chapter (David M. Freidenreich, *Foreigners and Their Food: Constructing Otherness in Jewish, Christian, and Islamic Law* [Berkeley: University of California Press, 2011], 136–143). However, there is much here in the *sūrah* that does not concern food; further, dietary rules and guidelines about commensality are not particularly prominent in the chapter as a whole. Still further, in the first two verses of the *sūrah* believers are enjoined to uphold strict behavioral standards regarding a number of things, including diet, but also the rites and taboos associated with the Sanctuary, the pretexts for entering into hostilities with enemies, and providing support to weaker members of the community.

ers, we here see a countervailing emphasis on Israel's total failure to shed blood appropriately in accordance with the divine will.

In the opening passages of the *sūrah*, it seems that the divine narrator's largely negative attention is directed at the People of Scripture in general, or Jews and Christians together, or even Christians specifically (e.g., Q 5:14 and 5:17). But the flow of the chapter diverts in a decidedly Israelite or Jewish direction in v. 20. Strikingly, this verse opens the passage that immediately precedes the Cain and Abel narrative: the qur'ānic version of the story of how the Israelites would not enter the Promised Land and fight when they were commanded to do so by Moses (vv. 20–26).[69] This account stands in sharp contrast with the subsequent story, that of the first murder, Cain's totally illegitimate spilling of the blood of his brother. One is clearly *jihād fī sabīl allāh*, here designating legitimate violence under specific conditions; this Israel were commanded to undertake, but refused to do. The other is *qatl al-nafs bi-ghayr nafs*, the unjustified homicide denounced in Q 5:32, which Cain, arguably a cipher for Israel, *did* do.[70]

Notably, after the Cain and Abel pericope (which again I have identified as the entire passage from v. 27 to 37) the text digresses to note the corporal punishment to be meted out to thieves (more authorized bloodshed), and then to once again assert God's singularity and omnipotence before undertaking another extended denunciation of the corruption of the Jews (vv. 41–45). The remaining eighty or so verses of the chapter then proceed

69. The obvious parallel is with the story of Saul (Q 2:246–253). For a strong historicist reading of this passage that deftly grounds it in the conjectured context of the qur'ānic prophet's mission, see Walid A. Saleh, "'What If You Refuse, When Ordered to Fight?': King Saul (Ṭālūt) in the Qur'ān and Post-Qur'ānic Literature," in Carl S. Ehrlich in association with Marsha C. White (eds.), *Saul in Story and Tradition* (Tübingen: Mohr Siebeck, 2006), 261–283. In Sūrah 2, the biblical story of Saul and Goliath is seemingly repurposed to critique the believers' reluctance to take up arms against their enemies; however, in Sūrat al-Mā'idah, the analogous story from the time of Moses (evoking the story of the spies from Numbers 13) is retold to establish a contrast with the story of Cain (juxtaposing a story about violence being shunned when legitimate with one in which it is indulged though illegitimate).

70. Cuypers is particularly concerned to vindicate the coherence of the qur'ānic account despite its rapid temporal shift from the account of the Mosaic era to the time of the protoplasts, and cites the remarks of classical commentators regarding Muḥammad's Jewish audience to support this (*The Banquet*, 197). However, if we identify legitimately sanctioned violence as the *Leitmotif* that explains the relationship between the two passages, this thematic continuity overrides any perceived disjunction between vv. 26–27 and the preceding section.

to range over a number of issues.[71] Most importantly, we must note that although the *sūrah*'s various statements about Jesus and Christianity have generally received the greatest amount of scholarly attention, much of the polemic that follows in subsequent sections of the chapter are directed either at the People of Scripture or Jews and Christians collectively, and there is no shortage of material in these subsequent passages that may be construed as criticism of Israel or the Jews specifically.

Overall, here in this *sūrah*, as elsewhere in the qur'ānic corpus, we see a direct association of Israel or the Jews with breaking their pledges (vv. 12–13, also a crime of the Christians, v. 14); with spreading corruption in the land (vv. 32–33); with treachery (and thus the believers should not take them or Christians as allies, v. 51); and with the killing of prophets (v. 70).[72] The last allegation is made a number of times in the Qur'ān, and is especially conspicuous here in the culminating passage in the *sūrah*, which re-

---

71. Like many of the other long *sūrahs* of the Medinan period, Sūrat al-Māʾidah appears at first glance to be a very heterogeneous collection of ruminations on a mixed bag of topics (cf. Robinson, "Hands Outstretched," 18, citing Neuwirth's characterization of the longer Medinan chapters as *Sammelkörbe* or "collection baskets"). The conspicuous heterogeneity of the later long chapters of the Qurʾān helps to explain the historical reluctance of scholars to see them as unitary compositions. It is easy to sympathize with the "mixed bag" view of Sūrah 5, for it does appear to be a strange combination of legal prescriptions of a very diverse sort with critique of the *ahl al-kitāb*. However, the efforts of scholars such as Robinson and Cuypers have shown that we need not necessarily conclude that diverse contents combined with exceptionally long verses in chapters such as al-Māʾidah means that they are just incoherent jumbles.

72. On this motif, see Gabriel Said Reynolds, "On the Qurʾān and the Theme of Jews as 'Killers of the Prophets,'" *Al-Bayān* 10 (2012): 9–32. As noted, for Cuypers the killing of the righteous is the main theme linking the Cain and Abel episode (specifically Abel's utterance in Q 5:28–29) with the precursor in Matt 23 (specifically the reference to the spilled blood of the holy in v. 35). Admittedly, the claim of the killing of the prophets does not sit well with qurʾānic prophetology as it is understood by the classical Islamic tradition, which generally sees the prophets as safeguarded by God on their missions and inevitably vindicated. The depiction of the apostles in Sūrat al-Māʾidah is typical of that of the Qurʾān as a whole, which sees the *ḥawāriyyūn* as sincere in their belief but eventually abandoning their faith, the implication being that Christians should return to the original message of Jesus by accepting the qurʾānic prophet—a message writ large over this *sūrah* (see Gabriel Said Reynolds, "The Quran and the Apostles of Jesus," *BSOAS* 76 [2013]: 209–227). As a recent contribution by Younus Mirza shows, the traditional exegetical approach to the qurʾānic disciples of Christ is more nuanced than one might expect; see "The Disciples as Companions: Ibn Taymiyya's and Ibn al-Qayyim's Evaluation of the Transmission of the Bible," *ME* 24 (2018): 530–560.

counts (expressing a clear anti-Christian sentiment) the story of Jesus and his followers and the miracle of the eponymous feast. Notably, no mention is made in this *sūrah* of the death of Jesus. The question of whether the Qur'ān denies the crucifixion of Christ entirely—the position of many Muslim exegetes—is an exceedingly complex one. There is a strong case to be made for another interpretation, namely, that the Qur'ān is here signaling that the events surrounding the execution of Jesus did not transpire as the main culprits, the Jews, intended or thought—though "it seemed so to them" (*shubbiha lahum*, Q 4:157).[73] For our present purposes, we will note only that it is difficult to imagine that a chapter that casts Cain as a symbol of Jewish violence and explicitly refers to the Jews killing their prophets invokes the name of Jesus without the crucifixion lurking in the background as a subtext—the preeminent example of Jewish violence targeting a prophet, whether or not the culprits were successful in their aim.[74]

I have highlighted the prominent themes of treachery, violence, and bloodshed (specifically legitimate versus illegitimate bloodshed) in Sūrat al-Māʾidah because this helps us to make sense of the rationale behind the Qur'ān's engagement of the mishnaic tractate Sanhedrin. The thematic parallels between the two are abundant. In particular, the emphasis in the mishnaic parallel on communal boundaries and stability that we previously remarked is significant, because these themes resonate throughout Sūrat al-Māʾidah as well, albeit refracted through the Qur'ān's distinct perspective and concerns.

If one accept's Donner's basic hypothesis of the trajectory of development of communal identity among Muḥammad's followers during the span of his career, then Sūrat al-Māʾidah was evidently composed at a time when this formerly more open and "ecumenical" *ummah* had matured and sought

73. Notably, it has recently been suggested that the point of the famous qurʾānic reference to the crucifixion is to provide a counter-narrative to the portrayal of the execution of Jesus in the Babylonian Talmud, itself a counter-narrative to the gospel tradition. Here (b. Sanh. 43a) Jesus is depicted as a heretic who was executed by a Jewish court by stoning, a depiction meant to contradict the gospel account and thus defang Christian claims about Jesus's messianic significance. Thus, it is the question of agency that is addressed by Q 4:167, not that of the fact of Jesus's death per se. See Ian Mevorach, "Qur'an, Crucifixion, and Talmud: A New Reading of Q 4:157–58," *Journal of Religion & Society* 19 (2017): 1–21.

74. This is especially likely given that the Gospel precursor for Abel's statement, Jesus's condemnation of the Pharisees for killing the prophets in Matt 23:35, hints at his own imminent death, which then serves to implicitly confirm the very indictment he issues here.

to establish not only social and political, but also religious, autonomy.[75] The *sūrah* repeatedly draws a sharp contrast between the believers and the Jews and Christians to whom they stand opposed, signaling directly that an inflection point in the distinction between communities—a parting of the ways—has been reached: "Today I have perfected your religion for you and made My grace complete, and chosen *al-islām* for you as your religion" (Q 5:3). Whether one sees *islām*/Islam as representing a coherent body of beliefs and practices here or not, *al-islām* is explicitly positioned as a criterion of difference, which corroborates a late date for the *sūrah*. Notably, the tradition itself posits that this verse was one of the last in the corpus, revealed during the Farewell Pilgrimage of 10/632, towards the end of the Prophet's life. The tradition also recognizes the supersessionist implications of this "perfecting," with the purification of the rites of the Kaʿbah as the fulfillment of the legacy of Abrahamic monotheism:

> Al-Shaʿbī reported: "The verse 'Today I have perfected your religion …' came down when the Prophet was standing at ʿArafāt, at *mawqif Ibrāhīm*, when idolatry was overcome and the beacon of Jāhiliyyah collapsed, and the people were forbidden from approaching the Kaʿbah naked."[76]

---

75. It is worth underscoring that Q 5 is, according to most chronological schemes, a very late composition in the qurʾānic corpus (possibly followed by only two more chapters, *sūrah*s 9 and 110). We may readily observe a strong thematic continuity between al-Māʾidah and al-Tawbah concerning what would become the *status quo* for the *ummah*'s relationships with other communities: Q 5 establishes what would become the mature position towards Jews and Christians mainly on a theological-ideological level, whereas Q 9 takes that position somewhat further, in particular by articulating what would eventually be understood as the Qurʾān's final policy on *jihād* against unbelievers. On the "ecumenical" nature of the early community, see the influential discussion of Fred Donner in *Muhammad and the Believers: At the Origins of Islam* (Cambridge, MA: Belknap, 2010). Donner's ideas about the permeable boundaries of the primitive *ummah* have now been developed, in strikingly different ways, by Stephen J. Shoemaker in *The Apocalypse of Empire: Imperial Eschatology in Late Antiquity and Early Islam* (Philadelphia: University of Pennsylvania Press, 2018) and Juan Cole, *Muhammad: Prophet of Peace amid the Clash of Empires* (Nation Books, 2018); see my review of Shoemaker's monograph in *RQR* 6.7 (2020).

76. Muḥammad Ibn Saʿd, *Kitāb al-Ṭabaqāt al-kabīr* [*Ibn Saad, Biographien Muhammeds*], ed. Eduard Sachau et al. (9 vols. in 16 parts; Leiden: Brill, 1904–1940), 2.1.135. The reference to the performance of pilgrimage naked is a metonym for the *jāhilī* religious order. A *ḥadīth* attested in al-Bukhārī and elsewhere notes that in former times pilgrims circumambulated the Kaʿbah naked (Abū ʿAbd Allāh Muḥammad b. Ismāʿīl al-Bukhārī, *al-Jāmiʿ al-musnad al-ṣaḥīḥ al-mukhtaṣar*, *al-ḥajj* 91, *bāb al-wuqūf bi-ʿArafah*, no. 1665); another—attested several times in al-Bukhārī—states that around the time of the Farewell Pilgrimage the Prophet stipulated that idolaters

Thus, this *sūrah* seems to represent a late summation of the qur'ānic author's perception of, and attitude towards, Jews and Christians, providing an extended critique of their claims and articulating a posture of separation and distinction from these communities. It is therefore not surprising that in vv. 17–18 of the chapter, in the lead-up to the Cain and Abel pericope, we see an explicit condemnation of Christians for their beliefs about Jesus. Those beliefs, the fundamental basis of their distinct sectarian identity, are decried as *kufr*, disbelief.

> 17 Those who assert that God is the Messiah, son of Mary, have disbelieved. Say to them: "Who could in the slightest impede Him if He wished to annihilate the Messiah, son of Mary, along with his mother, and everyone else on earth too! Mastery over heaven and earth and everything in between is God's. He creates as He pleases. God is the one who determines everything."

Among the verses of the Qur'ān that condemn Christian claims about Jesus, this one is unusual only for its assertion of God's ability to actually destroy Jesus, Mary, or any other created being as proof of His omnipotence. The passage then continues, explicitly drawing the Jews into the fray:

> 18 The Jews and the Christians have said: "We are the children of God, his favorites." Say to them: "So why does he punish you for your sins? No, you are just human beings He has created; He will forgive whomever He pleases, and punish whomever He pleases. Mastery over heaven and earth and everything in between is God's, and all paths lead to Him."

What is striking about these two verses is that they condemn the same offenses that are decried in m. Sanh 4:5. There, it will be recalled, the creation of humanity from the single protoplast Adam was intended "for the sake of maintaining peace among God's creatures, so that one person should not say to his fellow, 'My father was greater than yours'; and also so *mînîn* should not say, 'There are many powers in heaven.'" These verses in the Qur'ān similarly single out two kinds of wrongdoing, the association of lesser beings with God—implying that there are indeed many powers in Heaven—and the claim of favored status with the Deity, even that "we are the children of God"—implying that their father is indeed greater than others'. Beyond these parallels, a broader comparison of the two passages demonstrates conspicuous similarities between them, despite some structural differences. The Mishnah relates the Cain and Abel story, then con-

---

were no longer to perform the Ḥajj and no one would be permitted to circumambulate the Kaʿbah naked (see, e.g., nos. 4655–4657). See my further comments regarding the dating of Sūrat al-Mā'idah below.

demns those who exalt themselves over others (by saying "my father was greater than yours"), then those who cause strife (in the Jewish community) through associating others with God. In turn, reversing the two points of the critique, the Qur'ān condemns those who associate others with God, and then those who exalt themselves by claiming to be His children and so favored over others. Then, after the intervening passage about the Israelites' unwillingness to fight (not incidental to the larger argument of this section of the *sūrah*), it relates the Cain and Abel story. The constituent elements of the two passages are basically the same, only presented in a different order.[77]

In light of the larger themes of the *sūrah*, it is not surprising to see Jews and Christians condemned for their teachings here in the passage leading up to the Cain and Abel story. What is more surprising is that they are explicitly condemned both for associating others with God and for vaunting themselves over others—violating those very same principles that the Mishnah asserts in connection with the Cain and Abel story.[78] The polemic of the qur'ānic account appears to appropriate that of the Mishnah, inverting its structure and subverting its message. The lesson God sought to inculcate in Israel through the creation of humanity through Adam appears to have been forgotten, and so the Qur'ān castigates the Jews for neglecting God's lesson and vying with others over their putatively chosen status, employing a discursive pattern Jews presumably recognized and understood.[79]

Having appropriated and reoriented the mishnaic message about communal integrity, the qur'ānic passage proceeds to advise the recipients of older revelation where they should turn for correct guidance:

> 19 O People of Scripture: Our Messenger has come to you to make things clear to you after a break (*fatrah*) between messengers, so that you cannot say that no bearer of glad tidings or warner has come to you—for a bearer of glad tidings and warner has indeed come, and God is the one who determines everything.

77. Curiously, the question of who has legitimate authority to marshal the people to fight also surfaces in the mishnaic tractate, though it is mentioned there only obliquely, and not in connection with the Cain and Abel narrative (see 1:5, 2:4).
78. Here, of course, the focus is on Christian theological deficiency, whereas that of both Jews and Christians is asserted elsewhere, most notably in the famous statement about their claims about sons of God in Q 9:30. As with the theme of legitimate violence, this motif is yet another conspicuous linkage between the very late Sūrat al-Mā'idah and the (supposedly) penultimate revelation of Sūrat al-Tawbah.
79. In this, the Qur'ān itself replicates the discourse of competition at the very moment it castigates Jews and Christians for engaging in it; cf. Q 2:113.

As is so often the case in the Qur'ān (in distinction to later Muslim doctrine), this passage does not presuppose that the scriptures of older communities are corrupt or invalid. Rather, the message of the older revelations is validated, essentially recapitulated in the new one, with the qur'ānic prophet's continuity with older messengers underscored.[80] As if to drive home this point, the *sūrah* then segues to its presentation of the episode of Moses and the Israelites who were reluctant to fight, another appropriation that clearly illustrates the Qur'ān's compatibility with—or rather supplanting—of older scripture. As already noted, that episode then transitions to that of the two sons of Adam.

In keeping with this dynamic of appropriation and reorientation, it is striking that both the Mishnah and the Qur'ān explicitly anchor the rule or law concerning the value of life in revelation. The qur'ānic story of the sons of Adam emphasizes that Israel should know about this principle because it was ordained for them in their own scripture (v. 32). This is then reiterated by God asserting that "Our messengers have come to them with clear signs" (*wa-la-qad jā'athum rusulunā bi'l-bayyināt*, v. 32 continued), which again emphasizes Israel's previous reception of God's grace through revelation. This directly parallels the Mishnah's statement that "therefore was man created alone in the world initially, to teach you that the one who causes a single soul to perish, scripture imputes it to him (*ma'aleh 'alav ha-katūv*) as if he had caused an entire world to perish ..."[81] The Mishnah likewise asserts the principle's scriptural foundation: this lesson was the whole point of relating the story in Genesis, and the Mishnah even goes so far as to assert that it is scripture itself that indicts the murderer. Scripture holds the one who slays another responsible; there is no doubt that they are accountable because scripture makes the rule plain, through relating the narrative of Cain's killing of Abel.

In short, we here witness the Qur'ān deliberately echoing rabbinic tradition by alluding to a biblical story, to articulate—as rabbinic tradition does—a rule rooted in divine revelation. One might be tempted to infer that such a gesture communicates what we today would call an ecumen-

80. On the qur'ānic conception of *taḥrīf* in distinction to that articulated in later Muslim tradition, see Gabriel Said Reynolds, "On the Qur'anic Accusation of Scriptural Falsification (*taḥrīf*) and Christian Anti-Jewish Polemic," *JAOS* 130 (2010): 189–202.

81. Note that the Yerushalmi removes the reference to scripture, making it only implicit; thus, the Guggenheimer edition reads "the one who causes a single soul to perish, it is imputed to him (*ma'alîn 'alav*) as if he had caused an entire world to perish..." (*The Jerusalem Talmud*, ed. and trans. Guggenheimer, 165).

ical lesson: the Qurʾān asserts both the integrity of older revelation—what was ordained for Israel—and a basic commonality of moral sensibility here. Verse 32 is in fact often cited in popular discourse as expressing exactly this sentiment, usually intended to underscore both the fundamental respect for human life as primary in Muslim ethics and Islam's compatibility with "Western values." But reading the convergence of Mishnah and Qurʾān as a specimen of pre-modern ecumenism is clearly anachronistic if we conflate it with or project it onto the original historical milieu that the Qurʾān was revealed to address. Rather, given the overarching thrust of the *sūrah*, we must conclude that the rabbinic precursor has been deliberately appropriated and its major themes strategically reconstrued to propel a more strident, if not openly militant, message.

Verse 32 in the qurʾānic passage states, like m. Sanh. 4:5, that killing a single soul is like killing all of humanity, but the Qurʾān then goes on to add an important caveat as well. It makes exceptions to this principle in cases of retribution for murder or manslaughter or spreading corruption in the land (*faṣād fī ʾl-arḍ*). As we saw above, vv. 33–34 following then lay out the penalties for fighting God and His messenger or spreading corruption in the land, implying that the people who are doing so are a very proximate danger. The culprits are threatened with a series of grave penalties—death, crucifixion, mutilation, or exile. If they do not repent—and they can repent, for God is merciful and turns to those who offer sincere repentance—"their lot is humiliation in this world, and a tremendous punishment in the next" (v. 33). For numerous reasons, it is not implausible to conclude that this warning is here issued against the Jews—presumably not Jews in general, but rather a specific group that presented a manifest threat to the qurʾānic prophet's community.[82]

The message of the text here is quite clear: scripture not only relates a lesson to Israel in the story of Cain and Abel, but uses it as a medium to communicate what is essentially a divine law. In the Mishnah, whether the rule can be read as intended for all humanity is really immaterial; the text is concerned with its application to Israel specifically—Jews must understand the rule that God intended them to observe, whether or not it applies to gentiles. In the Qurʾān, the textual logic is inverted, and two crucial changes

82. The reference in v. 33 to "humiliation in this world and a tremendous punishment in the next" recurs at the conclusion of v. 41 as the penalty exacted from the Jews for their distortion of God's revelation. Further, the general theme of the Jews being punished by humiliation in this world, here conveyed by the term *khizy*, resonates with references to the disgrace (*dhillah*) visited on Israel or the *ahl al-kitāb* for their crimes elsewhere in the Qurʾān (e.g., Q 2:61, 3:112, 7:152).

in interpretation occur. First, the rule itself is here construed not simply as "thou shalt not kill" but rather as "thou shalt not kill except for legitimate reasons"—a more practical guideline for life in pre-Islamic Arabia (to say nothing of biblical Israel), with the specific crimes that actually do merit the penalty of death adumbrated here. The second shift in interpretation of the rule is even more consequential: it is not primarily the Jews to whom the rule about not killing is being communicated, though they were its original audience; rather, now it is the Jews who fall into the category of the express *exceptions* to the rule. They are no longer the subjects of its mandate, but rather its object. It is the shedding of Jewish blood that is now legitimated, because they have committed those crimes in response to which the rule is justifiably suspended. They should have known better, for their own scripture bears witness to the truth.[83]

Numerous aspects of the text corroborate this interpretation; the most conspicuous are the allusions to spreading corruption in the land in the passage, which is a *locus classicus* for the concept in the Qurʾān. The discourse surrounding "corruption" and "excess" reverberates throughout the corpus. In Meccan passages, *fasād* is often associated with the peoples of the past who were subjected to God's punishment and destroyed.[84] In earlier *sūrahs* it is sometimes at least implicitly connected to violence, as when Pharaoh is characterized as "one who spreads corruption" (*innahu kāna*

83. The notion that the Jews are indicted of various crimes by their own scripture is found throughout early and late antique Christian polemical literature. For example, in a passage from Ephrem's *Hymns on Faith*, he states bluntly of Israel's sin with the Golden Calf: "Behold, their Calf proclaims their sin; their scripture testifies to it"; see Ephrem, *Hymnen de Fide* 61.10, ed. and trans. Edmund Beck (2 vols.; Louvain: L. Durbecq, 1955), 1.190. This is not the only passage in the Qurʾān in which the authority of Torah is invoked to justify violence; compare Q 9:111, which cites Torah, Gospel, and Qurʾān alike to validate the everlasting covenant, the promise of reward to those who kill and are killed fighting in the cause of God that the Qurʾān articulates in the Medinan period (cf. Q 3:169, 33:23). But this passage in Sūrat al-Māʾidah is unusual in invoking the testimony of Torah to legitimate violence against the children of Israel themselves.

84. In perhaps the earliest passage to refer to *fasād* (according to the traditional chronology), it is mentioned as the crime of various wrongdoers who received severe chastisement from God: ʿĀd, Thamūd, and Pharaoh (Q 89:6–14). This characterization recurs throughout the Meccan *sūrahs* (see, e.g., Q 7:74.85.103, 27:48, 89:12). Further, in the Meccan *sūrahs* corruption is a cardinal sin that distinguishes believers from infidels as inheritors of paradise (see, e.g., Q 28:77, 28:83, 38:28), and the believers are often warned against it, just as peoples of the past were warned (and, failing to heed the warning, were destroyed).

mina 'l-mufsidīn) in connection with the slaughter of the Israelite children (Q 28:4).[85] However, it is in Medinan passages that an additional dimension emerges in the discourse surrounding *fasād*. While the motif continues to recur in the recollection of ancient peoples or general admonitions to believers, in later *sūrahs* it comes into focus as the activity of a community that opposes the qur'ānic prophet in the here and now. Insofar as *fasād* is still invoked in connection with figures of the past, this is done to underscore the gravity of transgressions being committed in the present. In Medinan chapters *fasād* implies violence both as a provocation that cannot be ignored and as the justified response to such provocation, as here in Sūrat al-Mā'idah, where the most drastic penalties against its perpetrators are not only sanctioned but mandated. This corruption is a crime against people, nature, and God alike that demands a resolute response.

Moreover, it is not an overstatement to say that in the Medinan period *fasād* becomes strongly associated with the Jews as a proximate threat to the qur'ānic prophet and his *ummah*. Already in the middle Meccan Sūrat al-Isrā', Israel is indicted of *fasād* in a most dramatic way: it was in response to their corruption that God ordained the destruction of the Temple, not once but twice (Q 17:4)—an exceedingly grave penalty for a grave crime. Notably—and rather reminiscent of Q 5:32—God decreed this in their scripture (*qaḍaynā ilā banī 'isrā'īla fī 'l-kitāb*), and so they were fairly warned. In *sūrahs* conventionally identified as Medinan, the linkage between the Jews and *fasād* becomes more frequent, and more momentous; it aligns Israel with wrongdoers of the past, like their former oppressor Pharaoh, or with the impending chaos and destruction of a possibly imminent apocalyptic age, like the *fasād* Gog and Magog are prophesied to wreak upon the earth (Q 18:94).[86]

85. Elsewhere, Pharaoh's role as a *mufsid* is confirmed by God at the moment of his death (Q 10:91). Pharaoh's *fasād* acquires an ironic tinge, since in multiple passages the Egyptians are said to have oppressed the Israelites out of fear that they would commit *fasād* in their land (e.g., Q 7:127, 40:26). In a previous age, Joseph's brothers were anxious to deny precisely the charge of having come to Egypt to commit *fasād* (Q 12:73); Abdel Haleem's rendering as "make mischief" downplays the gravity of the accusation.

86. The notion of *fasād* as a specifically apocalyptic type of corruption perpetrated by Jews—heralding or even precipitating the End Times—is developed in both classical and modern Islamic culture, for example in the jihadist rhetoric of Hamas. See Anne Marie Oliver and Paul Steinberg, *The Road to Martyrs' Square* (Oxford: Oxford University Press, 2005), 107–110.

A new emphasis on *fasād* is already conspicuous in the Medinan manifesto Sūrat al-Baqarah, and many of the pointed references to it here are clearly, if only implicitly, aimed at Jews (which would obviously be significant soon after the *hijrah* to Medina, if one accepts the traditional chronology of revelation). Thus, at the beginning of the *sūrah* those who profess to believe in God and the Last Day but do not really believe are warned not to spread corruption; in response they claim that they are just doing what is right, despite the fact that what they are doing is clearly *fasād* (Q 2:11–12).[87] Somewhat further on, we find a denunciation of those who have broken God's covenant after having sincerely pledged obedience (*alladhīna yanquḍūna ʿahda ʾllāhi min baʿdi mithāqihi*), and spreading corruption is then added to the charge (Q 2:27).

Sūrat al-Baqarah also contains the famous objection of the angels to God's creation of Adam (Q 2:30): "Will you create on earth one who will spread corruption in it, and shed blood (*man yufsidu fīhā wa-yasfiku ʾl-dimāʾa*)?" Like the objection to murder in Sūrat al-Māʾidah, this reference to primordial history may seem to imply a universalizing context.[88] However, if the particular conjunction of *fasād* and bloodshed here really is meant to be universal, then it is anomalous, as somewhat later on in the *sūrah*, Moses is depicted warning his people not to spread corruption, returning to an Israelite focus for the concept, and naturally implying that his people disobeyed and *did* spread corruption (Q 2:60).[89] We might also note the

87. Literally, they claim that they are "making things right," *muṣliḥīn*; it is tempting to think of this *iṣlāḥ* as *tîqqûn ʿôlam*, a concept generally associated with kabbalistic thought but with roots in the Mishnah, where it appears in chapter 4 of the tractate Gittin several times. Sometimes it seems to be a shorthand for what we would convey with the phrase "making the world a better place," though at other times it seems to mean something more like "maintaining good order" or even simply "best practices."

88. The traditions on the protoplasts in the Hebrew Bible are often read as naturally speaking to the experience of universal humanity. Against this, see Seth D. Postell, *Adam as Israel: Genesis 1–3 as the Introduction to the Torah and Tanakh* (Cambridge: James Clarke and Co., 2011), which emphasizes the commonsensical, but usually overlooked, conclusion that the protoplast traditions speak not to lessons about the general human condition but rather foreshadow major themes in God's relationship with Israel as articulated throughout the biblical corpus.

89. Note the contrast with the previously remarked Meccan passages in which Pharaoh accuses the Israelites of *fasād* or the brothers of Joseph anxiously deny the allegation. Here, *fasād* is something that is much more closely associated with Israel as perpetrators. As noted above, Q 2:60–61 contains a somewhat veiled allusion to the story of the spies that is more fully rehearsed in Sūrat al-Māʾidah, where it fore-

reference in the late Meccan or Medinan Sūrat al-Raʿd to those who spread corruption in the land being cursed and promised a "terrible abode," *sūʾ al-dār* (Q 13:25). The emphasis on natural phenomena as signaling divine sovereignty and peerlessness that predominates in the *sūrah* might at first suggest that the argument is staged against pagans, as would the reference to the prophet's interlocutors denying the resurrection (Q 13:5). However, in Q 13:25 those who are guilty of *fasād* are again said to have broken God's covenant after having sincerely pledged obedience, a recurrence of the allegation made against the Jews in Q 2:27 that uses the same terminology.[90]

The discourse surrounding *fasād* in the Qurʾān then reaches a crescendo in Sūrat al-Māʾidah, where it continues to be strongly associated with the Jews. As we have seen, in v. 32 *fasād fī 'l-arḍ* is one of the two major exceptions that justifies homicide. Later in that verse an allusion is made to those "who commit excesses in the land" (*fīʾ l-arḍ la-musrifīn*); then, in the very next verse, severe corporal punishment is prescribed for those "who spread corruption in the land," using phrasing slightly different from before (*yasʿawna fī 'l-arḍ fasādan*, v. 33).[91] The immediate context heavily implies that the Jews are meant here, and subsequent verses of the *sūrah* seem to bear this out.[92] For a moment, it may seem like a less focused denunciation of wrongdoing is being offered here, on the basis of vv. 38–39, where the

---

shadows the legitimate, obligatory violence commanded of the Israelites (Q 5:20–26) that is contrasted with the illegitimate violence perpetrated by Cain (vv. 27–31).

90. The specific mention of damnation here is reminiscent of the previously cited reference to the *fasād* of Israel in Sūrat al-Isrāʾ. There the Jews are offered the choice of mercy in exchange for sincere repentance or perdition; God avers that "We have made Hell a prison for unbelievers" (Q 17:8).

91. Immediately afterwards, damnation is again mentioned; here it is promised to those who disbelieve, but the context suggests that those who are guilty of *fasād* in vv. 32–33 are also those accused of *kufr* and so threatened with the penalty of the Fire in vv. 36–37.

92. Q 5:33 is conventionally termed the *ḥirābah* verse and has long been understood as the primary basis for the qurʾānic penalty for "brigandage" or robbery. In classical discussions of the verse, commentators recognize a variety of occasions for its revelation, and frequently dissociate it from the Jews (or *ahl al-kitāb*) as the specific referent. For an illuminating discussion of the often hair-raising reports on violent crime and its just deserts that comprises the early juristic discourse on the subject, see Khalid Abou El Fadl, *Rebellion and Violence in Islamic Law* (Cambridge: Cambridge University Press, 2001), 47–60. Similarly, in a recent discussion Juan Cole argues, on the basis of parallels with Justinianic law, that the *ḥirābah* verse is informed by the "logic of punishment" generally operative in the Roman Empire, and so he likeways downplays the specifically Jewish context of the verse; see "Muhammad and Justinian: Roman Legal Traditions and the Qurʾān," *JNES* 79 (2020): 183–196.

punishment for theft is declared. But the Jews come sharply back into focus in v. 40, where they are again explicitly mentioned as distorting scripture, with further deficiencies mentioned in vv. 41–43, leading up to the adumbration of the *lex talionis* in v. 44.

We have already noted the more generalized critique of the People of Scripture that unfolds in subsequent verses in this *sūrah*, alternating with more specific critique of the Jews for various failings. The link between the Jews and violence then recurs in the much-commented v. 64, which asserts directly that God's revelation to the Jews only increases their rebelliousness (*ṭughyān*) and disbelief; their enmity to the believers is everlasting; "every time they kindle the fire of war, God snuffs it out, yet still they spread corruption in the land (*wa-yasʿawna fī ʾl-arḍ fasādan*), though God does not love the corrupters." Sūrat al-Māʾidah's emphatic statements about the *mufsidīn* reach its climax here; the root *f-s-d* does not appear again in the *sūrah*, nor does it recur in the last two chapters of the corpus. We should thus see this cluster of references to *fasād* and related concepts in Sūrat al-Māʾidah as the Qurʾān's final word on the matter; while *fasād* is by no means exclusively connected with Israel in the Qurʾān, by the time of the final revelations, it is established as distinctly characteristic of them.

In short, the link between *fasād* and the Jews in Sūrat al-Māʾidah is the culmination of a longer discursive trajectory that develops gradually in the qurʾānic corpus. Older strata of the corpus emphasize failings and offenses of the Jews that are essentially theological in nature—their traducing the qurʾānic prophet, their disputing with him over various matters, their concealment and distortion of what was revealed to them.[93] By the time Sūrat al-Māʾidah is revealed, spreading corruption in the land is presented as a direct and tangible offense against God's law, a "subversion of God's created order," in opposition to the mandate of the community of the believers to promote peace and uphold the divine law.[94] It is an offense wrought not by words or in the heart but with actual deeds, and notably, Q 5:33–34 is the only passage in the Qurʾān that mandates actual this-worldly punishment for its commission.[95] This conception of how the Jews have transgressed

93. This discourse continues in Medinan *sūrah*s as well, however; for example, one might note that all of the qurʾānic references to *taḥrīf*, the misrepresentation of scripture, are Medinan (Q 2:75, 4:46, 5:13.41).

94. Frederick Mathewson Denny, "Corruption," *EQ*, s.v. (2001). Denny notes *fasād* as a direct and severe subversion of the divine order on earth, in contrast to the Jews' concealment and distortion of the truth (including, for example, *taḥrīf*), but he fails to remark the conspicuous linkage of the latter as well as the former with the Jews.

95. Thus Abou El Fadl (*Rebellion and Violence in Islamic Law*, 47–48).

the law revealed to them and so contemned the divine will by their actions and not just their words fits the martial and activist mentality exhibited in Medinan discourse well, especially its positioning of the qurʾānic prophet's community as the agents who will take up arms to exact divine retribution for these crimes.

This is all to say that there is much more at stake in the implicit analogy Sūrat al-Māʾidah draws between Cain and the Jews than previous commentators have recognized. There are, of course, multiple facets to the parallelism established between them in the chapter. Thus, early in the *sūrah*, mention is made of God's protecting the believers when a "group" (or "people," *qawm*) "stretched out their hands against you, but He kept their hands away from you" (v. 11). It is not difficult to imagine that this refers to the *ummah*'s Jewish opponents, and later, similar terminology is used to refer to Abel's anticipation of violence from Cain: "If you stretch out your hand against me to kill me, I won't stretch out my hand against you to kill you" (v. 28). The image of the outstretched hand recurs again later on, with quite a different valence, in a famous verse, in which God's power to restrain the hands of the community's enemies is certainly a subtext (v. 64): "The Jews say, 'God's hand is bound'—may their hands be bound instead! May they be cursed for what they say, for both His hands are outstretched. He dispenses His bounty as He pleases."[96] Triangulating between these verses, it is not difficult to read their import: Cain's violence against Abel recurs in that threatened by the Jews against the qurʾānic prophet and his community, but unlike that primordial precursor, now that violence is deflected by God, and the only outstretched hand that matters is God's, bestowing His largesse upon the faithful.[97]

A variety of other lexical symmetries and resonances throughout the *sūrah* reinforces the connection between Cain and the Jews. In v. 30, Cain murders Abel because "his soul urged him on" (*ṭawwaʿat lahu nafsuhu*); by murdering his brother, he "joined the ranks of the losers (*khāsirīn*)." In vv. 51–53, the believers are exhorted not to take Jews and Christians as allies; they will come to sorrow because of what they concealed in their souls, and have now "joined the ranks of the losers."[98] Another important point of

96. On this well-known verse in the Qurʾān, see below.
97. Notably, Robinson does not see v. 11 or 28 as symmetrical with 64. He observes a particularly prominent wordplay between "hand" (*yad*, also appearing here as *aydīhim*, "their hands") and "Jew" (*yahūd*) in v. 64 ("Hands Outstretched," 13). Presumably if *yad* is meant to bring to mind *yahūd* here in this verse, it would in vv. 11 and 28 as well.
98. Thus Robinson (ibid., 12–13).

thematic symmetry between Cain and the Jews is the reference to "recompense," *jazāʾ*. Before his death, Abel reminds Cain that wrongdoers receive recompense in the Fire (v. 29); the term *jazāʾ* again appears in v. 33, where it refers not to the afterlife but rather the corporal punishment inflicted on those who wage war on God and His messenger, though a terrible penalty (*ʿadhāb ʿaẓīm*) in the afterlife is mentioned here as well.[99]

All of these parallels and associations bolster the presentation of the *fasād* of the Jews who oppose the qurʾānic prophet and his community as an emblematic sin of Israel, a contemporary recurrence of the primordial violence and malice of their precursor Cain. The Qurʾān relates the story of the sons of Adam as a cautionary tale, intended to communicate a very specific message to its audience. On account of Cain's sin, God clearly prohibited killing for Israel; this rule implicitly applies to everyone, but especially to the Jews because this was communicated to them as revelation. But the Qurʾān adds exceptions to the mishnaic version of the rule, for killing is legitimate as a penalty for certain crimes, especially spreading corruption in the land. However, who is it that spreads corruption in the land? It is the Jews themselves; as they are guilty of grave transgressions, they deserve to have the penalty for *fasād* imposed on them. The Qurʾān's incorporation and reconstruing of the rabbinic principle, integrated into the argument that the Jews should know all this and accept the penalty for their behavior, can hardly be construed as ecumenical, as it has sometimes been read.

We should also note that even in adumbrating exceptions to the rule about homicide—and thus legitimating combat against a manifest Jewish threat—the Qurʾān here too follows the precedent set by the Mishnah, adapting it in keeping with its own perspective and context. In the later parts of the mishnaic tractate in which the Cain and Abel passage is found, the question of communal integrity raised by the previous reference to sectarians recurs, in terms that once again resonate quite clearly with numerous parallels in Sūrat al-Māʾidah.

Thus, chapter 10 of tractate Sanhedrin discusses those who are "real" Israelites (those who have a share in the world to come) and those who are not. Here contemporary and biblical history are telescoped as the text relates various examples of scriptural characters whose behavior put them beyond the bounds of redemption; this is a familiar feature of the Qurʾān, in Sūrat al-Māʾidah and elsewhere, and yet another way in which mishnaic

99. Notably, the term *jazāʾ* appears three more times in the *sūrah*, in reference to this-worldly punishment for the thief (v. 38); reward for the righteous in the afterlife (v. 75); and an atoning compensation believers must pay if they violate the sanctity of the *ḥaram* (v. 95).

discourse seems to anticipate it. Critically, the latter half of this chapter in Sanhedrin discusses an extreme example, the purgative violence in which loyal Israelites are licensed to engage when they take up arms to eliminate an erring city (*ʿîr ha-niddaḥat*; cf. Deut 13:13–18). This is the hypothetical case of an entire community meriting destruction by the righteous when led astray by hopelessly corrupt men; here, quite obviously, the rule to take care in exacting the penalty of death simply does not apply.[100]

The next chapter, the conclusion of tractate Sanhedrin, is mostly concerned with the problem of illegitimate authority. Communal elders who overstep their bounds in issuing rulings outside their jurisdiction are to be judged by the highest courts; further, false prophets are mentioned here as particularly dangerous, even if their judgments conform to the halakhah. Notably, like the denizens of the straying town and others whose crimes justify the suspension of the general rule against killing, false prophets are also directly prescribed the penalty of death.[101] As in Sūrat al-Māʾidah, here too in Mishnah tractate Sanhedrin there are clear limits to the idea that slaying a single soul is like slaying all humanity. Killing is in fact warranted, it seems, if the crime of those marked for death is extreme enough. Notably, those so marked are subversives, those whose claims might hold some appeal for the believing community, but must be stridently rejected—or even suppressed by force. This too seems to anticipate the Qurʾān's presentation of the Jews in Sūrat al-Māʾidah as the primary agents of corruption in the land.[102]

---

100. M. Sanh. 10:4–6. Earlier in the tractate authority to declare the blood of the denizens of such a city licit is reserved for the Sanhedrin (1:5).

101. As with the city led astray into godlessness, authority to mandate the death sentence for a false prophet is reserved for the Sanhedrin (1:5). It is perhaps significant that here the court's authority to administer capital punishment to both the denizens of the apostate city and the false prophet is asserted alongside that of sanctioning a king's declaration of war (*milḥemet ha-reshût*, that is, a war initiated by the king and not fought either by divine mandate or in self-defense; see note 77 above).

102. In his 2008 dissertation, Peter Matthews Wright argues that the point of the Qurʾān's allusion to the Mishnah here is that both seek "to limit the opportunities to impose capital sanctions upon specific crimes" ("Modern Qur'anic Hermeneutics," Ph.D diss., University of North Carolina at Chapel Hill, 2008, 160). I would suggest that this reading misses the point of both texts' approach to the question of when violence may be sanctioned, and against whom. I owe this reference to Marianna Klar.

Scriptural Virtuosity and Intercommunal Politics

Overall, the Cain and Abel pericope in Sūrat al-Māʾidah demonstrates why we must be as attentive as possible to the nuances of the Qurʾān's appropriation and deployment of the textual artifacts of pre-Islamic Jewish tradition. Naturally, the possible origin of any given tradition—the focus of much of the classic literature on source criticism of the Qurʾān, such as it is—tends to galvanize the scholar's attention, particularly for what it may reveal of the obscure origins of much of the qurʾānic corpus. But we must also consider how received material is adapted, rescripted, and recombined with other materials; in which literary settings within the qurʾānic corpus; and—most importantly—to what end. As I have shown, in this pericope, we have a biblical story that is viewed through the lens of a Jewish predecessor, but partially informed by the perspective of older Christian tradition as well. However, it is the dynamism and sophistication of the Qurʾān's engagement with the Jewish literary matrix that is most significant here: its presentation of the story reflects not only deep familiarity with the proximate context in which the story appears in the Mishnah, but is also designed to appropriate and subvert the specific claims of the rabbinic precursor in an extremely subtle, deft, and effective way.

In contrast to the former emphasis on Muḥammad's passive reception of influences drawn from his environment—"Abrahamic" scriptural traditions of which his pagan allies and adversaries were only superficially aware at best—contemporary scholars typically view qurʾānic appropriations and subversions of older scriptural and parascriptural materials as deliberate reconfigurations of discourses that were deeply familiar to its audience.[103] To revisit a point made at the beginning of this article, over the last ten to fifteen years, scholars have investigated numerous examples of this phenomenon, but generally in relation to Christian materials, usually in Syriac. It is here, many have argued, that we find the most plausible literary and

103. The shift in scholarly understanding of the Qurʾān's interlocutors from primarily pagan to acculturated in some form of monotheist tradition is perhaps one of the most lasting contributions of revisionism to the discipline of Qurʾānic Studies. See the classic discussion of G. R. Hawting, *The Idea of Idolatry and the Emergence of Islam* (Cambridge: Cambridge University Press, 1999), arguing that accusations of *shirk* represent a form of intra-monotheist polemical discourse; compare the studies collected in Patricia Crone, *The Qurʾānic Pagans and Related Matters: Collected Studies in Three Volumes*, vol. 1, ed. Hanna Siurua (Leiden: Brill, 2016), many of which argue that the qurʾānic "pagans" were entirely cognizant of, and even cited, standard monotheistic concepts but rejected them (thus the dismissal of the qurʾānic message as "tales of the ancients" and so forth).

religious horizons of qur'ānic discourse. Whereas scholars once emphasized the Qur'ān's origin as a wholesale, unsophisticated borrowing of rabbinic tradition, today many are convinced that the genesis of Islam's scripture lies in a persistent, subtle, and proficient engagement with late antique works of mainly Christian provenance such as the Didascalia Apostolorum, the Aramaic gospels and Acts traditions, the Alexander Romance, the *Diatesseron*, and the hymns and homilies of Ephrem, Aphrahat, and Jacob of Sarug.[104]

In certain ways, Sūrat al-Mā'idah fits this pattern. It is particularly concerned to refute Christian claims about Jesus, and (as Reynolds has shown in regard to the eponymous story of the heavenly table) it makes use of a subtle interweaving of pentateuchal, psalmic, and gospel traditions to polemicize against the errors and waywardness of Jesus's disciples, critiquing contemporary Christians as the heirs of the errant *ḥawāriyyūn* rather than true followers of Jesus. As regards the Cain and Abel pericope, here too we see a nuanced engagement with a traditional Christian portrayal of Abel as a prefiguration of Christ; and it is likewise possible that the association of the raven with the story has Christian roots as well. To many, it would seem irrefutable that the background and context for this *sūrah* must have been predominantly Christian.

Given the current popularity of such an approach—entirely justified, in this author's view—the qur'ānic engagement with rabbinic texts seems to fade as a concern. At the very least, the goal of uncovering the Jewish influences supposedly borrowed by Muḥammad now seems far less relevant, in comparison to its centrality for Geiger and his followers. However, our discussion here has shown the striking parallels between the overarching concerns of both the mishnaic tractate and the qur'ānic *sūrah* in question: the circumstances under which punitive violence, especially but not exclusively in the administration of justice, is legitimate; the necessary foundation of such legitimacy in revelation; and the rigorous defense of communal

104. The bibliography on the impact of Syriac literature on the Qur'an is sizeable and continues to grow. For representative treatments of this theme as pertains to the Didascalia, see Holger Zellentin, *The Qur'ān's Legal Culture: The Didascalia Apostolorum as a Point of Departure* (Tübingen: Mohr Siebeck, 2013) and Pregill, *Golden Calf*, 412–420; to the Aramaic gospels, see Emran El-Badawi, *The Qur'ān and the Aramaic Gospel Traditions* (Abingdon: Routledge, 2014); to the Alexander Romance, see Kevin van Bladel, "The *Alexander Legend* in the Qur'ān 18:83–102," in Gabriel Said Reynolds (ed.), *The Qur'ān in Its Historical Context* (Abingdon: Routledge, 2008), 175–203 and Stephen J. Shoemaker, *The Apocalypse of Empire: Imperial Eschatology in Late Antiquity and Early Islam* (Philadelphia: University of Pennsylvania Press, 2018), 79–86.

integrity. Both texts idealize a believing community that is distinguished by its submission to the divine will and seeks to regulate violence and bloodshed through the guidance of revelation, such that engaging in violence vindicates the authority of both revelation and communal leadership. It is not an overstatement to say that for both Mishnah and Qurʾān, violence as regulated through revelation becomes *constitutive* of community and identity. Through this process, the public sphere, in which the administration of justice through various means necessarily occurs, is rendered or reconfigured as holy through the explicit policing and governing of the collective according to a divinely mandated code of justice.

This is a quintessentially late antique nexus of concerns, and so it is not surprising to find it reflected in both Mishnah Sanhedrin and Sūrat al-Māʾidah, though they are separated by some three hundred years.[105] However, the finesse with which the Qur'ān elaborates on these themes by revisiting their treatment in the Mishnah, signaled most of all by the subversive recontextualization of the mishnaic portrayal of Cain and Abel and the ethical lesson drawn therefrom, provokes significant questions. It is perhaps not going too far to suggest that Sūrat al-Māʾidah seeks to establish its own authority and bona fides as a replacement for the Mishnah among both Jews and the followers of the qurʾānic prophet. At the very least, we must recognize that both texts serve as an elaboration on or recapitulation of Torah, and seek to renovate Torah for their respective audiences. But while the Mishnah speaks exclusively to Israel, the Qurʾān clearly speaks to Israel and *ummah* alike—or rather, it seeks to compel Israel to recognize its claims and subordinate itself to the *ummah*, threatening severe sanctions against recalcitrant Jews who do not submit: "humiliation in this world, and a tremendous punishment in the next, except for those who repent before you overpower them" (Q 5:33–34).

Sūrat al-Māʾidah is particularly important as evidence of a late stage of development of qurʾānic discourse (and presumably the attitude and ideology of the prophetic community on the eve of the Arab conquests). On the one hand, it adopts a strong rhetorical posture of distinction and separation from older communities who do not recognize the authority of its prophet and scripture. On the other, strategic use is made of the very scriptural traditions and materials cited by those older communities as warrant for

105. My debt to the work of Thomas Sizgorich, *Violence and Belief in Late Antiquity: Militant Devotion in Christianity and Islam* (Philadelphia: University of Pennsylvania Press, 2009), is no doubt conspicuous here. One of the panels on which I originally presented this research, "Violence and Belief in the Qur'anic Milieu," was devoted to papers inspired by or addressing Sizgorich's work.

their claims, appropriated and exploited for the qur'ānic author's own ends, on behalf of the fledgling *ummah*. This is reminiscent of how Jewish authors of the Second Temple period crafted apologia for Judaism by using the philosophical constructs, literary forms, and conceptual categories of their Greco-Roman interlocutors, or how Christian sources of late antique Syria and Mesopotamia (e.g., the Didascalia) drew on a rich body of traditions of clear Jewish ambience to legitimate their own community and delegitimize others. The necessity of forcing a distinction from *both* Jews and Christians is evident here in the *sūrah*, which may help to explain its simultaneous exploitation of conspicuously Jewish and Christian intertexts. In any event, the fundamental anchoring of Sūrat al-Māʾidah's arguments in a particular specimen of authoritative rabbinic tradition is difficult to deny; its engagement with the mishnaic tractate Sanhedrin seems neither accidental nor incidental.

I will conclude here by taking note of two recent trends in research on the Qurʾān. The first is that a number of other scholars have similarly revisited Geiger's thesis of a primary Jewish impact on the Qurʾān, recalibrating his observations, supplementing them in new ways, or otherwise seeking to illuminate the Jewish matrix in which various qurʾānic passages, themes, and claims were shaped. Sometimes these scholars' findings corroborate my own (or those of Geiger, for that matter). One example is Mehdi Azaiez's analysis of the dialogical form found in a number of qurʾānic passages concerning resurrection, for which he adduces a striking parallel in the Babylonian Talmud (notably, in tractate Sanhedrin); comparing these passages, one sees that "not only shared themes but also equivalent literary forms ... indicate the case for intertextuality."[106] Somewhat more broadly, Abdulla Galadari has postulated that the qurʾānic passages on the *qiblah* represent not the physical direction for prayer prescribed for the believers, but rather a discourse concerning the importance of purifying and properly directing the heart towards God when engaging in prayer. In support of this interpretation, he cites a number of passages from both the Pentateuch and talmudic tradition, implying an intertextual connection between them.[107] A

106. "The Eschatological Counter-Discourse in the Qur'an and in the Babylonian Talmud, *Sanhedrin* 90b–91a," in Holger M. Zellentin (ed.), *The Qur'an's Reformation of Judaism and Christianity: Return to the Origins* (Abingdon: Routledge, 2019), 261–270, 269.

107. "The *Qibla*: An Allusion to the *Shemaʿ*," *CIS* 9 (2013): 165–194. Unfortunately, inquiries into the significance of the term *qiblah* in qurʾānic discourse have fostered a rather freewheeling and at times even conspiratorial line of research arguing that the mosques of the proto-Muslim community were initially oriented in a variety of

third example is the recent research of Saqib Hussain, who stages a provocative argument concerning a much-discussed passage from Sūrat al-Nisāʾ; in his view, Q 4:34, long controversial for its apparent sanction of physical discipline against a disobedient wife, actually concerns suspicions of adultery, and should be read in proximity with—or even as an allusion to—the mishnaic discussion of the *sôṭah* ritual undertaken to ascertain the guilt or innocence of a woman accused of fornication.[108]

Each of the aforementioned studies argues that qurʾānic passages may be illuminated through reference to a parallel in a normative rabbinic source, including the Mishnah. Notably, their authors are generally agnostic regarding the implications for our larger understanding of how the Qurʾān relates to older scriptural forms and discourses—the how and the why that explains the instrumentality and intentionality behind intertextuality.

In another recent piece, Shari Lowin reaches conclusions that are in this respect closer to mine. In investigating the aforementioned claim in the Qurʾān that the Jews say God's hand is bound, Lowin identifies an important precursor in a piyyut or liturgical composition ascribed to Elʿazar ha-Qallir, a Jewish poet of the pre-Islamic period. Notably, the qurʾānic verse does not echo or allude to the poem, but rather critiques the language and imagery found therein: in the piyyut, as well as other, conceptually adjacent, Jewish traditions, God is said to have restrained Himself from protecting Israel at moments when they merited punishment for their sins, enacted against them through the depredations of their worldly enemies and persecutors. The qurʾānic verse deftly appropriates this idea, but shifts its context and alters its meaning in order to belittle the Jews for what they believe. Here the evident textual precursor cannot be understood as a mere "influence," but rather must be viewed as a critical stimulus that provoked a polemical response. Most significantly, the point of the qurʾānic riposte is not simply to challenge the theological integrity of the idea that God can be restrained somehow, but rather to subtly undermine the claim of a special covenantal relationship implied by the Jewish source material.[109]

Michael Graves reaches similar conclusions in his analysis of the image of God raising the mountain over Israel during the revelation of Torah at Sinai, a scene that is portrayed in four different *sūrah*s of the Qurʾān as well

different directions, or even that Islam originated in an Arab settlement north of the Ḥijāz, for example in Nabataea.

108. "The Bitter Lot of the Rebellious Wife: Hierarchy, Obedience, and Punishment in Q. 4:34," *JQS* 23.2 (2021): 66–111.

109. Shari L. Lowin, "*The Jews Say the Hand of God is Chained:* Q. 5:64 as a Response to a Midrash in a *piyyut* by R. Elʿazar ha-Kallir," *JQS* 21.2 (2019): 108–139.

as in two passages in the Babylonian Talmud. In the qurʾānic presentation, this motif is deployed in such a way as to insinuate that Israel only accepted the Torah under duress; notably, this is also the sentiment of the talmudic treatment of the episode.[110] However, the qurʾānic treatment subverts the basic message of the rabbinic depiction of the scene, which emphasizes Israel's special status among the nations. In the qurʾānic treatment, Israel's unique covenantal status is implicit, as it often is in the Qurʾān, but the punitive theme comes to the forefront.[111]

In these qurʾānic adaptations of Jewish precursor materials, we may detect a similar dynamic of appropriation and reversal to that we have observed in the relationship between Sūrat al-Māʾidah and Mishnah tractate Sanhedrin. Most of these cases pertain to material found in normative rabbinic sources, though the relevant Jewish precursor in the case discussed by Lowin is found in a genre that can at most be characterized as para-rabbinic. Perhaps more significantly, my case is unique in that here we appear to see a sustained engagement with a specific rabbinic literary composition—a putative source text that is directly evoked in a particular *sūrah*—and not a motif, theme, or discursive form that resonates more broadly in the qurʾānic corpus.

The second trend in recent research on the Qurʾān, which I have discussed at length elsewhere, is the contemporary revival of interest in the historical Muḥammad—an approach to the origins of the Qurʾān that anchors it in a framework by and large dependent upon the traditional Muslim account of the Prophet's life and mission.[112] The resurgence of such an approach—and the rejection of revisionist skepticism it implies—is a multifaceted issue that we cannot dwell upon here. Our main concern is whether we can invest credence in the Islamic tradition's accounts of Muḥammad's complicated, and eventually fractious—dare we say fratricidal—relations with the Jewish tribes of Medina.

Some scholars take the presence and prominence of the Jewish tribes in the Medinan milieu for granted, while others would decry the attempt to

---

110. As Graves notes, the Bavli treatments seem to elaborate upon a more positive depiction of the image in the halakhic midrash Mekilta de-Rabbi Yishmaʿel (which is itself grounded in a literal reading of Deut 4:11), but adapts it to the new, cosmopolitan context of Sasanian Iraq.
111. Michael Wesley Graves, "The Upraised Mountain and Israel's Election in the Qurʾan and Talmud," *CIS* 11 (2015): 141–177.
112. For an overview of the issues, see my "Positivism, Revisionism, and Agnosticism in the Study of Late Antiquity and the Qurʾān," *JIQSA* 2 (2017): 169–199, and also my recent review of Shoemaker's *The Apocalypse of Empire* in *RQR* 6.7 (2020).

correlate the evidence of the Qur'ān with what the *sīrah* tells us about these Jewish tribes and their relationship with Muḥammad as hopelessly misguided. Most germane for our concerns is the approach of Michael Lecker, who holds that the traditional Muslim sources present an image of Muḥammad's relations with the Jews that is basically reliable in its broad details, though that image is naturally colored by the ideology of a later time.[113] Moreover, Lecker has suggested, on the basis of the traditionally transmitted details pertaining to the clans and tribes mentioned as signatories to the Constitution of Medina and otherwise involved in the politics of the Ḥijāz after the *hijrah*, that the emigration of the Prophet and his community may ultimately have been orchestrated by the Byzantines in a deliberate attempt to counter the local hegemony of the Jewish tribes, agents of the Sasanian dominion.[114]

As previously noted, Muslim tradition usually dates Sūrat al-Mā'idah quite late, and sometimes recognizes that its message is embedded in the context of the Prophet's declining relations and ultimate hostilities with the Jews of Medina.[115] On this basis, scholars have typically dated the *sūrah* sometime in the period from 7/628 to 9/630, with parts of it perhaps as late

113. Lecker's approach, developed over a number of decades, is synthesized in his *Mûḥammad ve-ha-Yehûdîm* (Jerusalem: Yad Yitzḥaq ben Zvi and the Hebrew University of Jerusalem, 2014). While much of Lecker's work has been impactful on scholarship in Europe and the Americas, this synthesis and its implications have largely been overlooked.

114. Michael Lecker, "Were the Ghassānids and the Byzantines behind Muḥammad's *hijra*?," in Denis Genequand and Christian Julien Robin (eds.), *Les Jafnides: Des rois arabes au service de Byzance (VIe siècle de l'ère chrétienne)* (Paris: De Boccard, 2015), 277–293; cf. G. W. Bowersock, *The Crucible of Islam* (Cambridge, MA: Harvard University Press, 2017), 106–114. For specific details on the implications of Lecker and Bowersock's argument, as well as observations on the irreconcilability of this approach with much of contemporary qur'ānic scholarship, see my comments in "Positivism, Skepticism, and Agnosticism." For a provocative discussion of anti-Judaism in the context of the Roman-Persian Great War, see Sarah Gador-Whyte, "Christian-Jewish Conflict in the Light of Heraclius' Forced Conversions and the Beginning of Islam," in Wendy Mayer and Bronwen Neil (eds.), *Religious Conflict from Early Christianity to the Rise of Islam* (Berlin: De Gruyter, 2013), 201–214.

115. Interestingly, Ibn Kathīr identifies "those who commit excesses in the land" (*fī 'l-arḍ la-musrifīn*, Q 5:32) as the Jews of Medina, but on the basis of their practices in the pre-Islamic past, in particular their participating in warfare with their allies the Aws and Khazraj. According to his account, the Jewish tribes would fight each other alongside their pagan confederates and then offer and accept ransom and bloodwit for the captives and the slain, a practice for which God chastised them in Q 2:84–85. See Abū 'l-Fiḍā' Ismā'īl Ibn Kathīr, *Tafsīr al-Qur'ān al-'aẓīm*, ed. Sāmī b. Muḥammad

as 10/632. Thus, to take but one example, Theodor Nöldeke saw Q 5:15–38 as a discrete passage that must date to sometime after the intensification of hostilities between Muḥammad and the Jews, probably close to the campaign against Khaybar in 7/628.[116] The traditional location of the revelation of at least part of the *sūrah* at the time of the Prophet's Farewell Pilgrimage in 10/632 is significant because during this time he is also said to have declared the blood of believers to be illicit to other believers.[117] This stands in sharp contrast to the guidelines established in Sūrat al-Māʾidah to justify war against the Jews as unbelievers, making their blood licit on account of their crimes.

This timing is plausible not only in terms of the *sūrah*'s rejection of the Jews and authorization of violence against them on the basis of their *fasād* and other transgressions, but also possibly in terms of an appeal to Christians, whom the qurʾānic prophet may have countenanced as potential replacement allies at this time.[118] Similar to the articulation of a threat against the Jews in terms they would understand in this *sūrah*, it is possible that the various echoes of Christian tradition we have detected here are intended as flourishes that the qurʾānic community would recognize as familiar and thus appealing. This conjecture may help to explain aspects of the *sūrah* that seem anomalous or superfluous in terms of its overarching message. For example, if the point of the *sūrah* is to justify hostilities against those who spread corruption, Abel's insistent nonviolence—or rather, his forgoing of retaliation—in vv. 28–29 appears somewhat maladroit if he is to serve as a cipher for an *ummah* girding itself for war against the Jews.[119] At the same time, even if we follow Cuypers and others who read the real thrust of Sūrat

al-Salāmah (8 vols.; Riyadh: Dār Ṭaybah li'l-Nashr wa'l-Tawzīʿ, 1418/1997), 3.94, *ad* Q 5:32.

116. *GdQ*, 1.229–230.

117. For the account of Ibn Isḥāq, see Abū Muḥammad ʿAbd al-Malik Ibn Hishām, *Al-Sīrah al-nabawiyyah*, ed. ʿUmar ʿAbd al-Salām Tadmūrī (4 vols.; Beirut: Dār al-Kitāb al-ʿArabī, 1410/1990), 4.248.

118. Obviously, such a hypothesis would oblige us to explain Q 5:51, the famous verse that urges the believers "do not take Jews and Christians as allies, for they are only allies to each other." In fact, one must acknowledge that the entire passage from vv. 51–69 seems stridently hostile to the *ahl al-kitāb* on the whole.

119. Notably, Bell proposed an earlier date for the entire *sūrah* based on the incongruity of the "pacific attitude" of these verses in a martial conquest; see Richard Bell, *A Commentary on the Qurʾān* (2 vols.; Manchester: University of Manchester Press, 1991), 1.154. We might also note Q 2:178, where retaliation (*qiṣāṣ*) is similarly "prescribed" (*kutiba ʿalaykum*), but with a recommendation for leniency that is perhaps ultimately drawn from Matt 5:38–39.

al-Māʾidah as an appeal to Christians to accept the qurʾānic prophet and subordinate them to his authority, one must acknowledge that vv. 27–37, on which I have focused here, are more than just a mere momentary diversion or aside addressing the question of the Jews. Rather, this passage must be read as presaging an intensification of hostilities that would reshape the multilayered social and religious terrain surrounding the *ummah.*[120]

A final detail drawn from the traditional sources in connection with this *sūrah*, albeit indirect, is worth noting. According to a famous account in the *Sīrat Rasūl Allāh* of Ibn Isḥāq, when Muḥammad and his followers turned against their former allies the Banū Qurayẓah after their betrayal during the Battle of the Trench (5/626–627), the fate of the defeated tribe was put in the hands of one Saʿd b. Muʿādh, a Qurazī who embraced Islam and fought for the Prophet, and who was injured during the preceding battle. Saʿd's judgment against his former coreligionists was that the men should be killed, the women and children taken as slaves, and their property divided as spoils of war.[121]

As Martin Lings notes regarding this episode, Saʿd's judgment against the Qurayẓah conforms to the fate legislated for the denizens of an enemy city defeated by Israel in Deut 20:13–14.[122] It is striking in the light of our reading of Sūrah 5, so closely aligned with the mishnaic legitimation of violence, that Islamic tradition should present an analogous justification for the decree against Banū Qurayẓah, anchored in a different register of Jewish scriptural tradition, but one that is conceptually and thematically congruous with the mishnaic one. Noteworthy as well is that this is actually the more *lenient* penalty prescribed for defeated enemies in this chapter of Deuteronomy: the following passage (20:16–18) addresses the case of defeated

120. I borrow the term "multilayered" from Holger Zellentin, who applies it to the Medinan milieu. See his "Trialogical Anthropology: The Qurʾān on Adam and Iblīs in View of Rabbinic and Christian Discourse," in Rüdiger Braun and Hüseyin I. Çiçek (eds.), *New Approaches to Human Dignity in the Context of Qurʾānic Anthropology: The Quest for Humanity* (Newcastle upon Tyne: Cambridge Scholars Publishing, 2017), 59–129. Here Zellentin shows quite clearly that the Medinan narrative of Adam and the angels in Sūrat al-Baqarah (2:28–39) builds on the previous elaborations on the episode from the Meccan period, but also draws in unique traditions of clear Jewish ambience as well. Zellentin infers that this textual dynamic speaks not only to a largely oral milieu, in which different textual traditions freely intermingled, but may have specifically been tailored to address multiple constituencies, including both Jews and Christians.

121. Ibn Hishām, *Al-Sīrah al-nabawiyyah,* 3.190.

122. Martin Lings, *Muhammad: His Life Based on the Earliest Sources* (Rochester, VA: Inner Traditions, 1983), 232 (mistakenly citing the passage as Deut 20:12).

cities of the Canaanites and mandates that they should be utterly destroyed, with none left alive whatsoever. This is the also the pitiless fate decreed for an erring city in Deut 13:13–18, one of the sanctions discussed in the mishnaic tractate Sanhedrin. In contrast, the invocation of Deut 20:13–15 here admits at least some small quantum of mercy rather than total annihilation; this is also the judgment of the Qur'ān, which threatens gruesome punishments for those who wage war against God and His Prophet, but also admits the possibility of mercy in response to repentance (5:33).

It is ultimately unclear how much confidence we can invest in what the tradition reports about the Jews of Medina and whether the information we glean from the sources really illuminates the authentic revelatory context of the Qur'ān. I would certainly not go so far as to suggest that my interpretation of Sūrat al-Mā'idah validates or corroborates every detail of the *sīrah*'s account of Muḥammad's relations with the Jews of Medina. However, a breakdown in the *ummah*'s relationship with Jewish tribes in the vicinity, eventually accelerating into open conflict, provides a broadly plausible context for the emergence of the messaging of the *sūrah* as I have understood it here. Given circumstances in which the qur'ānic prophet's appeal to Jews in his social ambit was purportedly abandoned in favor of open confrontation—culminating, according to the *sīrah*, in the purging of Banū Qurayẓah and the campaign against Khaybar in 5–7/627–628—it strains credulity to think that the legitimation of violence against Jews in Sūrat al-Mā'idah is merely coincidental. This is the entire point of Sūrat al-Mā'idah, especially its reorientation of the Cain and Abel story, which tradition dates to approximately this point in the Prophet's career.

As I have shown here, this messaging is intrinsically tied to the strategic appropriation and reorientation of rabbinic Jewish tradition, more direct and concrete in Sūrat al-Mā'idah than perhaps anywhere else in the Qur'ān. Some would conclude from this that the Jews of Medina must have been halakhically observant and linked to the rabbinic communities of Palestine and Iraq.[123] This is surely an overinterpretation, especially given the variety of the echoes of ancient Jewish tradition exhibited by the qur'ānic corpus. But given the proximate, even intimate, knowledge of a normative rabbinic source that appears to be reflected throughout the *sūrah*, a reconsideration

123. A hypothesis most recently advanced by Haggai Mazuz in *The Religious and Spiritual Life of the Jews of Medina* (Leiden: Brill, 2014), a work that has been widely critiqued for its overconfidence in seeking to recover information about the religiosity and traditions of its subjects. For a countervailing position, see Aaron W. Hughes, *Shared Identities: Medieval and Modern Imaginings of Judeo-Islam* (Oxford: Oxford University Press, 2017), ch. 2, esp. 55–57.

of the connection between the evidence of the Qurʾān and what the traditional sources tell us about the relations between the *ummah* and the Jews towards the end of the Medinan period—at least in broad terms—comes into focus as an especially urgent task. Perhaps the most provocative question remains unanswered, and brings us back full circle to Geiger: how to square the fact of the profound knowledge of rabbinic Judaism and sheer scriptural virtuosity of the qurʾānic prophet with the portrait of Muḥammad that the tradition offers us.

JIQSA 6 (2021): 225–253

إسماعيل، ذو الكفل، وإدريس: قراءة في النّصّ القرآنيّ وفي التّفسيرات الإسلاميّة

إقبال عبد الرازق
باحثة مستقلة

ملخص

إن العديد من الشخصيات النبوية الوارد ذكرها في القرآن الكريم كأنبياء بني إسرائيل هي ممّن ورد ذكرها في الكتب اليهودية والمسيحية المقدسة، نحو إبراهيم وإسحاق ويعقوب ويوسف وموسى وهارون وداود وسليمان وزكريا ويحيى وعيسى وآخرين. لكن بعض هذه الشخصيات يحفها الغموض واللبس، نحو إسماعيل وذي الكفل وإدريس. وذلك أن إسماعيل يظهر في بعض الآيات المكية منفصلاً عن إبراهيم، بخلاف ما نجده في الآيات المدنية المتأخرة حيث يُذكر معه في نفس الآيات. أما ذو الكفل وإدريس فإننا لا نجد لتسميتهما نظائر في التناخ أو في العهد الجديد.

تبحث هذه الدراسة في الشخصيات إسماعيل وذي الكفل وإدريس في شقين منفصلين. الشق الأول يبحث في هوية الشخصيات الثلاث وصفتها كما تنعكس في القرآن، وذلك بقراءة النص القرآني قراءة فيلولوجية وباعتبار السياقات التي تظهر فيها هذه الشخصيات، وأيضاً من خلال مقارنة الآيات القرآنية بآيات أخرى من التناخ العبري. الشق الآخر يتتبع تفسيرات العلماء المسلمين القدماء فيما يتعلق بإسماعيل وذي الكفل وإدريس وكيفية توظيف العلماء لهذه الشخصيات في السياقات المختلفة. تقدم الدراسة تصوراً للشخصيات القرآنية الثلاث مختلفاً عمّا قدمه الباحثون المعاصرون من قبل، وتربطها بشخصيات شموئيل وإلياس واليسع التناخية. وتبيّن الدراسة أن هذا التصور يتوافق مع بعض التفسيرات الإسلامية القديمة والتي تلاشى صداها في المصادر والكتب المتأخرة. ففي هذه المرحلة اهتمّ العلماء بتبيان سبب فصل إسماعيل عن إبراهيم في بعض آيات القرآن، وقدموا تفسيرات متضاربة بشأن هوية ذي الكفل، بينما أجمعوا على أن إدريس هو حنوخ التناخي.

ISMĀʿĪL, DHŪ ʾL-KIFL, AND IDRĪS: A READING OF THE QURʾĀNIC TEXT AND MUSLIM EXEGESIS

IQBAL ABDEL RAZIQ
Independent Scholar

doi: http://dx.doi.org/10.5913/jiqsa.6.2021.a007

Abstract

Several figures whom the Qurʾān names as Israelite prophets are also mentioned in Jewish and Christian scriptural literature, such as Abraham, Isaac, Jacob, Joseph, Moses, Aaron, David, Solomon, Zachariah, John, and Jesus. But some of these prophetic figures are shrouded in obscurity, such as Ismāʿīl, Dhū ʾl-Kifl, and Idrīs. Ismāʿīl, for one, figures separately from Abraham in some Meccan verses, in contrast to Medinan verses that mention him alongside Abraham. As for Dhū ʾl-Kifl and Idrīs, their names have no equivalent in the Hebrew Bible or the New Testament.

The present study investigates the figures of Ismāʿīl, Dhū ʾl-Kifl, and Idrīs. It proceeds in two stages. The first section investigates the identity of the three figures and their characteristics as reflected in the Qurʾān through a philological reading of the qurʾānic text and by examining the context in which these figures appear. I also compare the qurʾānic verses with passages from the Hebrew Bible. The second section examines how classical Muslim scholars interpreted Ismāʿīl, Dhū ʾl-Kifl, and Idrīs, and how these figures were utilized in various contexts. This study offers a new understanding of the three figures and connects them with the biblical Samuel, Elijah, and Elisha. The study shows that this understanding accords with some classical Islamic exegetical opinions, whose echoes faded away in later books and sources. In the early phase the *ʿulamāʾ* were concerned to explain the reason for the separation of Ismāʿīl from Abraham in some verses of the Qurʾān and offered conflicting exegeses regarding the identity of Dhū ʾl-Kifl. They agreed, however, that Idrīs was the Enoch of the Hebrew Bible.

ترتكز العقيدة الإسلامية على مفهوم النبوة والوحي الذي أُنزل إلى محمد، رسول الله إلى العرب. وبحسبها فإن محمداً هو آخر الأنبياء والرسل على وجه البسيطة. وفي المصادر الإسلامية، بدءا من القرآن الكريم، العديد من الأنبياء هم ممّن ورد ذكرهم في الكتب اليهودية والمسيحية المقدسة، نحو نوح وإبراهيم وإسحاق ويعقوب ويوسف وموسى وهارون وسليمان وداود وعيسى وزكريا وآخرين. غير أننا لا نجد لأوصاف بعض الأنبياء أو لأسماء بعضهم في القرآن نظائر صريحة واضحة في الكتب المقدسة السابقة، نحو إسماعيل المذكور في بعض الآيات المكية منفصلاً عن إبراهيم وإسحاق على نحو مغاير لما نجده في الآيات المدنية المتأخرة أو في التناخ، ونحو ذي الكفل وإدريس اللذين لا نجد لتسميتهما تسميات شبيهة في التناخ أو في العهد الجديد. وقد نتج عن ذلك آراء متعددة وتحليلات مختلفة قدمها المفسرون المسلمون القدماء والباحثون المعاصرون، على حد سواء.

تسعى هذه المساهمة أولاً إلى الاستدلال على هوية الأنبياء الثلاثة إسماعيل وذي الكفل وإدريس من خلال قراءة النص القرآني وسياقاته وفهم ألفاظه وتعابيره ومقارنته بالكتب السابقة، خاصة التناخ. ومن ثم تتتبّع كيف صُورت هذه الشخصيات وكيف وُظفت في التفسيرات الإسلامية اللاحقة، السنيّة تحديداً على اختلاف مشاربها الفكرية والعقدية، وذلك بحسب ما يتطلبه النقاش ابتداء من مؤلفات مفسري القرن الثاني والثالث هجري (الثامن والتاسع ميلادي)، نحو مقاتل بن سليمان وعبد الرزاق الصنعاني، وحتى المتأخرين منهم، نحو البقاعي الذي عاش في القرن التاسع هجري (الخامس عشر ميلادي). سأتناول كل واحد

من الأنبياء إسماعيل وذي الكفل وإدريس، على حدة، مستعرضة أولاً بعض المقترحات التي قدمها الباحثون المعاصرون لتحديد هويتهم كما تنعكس في القرآن، ثم أقدم تصوري لها. بعد ذلك سأستعرض التفسيرات الإسلامية المختلفة لكل شخصية من هؤلاء، أيضاً على حدة، مبينة كيف عُرفت وكيف وُظفت في سياقات مختلفة لترتبط بشخصيات عدة مختلفة. لكن، في المستهلّ سأتناول باختصار مفهوم "النبي" مقارنة بـ"الرسول" كما ينعكسان في القرآن؛ ذلك أن إسماعيل وذا الكفل وإدريس قد ورد ذكرهم مع أنبياء بني إسرائيل، فتحديد مفهوم "النبي" ووظيفته بحسب النص القرآني سيساعدنا على فهم هذه الشخصيات.

مفهوم "الرسول" و"النبي" في النص القرآني

يصور النص القرآني محمداً رسولاً بعثه الله إلى المشركين من العرب، ويستخدم لفظين مختلفين، "رسول" و"نبي"، للإشارة إليه وإلى مبعوثي الله إلى الأمم لدعوتهم إلى الإيمان بالله. قُدمت تفسيرات مختلفة، إسلامية وغربية، فيما إذا كان هذان اللفظان يتعلقان بذات المعنى ويحيلان إلى نفس الوظيفة التي أوكلها الله للرسل والأنبياء، أم أن اختلافاً ما يُفرّق بينهما. هناك من اقترح أن الرسول والنبي يحيلان إلى نفس الوظيفة وأن اللفظين مترادفان أو متقاربان. واقترح آخرون أن الرسول يختلف عن النبي، نحو أن الرسول هو من يؤسس شريعة وأمة مؤمنة، في حين أن النبي هو من يتابع عمل الرسول ويكمله. ولقد بينت سابقاً أن تحولاً ما طرأ على استخدام مفهومي "الرسول" و"النبي" فيما بين السور المكية والأخرى المدنية.[1] ويمكن تلخيص هذا التحول كالآتي: في السور المكية يظهر الرسول كمبعوث الله إلى الأمم الكافرة المشركة، وترتكز رسالته على الوعظ عن الله الواحد الخالق وعن البعث والقيامة والحساب والعقاب والجزاء يوم الدين، وكذلك عن عقاب الله في الحياة الدنيا. ومن الرسل الذين تكرر ذكرهم في القرآن نوح وهود وصالح ولوط وشعيب وموسى.[2] أما النبي، فإن من أهم سماته أنه من ذرية إبراهيم من نسل ابنه إسحاق وحفيده يعقوب، أي أنه ينتسب إلى بني إسرائيل، وهم أمة موحدة غير مشركة، ومنهم، مثلاً، موسى وهارون ويوسف وداود وسليمان وأيوب وإلياس وعيسى وزكريا ويحيى.[3] إن وظيفة النبي في بني إسرائيل هي قيادتهم وإدارة شؤونهم الحياتية، خاصة الدينية والقضائية، باعتباره مصطفى من الله صدّيقاً مخلصاً. ويعتمد النبي في أحكامه وإدارة شؤون أمته على الوحي الإلهي وعلى الكتب السماوية التي أنزلت إلى أمته، وأهمها توراة موسى ومن بعدها إنجيل عيسى، وهو في القرآن نبي في بني

1. إن قراءتي للنص القرآني هي قراءة دياكرونية تتتبع الأفكار والمعاني القرآنية ابتداء بالسور المكية وانتهاء بالمدنية. وتعتمد هذه القراءة على ترتيب السور بحسب ثيودور نولدكه (Theodor Nöldeke) كأداة ووسيلة بحثية. يصنف نولدكه السور القرآنية إلى سور مكية وهي الأقدم وأخرى مدنية وهي المتأخرة، كما ويقسم السور المكية إلى ثلاث مراحل زمنية: المكية الأولى، المكية الثانية، والمكية الثالثة.

2. انظر مثلاً قصص هؤلاء في سورة هود، تباعاً، في الآيات 25–48، 50–60، 61–68، 77–83، 84–95، 96–99؛ وفي سورة الأعراف في الآيات 59–64، 65–72، 73–79، 80–84، 85–93، 103–136. وفي بعض السور يقدّم هارون أيضاً كرسول يساند أخاه موسى في رسالته إلى فرعون، كما جاء، مثلاً، في سورة طه (الآية 30) والقصص (الآية 34) والصافات (الآية 114–122). ويضاف إلى الرسل المذكورين أيضاً إبراهيم، وذلك أنه أرسل إلى قومه الذين عبدوا الأصنام والتماثيل، كما جاء، مثلاً، في الشعراء 26: 69–87، والصافات 37: 83–100. وفي بعض الآيات أن رسلاً آخرين قد بعثهم الله للأمم ولم يُذكروا في النصّ القرآنيّ (النساء 4: 164؛ غافر 40: 78).

3. يعدّ النص القرآني شخصيات مقدسة من العهد الجديد نحو عيسى وزكريا ويحيى (يوحنا المعمدان) أنبياء بُعثوا في بني إسرائيل.

إسرائيل. وعليه، فإن "الرسول" و"النبي" يتجليان في القرآن المكي كنظيرين من حيث أنهما مبعوثا الله وسفيراه إلى أممهم، ولكن في حين أن النبي سليل بني إسرائيل ويُبعث فيهم، فإن الرسول يُبعث إلى غيرهم من الأمم، ولا يُشترط فيه انتسابه إلى بني إسرائيل. يتجلى هذا المفهوم من خلال تقديم محمد في الفترة المكية كرسول فقط، في حين أن موسى يُقدم كرسول وكنبي أيضاً، هذا باعتباره رسولاً إلى فرعون والمصريّين ونبياً في بني إسرائيل. غير أن تحولاً طرأ على هذا المفهوم لاحقاً، ويظهر جلياً في السور المدنيّة في القرآن حيث يُقدم محمد كنبي، لا رسول فحسب، وذلك أن صفة النبي أريد بها مخاطبة اليهود والنصارى في المدينة وما حولها؛ فمحمد رسول الله إلى العرب يُقدم ها هنا كنبي أي مبعوث الله إلى اليهود والنصارى. وهكذا فإن مفهوم انتساب النبي إلى سلالة إبراهيم من نسل إسحاق قد توسع ليشمل أيضاً سلالته من نسل إسماعيل، كما يظهر بوضوح في الآيات المدنية (فيما يلي). وفي هذه المرحلة أيضاً، وعلى غرار محمد، قُدم الرسل كأنبياء والأنبياء كرسل ليصبح التمييز بين هاتين المجموعتين أمراً صعباً.[4]

إسماعيل في النص القرآني

عند تتبع ملامح شخصية إسماعيل في القرآن نواجه إشكالية كبيرة، ذلك أن إسماعيل بن إبراهيم لا يظهر في النص القرآني منذ البداية كنبي بوضوح مقارنة بإسحاق الذي يُشار إلى نبوته حتى قبل مولده.[5] تتجلى في القرآن صورة لإسماعيل مثيرة للجدل: في جميع الآيات المدنية يُذكر دون لَبس مع أبيه إبراهيم (في سياق الحديث عن تطهير البيت وبنائه؛ البقرة 2: 125، 127) ومع إسحاق أخيه ويعقوب (البقرة 2: 132، 133، 136، 140؛ آل عمران 3: 84؛ النساء 4: 163)، ولكن في الآيات المكية يُذكر مع أنبياء بني إسرائيل، لا بمحاذاة إبراهيم (وإسحاق ويعقوب) المذكور في نفس السياق، بل منفصلاً عنه منقطعاً.[6]

اختلف الباحثون المعاصرون في تفسير هذا التناقض في ملامح شخصية إسماعيل في القرآن. يفسر سنوك هرخرونيه (Snouck Hurgronje) هذه الإشكالية بأن النبي محمداً لم يكن في البداية (الفترة المكية) على دراية بالعلاقة الصحيحة التي تربط إسماعيل بإبراهيم، معتقداً خطأ أن أبناء إبراهيم هم إسحاق ويعقوب.[7] وفي رأي هاينريش شباير (Heinrich Speyer) أن إسماعيل لا يظهر كابن إبراهيم إلا في الفترة المدنية.[8] ويعتقد رودي بارت

4. انظر بتوسع: إقبال عبد الرازق، "التجلّي الإلهيّ لأنبياء بني إسرائيل بحسب الإسلام المبكّر والكلاسيكي [بالعبرية]،" (رسالة دكتوراه، جامعة تل أبيب، 2019)، ص 32–42.

5. ذلك في الآيات التي تروي لنا قصة الرسل (الملائكة) الذين جاءوا إلى إبراهيم ليبشروه وزوجته بابن "عليم" (الحجر 15: 53؛ الذاريات 51:28). و"العلم" في السياق القرآني يرتبط ارتباطاً وثيقاً بالنبوة والوحي الإلهي، مثلاً: البقرة 2: 120، 247؛ النحل 16: 27؛ الإسراء 17: 85؛ مريم 19: 43؛ النمل 27: 42؛ القصص 28: 80؛ الجاثية 45: 17؛ الأحقاف 46: 23.

6. يُستثنى من ذلك الآية 39 من سورة إبراهيم، والتي يدرجها نولدكه في المكية الثالثة.

7. يعتقد هرخرونيه أيضاً أن إبراهيم لا يحظى باهتمام كبير في السور المكية، فهو يجد أن الكعبة والعرب عموماً لم يحظوا في هذه المرحلة بذلك الاهتمام. يقول إن النظرة إلى إبراهيم وإسماعيل قد تغيرت في السور المدنية في سياق ردّ فعل محمد على رفض اليهود لنبوته. انظر: Willem A. Bijlefeld, "Controversies around the Qur'anic Ibrāhīm Narrative and Its 'Orientalist' Interpretations," *MW* 72 (1982): 81–94, 83–85.

8. Heinrich Speyer, *Die biblischen Erzählungen im Qoran* (Hildesheim: Georg Olms Verlag, 1988), 170–171.

(Rudi Paret) أن إسماعيل المذكور في بعض السور المكية يرتبط بصورة ما بإبراهيم، وإن لم يكن هذا الرابط صلة نسب. يرى بارت أن إسماعيل ليس ذا حضور بارز في القرآن إذ أنه يُقدّم كابن إبراهيم وكأحد أجداد يعقوب، لا غير.[9] أما يواكيم مبارك فيرى أن العلاقة بين إسماعيل وإبراهيم تتجلى في السور المكية كما في السور المدنية، ولكنه يُقرّ أن تلك الصلة لا تبدو مباشرة في المكية.[10] وفي رأي رؤوبين فيرستون (Reuven Firestone)، إن إسماعيل الموصوف بصادق الوعد في سورة مريم (54:19) لربما يشير إلى شخصية مغايرة لإسماعيل المذكور في التناخ العبري.[11] في تفسير مشابه لما سأطرحه في هذه الورقة، يقول إركان تشيليك (Ercan Celik) إن إسماعيل المذكور في السور المكية هو النبي شموئيل.[12] ويعتمد تشيليك في ذلك على حقيقة ذكره في القرآن مع النبيّيْن إلياس واليسع، فجميعهم يرتبطون بما يسمى بـ"جماعة الأنبياء" أو "أبناء الأنبياء" المذكورين في التناخ، ويعتمد كذلك على التشابه في الاسمين إسماعيل وشموئيل.[13]

من المهم الوقوف بداية على مواضع ظهور إسماعيل في قصص الأنبياء وتسلسل أسمائهم في السور القرآنية المكية لتبيان بعض خصائص هذه الشخصية وعلاقتها بالأنبياء الآخرين. وقد أشير إلى إسماعيل في آيتين من سورة مريم (19: 54–55)، يلي ذلك آيتان تشيران إلى إدريس (19: 56–57). أما الآيات الثلاث السابقة ففيها إشارة إلى موسى وهارون (19: 51–53). وقبل ذلك، جاءت قصة إبراهيم مختومة بتبشيره بنبوة إسحاق ويعقوب (19: 41–50). وهكذا فإن قصة إبراهيم جاءت أولاً، ثم الإشارة إلى موسى وهارون، ثم الإشارة إلى إسماعيل فإدريس. وظهور إسماعيل بعد الحديث عن موسى في سورة مريم مهم لفهمنا لهذه الشخصية كما سأبيّن لاحقاً. وفي سورة الأنبياء يُذكر موسى وهارون في الآية 21: 48، يلي ذلك قصة تحطيم إبراهيم الأصنام التي تنتهي بالإشارة إلى نبوة إسحاق ويعقوب (21: 51–72)، يلي ذلك إشارة إلى لوط (21: 74–75) ونوح (21: 76–77) وقصة داود وسليمان (21: 78–82)، وقصة أيوب مختصرة (21: 83–84)، ثم يُذكر إسماعيل مع إدريس وذي الكفل في الآية 21: 85. أما في سورة ص، فتأتي قصص داود (38: 17–26) وسليمان (38: 30–40) وأيوب (38: 41–44)، ويليها إشارة إلى إبراهيم وإسحاق ويعقوب في ثلاث آيات (38: 45–47)، منفصلاً عنهم يُذكر إسماعيل في الآية التالية مع اليسع وذي الكفل (38: 48). وفي سورة الأنعام، يُذكر إسماعيل في سلسلة أسماء لبعض الأنبياء جاءت بعد قصة بحث إبراهيم عن

9. Rudi Paret, "Ismāʿīl," *EI*², s.v. (1978).

10. Youakim Moubarac, *Abraham dans le Coran* (Paris: Librairie Philosophique J. Vrin, 1985), 55, 64–67.

11. Reuven Firestone, "Ishmael," *EQ*, s.v. (2002).

12. استغنيت في هذه الورقة عن استخدام المزيد من صيغ الأسماء لنفس الشخصية تجنباً للإرباك. اقتصرت، مثلاً، على استخدام "شموئيل" دون "صموئيل"، و"إلياس" دون "إلياهو"، و"اليسع" دون "إليشع"، و"شاؤول" دون "شاول"، و"حزقيل" دون "حزقيال". ذلك أن النقاش في هذه الورقة يدور غالباً حول تسمية إسماعيل وذي الكفل وإدريس في المصادر الإسلامية، ولأن هذه المصادر تستخدم "شموئيل"، و"إلياس"، و"اليسع" للإشارة إلى هؤلاء، وتستخدم كذلك "حزقيل"، التزمت بها واستخدمتها كذلك. ويستثنى من ذلك الإحالات إلى الأسفار التناخية، نحو سفر صموئيل، سفر حزقيال، إلخ.

13. Ercan Celik, "The Enigmatic Prophets of the Qur'an: Is'mā'īl [sic], Id'rīs [sic]/al-Yasaʿa [sic] and Dhul-Kifl," February 2016, (https://www.academia.edu/28557980/The_Enigmatic_Prophets_of_the_Quran_Ism%C4%81%C4%ABl_Idr%C4%ABs_al-Yasa%CA%BFa_and_Dhul-Kifl_and_The_Companies_of_Prophets_of_the_Hebrew_Bible_Samuel_Elijah_and_Elisha_)

الله الحق ومحاربته الوثنية في أبناء قومه، والتي تُختتم بالإشارة إلى نبوة إسحاق ويعقوب (6: 74–84). وجاءت أسماء الأنبياء هناك بالترتيب التالي: إسحاق ويعقوب، وداود وسليمان وأيوب ويوسف وموسى وهارون (6: 84)، وزكريا ويحيى وعيسى وإلياس (6: 85)، وإسماعيل واليسع ويونس ولوط (6: 86).

إن مواضع ظهور الأنبياء في السور القرآنية ذات أهمية لفهمنا هذه الشخصيات من حيث الروابط والقواسم والسياقات التي تجمعها. وإسماعيل ليس استثناء هنا، فالوقوف على مواضع ظهوره في الآيات المكية من حيث الترتيب ومن حيث اقترانه بالأنبياء الآخرين في سلاسل الأنبياء أو قصصهم (أي مع من يُذكر، وقبل من، وبعد من؟) سيساعدنا على فهم هذه الشخصية. فنحن نستخلص، مثلاً، أن إسماعيل الوارد ذكره في المواضع أعلاه منفصلاً عن إبراهيم هو ليس ابن إبراهيم، وذلك أنه لا يظهر في خواتم القصص، المشار إليها أعلاه، مع إسحاق الذي يُفترض أنه أخوه. وعوضاً عن ذلك يظهر إسماعيل مع أنبياء آخرين، فهو إذا نبي من بني إسرائيل، أي أنه من سلالة إبراهيم ولكنه من الأجيال المتأخرة من نسل يعقوب بن إسحاق. ومن اللافت أن هناك مجموعات من الأنبياء تظهر كـ"ثلاثيّات" في عدة مواضع في النص القرآني. فعادة ما يظهر إسحاق ويعقوب في سياق الحديث عن إبراهيم، وهؤلاء الثلاثة يرتبطون بعلاقة الأب والابن وابن الابن. وتظهر قصة عيسى في عدة مواضع بمحاذاة قصة زكريا ويحيى (19: 2–34؛ 21: 89–91)، وهؤلاء الثلاثة يظهرون معاً في سلسلة الأنبياء في سورة الأنعام (6: 85)، وليس هناك خلاف على أهمية هذه الشخصيات في العهد الجديد وفي التقليد المسيحي القديم. وهناك ثلاثي آخر في القرآن، داود وسليمان وأيوب، ذلك أن قصص هؤلاء تظهر بالتتابع في سورة ص (38: 17–44) وسورة الأنبياء (21: 78–84)، كما وتظهر أسماؤهم في سلسلة الأنبياء في سورة الأنعام بنفس التتابع (6: 84). ويرتبط داود بسليمان برابط الأبوة، وليس من الواضح تماماً كيف يرتبط أيوب بهاتين الشخصيتين،[14] غير أنه من الصعب تجاوز حقيقة أن أيوب المذكور في أربعة مواضع فقط في النص القرآني يظهر فيها جميعاً بمحاذاة داود وسليمان.[15] وهناك مجموعة رابعة مكوّنة من موسى وهارون

---

14. من الجدير بالذكر أن سفر المزامير وسفر الأمثال المرتبطيْن في التقليد اليهودي والمسيحي بشخصية داود وسليمان، يظهران في التناخ العبري بالتتابع ويليهما سفر أيوب. وقد وقف الباحثون على علاقة بعض السور والآيات القرآنية بنصوص من المزامير التناخية، فمثلاً، بيّنت أنجليكا نويفرت هذه العلاقة في أبحاث مستفيضة. أما العلاقة بين آيات قرآنية وأخرى من سفر الأمثال وسفر أيوب فإنها قائمة، غير أنها لم تدرس إلى الآن دراسة معمقة. ما أريد قوله هنا وجوب انتباهنا إلى أن مواضع التشابه والتقارب بين النص القرآني والنصوص التناخية من الأسفار المذكورة (المزامير، الأمثال، أيوب) يقوي الاحتمال أن ترتيب ظهور داود وسليمان وأيوب معاً في السور القرآنية لا يحتكم إلى العشوائية والصدفة، وهذا الأمر يحتاج إلى المزيد من التقصّي والبحث. عن العلاقة بين النص القرآني والمزامير التناخية، انظر مثلاً: Angelika Neuwirth, "Qur'anic Reading of the Psalms," in Angelika Neuwirth, Nicolai Sinai, and Michael Marx (eds.), *The Qur'ān in Context: Historical and Literary Investigations into the Qu'ānic Milieu* (Leiden: Brill, 2011), 733–778.

15. بالإضافة إلى المواضع الثلاثة المبيّنة هنا، يُذكر أيوب في موضع رابع في سورة النساء المدنية بعد عيسى، وقبل يونس وهارون اللذيْن يفصلانه عن سليمان وداود، على النحو الآتي: "إِنَّآ أَوْحَيْنَآ إِلَيْكَ كَمَآ أَوْحَيْنَآ إِلَىٰ نُوحٍ وَٱلنَّبِيِّينَ مِن بَعْدِهِ وَأَوْحَيْنَآ إِلَىٰ إِبْرَاهِيمَ وَإِسْمَاعِيلَ وَإِسْحَاقَ وَيَعْقُوبَ وَٱلْأَسْبَاطِ وَعِيسَىٰ وَأَيُّوبَ وَيُونُسَ وَهَارُونَ وَسُلَيْمَانَ وَآتَيْنَا دَاوُودَ زَبُوراً" (4: 163). ويحتمل أن تقديم أيوب في هذا الموضع وفصله عن داود وسليمان جاء ليتناسب مع الايقاع الداخلي في الآية، حيث ينسجم "أيوب" مع إيقاع الاسم "يعقوب" السابق له في ذات الآية. لاحظ أيضاً أن موضع سليمان يتقدم على داود، على ما يبدو، أيضاً محكوماً بإيقاع الكلام (والنفس الشعريّ، إن جاز التعبير) في الآية.

الأخوين (19: 51–53؛ 21: 48) اللذين يشكّلان ثلاثياً مع يوسف في سورة الأنعام (6: 84). ويشترك يوسف معهما في كونه نبياً إسرائيلياً وكونه رسول الله إلى فرعون والمصريّين، كما يُستدل من سورة غافر (40: 34).[16]

ما يهمنا هنا في هذا السياق مجموعة أخرى من الأنبياء، ثلاثي، فيها يشكّل إسماعيل (المنفصل عن إبراهيم) عنصراً أساسياً. ومن هذا المنطلق، فإن الاستدلال على العلاقة التي تربط الثلاثي سيساعدنا في التعرف على شخصية إسماعيل. غير أننا نواجه إشكالية في تحديد هوية النبيّين الآخريْن في هذا الثلاثي، لأنهما يتبدّلان في المواضع المختلفة من حيث المسمى. فإسماعيل في سورة ص يظهر مع اليسع وذي الكفل (38: 48)، وفي سورة الأنبياء يظهر مع إدريس وذي الكفل (21: 85)، وفي سورة مريم جاء وصفه في آيتيْن (19: 54–55) يليه بالذكر إدريس (19: 56–57). أما في سورة الأنعام فإن إسماعيل يظهر بعد إلياس المذكور في الآية السابقة (6: 85) ومع اليسع في ذات الآية (6: 86). وإذا ما تمعّنّا في الثلاثيات التي يظهر فيها إسماعيل معتبرين ارتباط شخصياتها برابط ما على غرار الثلاثيات إبراهيم وإسحاق ويعقوب، زكريا ويحيى وعيسى، داود وسليمان وأيوب، موسى وهارون ويوسف، فإنه يمكن الافتراض أن الثلاثيات المختلفة التي يشترك فيها إسماعيل (وهي: إسماعيل واليسع وذو الكفل؛ إسماعيل وإدريس وذو الكفل؛ إسماعيل وإلياس واليسع)، تحيلنا إلى نفس الشخصيات الثلاث، والتي تتجلى بوضوح في سورة الأنعام بصفة إسماعيل وإلياس واليسع. هذا الثلاثي سيساهم أيضاً في تحديد هوية شخصيتي ذي الكفل وإدريس الغامضتين، كما سأبيّن في التحليل المخصص لكل منهما.

يبدو أن المقصود بإسماعيل المذكور في السور المكية منفصلاً عن إبراهيم هو شموئيل النبي. إن هذه الفرضية تستند إلى التشابه الحاصل في لفظي الاسمين العربي إسماعيل والعبري شموئيل. وينعكس مثل هذا التشابه في الاسمين *su-mu-ʿil* و*shu-mu-ʿil* الموثقين في كتابات ومصادر آشورية قديمة، فيما يعتقد بعض الباحثين أن هذين الاسمين يحيلان إلى إسماعيل.[17] وبما أن اللغات الأشورية هي لغات سامية كالعربية والعبرية، فإن استخدام الاسم "شموئيل" للتدليل على إسماعيل محتمل أيضاً بالعربية. ويدعم هذا الافتراض أحاديث وتفسيرات إسلامية قديمة تشير إلى أن الصورة العربية للاسم "شموئيل" هي "إسماعيل" (سيأتي).

يضاف إلى التشابه في الأسماء، أن صفة إسماعيل كنبي صادق في وعوده، كما جاءت في الآية 19: 54، تتشابه مع صفة النبي شموئيل الواردة في التناخ في سفر صموئيل الأول، وجاء فيها أن أيّاً من كلام شموئيل لم يسقط إلى الأرض، وفي هذا إشارة إلى صدق وعوده وتحققها، وجاء فيها أيضاً تأكيد على نبوته في بني إسرائيل.[18] وللمقارنة، تقول الآية 19:

---

16. تقول الآية 40: 34 التي جاءت في سياق قصة مبعث موسى إلى فرعون: "وَلَقَدْ جَآءَكُمْ يُوسُفُ مِن قَبْلُ بِٱلْبَيِّنَاتِ فَمَا زِلْتُمْ فِي شَكٍّ مِّمَّا جَآءَكُم بِهِ حَتَّىٰٓ إِذَا هَلَكَ قُلْتُمْ لَن يَبْعَثَ ٱللَّهُ مِن بَعْدِهِ رَسُولاً كَذَٰلِكَ يُضِلُّ ٱللَّهُ مَنْ هُوَ مُسْرِفٌ مُّرْتَابٌ."

17. يعقوب ليفار، "إسماعيل [بالعبرية]،" *الموسوعة التناخية* (القدس: مؤسسة بياليك، 1950–1988)، ج 3، عمود 902–906، 906؛ Israel Finkelstein and Thomas Römer, "Comments on the Historical Background of the Abraham Narrative: Between 'Realia' and 'Exegetica,'" *Hebrew Bible and Ancient Israel* 3 (2014): 3–23, 13–14; Jan Retsö, *The Arabs in Antiquity: Their History from the Assyrians to the Umayyads* (Abingdon: Routledge, 2003), 165–168.

18. يدعم تشيليك مقاربته المشار إليها بين إسماعيل في القرآن وبين النبي شموئيل بآيات مختلفة من التناخ هي:

54: "وَٱذْكُرْ فِي ٱلْكِتَابِ إِسْمَاعِيلَ إِنَّهُ كَانَ صَادِقَ ٱلْوَعْدِ وَكَانَ رَسُولاً نَّبِيّاً." وتقول الآيات في صموئيل الأول 3: 19–20: "وكبر شموئيل وكان الله معه، ولم يُسقط من جميع كلامه شيئاً إلى الأرض. وعرف جميع إسرائيل من دان إلى بئر سبع أنه قد اؤتمن شموئيل نبياً لله."[19] وجاء في موضع آخر، في صموئيل الأول 7: 9، أن شموئيل دعا الله أن يرد الفلستينيّين عن بني إسرائيل "فاستجاب الله له". قد يكون تصوير شموئيل رسولاً، بالإضافة إلى كونه نبياً، في الآية القرآنية مستوحى من أهميته في التقليد اليهودي القديم الذي كثيراً ما يُقارن فيه شموئيل بموسى وهارون من حيث الرفعة والأهمية.[20] وفي القرآن موسى وهارون هما نبيان ورسولان. ويحتمل أن يكون ذلك نابعاً من دور شموئيل في محاربة أعداء بني إسرائيل (العماليق والفلستينيون) على غرار محاربة موسى وهارون فرعون والمصريين وقد بُعثا رسولين إليهم. وفي رأيي إن مجيء الآيتين اللتين تذكران إسماعيل في سورة مريم بعد ذكر موسى لم يكن عشوائياً، بل له دلالات، نحو أن إسماعيل، هو شموئيل، هو نبي مهم أيضاً. وقد يعكس التقارب في الموضع بين ذكر موسى وإسماعيل المقاربة الحاصلة بين الشخصيتين في التقليد اليهودي القديم. والدلالة الأخرى هي دلالة زمنية حيث يعكس ظهور إسماعيل بعد موسى ترتيباً زمنياً، ويظهر هذا البعد بوضوح في قصة شموئيل في سورة البقرة إذ جاء فيها أنه نبي بُعث في بني إسرائيل "مِنْ بَعْدِ مُوسَى" (2: 246).

والسؤال الذي يطرح نفسه هو لماذا قُدّم شموئيل في النص القرآني باسم إسماعيل، وخاصة أن هناك اسماً عربياً نظيراً لاسمه كان مستخدماً قبل الإسلام، وهو السموأل؟[21]

من المحتمل أن تكون الغاية من استخدام الاسم إسماعيل في القرآن للإشارة إلى شموئيل هي التلميح إلى جانب في شخصيته أو في قصته النبوية. الافتراض الأول يميل إلى أن الاسم إسماعيل ينسجم مع وصف هذا النبي في القرآن كمَن يصدق في وعوده، تحديداً في الآية 19: 54. وفي السياق القرآني لا تتحقق وعود الأنبياء إلا بإرادة الله تصديقاً لهم، ومن هذا المنطلق فإن اللفظ إسماعيل يشير إلى أن الله قد سمع وعود شموئيل لقومه أو وعيده لأعدائه فأثبتها وحققها فصدّقه. هذا باعتبار امتزاج مركبين في اسمه هما "سمع" و"ئيل" (= الله)، أي "سمع الله". إن وصف شموئيل في التناخ، المشار إليه آنفاً، ينسجم أيضاً مع هذا المعنى: إن الله لم يُسقط أيّاً من كلامه إلى الأرض، أي لم يُسقط أيّاً من وعوده للناس، وإن الله استجاب لصلواته.[22] الافتراض الآخر يميل إلى ارتباط الاسم إسماعيل بقصة مولد شموئيل كما وردت في التناخ. وفيها أن حنة زوجة ألقانة كانت بداية عاقراً لا تلد فدعت الله وسألته أن يرزقها ولداً (صموئيل الأول 1: 20، 27)،[23] فاستجاب لها الله ووهبها شموئيل، أي سمع سؤالها واستجاب

إرميا 15: 1؛ مزامير 99: 6. انظر: Celik, "The Enigmatic Prophets."

19. ترجمت هذه الآيات بنفسي مستعينة بترجمات العهد القديم العربية الحديثة. فضّلت استخدام "الله" لترجمة "يهوه"، وأبقيت على صورة الاسم "شموئيل" لأنها الأقرب للصورة المستخدمة في المصادر الإسلامية القديمة.

20. انظر، مثلاً: تلمود بابلي، روش هشاناه 25 ب؛ حجيجاه 4 ب.

21. مثلاً، السّموأل بن عادياء هو شاعر يهودي عاش قبل الإسلام. انظر: أبو الفرج علي بن الحسين الأصفهاني، *كتاب الأغاني* (13 مجلداً؛ بيروت: دار إحياء التراث العربي، 1994)، ج 11، ص 350–352.

22. بحسب النبوات القديمة في إسرائيل، إن إحدى الميّزات التي يمكن من خلالها التعرف على النبي الكاذب هي عدم تحقق كلامه ووعوده. انظر: David Noel, "Between God and Man: Prophets in Ancient Israel," in Yehoshua Gitay (ed.), *Prophecy and Prophets: The Diversity of the Contemporary Issues in Scholarship* (Atlanta: Scholars Press, 1997), 57–87, 64.

23. إن الاسم العبري "شموئيل" لا يتفق في أصله ومعناه مع موتيف "سماع الله" لسؤال حنة. وقد ناقش دارسو التناخ هذه الإشكالية، انظر: شاؤول أحيطوب، "شموئيل [بالعبرية]،" *الموسوعة التناخية*، ج 8، عمود 71–80، 73؛ بنيامين أوبنهايمر، *النبوة القديمة في إسرائيل* [بالعبرية] (القدس: دار إصدار الكتب على اسم ي.ل. ماجنس،

لصلواتها. وفي كلا الافتراضين المذكورين لتسمية شموئيل في القرآن بإسماعيل، فإن الصورة العربية للاسم "السموأل" لا تخدم معنى "سمع الله". إن استخدام أسماء الشخصيات والكنى ذات الدلالات في القرآن، على نحو ما بيّنت فيما يتعلق بالاسم إسماعيل هنا، ليس أمراً مستغرباً، بل هو وارد في مواضع أخرى. ففي القرآن يستخدم الاسم "طالوت" للإشارة إلى شخصية شاؤول (2: 247)، على ما يبدو مستوحى من صفة "الطول" المنسوبة له في التناخ (صموئيل الأول 9: 2)، وقد صيغ على وزن اسم "جالوت" المذكور في نفس السياق (2: 249–251).[24] وفي القرآن تستخدم الكنية "ذو القرنين" عوضاً عن تعريف هذه الشخصية باسم علم (الكهف 18: 83). وهذه الصيغة تشبه استخدام الكنية "ذي النون" للإشارة إلى النبي يونس (الأنبياء 21: 87)، وقد أشير إليه في موضع آخر بوصفه "صاحب الحوت" (القلم 68: 48). ومثل هذه الكنى والمسميات "ذو الكفل" و"إدريس" والتي سأتناولها بالتفصيل أدناه. وفي القرآن يشار إلى مريم أم المسيح "كأخت هارون" (مريم 19: 28) و"ابنة عمران" (التحريم 66: 12)، وفي ذلك دلالة ما مقصودة.[25] وكذلك الحال بالنسبة لـ"هامان"، ففي حين أنه يظهر في التناخ في سفر أستير كوزير للملك الفارسي أحشويروش، يبدو ظهوره في القرآن في سياق قصة موسى كواحد من أعوان فرعون (القصص 28: 8، 38)، من قبيل استخدام "نموذج" الشخصية، لا الشخصية التناخية ذاتها. أما الاستخدام المزدوج للاسم إسماعيل في القرآن، فقد يكون الاسم "موسى" مثالاً شبيهاً لذلك؛ إن شخصية موسى الوارد ذكرها في سورة الكهف (18: 60–82) لا تشبه شخصية موسى بن عمران كما نعرفها في مواضع أخرى في القرآن وكما نعرفها من قصته في التناخ العبري.

أما في السور المدنية، فلا يظهر شموئيل إلا مرة واحدة دون التصريح باسمه، لكن بالإشارة إليه كنبي في بني إسرائيل (2: 246–248). في هذه المرحلة استُخدم الاسم "إسماعيل" للإشارة إلى إسماعيل بن إبراهيم دون لَبس، فهو يُذكر مع أبيه في جميع الآيات المدنية. وقد يكون الامتناع عن استخدام الاسم "إسماعيل" في سورة البقرة للإحالة إلى شموئيل تجنباً للخلط والالتباس، أي الخلط بين شموئيل وبين إسماعيل بن إبراهيم الذي يظهر في نفس السورة بشكل مكثف (في خمس آيات من سورة البقرة). ويحتمل أن السبب هو الرغبة في تسليط الضوء على شخصية إسماعيل بن إبراهيم وإبرازها، وذلك من خلال الاكتفاء بالتلميح إلى شموئيل دون ذكر اسمه.

الجامعة العبرية، 1984)، ص 143؛ موشيه جرسيئل، *سفر صموئيل الأول: دراسة أدبية في المقارنات، في النظائر، وفي المقاربات* [بالعبرية] (رمات جان: ربيبيم، 1983)، ص 77–79.

24. عن طالوت في القرآن وفي الحديث الإسلامي، انظر: Walid Saleh, "'What if You Refuse, When Ordered to Fight?': King Saul (Ṭālūt) in the Qur'ān and Post-Quranic Literature," in Carl S. Ehrlich and Marsha C. White (eds.), *Saul in Story and Tradition* (Tübingen: Mohr Siebeck, 2006), 261–283.

25. انظر، مثلاً، تفسير نويفرت لنسبة مريم إلى آل عمران في المقال: Angelika Neuwirth, "The House of Abraham and the House of Imram: Genealogy, Patriarchal Authority, and Exegetical Professionalism," in Neuwirth, Sinai, and Marx, *The Qur'ān in Context*, 499–531.

إسماعيل في التفسيرات الإسلامية

في ظل تعاظم أهمية إسماعيل بن إبراهيم في العقيدة الإسلامية وفي تشكل الهوية الإسلامية، وباعتباره أبا العرب الذي ورث النبوة عن أبيه، من غير المتوقع أن يذهب العلماء والمفسرون القدماء إلى القول بوجود إسماعيل آخر في القرآن مغاير لابن إبراهيم، وتحديداً في أربع آيات (مكية) من مجمل اثنتي عشرة آية جيء فيها على ذكر إسماعيل.

إن الرأي القائل بوجود إسماعيل آخر في القرآن غير ابن إبراهيم نجده مبكراً عند مقاتل بن سليمان (ت 767/150)، غير أن المصادر المتأخرة همشته واستبعدته. يشير مقاتل إلى أن الصورة العربية لاسم النبي الإسرائيلي شموئيل هي "إسماعيل". في تفسير الآية 2: 246 التي تروي قصة هذا النبي دون ذكر اسمه،[26] وفيها أن الله قد بعثه نبياً في بني إسرائيل من بعد موسى، يقول مقاتل إن المقصود هنا هو "اشماويل وَهُوَ بِالعَرَبِيَّةِ إِسْمَاعِيلُ بنُ هلقابا [ألقانة]، وَاسْمُ أُمِّهِ حَنّةُ، وَهُوَ مِنْ نَسْلِ هارُونَ بنِ عِمرانَ أخو مُوسَى."[27] ويتكرر مثل هذا التفسير في الكتب اللاحقة، فمثلاً يصوغ أحمد بن محمد بن إبراهيم الثعلبيّ (ت 1035/427) أحد عناوين قصصه في كتابه *قصص الأنبياء* كالآتي: "مَجْلِسٌ في قِصَّةِ عيلي وَشمويل وَهُوَ إِسْمَاعِيلُ بِالْعِبْرَانِيَّةِ."[28] وفي *كتاب الطبقات الكبير* لمحمد بن سعد (ت 845/230) إشارة مثيرة إلى العلاقة بين الاسمين العربي "إسماعيل" ونظيره العبري "شموئيل"، إذ يقول في ذكر أخبار إسماعيل بن إبراهيم إن إسماعيل عندما ولدته هاجر "كانَ اسمُهُ أشمويل فأُعْرِبَ."[29]

لكن مقاتل بن سليمان يذهب إلى أبعد من ذلك في قوله إن إسماعيل المذكور في الآية 38: 48 مع اليسع وذي الكفل "هُوَ أشوبل بنُ هلقانا".[30] إن هذا التفسير استثنائي منفرد ولم يكن مقبولاً على المفسرين والعلماء المتأخرين، فأُهمل وأُقصي إلى حد بعيد. يجدر التنويه إلى أن اعتراض العلماء على مثل هذا التفسير لم يكن من باب ربط اسم شموئيل بالاسم العربي إسماعيل، فمثل هذا يتكرر عندهم، بل من باب القول إن "إسماعيل" المذكور في بعض الآيات القرآنية هو ليس إسماعيل بن إبراهيم. فمثلاً، يقول أبو الفرج عبد الرحمن بن علي

26. قصته مع بني إسرائيل والملك طالوت ومقتل جالوت على يد داود (2: 246–251)، ونظيرها في صموئيل الأول 17.

27. مقاتل بن سليمان، *تفسير القرآن*، تحقيق عبد الله محمود شحاتة (5 مجلدات؛ بيروت: مؤسسة التاريخ العربي، 2002)، ج 1، ص 205. "أخو موسى"، هكذا في طبعة شحاتة، ويُفترض نحوياً أن تكون الصورة "أخي موسى" بالجرّ.

28. أحمد بن محمد بن إبراهيم الثعلبي، *قصص الأنبياء* (*عرائس المجالس*) (القاهرة: المطبعة البهية المصرية، 1951)، ص 216. وفي تفسيره الآية 2: 246: أحمد بن محمد بن إبراهيم الثعلبي، *الكشف والبيان*، تحقيق أبي محمد بن عاشور (10 مجلدات؛ بيروت: دار إحياء التراث العربي، 2002)، ج 2، ص 208. انظر أيضاً: هود بن محكَّم الهواري، *تفسير كتاب الله العزيز*، تحقيق بالحاج بن سعيد شريفي (4 مجلدات؛ بيروت: دار الغرب الإسلامي، 1990)، ج 1، ص 233؛ أبو الليث نصر بن محمد بن أحمد بن إبراهيم السمرقندي، *بحر العلوم*، تحقيق علي محمد معوض، عادل أحمد عبد الموجود، وزكريا عبد المجيد النوتي (3 مجلدات؛ بيروت: دار الكتب العلمية، 1993) ج 1، ص 218؛ أبو القاسم سليمان بن أحمد بن أيوب الطبراني، *التفسير الكبير* (*تفسير القرآن العظيم*)، تحقيق هشام بن عبد الكريم البدراني الموصلي (6 مجلدات؛ الأردن: دار الكتاب الثقافي، 2008)، ج 1، ص 448؛ أبو عبد الله محمد بن أحمد بن أبي بكر القرطبي، *الجامع لأحكام القرآن*، تحقيق عبد الله بن عبد المحسن التركي (24 مجلداً؛ بيروت: مؤسسة الرسالة، 2006)، ج 1، ص 229.

29. محمد بن سعد بن منيع الزهري، كتاب *الطبقات الكبير*، تحقيق علي محمد عمر (11 مجلداً؛ القاهرة: مكتبة الخانجي، 2001)، ج 1، ص 32.

30. مقاتل، *تفسير*، ج 1، ص 649. وقد وقع هنا تصحيف في الاسم شموئيل بن ألقانة.

بـن محمـد الجـوزي (ت 1201/597) فـي تفسـيره الآيـة 38: 48: "وَزَعَـمَ مُقاتِـلٌ أَنَّ إِسْـماعيلَ هـذا لَيْـسَ بِابْـنِ إِبْراهيـمَ."[31] وفـي قولـه "زَعَـمَ" تشـكيك فـي كلام مقاتـل أو تكذيـب بـه.[32]

وفـي بعـض التفسـيرات أن إسـماعيل المذكـور فـي الآيـة 19: 54 ليـس ابـن إبراهيـم، بـل هـو إسـماعيل بـن حزقيـل، هـذا لأن إسـماعيل بـن إبراهيـم قـد مـات قبـل أبيـه.[33] إن هـذا التبريـر يعنـي أن ترتيـب ظهـور الأنبيـاء فـي سـورة مريـم يفيد ترتيبـاً زمنيـاً أيضـاً؛ ظهـور إسـماعيل فـي الآيـة 54 بُعيـد ظهـور إبراهيـم فـي الآيـة 41، فيمـا يفصـل بينهمـا موسـى وهـارون فـي الآيـات 51–53، يعنـي أن إسـماعيل هنـا قـد ظهـر فـي زمـن متأخـر بعـد إبراهيـم وبعـد موسـى وهـارون، لـذا فهـو ليـس إسـماعيل بـن إبراهيـم. وفـي رأيـي إن المقصـود بإسـماعيل بـن حزقيـل هـو النبـي شـموئيل وذلـك لاعتباريـن. الأول أن الاسـم إسـماعيل بحسـب المصـادر الإسـلامية القديمـة يـدل علـى شـموئيل، إذا فالمقصـود بإسـماعيل بـن حزقيـل هـو شـموئيل بـن حزقيـل. والاعتبـار الآخـر أن نسـبة شـموئيل إلـى حزقيـل تعتمـد علـى مجـيء قصـة شـموئيل النبـي فـي سـورة البقـرة مباشـرة بعـد الآيـة 2: 243 والتـي بحسـب المصـادر الإسـلامية تشـير إلـى قصـة حزقيـل النبـي،[34] مـع الملاحظـة أن كلتـا القصتيـن تفتتحـان بنفـس التعبيـر "أَلَـمْ تَـرَ إِلَـى". هـذا يعنـي أن ترتيـب ظهـور القصتيـن هنـاك (قصـة حزقيـل أولاً ثـم قصـة شـموئيل) اعتُبـر ترتيبـاً زمنيـاً لجيليـن متتابعيـن مـن الأنبيـاء الأب حزقيـل والابـن شـموئيل أو بالمسـمى العربـي إسـماعيل. ويدعـم هـذا مـا يقولـه أبـو منصـور محمـد بـن محمـد بـن محمـود الماتريـدي (ت 945/333) فـي تفسـيره الآيـة 19: 54، مـن أن المفسـرين اختلفـوا فيمـن يكـون إسـماعيل المذكـور فـي الآيـة؛ فمعظمهـم قالـوا بأنـه إسـماعيل بـن إبراهيـم، والبعـض قالـوا بأنـه مـن

31. أبو الفرج عبد الرحمن بن علي بن محمد الجوزي، *زاد المسير في علم التفسير* (بيروت: دار ابن حزم، 2002)، ص 1218. يشير السمرقندي (ت 986/375) إلى تفسير مقاتل هذا في كتابه. وينسب إسماعيل حقي البروسوي (ت 1715/1127) تفسيراً مشابهاً لقتادة بن دعامة (ت 735/117)، انظر: السمرقندي، *بحر العلوم*، ج 3، ص 139؛ إسماعيل حقي البروسوي، *روح البيان* (10 مجلدات؛ بيروت: دار إحياء التراث العربي، بغير تاريخ)، ج 8، ص 47.

32. يُقالُ "زَعَمَ يَزْعُمُ زَعْماً إذا شَكَّ في قَوْلِهِ": الخليل بن أحمد الفراهيدي، *كتاب العين*، تحقيق مهدي المخزومي وإبراهيم السامرائي (8 مجلدات؛ بيروت: دار ومكتبة الهلال، 1988)، ج 1، ص 364. انظر أيضاً: جلال الدين محمد بن مكرم بن منظور، *لسان العرب* (15 مجلداً؛ بيروت: دار صادر، 1990)، ج 12، ص 264.

33. أبو الحسن علي بن محمد بن حبيب الماوردي، *النكت والعيون*، تحقيق السيد بن عبد المقصود بن عبد الرحيم (6 مجلدات؛ بيروت: دار الكتب العلمية ومؤسسة الكتب الثقافية، بغير تاريخ)، ج 3، ص 377؛ القرطبي، *الجامع*، ج 13، ص 462؛ أبو حيان محمد بن يوسف الأندلسي، *البحر المحيط*، تحقيق عادل أحمد عبد الموجود وعلي محمد عوض (8 مجلدات؛ بيروت: دار الكتب العلمية، 1993)، ج 6، ص 188. ولا ينسب الماوردي أو القرطبي أو ابن حيان هذا القول لمحدّث أو مفسّر معيّن، لكنهم يشيرون إلى أن جمهور المفسرين يرون أن إسماعيل المذكور في الآية هو ابن إبراهيم. وأورد الماوردي (هناك) أن إسماعيل بن حزقيل هذا "بَعَثَهُ اللهُ إلى قَوْمِهِ فَسَلَخُوا جِلْدَةَ رَأسِهِ، فَخَيَّرَهُ اللهُ فيما شَاءَ مِنْ عَذابِهِمْ فَاسْتَعْفاهُ وَرَضِيَ بِثَوابِهِ وَفَوَّضَ أَمْرَهُمْ إلَيْهِ في عَفْوِهِ أَوْ عُقُوبَتِهِ." وقد ناقش رؤوبين فيرستون هذا الحديث في مقال له مبيّناً أن شخصية إسماعيل بن حزقيل تشكلت نموذجاً شبيهاً بشخصية "يشمعئيل بن إليشع" في التقليد اليهودي الرباني، وهو واحد من عشرة ربانيّين طوردوا وعُذبوا بأيدي حكام الإمبراطورية الرومانية في سياق الحديث عن ثورة بار كوخبا. يشير فيرستون إلى أن قصة مقتل إسماعيل بن حزقيل بأيدي أبناء قومه وُظفت في الحديث الشيعي في المقاربة مع حدث مقتل الحسين بن عليّ، ولهذا أهمية سياسية في سياق الصراع على الحكم ورفض الشيعة لسلطة أهل السنة. انظر بتوسع: Reuven Firestone, "The 'Other' Ishmael in Islamic Scripture and Tradition," in Mark G. Brett and Jakob Wöhrle (eds.), *The Politics of the Ancestors: Exegetical and Historical Perspectives on Genesis 12–36* (Tübingen: Mohr Siebeck, 2018), 419–432, 423–431.

34. 2: 243: "أَلَمْ تَرَ إِلَى ٱلَّذِينَ خَرَجُواْ مِن دِيَٰرِهِمْ وَهُمْ أُلُوفٌ حَذَرَ ٱلْمَوْتِ فَقَالَ لَهُمُ ٱللَّهُ مُوتُواْ ثُمَّ أَحْيَٰهُمْ إِنَّ ٱللَّهَ لَذُو فَضْلٍ عَلَى ٱلنَّاسِ وَلَٰكِنَّ أَكْثَرَ ٱلنَّاسِ لاَ يَشْكُرُونَ."

قال له قومه "ٱبْعَثْ لَنَا مَلِكاً نُّقَاتِلْ فِي سَبِيلِ ٱللَّهِ" (2: 246)، أي هو النبي شموئيل.[35] يبدو أن هذا التفسير يأخذ بعين الاعتبار ظهور إسماعيل في سورة مريم بعد ذكر موسى (الآية 19: 51)، على أنّ هذا الترتيب يعكس ما جاء في وصف شموئيل في الآية 2: 246 أنه نبي ظهر في بني إسرائيل "مِنْ بَعْدِ مُوسَىٰ".

من المثير أن نجد تفسيراً يربط إلياس المذكور في الآية 6: 85 (بعد زكريا ويحيى وعيسى) من حيث النسب بإسماعيل، ففي حديث يُنسب إلى الضحاك بن مزاحم (ت 720/102) أن إلياس من ولد إسماعيل.[36] وباعتبار إلياس نبياً من بني إسرائيل، لا يُتوقع أن يكون المقصود في حديث الضحاك نسبته إلى إسماعيل بن إبراهيم أبي العرب. لربما يُقصد بذلك ربط إلياس بالنبي شموئيل المسمى بالعربية "إسماعيل" بالاعتماد على الآيات القرآنية التي تقرن إلياس بإسماعيل، نحو الآيات 6: 85–86. وسأبيّن لاحقاً أن العلاقة بين هاتين الشخصيتين تنعكس أيضاً في الآيات 19: 54، 56؛ 21: 85، والتي تشير إلى إلياس بتسميته إدريس؛ والآية 38: 48 التي تشير إليه بوصفه بذي الكفل.[37] وإن صحّ ذلك، فإننا أمام دليل بوجود تفسير قديم آخر يستخدم الاسم إسماعيل للدلالة على شموئيل.

يتجاهل معظم المفسرين القدماء مسألة انفصال إسماعيل عن إبراهيم في بعض الآيات القرآنية، ولا يبدو ذلك جهلاً، فتفسير مقاتل الذي يربط إسماعيل بشموئيل كان معروفاً عندهم كما بيّنت، وكذلك التفسير الذي يُعرّف إسماعيل بابن حزقيل وارتباطه بشموئيل. لكن بعض المفسرين قد انبروا لتبرير ذلك الانفصال، ومنهم مقاتل حيث يقول في تفسيره للآية 38: 45 وفيها يوصف إبراهيم وإسحاق ويعقوب بأولي الأيدي والأبصار: "وَلَمْ يُذْكَرْ إِسْمَاعِيلُ بنُ إبْراهيمَ لأنّه لَمْ يُبْتَلَ."[38] يريد أنه ليس من دليل على أن إسماعيل قد ابتلي بلاء عظيماً مثل أبيه إبراهيم عندما أُلقي في النار وعندما أُمر بذبح ابنه، ومثل أخيه إسحاق الذبيح.[39] ويقصد أن إسماعيل بن إبراهيم لم يُذكر بتاتاً في هذا السياق، فمقاتل يُعرّف إسماعيل المذكور في نفس السورة (الآية 38: 48) بأنه شموئيل بن ألقانة (أعلاه).

يأتي فخر الدين محمد بن عمر الرازي (ت 1210/606) بتفسير آخر لسبب انفصال إسماعيل عن إبراهيم في بعض الآيات القرآنية، وذلك في تفسيره للآية 6: 84 وفيها أن الله وهب إبراهيم إسحاق ويعقوب من بعده.[40] يقول الرازي إن المقصود بالذكر في ذلك السياق هم أنبياء بني إسرائيل تحديداً، وهم بأسرهم أولاد إسحاق ويعقوب. أما إسماعيل، فلم يكن من سلالته نبي سوى محمد فلا يجوز ذكره في هذا المقام. وبما أن محمداً قد بُعث للاحتجاج على العرب المشركين واتخذ من منهج إبراهيم حجة في وعظه ودعوته، وقد وهبه الله لتركه

35. أبو منصور محمد بن محمد بن محمود الماتريدي، *تأويلات أهل السنة*، تحقيق مجدي باسلوم (10 مجلدات؛ بيروت: دار الكتب العلمية، 2005)، ج 1، ص 244.

36. السمرقندي، *بحر العلوم*، ج 1، ص 499؛ القرطبي، *الجامع*، ج 8، ص 448.

37. وسأبيّن كذلك أن ذا الكفل المذكور في الآية 21: 85 يحيل إلى اليسع لا إلياس.

38. مقاتل، *تفسير*، ج 3، ص 649. يقتبس بعض المفسرين المتأخرين تفسير مقاتل، أحياناً دون الإحالة إليه. انظر، مثلاً: الطبراني، *التفسير الكبير*، ج 5، ص 353؛ السمرقندي، *بحر العلوم*، ج 3، ص 138؛ الماوردي، *النكت*، ج 5، ص 105.

39. مقاتل من المفسرين الذين قالوا بأن ابن إبراهيم المذكور في الصافات 37: 101–102 والذي ابتلي بالأمر بذبحه هو إسحاق. انظر: مقاتل، *تفسير*، ج 3، ص 614. انظر مقال يونس ميرزا يبيّن فيه التحول الذي طرأ على هذه الرؤية في التفاسير الإسلامية: Younus Y. Mirza, "Ishmael as Abraham's Sacrifice: Ibn Taymiyya and Ibn Kathīr on the Intended Victim," *ICMR* 4 (2013): 277–298.

40. 6: 84: "وَوَهَبْنَا لَهُ إِسْحَاقَ وَيَعْقُوبَ كُلًّا هَدَيْنَا وَنُوحاً هَدَيْنَا مِن قَبْلُ وَمِن ذُرِّيَّتِهِ دَاوُودَ وَسُلَيْمَانَ وَأَيُّوبَ وَيُوسُفَ وَمُوسَىٰ وَهَارُونَ وَكَذَٰلِكَ نَجْزِي ٱلْمُحْسِنِينَ."

الشرك وإصراره على التوحيد أولاداً أنبياء وملوكاً، امتنع محمد عن ذكر نفسه معه، ولنفس هذا السبب لم يُذكر إسماعيل مع إسحاق في الآية المذكورة.[41] ويرى الرازي أن ترتيب ظهور الأنبياء في سورة الأنعام في الآيات 6: 83–86 ليس بعشوائي، ولهذا لزم تبيان سببه، وخصوصاً سبب ذكر إسماعيل مع اليسع ويونس ولوط (في الآية 86). يرفض الرازي القول بأن ترتيب الأنبياء هناك (عددهم تسعة عشر) جاء بحسب فضلهم ودرجتهم أو زمنهم ومدتهم، ويقول إن الترتيب جاء معتبراً صفات فضل وإكرام مشتركة لبعض الأنبياء. وهكذا يبرر ذكر إسماعيل مع اليسع ويونس ولوط بأن هؤلاء هم الأنبياء "الّذينَ لَمْ يَبْقَ لَهُمْ فيمَا بَيْنَ الْخَلْقِ أَتْبَاعٌ وَأَشْيَاعٌ."[42]

يقدم برهان الدين أبو الحسن إبراهيم بن عمر البقاعي (ت 885/1480) تفسيراً مختلفاً لانفصال إسماعيل عن إبراهيم وإسحاق ويعقوب في بعض آيات القرآن. في تفسيره للآية 6: 84 يقول إن الاقتصار على ذكر إسحاق ويعقوب هنا يخضع لسياق الآيات التي تركز على الامتنان على الخليل، أي نعم الله على إبراهيم، ومنها تمتعه بابنه إسحاق بعدم حمله على فراقه بأمر من الله، وتمتعه بيعقوب حفيده الذي كان أكثر مَن دعا إلى الله من الأنبياء ممّن هم من نسل إبراهيم. ومن ذلك أن إسحاق ويعقوب أول من طهّر الأرض المقدسة، مُهاجر إبراهيم.[43] بهذا يلمح البقاعي إلى أن إسماعيل لم يُذكر في هذا السياق لأنه قد فارق أباه وهو طفل بأمر من الله، وإن كان ذلك خيراً فقد كان مدعاة لحزن أبيه وأساه، ويلمح كذلك إلى دور إسماعيل في تطهير بيت الله في مكة (كما جاء في الآية 2: 125). ويدعم البقاعي تفسيره ذاك بفصل يوسف عن أبيه يعقوب في الآية 6: 84، قائلاً: "لِمِثْلِ ذَلكَ فُصِلَ بَيْنَ إسْماعيلَ وَأَبِيهِ وَيُوسُفَ وَأَبِيهِ عَلَيْهِمُ السَّلامُ إشَارَةً إلى فِراقِ كُلٍّ مِنْهُمَا لِأَبِيهِ في الْحَيَاةِ."[44] ويعزو البقاعي سبب ذكر إسماعيل مع اليسع في سورة الأنعام لبعض الصفات المشتركة بينهما؛ فإن كان المقصود باليسع خليفة النبي إلياس، فإن الله قد نبّأه وبعثه في بني إسرائيل رسولاً، وهكذا بحسب البقاعي، يكون الرابط بين إسماعيل واليسع كونهما نبيّين ورسولين أيضاً. أما إذا كان المقصود باليسع هو يوشع بن نون، فإنه يشترك مع إسماعيل بصدق الوعد.[45] ويعزز البقاعي الرابط بينهما بالمقاربة بين عمارتهما لبيت الله، إسماعيل في مكة ويوشع في البلدة المقدسة، وكذلك من قبيل أن الله هدى بهما قوميهما من غير عذاب.[46]

لقد تقدم أن الآيات 246–248 من سورة البقرة تسرد قصة شموئيل مع بني إسرائيل وملكهم طالوت (شاؤول) دون التصريح باسمه، لكن بوصفه نبياً في بني إسرائيل، ثم تتابع الآيات 249–251 سرد خروج طالوت وجنوده لمحاربة جالوت الذي قتله داود.[47] لم تقتصر

41. فخر الدين محمد بن عمر الرازي، *مفاتيح الغيب* (32 مجلداً؛ بيروت: دار الفكر، 1981)، ج 13، ص 67.
42. نفسه، ج 13، ص 68–69.
43. برهان الدين أبو الحسن إبراهيم بن عمر البقاعي، *نظم الدرر في تناسب الآيات والسور* (22 مجلداً؛ القاهرة: دار الكتاب الإسلامي، 1984)، ج 7، ص 170. انظر كذلك تفسيره الآيات 19: 49؛ 38: 45: نفسه، ج 12، ص 209–210؛ ج 16، ص 398.
44. نفسه، ج 7، ص 172.
45. يعتمد البقاعي في هذه التفسيرات على الآية 19: 54 وفيها يوصف إسماعيل كنبي ورسول صادق الوعد. أما يوشع فلأنه أحد النقيبين اللذين وفيَا لموسى من بين اثني عشر نقيباً بعثهم يجسون بلاد بيت المقدس. وفي ذلك إشارة إلى المائدة 5: 12، ونظير هذه القصة في سفر عدد 13؛ التثنية 1: 22–24.
46. البقاعي، *نظم الدرر*، ج 7، ص 176–177. وعند البروسوي أن إسماعيل "فُصِلَ ذِكْرُهُ عَنْ ذِكْرِ أَبِيهِ وَأَخِيهِ لِلْإِشْعَارِ بِعَرَاقَتِهِ في الصَّبْرِ الذي هُوَ الْمَقْصُودُ في التَّذَكُّرِ وَذلكَ لِأَنَّهُ أَسْلَمَ نَفْسَهُ لِلذَّبْحِ في سَبيلِ اللهِ أَوْ لِيَكونَ أَكْثَرَ تَعْظيماً فَإِنَّهُ جَدُّ أَفْضَلِ الْأَنْبِياءِ وَالْمُرْسَلِينَ": البروسوى، *روح البيان*، ج 10، ص 47.
47. نظير هذه الآيات في صموئيل الأول 8: 4–22؛ 17. أما ابتلاء بني إسرائيل بالنهر في الآية 2: 249، فنظيره

تفسيرات العلماء المسلمين على الإشارة إلى شموئيل في هذا السياق، فهم يقدمون ثلاث شخصيات للتعريف بالنبي المشار إليه، فقيل إنه شموئيل، وقيل إنه يوشع بن نون، وفي تفسير ثالث أنه شمعون.[48] على ما يبدو فإن التفسير الثاني يأخذ لفظاً ما جاء في الآية أن هذا النبي بُعث من بعد موسى، أي بُعث مباشرة بعد موت موسى، إذا فهو يوشع بن نون. واعترض بعض المفسرين على هذا بدعوى أن القصة تشير إلى النبي شموئيل وأنه ليس من الضروري أن يحمل التعبير "من بعد موسى" معنى الزمن القريب المباشر، أضف إلى ذلك فإن داود المذكور في ذلك السياق ظهر بعد موسى بقرون، في حين أن يوشع بن نون عاصره وخلفه في بني إسرائيل بعد موته.[49] أما تعريف النبي المذكور في 2: 246 بشمعون فإنه يتعلق بقصة مولده المتكررة في كتب التفاسير، والتي تذكرنا تفاصيلها بقصة مولد شموئيل كما جاءت في سفر صموئيل (أشرت إليها أعلاه). ولهذا نجد أن بعض التفسيرات تربط بين الشخصيتين: شموئيل وشمعون، فيما تبدو تلك القصة تفسيراً للتسمية "شمعون". جاء عند أبي الفداء إسماعيل بن عمر بن كثير (ت 1373/774)، مثلاً، أنه بعد مدة من الزمن من موت موسى، فسق بنو إسرائيل وخرجوا عن الاستقامة وانقطعت النبوة فيهم، ولم يبق من سبط الأنبياء سوى امرأة حامل حبسوها لعلها تلد ابناً يكون فيهم نبياً، وكانت تدعو الله أن يهبها ولداً ذكراً، فسمع الله دعاءها، فسمته "شموئيل"، والذي يعني "سمع الله دعائي". وفي بعض الروايات أنها سمته "شمعون" وله ذات المعنى، أي سمع الله دعاءها.[50] ويشبه هذا حديث طويل أورده أبو جعفر محمد بن جرير الطبري (ت 923/310) فيه قصة مولد شموئيل وبعثه نبياً في بني إسرائيل، ولكنه يقدم في نفس الحديث "شموئيل" و"شمعون" كاسمين لذات الشخص، كالآتي:

> فَجَعَلَتِ الْمَرأةُ تَدْعو اللهَ أنْ يَرْزُقَها غُلاماً، فَوَلَدَتْ غُلاماً فَسَمَّتْهُ شمعُونَ. فَكَبُرَ الغُلامُ فأسْلَمَتْهُ يَتَعلَّمُ التَّوْراةَ في بَيْتِ الْمَقْدِسِ، وَكَفِلَهُ شَيْخٌ مِنْ عُلمَائِهِم وَتَبَنّاهُ. فَلَمَّا بَلَغَ الغُلامُ أنْ يَبْعَثَهُ اللهُ نَبِيّاً أتاهُ جِبريلُ وَالغُلامُ نائِمٌ إلى جَنْبِ الشّيْخِ، وَكانَ لا يَتَّمِنُ عَلَيْهِ أحداً غَيْرَهُ، فَدَعاهُ بِلَحْنِ الشّيْخِ: يا شماوِل.[51]

أما الاسم "شمعون" فيعكس قصة مولد النبي، كاسم مشتق من لفظ "شمع" باعتباره اللفظ العبري للفعل "سمع"،[52] أي سمع الله دعاء والدته، وأما "شماول"، ويراد به شموئيل، فجاء

في قضاة 7: 4–8.

48. انظر، مثلاً: جار الله أبو القاسم محمود بن عمر الزمخشري، *الكشاف عن حقائق التنزيل وعيون الأقاويل في وجوه التأويل*، تحقيق خليل مأمون شيحا (بيروت: دار المعرفة، 2009)، ص 141. غالباً ما تنسب المصادر القول بشموئيل إلى وهب بن منبّه (ت 728/110) ومحمد بن إسحاق (ت 767/150) ومقاتل، والقول بيوشع بن نون إلى قتادة، والقول بشمعون إلى السُّدي (إسماعيل بن عبد الرحمن، ت 746/128)، مثلاً: الماوردي، *النكت*، ج 1، ص 314؛ أبو محمد عبد الحق بن غالب بن عطية الأندلسي، *المحرر الوجيز في تفسير الكتاب العزيز*، تحقيق عبد السلام عبد الشافي محمد (6 مجلدات؛ بيروت: دار الكتب العلمية، 2001)، ج 1، ص 330.

49. انظر: ابن عطية، هناك؛ القرطبي، *الجامع*، ج 4، ص 229؛ الرازي، *مفاتيح الغيب*، ج 6، ص 183.

50. أبو الفداء إسماعيل بن عمر بن كثير، *تفسير القرآن العظيم*، تحقيق سامي بن محمد السلامة (8 مجلدات؛ الرياض: دار طيبة، 1999)، ج 1، ص 665.

51. أبو جعفر محمد بن جرير الطبري، *جامع البيان عن تأويل آي القرآن*، تحقيق عبد الله بن عبد المحسن التركي (25 مجلداً؛ القاهرة: دار هجر، 2001)، ج 4، ص 441–442.

52. لا يغفل المفسرون عن هذه الصلة، فمنهم من يوضح أن حرف السين بالعربية يقابله الشين بالعبرية، ومن هنا "شمعون" يقابله بالعربية "سمعون". انظر، مثلاً: الثعلبي، *الكشف*، ج 2، ص 208؛ الرازي، *مفاتيح الغيب*، ج 6، ص 184؛ القرطبي، *الجامع*، ج 4، ص 229.

من قبل أنه الاسم المألوف لهذا النبي كما ورد ذكره في التناخ، وللتوفيق بين الاسمين جُعلا نظيرين في لهجتين مختلفتين، وفي الحديث أن "شماول" هو اسم النبي بلحن شيخه (عيلي)، أي بلهجته ولغته.[53]

ذو الكفل في النص القرآني

من الشخصيات الغامضة أيضاً في القرآن شخصية ذي الكفل الذي ورد ذكره في موضعين اثنين فقط مع مجموعة من أنبياء بني إسرائيل (21: 85؛ 38: 48). لا نجد في التناخ ولا في العهد الجديد نظيراً لهذا الاسم أو هذه الكنية، ولا النص القرآني نفسه يفيدنا بمعلومات إضافية حيال هذه الشخصية، الأمر الذي يجعل تحديد هويتها مهمة صعبة ومركبة. وعلى غرار العلماء المسلمين القدماء، قدم الباحثون الغربيون عدة تفسيرات لهذه الشخصية سأوجز فيما يلي بعضاً منها تمهيداً للتحليل الذي سأقدمه.

للاستدلال على شخصية ذي الكفل، غالباً ما يعتمد الباحثون على معاني اللفظ العربي "كفل" وعلى التفسيرات الإسلامية. يقدم تشارلز توري (Charles Torrey) تصوراً لهذه الشخصية على أنها تشير إلى يوشع مرتكزاً على معنى "القسمة" أو "النصيب" المتضمن في لفظ "كفل". وبحسبه فإن لفظ "كفل" كثيراً ما جاء على لسان يوشع عند حديثه عن قسمة الأراضي بين قبائل العبريّين، وذلك في النسخة الإثيوبية من سفر يوشع.[54] يعتقد جون ووكر (John Walker) أن ذا الكفل يرتبط بشخصية أيوب.[55] أما أبراهام جيجر (Abraham Geiger) فيقدم اقتراحين لهوية ذي الكفل: عوبديا وحزقيل.[56] وفي رأي جيمس بيلامي (James Bellamy)، ذو الكفل هو تحريف للتعبير "ذو الطفل" ناتج عن خطأ في عملية النسخ. ويقول إن الخلط بين حرفي "ك" و"ط" في المخطوطات العربية شائع. بناء على ذلك، يرى بيلامي أن التعبير "ذو الطفل" ينعكس في بعض الآيات من سفر إشعياء (نحو إشعياء 9: 5؛ 11: 6)، فيها يُذكر "ولد" أو "صبي صغير".[57] لكن هذا التفسير لا يصمد أمام الأبحاث الكثيرة التي كتبت مؤخراً عن الدور المهم والأساسي للنقل الشفوي للنصوص القرآنية خاصة في الفترة الأولى المبكرة من ظهور القرآن. والنص القرآني نفسه يدلل على التناقل الشفوي له من باب قراءته على أسماع الناس وعظاً وقراءته في العبادات كالصلاة والقيام والتهجد، وهذه السمة تنعكس

53. نظير قصة تجلي الله إلى شموئيل في صموئيل الأول 3. وقد تكون هذه التفسيرات الإسلامية لأصل تسمية شموئيل مستوحاة من تفسيرات يهودية، وخاصة أن اسم شموئيل في التناخ لا ينسجم مع قصته التناخية (قصة مولده تحديداً، كما أشرت في الملاحظة 23)، وهذه الفرضية بحاجة إلى المزيد من البحث والاستقصاء في المصادر الإسلامية واليهودية.

54. Charles Torrey, *The Jewish Foundation of Islam* (New York: KTAV Publishing House, 1967), 71–72.

55. John Walker, "Who Is Dhu 'l-Kifl?," *MW* 16 (1926): 399–401.

56. Abraham Geiger, *Judaism and Islám: A Prize Essay*, trans. F. M. Young (Madras: M. D. C. S. P. C. K. Press, 1898), 155.

57. يُقر الباحث بأن الرابط بين ذي الكفل القرآني وشخصية الطفل في سفر إشعياء ضعيف وغير كاف. ولهذا فإن طرحه يعتمد بالدرجة الأولى على افتراضه أن اسم النبي "شعيب" في القرآن هو تصحيف لـ"إشعياء". ويعتمد كذلك على حقيقة أن الآيات المتعلقة بالولد أو الطفل من سفر إشعياء قد اقتُبست كثيراً في الكتب المسيحية القديمة كآيات تبشر بقدوم المسيح. يرمي الباحث بذلك إلى تعزيز الفرضية أن النص القرآني على معرفة بسفر إشعياء، وبالتالي تعزيز الفرضية أن النص القرآني على معرفة بالآيات هناك المتعلقة بالولد أو الصبي. انظر: James Bellamy, "Textual Criticism of the Koran," *JAOS* 121 (2001): 1–6.

أولا وقبل كل شيء في اللفظ "قرآن". وبالرغم من أن القرآن قد دُون كتابة في وقت مبكر من ظهوره، إلا أن النقل الشفوي ظل الأداة الأساسية لحفظه.[58] ومن هذا المنطلق فإن خطأ استبدال "كفل" بـ"طفل" يبدو مستبعداً. أما تشيليك فيرى أن ذا الكفل معناه "صاحب النصيبين" ويدلّ على اليسع الذي سأل إلياس نصيباً مضاعفاً من روحه النبوية بحسب سفر الملوك الثاني 2: 9. وفي هذا يعتمد تشيليك على معنى "الضعف" المتضمن في لفظ "كفل". غير أن هذا الاستنتاج، والذي أؤيده جزئياً بالاستناد إلى تفسير مختلف، قاد تشيليك إلى استنتاج آخر خاطئ فيما يتعلق بالآية 38: 48، والتي ذُكر فيها ذو الكفل مع اليسع، إذ يقول تشيليك إن اليسع في هذه الآية يدل على إلياس.[59] ويقول إجناتس جولدتسيهر (Ignaz Goldziher) في مقالته "ذو الكفل" في دائرة المعارف الإسلامية إن الباحث محمد مسعود (Meḥmet Mesʿūd) يربط في كتاب له صدر عام 1910 بين ذي الكفل وبين النبي إلياس بالاستناد إلى الآية 2: 8 من سفر الملوك الثاني، سأتطرق إليها لاحقاً.[60]

إن ظهور ذي الكفل في النص القرآني مع مجموعة من أنبياء بني إسرائيل، يُمكّننا من الافتراض أن ذا الكفل هو نبي من بني إسرائيل بمعنى أنه من ذرية إبراهيم من نسل إسحاق ويعقوب. في الآية 38: 48 يُذكر ذو الكفل مع شخصيتين نبويتين مهمتين في التراث اليهودي: اليسع وشموئيل المسمّى بالقرآن إسماعيل.[61] وفي التناخ يرتبط اليسع بالنبي إلياس ارتباطاً وثيقاً، من حيث أنه كان تلميذه ثم نبياً خلفاً له بعد صعوده في عاصفة إلى السماء (الملوك الثاني 2). وإلياس شخصية بارزة في التناخ وفي أدبيات الحاخامات القدماء.[62] بالاستناد إلى هذا فإن الكنية ذا الكفل في الآية 38: 48 تحيلنا إلى شخصية إلياس النبي في إشارة إلى معطفه الخارق. ويدعم هذا الافتراض أحد المعاني القديمة للفظ "كفل" الذي جاء بمعنى الكساء أو الرداء يوضع على الكاهل. وفي تفسيرات أخرى أن الكفل هو "شَيءٌ مُسْتَدِيرٌ يُتَّخَذُ مِنْ خِرَقٍ" أي القماش ليوضع على سنام البعير.[63] وقد جاء هذا المعنى الأخير في أبيات من الشعر

58. وقد كتب كثير من الباحثين عن هذه الخاصية للقرآن، انظر: William A. Graham, "The Earliest Meaning of the Qur'ān," *WI* 23 (1984): 361–377; Angelika Neuwirth, "Two Faces of the Qur'ān: *Qur'ān* and *Muṣḥaf*," *Oral Tradition* 25 (2010): 141–156; eadem, "From Recitation through Liturgy to Canon: Sura Composition and Dissolution during the Development of Islamic Ritual," in *Scripture, Poetry and the Making of a Community* (Oxford: Oxford University Press, 2014), 141–163; eadem, *The Qur'an and Late Antiquity: A Shared Heritage*, trans. Samuel Wilder (New York: Oxford University Press, 2019), 4–10, 76–78. وبيّن الباحثون أن لفظ "كتاب" في النص القرآني لا يوحي بالضرورة معنى التدوين بالكتابة، وقد تناول دنيال ماديغان هذه النقطة الأخيرة في كتاب له بالتفصيل. انظر: Daniel A. Madigan, *The Qur'ân's Self-Image: Writing and Authority in Islam's Scripture* (Princeton: Princeton University Press, 2001).

59. Celik, "The Enigmatic Prophets."

60. I. Goldziher, "Ḏhu 'l-Kifl," *EI*[1], s.v. (1913).

61. يجدر الإشارة هنا إلى أن دارسي التناخ المعاصرين يصنفون هؤلاء الأنبياء الثلاثة البارزين مع الأنبياء القدماء المبكرين، مقارنة بالأنبياء المتأخرين (نحو إرميا، إشعياء، حزقيل، والأنبياء الصغار) الذين نشطوا في أزمان لاحقة. ويتميّز الأنبياء المبكّرون بنشاطهم في قصور الملوك حيث يقدمون لهم النصح ويناصرونهم. يتميز هؤلاء الأنبياء أيضاً بمحاربتهم للوثنية. انظر: بنيامين أوبنهايمر، "نبوة، نبي [بالعبرية]،" *الموسوعة التناخية*، ج 5، عمود 690–732، 697–703.

62. انظر الملاحظة 106 أدناه.

63. جاء في مادة "كفل": "وَالكِفْلُ مِنْ مَرَاكِبِ الرِّجَالِ وَهُوَ كِساءٌ يؤْخَذُ فَيُعْقَدُ طَرَفاهُ ثُمّ يُلْقَى مُقدَّمُهُ عَلَى الكَاهِلِ وَمُؤَخَّرُهُ مِمَّا يَلِي الْعَجُزَ." انظر: ابن منظور، *لسان العرب*، ج 11، ص 588.

القديم،[64] ومنه جاء التعبير "اكْتَفَلَ الرَّجُلُ بِكِفْلٍ مِنْ كَذا أوْ مِنْ ثَوْبِهِ."[65] وفي القرآن ترد عدة تعابير مشتقة من لفظ "كفل" بمعان مختلفة كالتعهد بالرعاية والاهتمام والانفاق على شيء أو شخص ما، نحو ما جاء في تكفّل زكريا لمريم (3: 37)،[66] وكذلك بمعنى الضعف والمضاعفة كما جاء في النساء 4: 85 والحديد 57: 28. لكن، هذه المعاني قاصرة عن تزويدنا بما يفيد عن شخصية ذي الكفل.

يبدو أن النص القرآني يستخدم "ذا الكفل" بمعنى "صاحب الكساء" ككنية للدلالة على إلياس وعلى قصته العجيبة حينما ضرب النهر بكفله أي بكسائه ليفلقه ويعبره مع تلميذه اليسع (الملوك الثاني 2: 8). وفي بعض المواضع في التناخ يرمز الكساء إلى النبوة. فمثلاً، يأمر الله إلياس أن يمسح اليسع نبياً بعده، فتم ذلك بإلقاء كسائه النبوي إليه (الملوك الأول 19: 16، 19). ويتكرر هذا المشهد حين تلقى اليسع كساء إلياس الذي رُفع للتوّ إلى السماء ليصبح نبياً مكانه. وكما فعل إلياس من قبل، يضرب اليسع النهر بذلك الكساء ليشقه (الملوك الثاني 2: 13–14).[67] يبدو لي أنه لم تكن هناك غاية في النص القرآني لسرد قصة إلياس العجيبة تلك بإسهاب، ولذلك كان الايجاز بالتلميح والرمز باستخدام التعبير "ذي الكفل" بمعنى "صاحب الكساء" العجيب. ولا يبدو أن الغاية هي اشتقاق اسم جديد لإلياس، بل كنية أو لقب يحيل إلى موتيف أو ميزة في شخصية إلياس النبوية وقصته، وأيضاً لأن النص القرآني يستخدم اسم العلم لهذا النبي بصورة "إلياس".

لكن، لا يخلو توظيف النص القرآني للكنية "ذي الكفل" من التركيب والتعقيد. هذا لأن ذا الكفل في الآية 21: 85 يحيل في اعتقادي إلى اليسع وريث إلياس في النبوة، لا إلى إلياس نفسه، فاليسع أيضاً قد حظي بذلك الكساء العجيب، إذا فهو أيضاً صاحب الكساء، ومن هذا المنطلق هو أيضاً ذو الكفل. هذه الفرضية تستند بشكل أساسي إلى أن "إدريس" المذكور في ذات الآية هو إلياس، كما سأبيّن لاحقاً. وللتوضيح فإن الآية 21: 85 تشير إلى إسماعيل (شموئيل) وإدريس وذي الكفل، فإذا ما اعتبرنا أن إدريس هو إلياس، لا يصلح أن يكون ذو الكفل هو أيضاً إلياس، وهكذا فإن المرشح الأفضل لذي الكفل في هذه الآية هو اليسع. اليسع

---

64. يقول أبو ذؤيب، وهو شاعر جاهلي لحق بالإسلام، في وصف جلب الخمرة من مصر وغزة على ظهر ناقة: "تَزَوَّدَها مِنْ أهْلِ مِصْر وَغَزَّة / على جَسْرةٍ مَرْفوعةِ الذَّيلِ والكِفْلِ." وجاء في أشعار جرير (ابن عطية الخطفي، ت حوالي 114/732) الهجائية قوله: "لَقَدْ قَوّسَتْ أمُّ البَعيثِ، ولَمْ تَزَلْ / تُزَاحِمُ عِلْجَاً صَادِرينَ عَلى كِفْلِ." انظر: *ديوان الهذليّين*، تحقيق أحمد الزين ومحمود أبو الوفا (3 مجلدات؛ مصر: دار الكتب المصرية، 1965)، ج 1، ص 40؛ *ديوان جرير* (بيروت: دار بيروت للطباعة والنشر، 1986)، ص 371.

65. انظر: الفراهيدي، *كتاب العين*، ج 5، ص 373؛ ابن منظور، *لسان العرب*، ج 11، ص 588.

66. انظر مثل هذا المعنى أيضاً: آل عمران 3: 44؛ طه 20: 40؛ القصص 28: 12؛ ص 38: 23.

67. إن ارتباط الكساء بوظيفة النبي والنبوة يتجلى في التناخ في مواضع أخرى. يُروى، مثلًا، أن الملك شاؤول استطاع أن يتعرف على النبي شموئيل بتعرفه على كسائه (صموئيل الأول 28: 14)، ويُروى أن والدة شموئيل كانت تصنع له كل عام كساء عند حجها مع زوجها إلى معبد الله وتقديم القرابين هناك (صموئيل الأول 2: 19). وفي موضع آخر، في صموئيل الأول 18: 4، يخلع يوناثان ابن الملك شاؤول كساءه ويعطيه إلى داود. وإن لم يكن يوناثان نبيّاً، فإن كساءه، على ما يبدو، يرمز إلى القوة والسلطة ذات الصلاحية الإلهية (الله هو من يختار ملوك بني إسرائيل، كما يظهر، مثلاً، في صموئيل الأول 8؛ وهكذا في سورة البقرة في الآية 2: 247). كأن يوناثان بذلك يتنازل عن وراثة ملك أبيه لصالح داود. أشكر أورا بريزون للفت انتباهي إلى هذه الإشارات إلى كساء شموئيل وكساء يوناثان. وفي القرآن يُذكر الكساء مرتبطاً بالوظيفة التي أنيطت برسول القرآن (محمد) في مستهل سورتي المزمل 73 والمدثر 74. يناقش أوري روبين هاتين السورتين في مقال له يربط فيه كساء النبي محمد الذي كان يتدثر فيه مع بداية رسالته النبوية. انظر: Uri Rubin, "The Shrouded Messenger: On the Interpretation of *al-muzzammil* and *al-muddaththir*," *JSAI* 16 (1993): 96–107.

هو صاحب الكفل العجيب، وهو أيضاً واحد في مثلث الأنبياء: شموئيل، إلياس، واليسع. وللإجمال، إن الآيتين 38: 48 و21: 85 تذكُران الأنبياء الثلاثة: شموئيل، إلياس، واليسع، ولكن في حين أن الاسم "إسماعيل" يُشير في كلتا الآيتين إلى شموئيل، فإن الكنية "ذا الكفل" تشير في واحدة منهما إلى إلياس (38: 48)،[68] وفي الأخرى إلى اليسع (21: 85).[69] إن توظيف الكنية "ذي الكفل" في النص القرآني على هذا النحو، أي مرة للدلالة على إلياس ومرة للدلالة على اليسع، نابعة عن وعي وإدراك لا عن سهو أو خطأ ما، كما أسلفت الذكر أعلاه. ويدعم هذا الإشارة إلى اليسع بوضوح باسمه العلم في الآية 38: 48، فيما يبدو منعاً للبس والخلط، يعني كي لا يختلط على الجمهور المستمع (المعاصر للقرآن) من المقصود بصاحب الكساء في هذه الآية، ذلك أن التصريح باسم اليسع فيها يعني أن ذا الكفل في هذا الموضع يدل على إلياس. ويحتمل أن يكون الغرض من توظيف الكنية "ذي الكفل" مرة للإشارة إلى إلياس وأخرى للإشارة إلى اليسع هو تسليط الضوء على العلاقة الوثيقة التي تربط هاتين الشخصيتين وتتجلّى في وراثة اليسع كفل إلياس وخلافته في النبوة. هذه المقترحات تقتضي أنه في السياق القرآني يُستخدم "ذو الكفل" ككنية ووصف، لا كاسم علم يقتصر على شخصية واحدة فحسب، والهدف من ذلك الايجاز والتلميح وتجنّب الإسهاب في السرد والإطالة في الوصف، وهي مسألة بلاغية فنية. وإذا ما عدنا إلى ما يربط هؤلاء الأنبياء الثلاثة، شموئيل وإلياس واليسع، فإنهم من أبرز الأنبياء القدماء في التراث اليهودي القديم والذين نشطوا في زمن بعض الملوك (شموئيل زمن الملك شاؤول وداود، إلياس واليسع زمن الملك أخاب). ويمكن القول أيضاً إن كلاً منهم قد تميّز بكساء النبوة.[70]

لقد ذكرتُ أنه في النص القرآني قد استخدم أيضاً اسم العلم "إلياس" للإشارة إلى النبي،[71] ويبدو أنه مستوحى من مصادر مسيحية معاصرة له.[72] ويُلاحظ ظهور إلياس مع إسماعيل (شموئيل) واليسع في الآيات 6: 85–86. من المثير ذكر إلياس في هذا السياق مع شخصيات من العهد الجديد (مسيحية) هي زكريا ويحيى وعيسى في الآية 6: 85، وتليهم مباشرة شخصيات تناخية: إسماعيل (شموئيل) واليسع ويونس ولوط، على النحو الآتي: "وَزَكَرِيَّا وَيَحْيَىٰ وَعِيسَىٰ وَإِلْيَاسَ كُلٌّ مِّنَ ٱلصَّالِحِينَ/ وَإِسْمَاعِيلَ وَٱلْيَسَعَ وَيُونُسَ وَلُوطاً وَكُلاًّ فَضَّلْنَا عَلَى ٱلْعَالَمِينَ." إن الربط الحاصل في هذه الآيات بين إلياس وزكريا ويحيى وعيسى من جانب، وبين إلياس وشموئيل واليسع من جانب آخر، يوحي بإدراك الخطاب القرآني لأهمية إلياس في التقليد والتراث المسيحي، وليس فقط اليهودي.

68. وهكذا الآية: "وَٱذْكُرْ إِسْمَاعِيلَ [شموئيل] وَٱلْيَسَعَ وَذَا ٱلْكِفْلِ [إلياس] وَكُلٌّ مِّنَ ٱلْأَخْيَارِ."
69. وهكذا الآية: "وَإِسْمَاعِيلَ [شموئيل] وَإِدْرِيسَ [إلياس] وَذَا ٱلْكِفْلِ [اليسع] كُلٌّ مِّنَ ٱلصَّابِرِينَ."
70. انظر الإحالات إلى كساء شموئيل في الملاحظة 67 أعلاه.
71. في الآية الصافات 37: 123 يُشار إلى النبي بلفظ "إلياس" وفي الآية 37: 130 بلفظ "إل ياسين"، على ما يبدو لملائمة الايقاع مع ايقاع الآيات السابقة، بتكرار المقطع -ين.
72. صورة الاسم "إلياس" تنسجم لفظاً مع نظيره في اللغة اليونانية (وفي الإثيوبية)، كما ينعكس في السبعينية، الترجمة اليونانية للعهد القديم. انظر: A. J. Wensinck and G. Vajda, "Ilyās," *EI*², s.v. (1971); Josef Horovitz "Jewish Proper Names and Derivatives in the Koran," *Hebrew Union College Annual* 2 (1925): 145–227, 154, 170.

ذو الكفل في التفسيرات الإسلامية

إن كانت شخصية ذي الكفل في القرآن غامضة محيرة للقارئ الدارس، فإنها في التفسيرات الإسلامية اللاحقة أكثر غموضاً وتحييراً. من جهة، يقدّم لنا المفسرون القدماء العديد من الفرضيات بخصوص هوية ذي الكفل في القرآن، والتي عادة ما تُشير إلى شخصيات مألوفة لنا من الكتب اليهودية والمسيحية المقدسة. من جهة أخرى، يقدم لنا المفسرون العديد من الأحاديث التي تحكي سبب تسمية ذي الكفل دون الإشارة إلى هوية شخصية محددة. وتعتمد جميعها على المعاني المختلفة المتضمنة في لفظ "كفل". يعالج المفسرون بهذا الخصوص سؤالين أساسيّين: هل كان ذو الكفل نبياً أم رجلاً صالحاً؟ ومن المقصود بذي الكفل تحديداً أي ما اسمه العلم؟ هذه الأسئلة تفترض أن ذا الكفل كنية أو صفة له ألحقت به لسبب ما. سأبدأ أولاً بتقديم بعض التفسيرات التي تروي قصة ذي الكفل دون تحديد هويته، ذلك أنها كثيرة الانتشار في المصادر الإسلامية القديمة، وبعد ذلك سأتوقف عند بعض التفسيرات التي تعرف شخصية ذي الكفل من خلال ربطها بنبي من أنبياء بني إسرائيل أو بشخصيات أخرى.

أحد التفسيرات الوارد في أقدم تفسير متوفر بين يدينا عند عبد الرزاق بن همام الصنعاني (ت 827/211) والمتكرر في كتب التفاسير اللاحقة، ذلك المنسوب لأبي موسى الأشعري (ت حوالي 42–53/662–673). وبحسبه ذو الكفل لم يكن نبياً بل رجلاً صالحاً، وإنما سُمي ذا الكفل لأنه "كَفِلَ بِصلاةِ رَجُلٍ كانَ يُصَلّي كُلَّ يَومٍ مِائةَ صَلاةٍ فَتُوُفّيَ، فَكَفِلَ بِصَلاتِهِ."[73] مَن يتمعن في هذا التفسير يدرك أن غايته التعبير عن فكرة ما وترسيخ معنى مقصود، لا الكشف عن هوية ذي الكفل. يتّضح ذلك من خلال أمرين: الأول أن هذا التفسير لا يهتم بتعريفنا بالشخصية ولا يحاول الإدلاء باسم محدد لها ولكن يركز على سبب تسمية ذي الكفل؛ الأمر الآخر هو التأكيد على أن ذا الكفل كان رجلاً صالحاً لا نبياً. وباعتبار السياق القرآني وظهور ذي الكفل مع أنبياء آخرين، فإن هذا التفسير يرمي إلى رفع الرجل الصالح والعمل الصالح بتقريبه من درجة الأنبياء. وإذا ما بحثنا في المصادر القديمة عن معنى العمل الصالح والرجل الصالح سندرك أن التفسير المنسوب لأبي موسى الأشعري غايته الحث على العمل الصالح والقيام بالواجبات الدينية، وأهمها الصلاة، وهكذا فإن هذا التفسير بالدرجة الأولى هو تربوي تثقيفي ديني. ما أريد قوله هو إن تفسير الأشعري لا يسعى لكشف هوية ذي الكفل الغامضة، بل إنه يوظف هذه الشخصية وكنيتها لحث المؤمنين على العمل الصالح والقيام بواجباتهم الدينية. يدعم هذا المقترح حديث يُنسب إلى إسحاق بن بشر (ت 822/206)، وجاء فيه ما يلي:

> كانَ يونُسُ عَبْداً صَالحاً لَمْ يَكُنْ في الأنْبياءِ أحدٌ أكْثَرَ صَلاةً مِنْهُ، كانَ يُصَلّي كُلَّ يَوْمٍ ثلاثَمِائةِ رَكْعةٍ قَبْلَ أنْ يَطْعَمَ، وَقَلَّما كَانَ يَطْعَمُ مِنْ دَهْرِهِ. وَكانَ يُصَلّي كُلَّ لَيْلَةٍ قَبْلَ أنْ يَأخُذَ مَضْجَعَهُ ثلاثَمِائةِ رَكْعةٍ وَقَلَّما كانَ يَتَوَسَّدُ الأرْضَ. فَلمّا أنْ فَشَتِ المَعَاصي في أهلِ نينَوى، وَعَظُمَتْ أحْداثُهُمْ بُعِثَ إلَيْهِمْ.[74]

73. انظر: عبد الرزاق بن همام الصنعاني، *تفسير القرآن*، تحقيق محمود محمد عبده (3 مجلدات؛ بيروت: دار الكتب العلمية، 1999)، ج 2، ص 391؛ الهواري، *تفسير*، ج 3، ص 86؛ ج 4، ص 25؛ الطبري، *جامع البيان*، ج 16، ص 372–373؛ الماتريدي، *تأويلات*، ج 8، ص 637؛ الثعلبي، *الكشف*، ج 36، ص 300؛ ابن كثير، *تفسير*، ج 5، ص 365.

74. أبو القاسم علي بن الحسن بن هبة الله بن عساكر، *تاريخ مدينة دمشق*، تحقيق محب الدين أبي سعيد عمر بن غرامة العمروي (80 مجلداً؛ بيروت: دار الفكر، 2001)، ج 74، ص 281.

يربط هذا الحديث صفة الصلاح والرجل الصالح بالعبادات والورع والتقوى وخصوصاً القيام بالصلاة. ومن المحتمل أن الحديث يقصد أن يونس كان رجلاً صالحاً قبل أن يصبح نبياً وقبل أن يبعثه الله إلى أهل نينوى، أي أن الرجل الصالح أقل بدرجة من النبي. إن هذه الرؤية تتناسب بوضوح مع ما بيّنته بشأن نعت ذي الكفل بالرجل الصالح وأن صلاحه ينعكس في كثرة تعبده وصلاته مئات الركعات في اليوم الواحد، كما جاء في تفسير الأشعري. في المصادر القديمة يُعرّف العمل الصالح بالقيام بالواجبات الدينية والعبادات خصوصاً المواظبة على الصلاة والإكثار منها، ويندرج فيها أيضاً الدعاء والتسبيح.[75] فمثلاً، جاء في كتاب *فتح الباري بشرح صحيح البخاري*: "الْأَشْهَرُ فِي تَفْسِيرِ الصَّالِحِ أَنَّهُ الْقَائِمُ بِمَا يَجِبُ عَلَيْهِ مِنْ حُقُوقِ اللَّهِ وَحُقُوقِ عِبَادِهِ وَتَتَفَاوَتُ دَرَجَاتُهُ."[76] وفي تفسير معنى "وَٱلْبَاقِيَاتُ ٱلصَّالِحَاتُ" (الآية 18: 46)، يقول الطبري إنها جميع أعمال الخير تشمل الصلوات الخمس والصلوات بالدعاء.[77] وفي تفسيره للتعبير "وَعَمِلُوا ٱلصَّالِحَاتِ" (الآية 2: 82) أنه يعني "أَطَاعُوا اللهَ فَأَقَامُوا حُدودَهُ، وَأَدَّوْا فَرَائِضَهُ، وَاجْتَنَبُوا مَحَارِمَهُ." وفي تفسير الثعلبي يعني "أَخْلَصُوا الْأَعْمَالَ وَأَقَامُوا الصَّلَوَاتِ الْمَفْرُوضَاتِ."[78]

في المصادر القديمة تفسيرات أخرى تصف ذا الكفل، ومنها تفسير مجاهد بن جبر (ت 722/104) القائل: "ذو الكِفْلِ كانَ رَجُلاً صَالحاً وَلَيْس بِنَبِيٍّ. تَكَفَّلَ لِنَبِيٍّ بِأَنْ يَكْفَلَ لَهُ أَمْرَ قَوْمِهِ وَيُقيمَهُ لَهُمْ، يَقْضي بَيْنَهُمْ بِالعَدْلِ."[79] ويورد الطبري تفسيراً مشابهاً أكثر تفصيلاً يُنسب أيضاً لمجاهد، وفيه أن اليسع عندما كبر في السن أراد أن يعيّن خلفاً له في قومه، فجمع الناس وسألهم قائلاً: "مَنْ يَتَقَبَّلُ لِي بِثَلاثٍ أَسْتَخْلِفُهُ؛ يَصومُ النَّهارَ، وَيَقومُ اللَّيْلَ، وَلا يَغْضَبُ؟" فأجابه إلى ذلك رجل "تَزْدَريهِ الْعَيْنُ"، ثم أنه قد استخلفه. وقد سُمي بذي الكفل لأنه تكفل بأن يخلف اليسع في قومه بالشروط التي فرضها.[80] وفي صيغة أخرى، إن ملكاً صالحاً من بني إسرائيل قد كبر في السن فجمع الناس ليختار من بينهم من يستخلفه في ملكه على أن

75. مثلاً، في حديث نبوي، يحث النبي محمد المؤمنين على الصلاة بالدعاء والإكثار من التسبيح كل يوم لأجل الخلاص والغفران. انظر: أبو الحسين مسلم بن الحجاج بن مسلم النيسابوري، *الجامع الصحيح*، الذكر والدعاء والتوبة والاستغفار 48، باب فضل التهليل والدعاء والتسبيح، رقم 2691؛ أبوعبد الله محمد بن إسماعيل البخاري، *الجامع المسند الصحيح المختصر من حديث رسول الله وسننه وأيامه*، الدعوات 80، باب فضل التهليل، رقم 6403.

76. أحمد بن علي بن حجر العسقلاني، *فتح الباري بشرح صحيح البخاري*، تحقيق عبد العزيز بن عبد الله بن باز، محمد فؤاد عبد الباقي، ومحب الدين الخطيب (13 مجلداً؛ الرياض: المكتبة السلفية، 1390هـ [1970])، ج 2، ص 314.

77. الطبري، *جامع البيان*، ج 15، ص 281. ويقول مقاتل والصنعاني إن الباقيات الصالحات هي أربع كلمات: سبحان الله، والحمد لله، ولا إله إلا الله، والله أكبر. ويقول الماتريدي في مجمل هذه التفاسير إنها تجمع جميع أنواع العبادات والخيرات. أنظر: مقاتل، *تفسير*، ج 2، ص 588، 637؛ الصنعاني، *تفسير القرآن*، ج 2، ص 364؛ الماتريدي، *تأويلات*، ج 7، ص 176–177.

78. الطبري، *جامع البيان*، ج 2، ص 186–187؛ الثعلبي، *الكشف*، ج 13، ص 170.

79. الهواري، *تفسير*، ج 3، ص 86؛ ج 4، ص 25؛ السمرقندي، *بحر العلوم*، ج 2، ص 376؛ ابن الجوزي، *زاد المسير*، ص 939؛ ابن كثير، *تفسير*، ج 5، ص 363.

80. وفي القصة تفاصيل كثيرة مطولة، وبحسبها قد عرض اليسع سؤاله على قومه ثلاث مرات وفي كل مرة ينهض نفس الرجل ليتكفل بما اشترطه اليسع. ثم هناك تفاصيل أخرى عن محاولات إبليس إحباط عمل ذي الكفل وما أخذه على عاتقه من صيام النهار وقيام والليل وتجنّب الغضب. انظر: الطبري، *جامع البيان*، ج 16، ص 369–371؛ الثعلبي، *الكشف*، ج 6، ص 299–300؛ الرازي، *مفاتيح الغيب*، ج 22، ص 211؛ القرطبي، *الجامع*، ج 14، ص 264–265؛ ابن كثير، *تفسير*، ج 5، ص 363–364.

يصوم النهار ويقوم الليل ويحكم بين بني إسرائيل بما أنزل الله ولا يغضب.[81] تتكرر مثل هذه التفسيرات في المصادر الإسلامية بصيغ مختلفة.[82] ولا يخفى على القارئ الشبه بينها وبين تفسير الأشعري من حيث تشديدها على خلق ذي الكفل وعلى ورعه وتقواه، ولكنها أيضاً تختلف ببعض التفاصيل، وليس ذلك عشوائياً، فيما يبدو. ذلك أن التفسيرات المذكورة هنا نحو تلك المنسوبة لمجاهد تتوسع بوصف ذي الكفل، فلا تقتصر صفته على قيامه بمائة ركعة كل يوم، بل بصيام النهار وقيام الليل، وهي من العبادات والواجبات الدينية التي تجعل المرء إنساناً صالحاً. وأضف إلى ذلك صفة التحكم بالغضب أو القضاء بالعدل بين الناس. ووجب التوقف عند هذه النقطة تحديداً. في رأيي إن هذا التفسير فيه نقد مبطن للحاكم أو لولي أمر الأمة أو ملكها، إذ يلزم بحسب منطقه أن من يخلف النبي أو الملك الحاكم في قومه، وفي بعض الصيغ القاضي،[83] يجب أن يكون رجلاً صالحاً يقوم بواجباته الدينية ويحكم بالعدل بين الناس. بخلاف تفسير الأشعري الذي يحث على العمل الصالح وعلى التقوى والتقرب من الله، فإن تفسير مجاهد والتفسيرات الأخرى الشبيهة تلمح إلى أن حاكم الأمة وخليفة النبي يجب أن يكون تقياً ورعاً وعادلاً، وفي هذا انتقاد للملوك والسلاطين المخالفين في خلقهم وأخلاقهم لصفة الرجل الصالح.

إذاً، لم تكن غاية التفسيرات التي ناقشتها للتوّ الكشف عن هوية ذي الكفل ومن يكون تحديداً، ولكن تفسيرات أخرى كثيرة اجتهدت في معرفة هوية هذه الشخصية الغامضة، واعتمد المفسرون في ذلك على المعاني المختلفة للفظ "كفل" في اللغة وبالتالي ربطها بشخصية نبوية أو شخصية رجل صالح. وهكذا نجد أنفسنا أمام العديد من الفرضيات، سأعقّب على البعض منها للتدليل على منهج المفسرين في هذا السياق. فمثلاً جاء في حديث الآتي:

كَانَ إِلْيَاسُ فِي أَرْبَعِمَائَةِ نَبِيٍّ—عَلَيْهِمُ السَّلَامُ—فِي زَمَنِ مَلِكٍ، فَقَتَلَ الْمَلِكُ ثَلَاثَمِائَةٍ مِنْهُمْ فَكَفِلَ رَجُلٌ إِلْيَاسَ فِي مِائَةِ نَبِيٍّ فَكَفَلَهُمْ وَخَبَّأَهُمْ عِنْدَهُ يُطْعِمُهُمْ وَيَسْقِيهِمْ حَتَّى خَرَجُوا مِنْ عِنْدِهِ، وَكَانَ الْكِفْلُ بِمَنْزِلَةٍ مِنَ الْمَلِكِ فَلِذَلِكَ سُمِّيَ: ذَا الْكِفْلِ لِأَنَّهُ خَبَّأَهُمْ وَكِفَلَهُمْ.[84]

هذا الحديث استوحى شخصية ذي الكفل من قصة عوبديا مع الملك أخاب وإلياس (الملوك الأول 18). إن الحديث المقتبس لا يذكر اسم عوبديا للتعريف بذي الكفل ولكننا نستنتج ذلك من وصفه. والحقيقة أن الحديث يخلط بعض التفاصيل التي جاءت في القصة التناخية، والتي بحسبها أنقذ عوبديا مائة نبي خبأهم في كهفين وزودهم بالماء والطعام (الملوك الأول 18: 4). أما أن إلياس كان على رأس أربعمائة نبي، فإن هذا التفصيل مستوحى، فيما يبدو، من جموع الأنبياء الذين قتلهم إلياس (الملوك الأول 18: 40)، لا أخاب، وهم أنبياء بعل وعددهم أربعمائة وخمسون، وأنبياء أشيرا ممن يأكلون على مائدة إيزابل زوجة أخاب وعددهم أربعمائة (الملوك الأول 18: 19). وبعض التفاسير الإسلامية تُعرّف ذا الكفل على أنه إلياس، ولكن دون

---

81. الطبري، جامع البيان، ج 16، ص 371–373.

82. انظر، مثلاً: الطبراني، التفسير الكبير، ج 4، ص 308؛ ابن الجوزي، زاد المسير، ص 939؛ الرازي، مفاتيح الغيب، ج 22، ص 210–211.

83. في حديث عند ابن كثير أن قاضياً في بني إسرائيل قد حضره الموت، فسأل من يقوم مقامه على ألا يغضب، إلخ الرواية. انظر: ابن كثير، تفسير، ج 5، ص 364.

84. الماتريدي، تأويلات، ج 8، ص 637؛ الطبراني، التفسير الكبير، ج 5، ص 354؛ السمرقندي، بحر العلوم، ج 2، ص 376؛ ج 3، ص 139؛ ابن الجوزي، زاد المسير، ص 939؛ ناصر الدين أبو الخير عبد الله بن عمر بن محمد البيضاوي، أنوار التنزيل وأسرار التأويل، تحقيق محمد عبد الرحمن المرعشلي (5 مجلدات؛ بيروت: دار إحياء التراث العربي، بغير تاريخ)، ج 5، ص 32. يأتي الحديث في بعض هذه المصادر مختصراً.

توضيح سبب تسميته بذلك غير القول بأن في القرآن خمسة من الأنبياء ممّن سُموا باسمَيْن: يعقوب سمي أيضاً إسرائيل، إلياس سمي ذا الكفل، عيسى سمي المسيح، يونس سمي ذا النون، ومحمداً سمي كذلك أحمد.[85] بعض التفاسير ترشح النبي زكريا بكنيته ذي الكفل بناء على كفالته مريم،[86] ويعتمد هذا التفسير على الآية 3: 37 وفيها أن زكريا قد كفّل مريم.[87] ويأتي أبو الخير عبد الله بن عمر بن محمد البيضاوي (ت 1286/685) بسبب آخر لتسمية زكريا بذلك، كما يلي: "لأنّه كانَ ذا حَظٍّ مِنَ اللهِ تَعَالى أوْ تَكَفّلَ أمَّتَهُ أوْ لَهُ ضِعْفُ عَمَلِ أنْبِياءِ زَمَانِهِ وَثوابِهِمْ، وَالكِفْلُ يَجيءُ بِمَعْنى النَّصِيبِ وَالكَفَالَةِ وَالضِّعْفِ."[88] وفي بعض المصادر ذو الكفل هو اليسع بن أخطوب، وهو ليس ذات اليسع المذكور في القرآن.[89] والظاهر أن هذا الاستدراك يأخذ بعين الاعتبار ظهور اليسع وذي الكفل معاً في الآية 38: 48.

يبقى أن نذكر ما جاء في تفسير مقاتل للآية 2: 243 التي تقول: "أَلَمْ تَرَ إِلَى ٱلَّذِينَ خَرَجُواْ مِن دِيَٰرِهِمْ وَهُمْ أُلُوفٌ حَذَرَ ٱلْمَوْتِ فَقَالَ لَهُمُ ٱللَّهُ مُوتُواْ ثُمَّ أَحْيَٰهُمْ إِنَّ ٱللَّهَ لَذُو فَضْلٍ عَلَى ٱلنَّاسِ وَلَٰكِنَّ أَكْثَرَ ٱلنَّاسِ لاَ يَشْكُرُونَ." هذه الآية لا تصرح أي قوم هم المقصودون، ولا تأتي على ذكر نبي لهم، غير أن المفسرين يُجمعون على أنها تشير إلى قصة النبي حزقيل، والتي على اختلاف صيغها في المصادر الإسلامية، يمكن القول بأنها الرواية المقابلة لرؤيا العظام اليابسة التي جاءت في سفر حزقيال 37. يذكر مقاتل أن نبي هؤلاء القوم المذكورين في الآية المشار إليها هو "حِزقيلُ بنُ دوم، وَهوَ ذو الكِفْلِ بنِ دوم."[90] في رأيي، هناك عدة نقاط تُمكّننا من القول بأن مقاتلاً لم يرد بهذا التوضيح ربط حزقيل بذي الكفل المذكور في الآيات القرآنية. ومنها أنه يكرر نسب حزقيل كابن دوم في تسمية ذي الكفل ونسبته إلى دوم، وهذا لأجل تمييزه عن ذي الكفل القرآني. ومنها أن مقاتلاً لا يكرر هذا الكلام في تفسيره للآيات 21: 85 و38: 48، ولا يقول لنا إن ذا الكفل المذكور في هذه الآيات هو حزقيل. أضف إلى أننا – بقدر ما تتيحه المصادر المتوفرة بين أيدينا من الافتراض – لا نجد تفسير مقاتل (والحسن البصري – هكذا في المصادر) هذا مقتبساً في التفاسير اللاحقة في تفسير الآيات القرآنية التي تشير إلى ذي الكفل (في سورتي الأنبياء وص)، بالرغم من أنه معروف ويُقتبس كثيراً

85. الرازي، *مفاتيح الغيب*، ج 22، ص 211–212؛ الثعلبي، *الكشف*، ج 6، ص 301؛ الزمخشري، *الكشاف*، ص 685.

86. القرطبي، *الجامع*، ج 14، ص 266. والبعض لا يذكر سبب تسمية زكريا بذي الكفل، والبعض يعرف ذا الكفل بيوشع بن نون دون ذكر السبب. انظر: الزمخشري، ، *الكشاف*، ص 685؛ الرازي، *مفاتيح الغيب*، ج 22، ص 211–212؛ البقاعي، *نظم الدرر*، ج 12، ص 464؛ البيضاوي، *أنوار التنزيل*، ج 4، ص 58.

87. من الغريب ألا نجد إشارة إلى زكريا باعتباره ذا الكفل في تفسير هذه الآية، وخاصة لدى المفسرين المذكورين في الإحالة السابقة.

88. البيضاوي، *أنوار التنزيل*، ج 4، ص 58.

89. عمارة بن وثيمة، *بدء الخلق وقصص الأنبياء*، تحقيق رئيف جورج خوري (فيسبادن: أوتو هراسوبيتز، 1978)، ص 71. وفي رواية مناقضة أن اليسع بن أخطوب هو الذي استخلفه إلياس والذي أصبح نبياً بعده، أما ذو الكفل فهو ابن عم اليسع هذا أو هو بشر بن أيوب. انظر: البيضاوي، *أنوار التنزيل*، ج 5، ص 32.

90. مقاتل، *تفسير*، ج 1، ص 202. يبدو أن تسمية حزقيل بابن دوم مستوحاة من التسمية "حزقيل بن آدم"، وهو تجسيد لتعبير المناداة "ابن آدم" المتكرر في سفر حزقيال كما جاء في ترجمة يوناثان السريانية. وقد لاحظ الباحثون أن تعبير المناداة الذي عادة ما يترجم "بابن الإنسان" يظهر في ترجمة يوناثان كاسم علم يتعلق بحزقيل أي أن اسمه "حزقيل بن آدم". انظر مقدمة الترجمة: *The Targum of Ezekiel*, trans. Samson H. Levey (Delaware: Michael Glazier, 1987), 7.
انظر كذلك: Alinda Damsma, "From Son of Man to Son of Adam: The Prophet Ezekiel in Targum Jonathan," *Aramaic Studies* 15 (2017): 23–43, 24.

فـي المصـادر فـي تفسـير الآيـة 2: 243.[91] أريـد القـول إنـه كمـا أن مقاتلاً لا يُعرّف هويـة ذي الكفل المذكـور فـي القـرآن بحزقيـل، كذلـك المفسـرون المتأخـرون لا يُعرّفـون هويـة ذي الكفـل المذكـور فـي القـرآن بحزقيـل. ويُلاحـظ أن تفسـير مقاتـل لا يهـدف إلـى كشـف هويـة شـخصية غامضـة، بـل العكـس، فـإن حزقيـل (اسـم علـم) هويتـه معروفـة، لذلـك جـاءت تسـميته بـذي الكفـل مـن بـاب وصفـه والتلميح لموتيـف فـي قصتـه، لا تعريفـه وتحديـده. إن مقاتـلاً نفسـه لا يزودنـا بهـذه القصـة، ولكـن التفاسـير اللاحقـة تتداولهـا كثيـراً، وبحسـبها فـإن حزقيـل سُـمي ذا الكفـل لمـا يلـي: "لأنَّـهُ تَكَفَّلَ بسَـبْعِينَ نَبِيّـاً وَأنْجَاهُـمْ مِـنَ الْقَتْـلِ، فَقَـالَ لَهُـمْ: اذْهَبُـوا فَإنِّـي إنْ قُتِلْـتُ كَانَ خَيْـراً مِـنْ أنْ تُقْتَلُـوا جَمِيْعـاً، فَلَمَّـا جَـاءَ الْيَهُـودُ وَسَـألُوا حِزْقِيـلَ عَـنِ الأنْبِيَـاءِ السَّـبْعِينَ، فَقَـالَ لَهُـمْ: ذَهَبُـوا وَلَـمْ أدْرِ أيْـنَ هُـمْ. وَحَفِظَ اللهُ ذَا الْكَفْـلِ مِـنَ الْيَهُـودِ."[92] وهكـذا فـإن نعـت حزقيـل بـذي الكفـل جـاء مرتبطـاً بهـذه الروايـة أي لأنـه كفـل سـبعين نبيـاً ونجاهـم مـن المـوت.

لقـد قدمـتُ فـي القسـم السـابق الـذي ناقـش "ذا الكفـل" فـي النـص القرآنـي تفسـيراً يأخـذ بعيـن الاعتبـار أحـد معانـي لفـظ "كفـل" فـي المعاجـم القديمـة والـذي يربـط هـذه الشـخصية بكسـاء أو بـرداء النبـوة. وبالمجمـل هـذا التفسـير غيـر حاضـر فـي المصـادر الإسـلامية. ومـع ذلـك، يمكـن الإحالـة إلـى مصـدر، ولـو كان متأخـراً، يحفـظ لنـا هـذا المعنـى. جـاء فـي معجـم *لسـان العـرب* لجمـال الديـن محمـد بـن مكـرم بـن منظـور (ت 1312/711) ملخصـاً لتفسـيرات تبيّـن سـبب تسـمية ذي الكفـل القرآنـي، كمـا يلـي:

> وَذو الكِفْلِ: اسمُ نَبـيٍّ مِـنَ الأنْبِيـاءِ، صَلَـواتُ اللهِ عَلَيْهِـمْ أجْمَعيـنَ، وهـوَ مِـنَ الكَفالـةِ، سُـمّيَ ذا الكِفْلِ لأنـه كَفَلَ بِمِائَـةِ رَكْعَـةٍ كُلَّ يَـومٍ فَوَفَـى بِمـا كَفَلَ، وَقيـلَ: لأنَّـه كانَ يَلْبَـسُ كِسـاءً كَالكِفْلِ، وَقـالَ الزَّجَّـاجُ: إنَّ ذا الكِفْلِ سُـمّيَ بِهـذا الاسـمِ لأنَّـهُ تَكَفَّـلَ بِأمْـرِ نَبِـيٍّ فـي أمَّتِـهِ فَقَـامَ بِمـا يَجِـبُ فيهِـمْ، وَقيـلَ: تَكَفَّلَ بِعَمَلِ رَجُلٍ صَالِـحٍ فَقـامَ بِـهِ.[93]

يبـدو أن بيـن يـدي ابـن منظـور تفسـيرات قديمـة متعـددة مـن بينهـا تلـك التـي تشـير إلـى كفـل النبـي أي كسـائه الـذي سُـمّي بـه.

إدريس في النص القرآني

يظهـر إدريـس فـي موضعيـن فـي القـرآن فـي سـياق ذكـر أنبيـاء مـن بنـي إسـرائيل (19: 56؛ 21: 85)، ولا نعـرف لهـذه التسـمية أو الكنيـة نظيـراً فـي الكتـب المقدسـة السـابقة، التنـاخ والعهـد الجديـد. وقـد أثـارت هـذه المسـألة اهتمـام الباحثيـن والأكاديمييـن المعاصريـن. فيمـا يلـي سـأعرض بعـض التفسـيرات التـي قدمهـا الباحثـون لهـذه التسـمية القرآنيـة، ثـم سـأقدم مقترحـاً مغايـراً سـأبيّنه مـن خـلال تحليـل سـياق النـص القرآنـي وألفاظـه ومقارنتـه بنصـوص سـابقة، علـى غـرار مـا قدمتـه بخصـوص إسـماعيل وذي الكفـل.

---

91. عادة ما يُنسب هذا التفسير لمقاتل وللحسن البصري (ت 728/110)، انظر: الطبراني، *التفسير الكبير*، ج 1، ص 440؛ الثعلبي، *الكشف*، ج 2، ص 203؛ أبو محمد الحسين بن مسعود البغوي، *معالم التنزيل*، تحقيق محمد عبد الله النمر، عثمان جمعة ضميرية، وسليمان مسلم الحرش (8 مجلدات؛ الرياض: دار طيبة، 1409هـ [1989])، ج 1، ص 293؛ الرازي، *مفاتيح الغيب*، ج 6، ص 177.

92. انظر الإحالات في الملاحظة السابقة. إن تصوير اليهود كقتلة الأنبياء جاء في القرآن، نحو الآيات المدنية 2: 61؛ 3: 21، 112؛ 5: 70. عن ذلك انظر: Gabriel Said Reynolds, "On the Qur'ān and the Theme of Jews as 'Killers of the Prophets,'" *Al-Bayān* 10 (2012): 9–32.

93. ابن منظور، *لسان العرب*، ج 11، ص 590.

حاول الباحثون المعاصرون الوقوف على أصل التسمية القرآنية لإدريس، ومن ثم التعرف على هذه الشخصية وعلى حضورها في القرآن. ونتج عن هذه المحاولات آراء متعددة، منها أن الاسم إدريس نشأ من النظير اليوناني للاسم عزرا (Esdras)، وهو شخصية مهمة خاصة في الكتب المنحولة (أبوكريفا).[94] وفي رأي مخالف إن إدريس منبثق عن الصورة اليونانية للاسم أندرو (Andreas)، والذي بحسب نولدكه يحيل إلى القديس أندرو أحد رسل عيسى المسيح، وبحسب ريتشارد هارتمان (Richard Hartmann) يحيل إلى طباخ الإسكندر المقدوني، هو في الميثولوجيا اليونانية صدّيق مُخلّد.[95] ويذهب الباحث يورام إردر (Yoram Erder) إلى ربط إدريس القرآني بشخصية حنوخ التناخية وبهرمس الهرامسة، معتمداً بذلك على المصادر العربية. هو يعتقد أن الصورة "إدريس" ناتجة عن تصحيف للمقطعين الأخيرين في لفظ *poimandrēs*،[96] وهو اسم فصل مهم من المتون الهرمسية (الهرموتيكا).[97] مع ذلك يخالف إردر الرأي القائل بانبثاق الاسم إدريس عن الصورة اليونانية لاسم هرمس، باعتبار الاختلاف في أصل الاسمين. ويعتقد بأن مخطوطات كهوف قمران يمكن أن تساعدنا على فهم هذه الأحجية، وهكذا يربط بين إدريس وبين شخصية جيء على ذكرها في وثيقة دمشق تحت وصف "دارس التوراة" (بالعبرية: דורש התורה). من جهة، يرى إردر أن التشابه بين أصل الكلمة "إدريس" والجذر العبري د-ر-ش (لدارس التوراة) وتقديم إدريس في المصادر الإسلامية كمُشرّع، يمكّنان من الربط بين إدريس وحنوخ التناخي الموصوف في الأدب المنحول كمَن جاء بأسرار السماء ومَن دوّن كتب الوحي السماوية. من جهة أخرى، يربط إردر بين "دارس التوراة" وبين هرمس بالركون إلى المعنى "تفسير" الذي يتضمنه الاسم اليوناني لهذه الشخصية. ويضيف إردر بالقول إن "دارس التوراة" يرتبط في الوثيقة الدمشقية بكوكب عطارد (مركوري)، وفي الميثولوجيا اليونانية يرتبط هذا الكوكب بهرمس.[98]

إن المقترحات التي تربط إدريس القرآني بهرمس أو بالصورة اليونانية للأسماء عزرا وأندرو غير مرضية تماماً. أما قول إردر بأن المتون الهرمسية قد وصلت إلى المصادر الإسلامية من خلال قناتين: حرّان في العراق واليمن عبر المصادر اليهودية القرائية،[99] فإنه لا يوضح كيف للنص القرآني الذي ظهر في القرن السابع للميلاد في بلاد الحجاز، أن ينكشف على مثل هذه القنوات ليتحقق الربط بين "هرمس الهرامسة" و"دارس التوراة"، ثم لتُشتق الصورة "إدريس". كما وأن شخصية "دارس التوراة" لا تنعكس في النص القرآني

---

94. وهذا رأي كل من بول كزنوفا (Paul Casanova)، وريتشارد بل، وتشارلز توري، ويدعمه بيلامي معتقداً أيضاً أن الأسماء القرآنية "عُزيْر" (التوبة 9: 30) و"الرّسّ" (الفرقان 25: 38؛ ق 50: 12) منبثقة عن الاسم عزرا. انظر: James Bellamy, "Textual Criticism of the Koran," *JAOS* 121 (2001): 1–6. انظر نقداً لهذا الرأي: Yoram Erder, "The Origin of the Name Idrīs," *JNES* 49 (1990): 339–350, 341.

95. Erder, "The Origin," 340; Jeffery, *The Foreign Vocabulary of the Qurʾān*, 51–52.

96. وهو ليس مقترحاً جديداً، انظر: Jeffery, *The Foreign Vocabulary of the Qurʾān*, 52.

97. Yoram Erder, "Idrīs," *EQ*, s.v. (2002); G. Vajda, "Idrīs," *EI²*, s.v. (1971).

98. Erder, "The Origin," 342–344.

99. نفسه، ص 347–350. أضف إلى ذلك فإن المصادر الإسلامية التي تربط بين إدريس وهرمس والتي يعتمدها إردر حججاً ودلائل، نحو مؤلفات الأندلسي ابن جلجل (ت 383/994) والمصري ابن القفطي (ت 646/1248) هي مصادر متأخرة. انظر: نفسه، ص 341، ملاحظة 19. انظر عن هرمس الهرامسة في المصادر الإسلامية: A. E. Affifi, "The Influence of Hermetic Literature on Moslem Thought," *BSOAS* 13 (1951): 840–855.

بوضوح، ولا علاقتها بحنوخ وهرمس. فيما يلي سأقدم مقترحاً يفسر صورة اللفظ "إدريس" ومعناه المقصود وفقاً لسياق النص القرآني واستناداً لمعاني لفظ "درس" في العربية الكلاسيكية القديمة وكذلك بالمقارنة مع نص التناخ. وقد قدم تشيليك تفسيراً مشابهاً يشير فيه إلى معنى "الغياب" و"الاختفاء" الذي يتضمنه لفظ "درس".[100]

يظهر إدريس في الآية 21: 85 مع إسماعيل هو شموئيل وذي الكفل وهو في هذا الموضع اليسع، كما بيّنت أعلاه. ويُذكر إدريس مرة أخرى في الآيات 19: 56–57،[101] والتي جاء فيها: "وَٱذْكُرْ فِي ٱلْكِتَٰبِ إِدْرِيسَ إِنَّهُۥ كَانَ صِدِّيقاً نَّبِيّاً/ وَرَفَعْنَٰهُ مَكَاناً عَلِيّاً."

إن مفهوم النبوة كما أوجزته في مدخل هذه الورقة، سيساعدنا على فهم شخصية إدريس في سياقها القرآني. وبحسب النص القرآني فإن النبوة جُعلت في بني إسرائيل، والأنبياء هم من ذرية إبراهيم من نسل إسحاق ويعقوب. ولأن إدريس ذُكر في الآيات القرآنية في سياق الحديث عن أنبياء بني إسرائيل فهو منهم. ومن هنا، فإن ربط بعض الباحثين الغربيّين (وكذلك العلماء المسلمين القدماء) هذا النبي بشخصية حنوخ التناخية يبدو أكثر بعداً وأشدّ غرابة. إذا، لتحديد هوية إدريس كما يقدمها الخطاب القرآني، علينا البحث عن أحد أنبياء بني إسرائيل من الأجيال التي نشأت بعد يعقوب وليس قبله. يمكن القول ها هنا إن البحث عن معنى التسمية "إدريس" سيساهم في كشف الغموض وإزالة اللبس عن هذه الشخصية. لا شك أن النص القرآني يستخدم في بعض المواضع لفظ "درس" بمعنى شبيه للفظ العبري "درش" (דרש) أي بمعنى التعلم،[102] غير أن هذا المعنى لا يقدم تفسيراً مقنعاً لاشتقاق اللفظ "إدريس" في سياقه القرآني. ومن المعاني السائدة في اللغة العربية القديمة للفظ "دَرَسَ" هو اختفاء الأثر والمحو والاندثار.[103] وجاء هذا المعنى في الشعر العربي القديم في حديث الشعراء عن الرسم والطلل.[104] بهذا يمكن ربط معنى الاختفاء المتضمن في لفظ "إدريس" بقصة إلياس المذكورة في التناخ العبري، وتحديداً اختفاء أثره بعد أن رُفع في عاصفة إلى السماء (الملوك الثاني 2: 11). ولا تبرز شخصية إلياس ذات المعجزات وقصة صعوده إلى السماء في التناخ فقط، بل أيضاً في أدبيات الحاخامات القدماء (في التلمود والمدراش، مثلاً) في سياقات كثيرة ومتعددة.

---

100. Celik, "The Enigmatic Prophets."

101. الآيات السابقة لهذه تسرد لنا قصة الأنبياء زكريا ويحيى وعيسى وإبراهيم وموسى وهارون وإسماعيل (شموئيل).

102. نحو آل عمران 3: 79؛ الأنعام 6: 105، 156؛ الأعراف 7: 169؛ سبأ 34: 44؛ القلم 68: 37.

103. إن لفظ "إدريس" يتناسب مع وزن "إبليس" في القرآن. جاء في المعاجم اللغوية في مادة "درس": "دَرَسَ الشيءُ والرَّسْمُ يَدْرُسُ دُرُوساً: عَفَا ... وَقَالَ أَبو الْهَيْثَمِ: دَرَسَ الأَثَرُ يَدْرُسُ دُروساً ودَرَسَتْهُ الرِّيحُ تَدْرُسُه دَرْساً أَيْ مَحَتْه؛ وَمِنْ ذلك دَرَسْتُ الثوبَ أَدْرُسُه دَرْساً، فهو مَدْرُوسٌ ودَرِيسٌ، أَي أَخْلَقْتُهُ." انظر: ابن منظور، *لسان العرب*، ج 6، ص 79.

104. مثلاً، جاء في معلقة امرئ القيس قوله: "وإنّ شِفائي عَبْرةٌ مُهَراقةٌ / فهَلْ عِندَ رَسْمٍ دَارِسٍ مِنْ مُعوَّلِ." يريد بذلك أن لا فائدة من البكاء على المحبوبة عند الطلل الدارس الممحوّ. وجاء في أشعار الأخطل (غياث بن غوث، ت حوالي 711/92) قوله: "هَلْ عَرَفتَ الدّارَ يابنَ أوَيْسٍ / دَارِساً نُؤْيُها كخَطِّ الزَّبورِ"؛ وكذلك قوله: "أتَعرفُ مِنْ أسماءَ بالجُدِّ رَوْسَما / مُحيلاً وَنُؤياً دارِساً قدْ تَهدَّما." والنؤي الدارس والمهدم هو ما يُحفر حول الخيام لتجنيبها الماء والسيول. ويقول الفرزدق (همام بن غالب، ت 732/114): "كَمْ للمُلاءةِ مِنْ أطلالِ مَنْزِلَةٍ / بِالعَنْبرِيّةِ لَمْ يَدْرُسْ لهَا أثَرُ"؛ يعني لم يندثر لها أثرُ. وقال أيضاً: "ألِمَّا عَلى أطلالِ سُعْدى نُسَلِّمِ / دَوَارِسَ لَمَّا اسْتُنْطِقَتْ لَمْ تُكَلِّمِ"؛ والأطلال الدّوارس ما اندثر وزال من المعالم والأثر. انظر الأبيات الشعرية المذكورة بالتتابع: الحسن بن أحمد الزوزني، *شرح المعلقات السبع*، تحقيق محمد الفاضلي (بيروت: المكتبة العصرية، 1998)، ص 13؛ *ديوان الأخطل*، تحقيق مهدي محمد ناصر الدين (بيروت: دار الكتب العلمية، 1994)، ص 135، 311؛ *ديوان الفرزدق*، تحقيق علي فاعور (بيروت: دار الكتب العلمية، 1987)، ص 285، 524.

فهو يُصوّر مثلاً كمَن لم يمت ومن تجتمع فيه ماهيتان: إنسية وملكية؛ وهكذا فهو يكون في السماء كالملك ويجوب الأرض بهيئة طير، ويُعتقد أنه سيظهر في آخر الزمان.[105] في بعض الروايات يُعرّف إلياس بأنه فنحاس بن إليعازار بن هارون أخي موسى أو بشخصيات أخرى. وفي عشرات الروايات والقصص يتجلى إلياس للناس عموماً وللحاخامات خصوصاً ليؤدي أدواراً مختلفة في نصوص تعالج مسائل دينية روحانية واجتماعية أخلاقية وتشريعية وحياتية.[106] إذا إدريس يدل على إلياس. يدعم هذا القول ظهور إدريس في سورة الأنبياء مع إسماعيل (شموئيل) ومع اليسع، معاً يشكل هؤلاء ثلاثياً. ويظهر إدريس مرة أخرى في سورة مريم مباشرة بعد قصة إسماعيل (شموئيل). في رأيي إن الآية 19: 57 التي تشير إلى رفع إدريس إلى مكان عليّ إنما تحيل إلى قصة رفعه إلى السماء واختفائه، وهو المعنى المقصود في صياغة لفظ "إدريس". ويعزز هذا المعنى أن اللفظ "رَفَعْنَاهُ" المتعلق بإدريس مشتق من نفس جذر اللفظ "رَافِعُكَ" الذي يشير إلى رفع عيسى المسيح إلى السماء، كما جاء في الآية 3: 55 التي تقول: "إِذْ قَالَ ٱللَّهُ يَٰعِيسَىٰٓ إِنِّي مُتَوَفِّيكَ وَرَافِعُكَ إِلَيَّ". وقد يُقال إن حنوخ أيضاً قد رُفع إلى السماء بحسب سفر التكوين (5: 24)، لكن ما يحسم الأمر هنا اعتبار إدريس نبياً في بني إسرائيل وهي صفته في القرآن، وليس حنوخ نبياً، ولا يرتبط ارتباطاً وثيقاً بالأنبياء اليسع وشموئيل. أضف إلى كل هذا أسلوب الخطاب القرآني الذي يميل في بعض المواضع إلى الايجاز والتلميح دون الإسهاب والتصريح، كما رأينا في تسمية شموئيل بإسماعيل للإشارة إلى تصديق الله لوعوده وكلامه، ووصف إلياس مرة واليسع مرة أخرى بذي الكفل للإشارة إلى كساء النبوة العجيب. وهكذا فإن "إدريس" والذي يمكن اعتباره رمزاً وكنية يشير إلى اختفاء أثر إلياس ورفعه إلى السماء. لاحظ أن الآية 21: 85 تذكر الأنبياء الثلاثة بترتيبهم الزمني: أولاً إسماعيل (شموئيل)، ثم إدريس (إلياس) في إشارة إلى رفعه إلى السماء، وبعد ذلك ذا الكفل ها هنا اليسع في إشارة إلى كساء النبوة الذي تلقّاه من إلياس بُعيد اختفاء أثره.

إدريس في التفسيرات الإسلامية

يُجمع المفسرون المسلمون على أن إدريس المذكور في القرآن هو أخنوخ (حنوخ) جد أبي نوح،[107] ويعتمدون في ذلك على أمرين. الأول معنى الاسم إدريس واشتقاقه، فمعظم المفسرين يذهبون إلى أن إدريس سُمي بذلك لكثرة دراسته كتب الوحي السماوية، بهذا فإن اسمه مشتق من لفظ "درس" بمعنى التعلم والحفظ.[108] ويعترض جار الله أبو القاسم محمود بن

---

105. وذلك بالاعتماد على ما جاء في سفر ملاخي 3: 23–24.

106. فنحاس فلاي، "النبي إلياهو في بيت مدراش الحاخامات [بالعبرية]،" *بأوراح مداع: أبحاث في ثقافة إسرائيل مُكرسة لأهارون مرسكي بمناسبة مرور سبعين عاماً على مولده*، تحقيق تسفي ملاخي (اللد: معهد هبرمن للأبحاث الأدبية، 1986)، ص 141–168، 141–142، 148–149. انظر في المقال العديد من الروايات فيها يتجلى إلياهو للحاخامات والعلماء.

107. مقاتل، *تفسير*، ج 2، ص 631؛ الطبري، *جامع البيان*، ج 16، ص 368؛ السمرقندي، *بحر العلوم*، ج 2، ص 326؛ الطبراني، *التفسير الكبير*، ج 4، ص 215؛ الثعلبي، *الكشف*، ج 6، ص 219؛ الزمخشري، *الكشاف*، ص 640؛ البغوي، *معالم التنزيل*، ج 5، ص 237؛ ابن عطية، *المحرر*، ج 4، ص 21؛ الرازي، *مفاتيح الغيب*، ج 21، ص 234؛ القرطبي، *الجامع*، ج 13، ص 466–467؛ البقاعي، *نظم الدرر*، ج 12، ص 216.

108. وهذا التفسير سائد في كتب التفاسير، انظر على سبيل المثال فقط: السمرقندي، *بحر العلوم*، ج 2، ص 326. انظر أيضاً: الثعلبي، البغوي، والرازي في الإحالة السابقة.

عمر الزمخشري (ت 1144/538) على هذا التفسير من باب الاشتقاق، لا المعنى. في اعتقاده أن أصل الاسم ليس عربياً بل أعجمياً بدليل امتناعه عن الصرف، وهو بذلك يشبه الاسم "إبليس" من حيث وزنه وعجمته.[109] الأمر الثاني الذي يستدل المفسرون به على أن إدريس هو أخنوخ أن الآية 19: 57 التي تصف رفع إدريس إلى مكان عليّ ("وَرَفَعْنَاهُ مَكَاناً عَلِيّاً") تتعلق بقصة رفع أخنوخ إلى السماء التي يرد ذكرها في كثير من الأحاديث الإسلامية.[110] هذه الأحاديث عموماً تروي قصة قبض روح إدريس ورفعه إلى السماء حيث يموت هناك، وبعض الأحاديث تقول بأنه لا يزال حياً في السماء لم يمت.[111] ويؤيد البقاعي هذا التفسير باقتباس آية من التوراة تشير إلى رفع حنوخ إلى السماء، كالآتي: "أَخْنوخُ أَحْسَنَ قُدَّامَ اللهِ فَرَفَعَهُ إلَيْهِ" (تكوين 5: 24).[112] وفي المجمل فإن إدريس يوصف في هذه المصادر بأنه كان خياطاً، أو أول من خاط الثياب ولبس المخيط، أو أول من لبس القطن وقد كانوا من قبله يلبسون الجلود، وبأنه أول من خطّ بالقلم، وأول من نظر في علم النجوم والحساب، وكذلك أن الله قد أنزل إليه ثلاثين صحيفة.[113]

اقترحت أعلاه أن المقصود بإدريس في النص القرآني هو النبي إلياس وأن هذه التسمية تلمح إلى قصة رفعه إلى السماء، وهنا أشرتُ إلى إجماع المفسرين على تعريف إدريس بأخنوخ، ومع ذلك نجد في المصادر آراء أخرى خارجة عن هذا الإجماع. في تفسير منفرد يُنسب إلى عبد الله بن مسعود (ت 653/32) قوله إن إلياس المذكور في الآية 37: 123 هو إدريس،[114] وتُنسب إليه قراءة هذه الآية كالآتي: "وَإِنَّ إِدْرِيسَ لَمِنَ ٱلْمُرْسَلِينَ،" في حين أن صيغتها المعتمدة في المصحف العثماني هي كالآتي: "وَإِنَّ إِلْيَاسَ لَمِنَ ٱلْمُرْسَلِينَ."[115] بالرغم

---

109. الزمخشري، *الكشاف*، ص 640؛ القرطبي، *الجامع*، ج 13، ص 466.

110. وقد تعددت الروايات في سبب رفع إدريس إلى السماء. انظر، مثلاً: الطبري، **جامع** *البيان*، ج 15، ص 562–563؛ السمرقندي، *بحر العلوم*، ج 2، ص 326–328؛ الثعلبي، *الكشف*، ج 6، ص 219–220؛ مكي بن أبي طالب، *الهداية إلى بلوغ النهاية*، تحقيق مجموعة من الباحثين (13 مجلداً؛ الشارقة: جامعة الشارقة، 2008)، ج 7، ص 4555–4558. يوجز ابن الجوزي هذه الروايات في ثلاثة أقوال: ابن الجوزي، *زاد المسير*، ص 889. ينتقد ابن كثير الطبري للحديث الذي أورده في هذا السياق ويقول إنه أثر غريب عجيب، معتبراً إياه خبراً منكراً من أخبار كعب الأحبار الإسرائيليات، انظر: ابن كثير، *تفسير*، ج 5، ص 240–241.

111. قيل، مثلاً: "إنّ اللهَ جَلَّ ذِكْرُهُ جَعَلَهُ في السّمَاءِ الرّابِعَةِ قاضِياً كَالمَلِكِ في وَسَطِ مُلْكِهِ وَجَعَلَ خَزائِنَ السَّماواتِ بِيَدِهِ." وقال مجاهد: "رُفِعَ إدريسُ وَلَمْ يَمُتْ كَمَا رُفِعَ عِيسى": مكي، *الهداية*، ج 7، ص 4556. وينسب القرطبي لوهب بن منبه قوله: "فإدريسُ تارَةً يَرْتَعُ في الجَنّةِ، وَتارَةً يَعْبُدُ اللهَ تَعالى مَعَ المَلائِكَةِ في السَّماءِ": القرطبي، الجامع، ج 13، ص 470.

112. يأتي البقاعي بعدة تراجم لهذه الآية: البقاعي، *نظم الدرر*، ج 12، ص 216–217.

113. انظر، مثلاً: الطبراني، *التفسير الكبير*، ج 4، ص 215؛ الزمخشري، *الكشاف*، ص 640؛ الرازي، ***مفاتيح الغيب***، ج 21، ص 234؛ القرطبي، *الجامع*، ج 13، ص 466. انظر أيضاً: الثعلبي، *الكشف*، ج 6، ص 219؛ ابن عطية، *المحرر*، ج 4، ص 21؛ السمرقندي، *بحر العلوم*، ج 2، ص 326.

114. بالرغم من أن هذه القراءة لا ترد إلا في المصادر المتأخرة، إلا أن أهميتها – إن صحت نسبتها لابن مسعود – تكمن في كون ابن مسعود أحد الصحابة المقربين من النبي محمد الذي تعلم القرآن منه. وقد وقف الباحثون المعاصرون على الفرق بين نسخة القرآن المنسوبة لابن مسعود ونسخة المصحف العثماني المعتمدة اليوم. تتلخص هذه الاختلافات في ترتيب السور وبعض الألفاظ والتعابير. وفي نظر الباحثين أن هذه الاختلافات ليست ذات أهمية كبيرة. انظر: J.-C Vadet, "Ibn Masʿūd," *EI*², s.v. (1971).

115. وكذلك قراءة ابن مسعود للآية 37: 130 كالآتي: "سَلَامٌ عَلَىٰ إدْرَاسين." انظر، مثلاً: الطبري، **جامع** *البيان*، ج 19، ص 622؛ الماوردي، *النكت*، ج 5، ص 65؛ البغوي، **معالم** *التنزيل*، ج 7، ص 59؛ ابن كثير، *تفسير*، ج 7، ص 37. وذكر القرطبي قراءة "وإدْرِيسينَ وإدْرسينَ وإدْرَاسِينَ"، دون أن ينسبها: القرطبي، *الجامع*، ج 18، ص 59. من المحتمل أن تكون قراءة "إدريس" مكان "إلياس" في الآية 37: 123 هي الأقدم، ذلك أنه في

من أن قراءة ابن مسعود "إدريس" مكان "إلياس" في سورة الصافات تُعدّ شاذة ومخالفة للإجماع، إلا أنه يكاد لا يكون هناك كتاب تفسير لم يذكرها أو يوثقها.[116]

من جانب آخر فإن المصادر الإسلامية تروي أيضاً قصة صعود إلياس إلى السماء على فرس من نار (نظيرها في الملوك الثاني 2). وفي رواية عند الطبري جاء ما يلي:

> فَلَـمّا رَأى ذلك إلْـياسُ مِنْ كُفرهِمْ، دَعا رَبَّـهُ أنْ يَقْبِضَـهُ إلـيْهِ، فَـيُريحَهُ مِنْهُمْ، فَقيـلَ لَـهُ – فِيـما يَزْعُمونَ –: انْظُرْ يَومَ كَذا وَكَذا، فَـاخْرُجْ فـيهِ إلـى بَلَدِ كَذا وَكَذا، فَماذا جاءَكَ مِنْ شَيْءٍ فَـارْكَبْهُ وَلا تَهَبْهُ. فَخَرَجَ إلْـياسُ، وَخَـرَجَ مَعَـهُ الـيَسَعُ بنُ أخْطـوبَ، حتّـى إذا كانَ فـي البَلَدِ الـذي ذُكِرَ لَـهُ، فـي الـمَكَانِ الـذي أُمِرَ بِـهِ، أقْبَلَ إلـيْهِ فَرَسٌ مِنْ نـارٍ حتّـى وَقَـفَ بَـيْنَ يَدَيْـهِ، فَوَثَبَ عَلَـيْهِ، فَـانْطَلَقَ بِـهِ، فَنـاداهُ الـيَسَعُ: يـا إلْـياسُ، يـا إلْـياسُ، مَـا تَأمُرُنـي؟ فَكانَ آخرَ عَهْدِهِم بِـهِ، فَكَساهُ اللهُ الرِّيشَ، وَألْبَسَـهُ النُّـورَ، وَقَطَـعَ عَنْـهُ لَـذّةَ الـمَطْعَمِ وَالـمَشْرَبِ، وَطـارَ فـي الـمَلائِكَةِ، فَكانَ إنْسِيّاً مَلَكِيّـاً، أرْضِيّاً سَـمَاوِيّاً.[117]

ويسرد الثعلبي رواية مشابهة مطولة وفيها تفصيل مثير لافت وهو أن إلياس عندما انطلق به الفرس إلى السماء ألقى بكسائه إلى اليسع "وَكانَ ذَلكَ عَلامَةَ اسْتِخْلافِهِ إيّاهُ عَلى بَني إسْرائيلَ"،[118] أي أن الكساء يمثل "النبوة" ويرمز لها. غير أن المفسرين لا يربطون قصة صعود إلياس إلى السماء على فرس من نار بشخصية إدريس باعتبار رفعه إلى مكان عليّ بحسب الآية 19: 57، وباعتبار قراءة ابن مسعود التي تربط بين إلياس وإدريس. ويبدو أن هذه الأحاديث تعتمد على الروايات اليهودية القديمة، فقد رأينا أعلاه أحاديث بعض الحاخامات من قبيل أن إلياس لم يمت وأنه أصبح بعد صعوده إلى السماء ذا ماهيتين: إنسية وملكية. ويشذ عن هؤلاء مكي بن أبي طالب (ت 1045/437) الذي جاء في تفسيره للآية 37: 123 بقصة صعود إلياس إلى السماء، حيث كساه الله ريشاً وألبسه نوراً، وقطع عنه لذة الطعام والشراب فكان بين الملائكة إنسياً ملكياً وأرضياً سماوياً، أي أن إلياس أصبح في ماهيته ملَكاً وبشراً في

النص القرآني يُستخدم الاسم "إلياس" في موضع آخر فقط، في سورة الأنعام، وهي من المكية الثالثة أي المتأخرة. بينما يُستخدم "إدريس" في السور الأقدم، نحو سورة مريم وسورة الأنبياء. وبحسب نولدكه فإن سورة الصافات أقدم من جميع هذه السور.

116. عادة ما تُذكر قراءة ابن مسعود في تفسير الآية 37: 123، انظر: السمرقندي، *بحر العلوم*، ج 3، ص 123؛ الثعلبي، *الكشف*، ج 8، ص 158؛ الزمخشري، *الكشاف*، ص 913؛ البغوي، *معالم التنزيل*، ج 7، ص 52؛ ابن عطية، *المحرر*، ج 4، ص 240، 483؛ ابن الجوزي، *زاد المسير*، ص 1194؛ الرازي، *مفاتيح الغيب*، ج 26، ص 161؛ القرطبي، *الجامع*، ج 18، ص 84؛ ابن كثير، *تفسير*، ج 7، ص 36؛ البقاعي، *نظم الدرر*، ج 16، ص 283. ويذكر الطبري ذلك في تفسيره للآية 6: 85، انظر: الطبري، *جامع البيان*، ج 9، ص 383. يذكر بعض هؤلاء المفسرين في هذه المواضع علماء آخرين يميلون لرأي ابن مسعود أو يقدمون تفسيراً مشابهاً لتفسيره، نحو عكرمة (مولى ابن عباس، ت 723/105)، كما جاء عند الثعلبي، البغوي، الرازي، القرطبي، والبقاعي؛ ونحو قتادة، كما جاء عند ابن عطية، ابن الجوزي، وابن كثير، وكذلك في: الطبري، *جامع البيان*، ج 19، ص 612؛ مكي، *الهداية*، ج 9، ص 6150. ينسب ابن كثير هناك تفسيراً مشابهاً لابن إسحاق والضحاك بن مزاحم. وينسب ابن الجوزي قراءة مشابهة لقراءة ابن مسعود لأبي العالية (رُفيع بن مِهران الرياحي، ت حوالي 90–709/93–712) ولأبي عثمان النهدي (ت حوالي 95–714/100–719).

117. الطبري، *جامع البيان*، ج 19، ص 617. يقتبس الطبري القصة مطولاً عن ابن اسحاق: نفسه، ج 19، ص 615–617. ويسرد ابن كثير رواية مشابهة بنوع من الريبة على أن وهب بن منبه قد أخذها عن أهل الكتاب. انظر: ابن كثير، *تفسير*، ج 7، ص 37.

118. الثعلبي، *الكشف*، ج 8، ص 167. يظهر هذا التفصيل في الرواية التي دوّنها القرطبي، انظر: القرطبي، *الجامع*، ج 18، ص 84.

ذات الوقت. وتعقيباً على هذه التفاصيل يقول مكي كالآتي: "وَهذا الخَبَرُ إذا صَحَّ فَإنَّما يَصِحُّ عَلَى قَوْلِ مَنْ قَالَ: إنَّهُ إدْريسُ صَلَى اللهُ عَلَيْهِ وَسَلّمَ لِقَوْلِهِ تَعَالى ذِكْرُهُ في إدْريسَ: 'وَرَفَعْنَاهُ مَكَاناً عَلِيّاً'."[119] وهكذا فإن مكي يرى أن قصة صعود إلياس إلى السماء تدعم من يقول بأن إدريس المذكور في القرآن هو إلياس، خاصة الآية 19: 57 التي تشير إلى رفعه إلى مكان عليّ، فالمكان العليّ هنا هو السماء أو الجنة في السماء.

إجمال

لقد ناقشت في هذه الورقة ثلاث شخصيات نبوية غامضة في القرآن هي شخصيات إسماعيل وذي الكفل وإدريس، وخلصت إلى أن النص القرآني وسياقه يحيل من خلال هذه التسميات إلى الأنبياء شموئيل وإلياس واليسع. لقد اعتمدت في ذلك على مفهوم "النبي" و"النبوة" كما ينعكس في الخطاب القرآني؛ لأن إسماعيل (المذكور في بعض الآيات منفصلاً عن إبراهيم) وذا الكفل وإدريس قد قُدموا كأنبياء وذُكروا مع أنبياء بني إسرائيل. كما أنني استعنت بالمعاجم اللغوية القديمة والمعاني التي توفرها لنا لفهم التسميات "ذي الكفل" و"إدريس". أضف إلى مقارنة النص القرآني بنصوص وردت في التناخ وفي التقليد اليهودي القديم، نحو وصف إسماعيل بنبي صادق الوعد مقارنة بتمييز شموئيل في بعض الآيات التناخية بصدق كلامه، والإشارة إلى رفع إدريس مقارنة برفع إلياهو إلى السماء كما جاء في التناخ. تطرقت كذلك إلى ارتباط هذه الشخصيات كثلاثي مقارنة بأنبياء إسرائيليين آخرين ورد ذكرهم في القرآن كثلاثيات. ومن ثم ناقشت الشخصيات الثلاث كما جاءت في المصادر الإسلامية اللاحقة وخصوصاً كتب تفسير القرآن السنيّة. لاحظت أن جميع التفسيرات التي اقترحتها في هذه الورقة، أعني أن إسماعيل يدل على شموئيل، وذا الكفل يدل على صاحب الكساء في إشارة إلى كساء النبوة، وإدريس يدل على إلياس وقصة رفعه إلى السماء، قد وردت في المؤلفات الإسلامية القديمة. ولا نستطيع القول إن التوافق المذكور بين التفسيرات المتأخرة وبين الآيات القرآنية يعني بالضرورة الارتباط الوثيق، من قبيل الاستمرارية بين التقليديْن. لكننا من ناحية أخرى لا نستطيع تجاهل التوافق الحاصل بين النص القرآني وقراءة عبد الله بن مسعود التي تربط إدريس بإلياس وحديث مقاتل بن سليمان عن تسمية شموئيل بإسماعيل، أضف إلى اعتبار مقاتل "ذا الكفل" صفة وكنية لا اسم علم (ولهذا أمكن استخدامها لوصف "حزقيل بن دوم")، وكذلك حديث الضحاك بن مزاحم الذي يربط إلياس بإسماعيل من حيث النسب، وذلك لقدم هذه التفسيرات. ونحن بحاجة إلى المزيد من البحث والتقصي للوقوف على طبيعة العلاقة بين نص القرآن والتفسيرات القديمة المذكورة. وقد بيّنت أن مثل هذه التفسيرات قد أهملت وهُمشت مع مرور الوقت لسبب أو غاية ما، نحو تسليط الضوء على إسماعيل بن إبراهيم أبي العرب لرفع شأنه، ونحو توظيف شخصية ذي الكفل لترسيخ فكرة الصلاح والقيام بالواجبات الدينية والحكم الرشيد العادل، ونحو تعدد الآراء وكثرتها كما هو الحال مع ذي الكفل، وكذلك لغلبة الإجماع على رأي مثل الإجماع على أن إدريس هو أخنوخ أي حنوخ التناخي.

119. مكي، *الهداية*، ج 9، ص 6155.

JIQSA MISSION AND CALL FOR PAPERS

The *Journal of the International Qur'anic Studies Association* (*JIQSA*) is a peer-reviewed annual journal devoted to the scholarly study of the Qur'ān. Our goals are:

- to publish scholarship of high technical quality on the Qur'ān, addressing such concerns as its historical context; its relationship to other scriptural, parascriptural, and commentary traditions; and its literary, material, and cultural reception;
- to cultivate Qur'ānic Studies as a growing field with a distinctive identity and focus, while acknowledging relevant linkages to the study of the Bible as well as Islamic tradition, including *tafsīr*;
- to facilitate crucial conversations about the state of the field in Qur'ānic Studies and its future;
- to connect diverse scholarly communities from around the world on issues of common concern in the study of the Qur'ān.

We invite submission of original, quality research articles for consideration for publication in *JIQSA*. Methodologies of particular interest to the journal include historical-critical, contextual-comparative, and literary approaches to the Qur'ān. We especially welcome articles that explore the Qur'ān's origins in the religious, cultural, social, and political contexts of Late Antiquity; its connections to various literary precursors, especially the scriptural and parascriptural traditions of older religious communities; the historical reception of the Qur'ān in the West; the hermeneutics and methodology of qur'ānic exegesis and translation (both traditional and modern); the transmission and evolution of the *textus receptus*; Qur'ān manuscripts and material culture; and the application of various literary and philological modes of investigation into qur'ānic style, compositional structure, and rhetoric.

The field of Qur'ānic Studies is rich, diverse, and dynamic, and currently comprises a wide array of approaches and concerns. Articles to be considered for publication may reflect a variety of disciplinary perspectives, but should be:

- located in and engaged with the relevant scholarly literature, building on existing knowledge;
- conscious of authorial perspective and positionality, and explicit about aims, theoretical posture, and methodology;
- reflective about their potential impact on larger issues and debates in the academic field of Qur'ānic Studies and in broader scholarly and public discourses around the Qur'ān and Islam.

To submit an article for consideration for publication in *JIQSA*, please see the style guidelines and instructions for submission of articles at http://lockwoodonlinejournals.com/index.php/jiqsa.

Submissions should be in the range of 10,000–20,000 words and include an abstract of no more than 250 words and three to six indexing keywords. Authors are urged to conform their submissions to our style guidelines, available for download at the above URL.